NEGOTIATING SECURITY

NEGOTIATING SECURITY

An Arms Control Reader

Edited by William H. Kincade and Jeffrey D. Porro

Œ The Carnegie Endowment for International Peace

All of the articles in this collection appeared first in *Arms Control Today,* the newsletter of the Arms Control Association, and are reprinted by permission.

I.S.B.N. 0-87003-012-4

Library of Congress Catalog Card Number: 78-74185

Printed in the United States of America.

Contents

Acknowledgements

The task of an editor is lightened when the quality of the original material is high. In this, the present editors have indeed been fortunate. We owe a primary debt of gratitude to those who contributed their work to *Arms Control Today,* from which these essays are drawn. Our particular thanks go to Senator Frank Church, who, during a busy legislative season, took time to prepare an introduction for the collection.

No less indebted are we to Thomas A. Halsted, former executive director of the Arms Control Association, and to John C. Baker, the first editor of *Arms Control Today,* for establishing high standards for the publication in their tenures. To enhance the essays as they originally appeared, Tom and John added graphics and short "Perspectives," some of which are reprinted here, and we are grateful for these, as we believe the reader will be. For its generous grants to the association for *Arms Control Today,* we are likewise grateful to the Public Welfare Foundation.

Special thanks are due the Carnegie Endowment for International Peace, and to its president, Thomas L. Hughes, for continuing support of the association's educational efforts generally and, in particular, for publishing this volume. The publication itself owes much to the inspiration and energy of Diane B. Bendahmane, associate director of publications, who originally proposed the project and was tireless in assuring its implementation. Important contributions were also made by Betsy Andrews and Lee Halper of Publications, by Carnegie research assistants John M. Herzberg, who prepared the bibliography, and John Packs, who developed the glossary and several of the tables in the volume, and by Christopher Makins, director of the Endowment's West European Trends Program, who inspired the title. To them, and to many others at the Endowment who sustained our efforts, we wish to express our thanks.

Whatever merit this volume may have in conveying the substance of arms control other than through words is largely due to the cooperation of private citizens and government agencies. In particular, we are grateful to Ruth Leger Sivard, author of the annual *World Military and Social Expenditures,* for the use of tables and charts from the 1978 edition and to the U.S. Arms Control and Disarmament Agency for similar material from *World Military Expenditures and Arms Transfers 1967-1976.* It should be noted that seeming discrepancies between these two sources of graphic material arise from the use of different data, base years, and methodologies. The reader is advised to consult both of these reports for more detailed information on patterns of military expenditures and arms transfers. We wish also to thank officials in the Department of

Defense and the Department of Energy for their assistance in providing photographs to accompany the text.

For the defects in conception and organization, for any technical errors that may have crept in, and for lacunae in the subject matter, as well as our interpretation of it, the editors assume full responsibility.

A final word: as editors, we have been struck by how well these essays—several of them now four years old—have retained their relevance. Although the aim of *Arms Control Today* was, and is, to be more topical than definitive, the information and insights in many of its articles are as valid today as when they were first committed to print. While this condition, too, has eased our task as editors, it should not be forgotten that the lasting quality of these articles owes as much to the slow progress of arms limitation as to the prescience and acumen of the authors.

The ultimate rationale for both military preparedness and arms control, as, indeed, for the nation-state itself, is the safety of human life and property. While sound arms limitation and national security policies complement one another, they are often treated as though they were contradictory. We hope that this volume, by clarifying the relationship between limitations on arms and national defense, will contribute to further progress in achieving international security through arms control.

As is the case for all Endowment publications, the publication of this collection of articles implies a belief only in the importance of their subjects. The views expressed are those of the authors.

Washington, D.C.   William H. Kincade
December 1978   Jeffrey D. Porro

Introduction

This volume is being published at an important point in the search for strong, effective arms control. The arms limitation negotiation at the center of public interest—SALT II—may be close to completion. Major issues have been resolved, and agreement on the remaining issues appears to be within grasp. If the administration is successful in achieving a SALT II treaty and protocol which merit—and receive—Senate consent to ratification, the way will be open for progress on other initiatives.

Success in SALT II could open the way to an early conclusion of a comprehensive ban on nuclear explosions. SALT II should serve to reassure other nations as to the willingness of the United States and the Soviet Union to continue efforts to control the arms race and should encourage them to join with us in finding the means to reduce further the threat posed by the spread of nuclear weapons. Of course, a successful SALT II could lead to additional qualitative and quantitative controls and, possibly, significant reductions in nuclear weapons as a result of SALT III.

There are also negotiations under way with the Soviet Union and other nations on the limitation of chemical weapons and the control of anti-satellite activities. New undertakings to promote security through restraint may be sought on a regional basis, in keeping with recommendations made, for example, regarding naval forces in the Indian Ocean or nuclear weapon-free zones in Africa or South Asia.

Any assessment of the future of weapons limitation requires recognition of past achievement. Efforts on our part to obtain arms control are not new. The first such agreement was the Rush-Bagot Treaty of 1817, which applied certain limits to American and British naval forces on the Great Lakes. In modern times, the United States has become party to the Geneva Protocol outlawing poison gas and bacteriological warfare, to the Antarctic Treaty, the Outer Space Treaty, Protocol II to the Treaty for the Prohibition of Nuclear Weapons in Latin America, the Non-Proliferation Treaty, the Seabed Arms Control Treaty, the Biological Weapons Convention, the Limited Test Ban Treaty, and the SALT I treaty on the limitation of anti-ballistic missile (ABM) systems.

Despite this history, the American view of arms control remains divided. The majority of our people appear to support it, according to consistent findings of opinion surveys, and even to place it among the nation's highest priorities. Yet there are many who question its practicality, and some who believe it is undermining our security. Too few seem aware of the significant and indisputable achievements of arms control. The Limited Test Ban Treaty of 1963 has served to reduce the poisoning of our atmosphere by radioactive fallout. Without endangering our security, the Non-Proliferation Treaty of 1968 has functioned as a deterrent to the further spread of nuclear weapons—a development which the law of probabilities suggests could only jeopardize the security of our own and other nations. And the ABM Treaty of 1972 has helped to preserve mutual deterrence and stabilize the strategic environment while forestalling increased investment in missile defenses that would not be effective.

If certain benefits of arms control have been neglected, some opportunities for it have been missed, to the detriment of our national security. Had we limited the deployment of multiple independently-targetable re-entry vehicles (MIRVs) in SALT I, we would not have become so concerned later about the larger throw-weight capacity of Soviet missiles, and their concomitant capacity to carry more warheads than our own. Had we concluded SALT II earlier, we would have reduced the strategic threat each side now poses to the other, as well as uncertainties as to the future strategic environment.

If we are to reduce the danger of future annihilation, the United States and the Soviet Union, together with other nuclear powers, must be willing to go much further than SALT II. The two superpowers have each spent a trillion dollars amassing huge nuclear arsenals, only to make themselves, not the most secure, but the two most insecure nations in the world today. Thus far, for the most part, nations have only been willing to sign arms limitation agreements that do not impinge upon their own weapons building plans. Obviously, this falls far short of the need, if we are to improve the chances for a peaceful world for ourselves and future generations.

As technology has led to the development of weapons of incredible potency, the necessity for arms restraint has become more apparent and imperative. The higher we pile the chips, nuclear and conventional, the greater the likelihood they will topple and fall. History tells us that the means of waging war furthers not only the purpose of defense or deterrence, but can also serve as a contributory cause of unwanted conflict. World War I is a notable example. Yet it is not the skeptics of arms control nor the advocates of more weaponry who can provide solutions to this dilemma. The burden for developing effective instruments of restraint in a world that is increasingly complex lies with the proponents of arms control.

It is time for a reassessment of the assumptions, tools, and techniques of arms control, in the light of what we have learned from fifteen years of slow but steady movement. The future course of arms control may well depend on the cogency of this evaluation and whether it leads to improved measures for reducing the risks of war.

This volume, I hope, will encourage affirmative action. It brings together authors who are committed to arms control but differ, in many cases, on the specific ways to achieve the goal. Not all of the authors agree completely on such subjects as enhanced radiation warheads (the "neutron bombs"), the impact of the cruise missile, or the standards for verifying compliance with arms control agreements. For example, I find myself in disagreement with some of the opinions expressed concerning the breeder reactor and the reprocessing of spent fuel. It seems to me that our efforts to check the proliferation of nuclear weapons would be better served by the establishment of multinational nuclear fuel recycling centers and the improvement of international inspection of nuclear power plants.

However, I believe this diversity of opinion is a strength, encouraging critical thought and creativity. For it is only through a searching and innovative approach to the existing legacy of arms control that we will be able to find answers for the difficult problems that lie ahead. This compilation of articles, I believe, will serve to aid the on-going debate over arms control and to encourage the free flow of ideas and information so essential to our democratic process.

Frank Church
January 24, 1979

NEGOTIATING SECURITY

The basic aims of modern arms control are to reduce the likelihood of war, the damage of war, and the costs of preparing for war. Predicated upon the experience that preparing for conflict can be a cause of conflict, these aims have guided theorists and practitioners since the advent of the nuclear age revealed that the survival of society as we know it could depend on limiting the use of force and weapons of mass destruction.

As a first priority, the major nuclear powers have attempted to prevent the occurrence of "accidental" or "unintended" war—conflict growing out of technical failures, misunderstandings, or minor disagreements. The 1963 Washington-Moscow "hotline" and the 1972 Soviet-American Incidents at Sea Agreement exemplify these attempts.

The 1960s saw two major efforts to constrain the testing and spread of nuclear weapons, the Limited Test Ban Treaty and the Non-Proliferation Treaty. The 1970s, on the other hand, have been marked chiefly by complex negotiations to limit and then reduce existing stockpiles of nuclear and thermonuclear weapons. Cost factors and technological limitations made it comparatively easy to negotiate limits on defensive weapons in the Anti-Ballistic Missile Treaty of 1972. Progress on limiting offensive weapons has proved much harder to achieve. A permanent treaty (SALT II) to succeed the five-year Interim Offensive Weapons Agreement (part of SALT I) eluded negotiators for seven years, even after the so-called "conceptual breakthrough" of the 1974 Vladivostok Accord which created an offensive-weapons treaty framework.

Many of the factors which illustrate the need for, and the difficulty of, negotiating limits on offensive weapons are reviewed here: bureaucratic and domestic pressures in both the United States and USSR; weapons that make strategic miscalculations more, not less, probable; demands for perfection in verification confounded by weapons designed to make verification harder; and the negotiating process itself, which has sometimes even spurred the development of new weapons or increases in inventories. A decade after its beginning, the SALT process is being reviewed to determine whether it is meeting the goals of arms control and, if not, how it might be modified. The articles here provide the background for such an appraisal.

Preventing Nuclear War

SALT II, Linkage, and National Security
Frank Church

Since 1973, the United States and the Soviet Union have been endeavoring, slowly and haltingly, to achieve a new treaty limiting strategic offensive arms. Now, on the verge of agreement, the SALT (Strategic Arms Limitation Talks) process itself is under attack.

The strategic arms limitation effort has been caught up in the maelstrom of our stormy relationship with the Soviet Union. As a result, no one knows whether a new agreement will emerge in weeks, in months, or at all.

Some of my Senate colleagues have suggested that the United States should unilaterally break off the SALT negotiations to protest the political trials of Soviet dissidents, Anatoly Shcharansky and Aleksandr Ginzburg. The Carter administration says it is opposed to using the SALT talks as a tool for pressuring the Kremlin on its internal human rights policies. However, the President, himself, may have opened the door to this kind of linkage, when he suggested that the successful conclusion of SALT II could be jeopardized by Soviet and Cuban activities in Africa. Once the concept of linkage between strategic arms negotiations and other extraneous political developments has been legitimized, it is inevitable that this same principle will be invoked by others to argue in favor of suspending the arms control talks for a myriad of other reasons. In the process, the hope of ever negotiating an end to the nuclear arms race may fade altogether.

If we persist in tying SALT to Russian behavior in the Horn of Africa, in Central Africa, or even in Moscow, we are quite unlikely to find that perfect moment in the flow of events at which we can say, "At last, our persistent competitor, the Soviet Union, is comporting itself to our complete satisfaction. Now, we should discuss the conclusion of a SALT agreement."

And if we hold the Kremlin responsible for Castro's every move in Angola or Ethiopia, then what is to stop the Russians from arguing that SALT cannot proceed until our allies, the French and Belgians, pull out of Zaire or Chad? Once you espouse the theory of linkage, where do you break the chain?

Finally, the notion that SALT II can be held hostage for changes in Soviet behavior in other areas flies in the face of the fundamental precept that makes the arms limitation talks possible at all: that is, that an agreement to limit strategic arms equally serves the vital interests of both powers and, further, is mutually perceived to do so. The linkage theory presumes that an agreement is more in the interest of the Soviets than of the United States, and we can therefore "punish" the Kremlin by delaying conclusion of the talks. But if the SALT talks are more in the interest of the Soviet Union than our own country, why are we engaging in them?

I agree wholeheartedly with Secretary of State Cyrus Vance that this issue must be treated differently from others:

> The imperatives to go to Geneva now are that we are
> dealing with negotiations that affect the national security
> of our nation and the security and well-being of the
> world in general. . . . It is a question which deals with
> the prospect of mutual annihilation. . . .

SALT is the only realistic alternative to a senseless nuclear arms race which neither side can win. We have already assembled a nuclear arsenal of such staggering proportions that the United States could destroy the Soviet Union several times over, even after enduring an attack upon itself. This ability to strike back devastatingly if attacked—an ability the Soviet Union also possesses—has brought the two sides to a state of mutual deterrence, and a suicidal holocaust has thus far been averted.

But we are on the verge of a new, even more dangerous stage of the arms race. The United States and the Soviet Union are developing new counterforce weapons which could enable each side to destroy the other's intercontinental ballistic missiles (ICBMs). If these weapons are deployed, each nation's fear of a first strike will be dramatically increased. The psychology of the arms race is such that without a mutual agreement between the United States and the USSR to limit these new weapons developments, the race will escalate—even though it is obvious that we would never reach a point through competition at

SALT II Ceilings and Subceilings

All strategic launchers: Bombers with or without ALCMs; Missiles with or without MIRVs (2250)

Missiles without MIRVs and Bombers without ALCMs (930)

With MIRVs and ALCMs (1320)

Strategic bombers with ALCMs and missiles with MIRVs (1320)

Bombers with ALCMs (120)

Missiles with MIRVs (1200)

Strategic missiles with MIRVs (1200)

Sea-based missiles with MIRVs (380)

Land-based missiles with MIRVs (820)

Land-based strategic missiles with MIRVs (820)

Ceilings or subceilings in boldfaced type represent the upper limit permitted for these classes of strategic weapons under the terms of the SALT II treaty. Ceilings or subceilings in regular type are the numbers of strategic weapons in other classes which either side *may* attain if it chooses to deploy the maximum allowed under the upper limit shown in boldface.

Current U.S. and Soviet Force Levels Under SALT II Criteria

	U.S.	USSR
All Strategic Launchers:	2059	2500
Missiles without MIRVs and/or bombers without ALCMs	1013	2130
Missiles with MIRVs and/or bombers with ALCMs:		
missiles	1046	370*
projected bombers	165	?
total	1211	370
Missiles with MIRVs:		
land-based	550	370
sea-based	496	
total	1046	370

* In calculating the number of Soviet MIRVed missiles the SS-NX-18, a Soviet MIRVed SLBM in the process of deployment, has been excluded due to the unavailability of data. Another recently developed Soviet SLBM, the SS-NX-17, has been excluded due to uncertainty about its MIRV capabilities.

which we would feel secure enough to stop. In fact, a new counterforce competition would make us feel less secure, because the stability of mutual deterrence would be weakened. In short, the only practical way to achieve stability, enhance our national security and, simply put, keep the lid on is through strategic arms limitation agreements.

Secretary of Defense Harold Brown said in his presentation this year to the Senate Armed Services Committee:

> We want mutual deterrence to be so stable that it cannot be upset in a crisis. We want it to be so well designed that neither side will be tempted to try to upset it over the longer term. These are the two essential types of strategic stability that we seek.

There is no question in my mind that strategic arms limitation agreements are indispensable if we are ever to achieve this kind of strategic stability.

The value of arms limitation is much more obvious when we consider how indefatigably we and the Soviets have pursued the other path— only to secure a stalemate. We kicked off the nuclear weapons age in 1945 and outdistanced the Soviets throughout the 1950s. We maintained both a quantitative and qualitative lead in the 1960s, and we still hold a qualitative lead. But from the start, the Soviet catch-up has only been a matter of time.

In 1966, the Soviet Union had 244 ICBMs. We were then approaching our present total of 1,054 land-based ICBMs. The Russians had 29 submarine-launched ballistic missiles (SLBMs) and we had almost finished our program of 656 such missiles.

In the late 1960s, with forces more than adequate for deterrence, we decided to stick with our missile totals, at least for the near future. Meanwhile, the Soviet Union was coming from behind, and its land-based missile force exceeded ours by the end of the decade. Their submarine force grew larger than ours a few years ago.

But we were not idle while the Soviet Union was increasing its missile totals. In 1970, we began installing multiple independently-targetable re-entry vehicles (MIRVs)—a technical name for strategic warheads— atop both our land-based Minuteman missiles and our submarine-based Poseidon missiles. (We also installed less sophisticated multiple warheads on our Polaris submarine missiles.) The Soviet Union did not start MIRVing its land-based missiles until 1975, and only recently acquired the ability to deploy MIRVs on submarine-based missiles. By comparison, every one of our submarine-based ballistic missiles boasts a multiple warhead.

As a result of our earlier start and better technology, we possess at present more than twice as many deliverable strategic nuclear warheads as the Soviet Union. Our analysts tell us that we will maintain a war-head lead for the foreseeable future.

Some discount this lead by pointing out that the Soviets have developed generally larger ICBMs and more of them—about 1,500 compared to our 1,054. They have also installed more submarine-launched ballistic missiles, although we have built more bombers. The total forces, as measured by the number of strategic delivery systems, compare at more than 2,500 for the Soviets to about 2,100 for us. But the numerical disparity is not in itself a cause for concern, since our current forces are capable of hitting twice as many targets as theirs, with a punch many times larger than the blasts which destroyed Nagasaki and Hiroshima.

To understand why we should welcome the prospective new treaty now being negotiated, we should look at some of the contemplated controls and limitations. We should also consider both the added cost and uncertainty that would face us without a new treaty.

The basic element of a new SALT package will be a treaty to last until 1985, which will establish certain ceilings on overall strategic delivery systems, as well as sublimits on missiles with MIRVs, upon heavy bombers carrying cruise missiles, and upon land-based MIRVed ICBMs. The second component will be a protocol applying temporary additional limitations until around the end of 1980. The third component will be a statement of principles and guidelines for SALT III.

The emerging three-part SALT agreement would hold many benefits for the national security interests of the United States:

—The maximum limit of 2,250 on strategic delivery systems will force the Soviet Union to dismantle about 300 of its missiles and/or bombers. This reduction is even more striking by comparison with what the Soviets might add without SALT. The Department of Defense projects more than 3,000 Soviet strategic weapons by 1985 without a treaty. If so, then we can correctly credit SALT II with removing the threat that an additional 800 Soviet intercontinental bombers and/or ballistic missiles would pose. By contrast, the ceiling will not force us to make any reductions in the number of our strategic weapons. Indeed, if we choose to do so, we can add new weapons in sufficient number to equate our total force with that of the Russians.

—The ceiling of about 1,200 on missiles with MIRVs will constrain the United States only slightly. However, it will hold the Soviet side to a total hundreds below what we believe they would otherwise install.

—We benefit most immediately from the expected allowance above the MIRV ceiling of 120 heavy bombers equipped with air-launched cruise missiles (ALCMs), as we are well along with our cruise missile program.

—Since a far smaller proportion of our forces are on land, the Soviet side will be most affected by the limit of 820 on land-based ICBMs with MIRVs. Our intelligence believes that the Russians would deploy hundreds more land-based missiles with MIRVs by 1985 without a treaty.

—The treaty limitations may cause the Soviets to give greater emphasis to sea-based forces at the expense of land-based forces, a move which will be inherently less threatening and more stabilizing.

—The mobile missile provisions in the protocol are decidedly in our interest. A Soviet mobile missile now ready to be deployed, the SS-16, would be banned for the period of the protocol, while the development of our own mobile missile, the MX, would not be constrained, should we decide to proceed with it.

—The cruise missile provisions in the protocol will allow us to proceed as quickly as we are able with cruise missile development and deployment. The Soviets will not derive similar benefits, since they have no comparable program.

Against this background, one might ask, what is in this package for the Soviet Union that does not increase the danger to us?

First, the land-based missile forces of the Soviet Union possess a greater throw-weight in megatonnage than the comparable forces of the United States. This will compensate them for the threat posed by us of our far superior submarine missiles and our larger force of penetrating bombers with ALCMs. Second, SALT II, by incorporating the principle of equal aggregates, will acknowledge the fact that the Soviet Union has become the relative equal of the United States in strategic nuclear arms. Third, the new agreement will save the Russians—as it will us— the heavy financial burden and the needless diversion of resources which would be entailed in an unrestrained continued competition.

To sum up, in no case will SALT II cause the United States to yield any advantage whatever to the Soviet Union in strategic nuclear arms. On the contrary, SALT II will leave the United States relatively better off, for the life of the treaty, than it would be if there were no treaty and each side continued to proceed through 1985 according to current plans.

Obviously, if there were no SALT II agreement, the United States would not sit still militarily. If the Russians continued to expand their strategic force at the current rate, we could expect upward revisions in our own military budget.

Even if the Russians did not step up their own strategic program in the event of a SALT breakdown, the United States would have to spend an extra $20 billion, at the very least, between now and 1985, just to maintain the relative force strength that would be guaranteed by SALT II. This amount would cover the construction of 100 FB-111 bombers and modernization of existing ones, the deployment of additional sea-launched cruise missiles, the replacement of the remaining 450 Minuteman IIs, with MIRVed Minuteman IIIs, and the installation of more ICBMs.

If, in addition, we were to speed up development of the M-X mobile missile by two years, and restart the B-1 bomber program, we would have to pile on another $24 billion over the next ten years. The Senate Budget Committee staff has estimated that over thirteen years, the incremental cost to the United States of building a maximum force reasonably envisioned in the absence of a SALT agreement could be $90 to $100 billion!

The willingness of the American people to bear whatever cost is necessary is not in doubt, nor is the ability of our military to keep pace with the Russians. The question is, why should we pour additional billions of dollars for defense into a federal budget already deep in deficit and further inflame inflationary pressures, when precisely the same measure of security can be achieved by concluding a sensible arms agreement with the USSR? *(August-September 1978)*

The Challenge to Arms Control *Dick Clark*

These remarks are taken from Senator Clark's speech to the Arms Control Association at its 1977 annual meeting.

I am fortunate to be able to appear before this distinguished group today since prospects for arms control appear brighter now than they have for years. In fact, we have had very few arms control achievements to date. The arms control atmosphere which began dramatically with the Limited Test Ban Treaty of 1963 has diminished with the passage of time. We can hope—and do our best to insure—that this bleak period for arms control is behind us. Due to the President's personal interest, new life has been breathed into arms control.

I would like to focus on SALT (Strategic Arms Limitation Talks). Let me state my central contention at the outset: We have a stronger case for SALT than we have so far succeeded in publicly projecting. We have a broad base of support in the United States. The key to our awakening this broad constituency is ourselves.

Specifically, I contend that we in the arms control community have failed to frame the debate and, thereby, have forfeited this advantage to the critics. Second, we have permitted the false impression to arise that our approach to national security issues is less realistic than the approach of the critics. Third, we have failed to make clear the national security advantages of SALT. Fourth, we have failed to show the weakness of the contentions of the critics. Finally, we have failed to make clear the danger to our nation which would arise if there were no SALT agreement.

We have allowed what is essentially a debate over the fundamental strategic interests of this nation to be distorted by those who are hostile to the objectives of arms control. The result is that many people believe that arms control is the enemy of our security instead of an effective and necessary way to reinforce our security.

The critics argue that SALT II is too restrictive, that it seriously limits United States military programs. That, simply, is untrue. In fact, the opposite is more nearly the case. Those of us who support SALT in its emerging form do so without any certain sense that SALT II is a significant achievement toward controlling the arms race. Simply put, SALT II, like the SALT I and Vladivostok agreements, still allows the two sides to move ahead with most of the existing programs. While SALT II will certainly be an achievement meriting public support, it is a good—rather than a great—achievement. We will not really have a significant SALT agreement until both sides are willing to cross over that painful threshold which requires reductions and constraints that actually curtail favored and approved programs in a meaningful way.

All too often, the critics of SALT have done a disservice to public understanding by focusing selectively on narrow, hardware issues, neglecting those provisions which benefit the United States and brushing aside the broader military and political advantages of SALT. Fears are being fed by simplistic ratios and projections of strategic threats and by farfetched, alarmist and unrealistic scenarios which overlook the distinction between a fantastic, paranoid nightmare on the one hand, and the military planner's "worst *plausible* case" on the other. Verifications issues in particular have lent themselves to demagogy, when they should be discussed as difficult and complex matters.

Opponents of arms control have consistently poor-mouthed and downgraded our very substantial, capable, flexible, and durable nuclear forces. They propagate these distortions in spite of the testimony of the President, the Secretary of Defense, the Joint Chiefs of Staff and the intelligence community. These self-defeating distortions can help neither our negotiators nor our allies. All too often, they poison the climate of the domestic debate with half-truths and untruths—and degrade the credibility of our deterrent. The critics of SALT imply thereby, that our security is only to be guaranteed by more and more military weaponry.

What we must do is to put the debate on a new, clearer, and more realistic footing. While not for a moment neglecting the hard technical issues, we should make sure that people realize that these are *not* the *only* issues. We must view SALT in terms of its contribution to our overall national security, not just seeing numbers of delivery vehicles on each side, but also seeing the relevant strategic incentives, constraints, and interests on both sides. We must not see SALT as freezing either nation in awkward positions but as a step in a process from which both parties gain in their security.

We must enter the debate forcefully and maintain a tenacious and continuing involvement in SALT II and later SALT efforts to activate the broad national constituency in our nation for these agreements. Otherwise, we shall find ourselves battling for support each time a treaty or agreement comes around simply because what is in hand is better than the alternative. The members of the Arms Control Association must understand that the Senate cannot carry alone the burden of consideration of SALT. The Senate will not go ahead of the American people on SALT—and no one can expect otherwise in a democracy. But once the national support for SALT becomes apparent in a properly framed debate, neither will the Senate fall behind the American people on SALT.

This brings me to my second major point: We must reject the implications that arms control is less tough-minded than the critics' view. Ours *is* the realistic and practical view. Our calculations about nuclear deterrence show more realism and a better understanding of how nations behave than the estimates of those who glibly attribute a first-strike or war-winning strategy to the Soviet Union.

We all remember what happened to Hiroshima with a single, small atomic bomb, yielding less than 20 kilotons. By comparison, each side can now create thousands of Hiroshimas on the other's territory. And nothing the Soviets can do can deny that terrible power to us. I find it more than a little ludicrous when people suggest that the Soviet leadership would find a far more devastating retaliatory attack acceptable— economically, politically, or militarily.

Much of the effort to generate fear about SALT is based on the fact that we have only a dim view of Soviet nuclear strategy and of Soviet intentions. Soviet writings permit contradictory interpretations which create all kinds of fantasies that pass for knowledge. While I can agree that we do not fully understand Soviet strategy and intentions, I *cannot* agree with the suggestions that we must therefore expect the Soviets to act *contrary* to their own national or party interests. I have no doubt that the Soviet leadership wants to stay in power and that they want to preserve their political system, their economic status, and their territorial integrity. So long as the Soviets have these real and tangible interests, I doubt their willingness to risk these fundamental values in the forlorn hope that, by some miracle of planning, a nuclear war can be won, in the sense that they will escape major retaliatory destruction. In my judgment, the opposite view is nonsense, and we should say so plainly.

There is further ground on which I would challenge the realism of many SALT critics. Somehow, these critics seem to believe that we must "win" this negotiation with the Soviet Union, that we must "outfox" the Soviet negotiators and obtain terms which enhance our strategic advantages and undermine theirs, and, failing this, that we should forego a treaty.

This is either naive or deceitful. Certainly, it is a fundamental principle of diplomacy that you cannot negotiate an agreement which is clearly prejudicial to the interests of one of the negotiating parties. In the case of SALT, if one side can't live with the contract, then it won't be concluded. In short, we cannot change the strategic balance in our favor through negotiations. Nor are we going to "give away the store" in unsuspecting concessions to the Soviets.

Even if one *were* able to gain a strategic advantage at the bargaining table, the other party would shortly awaken to this and either violate the agreement or renounce it. No treaty we can possibly negotiate will reduce the Soviets or us to an inferior position. As the director of the Arms Control and Disarmament Agency, Paul Warnke, emphasizes, you must begin with the recognition that you are striving for an arms agreement which is fair, which is balanced, which has equal restrictions on both sides, and which provides equal security for both nations. Our rejection of the fantasies of nuclear war-fighting, our appreciation of SALT as a tool to our military planners, and our more practical expectations of the opportunities and pitfalls of the bargaining process demonstrate our realism and practicality. The failure of the public to appreciate this is due to our lack of energy and assertiveness, not to the skill of the critics.

The same is true about our case for the current SALT package under negotiation. Our case for the emerging agreement is stronger than we have appreciated, more commanding of broad public support than we have realized.

After all, the fundamental test of SALT is whether it serves our national interest, primarily our national security interest, broadly understood. We need not and should not argue that a SALT agreement is the millennium. Once we demonstrate clearly that a SALT accord is a means of enhancing our vital national defense; once we show, as such, SALT is a far less dangerous and less costly option than an unregulated arms race; once we make it clear that arms controls are not opposed to national security, but rather bolster it, then the American public and the Senate will rally to the support of SALT. The package under negotiation promises to enhance our national security in several ways.

For the first time in strategic arms control, there will likely be a reduction of deployed weapons. *Some 300 fewer Soviet missiles and heavy bombers will be aimed at the United States.* This may not be the sizable reduction many of us would like to see, but it is nevertheless a significant achievement and clearly in our national security interest.

The agreement will provide for equal aggregates of strategic nuclear forces on both sides. This accomplishes the objectives defined in 1972 for SALT II. It, too, is an important achievement, when you consider the difficulty of achieving this type of equality between forces which are responsive to different geopolitical circumstances and different technological capacities. When you consider that the Soviet Union faces four nuclear forces on or within reach of its borders, this becomes an even more significant accomplishment.

The expected limitations on missiles with multiple independently-targetable re-entry vehicles (MIRVs) and particularly the sublimit on MIRVed ICBMs are important steps to a more stable balance. A limit to Soviet land-based MIRVs will force them to a greater proportion of MIRVs at sea and to thereby rely on a more balanced, more survivable, and more stable force than in the past.

The agreement will tell us just how many missiles in each category to expect the Soviets to build. This will curb the strategic guessing game that leads to uncertainty, worst-case estimates, and hedges.

By putting limits on the Soviet systems which concern us the most in the eight-year treaty and by putting limits on our systems which concern the Soviets the most in the three-year protocol, the SALT package is shrewdly conceived to enhance our bargaining leverage in the next round.

Depending on the final content of the protocol, the agreement may ban their mobile missile which is ready for deployment and may delay the development of the fifth generation of Soviet intercontinental ballistic missiles (ICBMs).

These are all sound, understandable arguments for SALT. Taken together, they make a compelling case that SALT II is assuredly in our national interest. It is not enough, however, to have a positive case. Presenting our case positively is the most important thing, but we must also deal with the criticisms in a serious and forthright way. We must disabuse the public of any notion that SALT would affect our national security adversely.

To begin with, we must make it clear that the press reports indicating the United States has conceded too much to the Soviet Union are the product of highly selective leaking which focuses on those features of the negotiation document that bind the United States in some form or other. People should remember the cynicism of this effort when the final document itself becomes available, because it will then be clear that the Soviets have come a long way toward meeting our security interests by binding themselves to certain provisions. But let me address some specific charges:

On the question of Minuteman vulnerability—it has been alleged by the critics of arms control that the levels for MIRVed ICBMs in this agreement have been set too high, so that the Soviets could destroy a large portion of our Minuteman ICBM silos. First of all, those who make this charge have failed to be completely frank and to acknowledge that Minuteman missile silos are vulnerable in any case and that they would be even more vulnerable *without* SALT II. The critics are not being exactly candid in stressing what has long and intentionally been the smallest part of our deterrent force while ignoring our large and durable bomber and submarine-based delivery vehicles.

Even now, there is considerable disagreement over just how vulnerable Minuteman is now and how vulnerable it will be in the future. Even if vulnerability can be demonstrated at some future point, it is hard to translate that threat into something bearing upon the real world. To be confident of eliminating our Minuteman force, an adversary must deliver on each silo two re-entry vehicles with precise timing, and with near-perfect reliability and accuracy. I find it very hard to believe that any Soviet military official or leader would stake the future of the regime, the Soviet economy, or the Russian people on a technically perfect attack involving some 2,000 separate re-entry vehicles and 300 or so missiles which even then would not touch our sea-based retaliatory forces or our bomber forces. To seriously propose such a scenario is to enter the realm of mystic philosophy.

In the final analysis, we can conclude that Minuteman vulnerability is a matter which cannot be resolved by SALT. Of course, SALT can help. It certainly will not increase Minuteman vulnerability.

One final note on this—the poverty and narrowness of this brouhaha over Minuteman vulnerability in the SALT context can be seen in the proposed solution—the MX. This proposed mobile missile would have much greater throw-weight as well as more, and more accurate, warheads in each deployed missile than in our existing Minuteman III. Thus, the MX program would increase the hard-target threat to the Soviet Union under the guise of decreasing the hard-target threat to us. How could the Soviet Union fail to react as our hardliners would expect us to do under the same circumstances?

Related to the vulnerability issue is the question of Soviet heavy missiles, that is, ICBMs with a large lift capacity or throw-weight which gives them the ability to carry numerous MIRVs. What bothers people is that the so-called heavy missiles have more than doubled the throw-weight of standard missiles. The Soviet SS-18 has 15,000 pounds of throw-weight, as compared to the 7,000 pounds of the SS-19. Though the Soviets are having difficulties with their MIRV program and though it is not clear they will MIRV all of these heavy ICBMs to their maximum extent, I think the more important considerations are accuracy, reliability, and the practical utilization of throw-weight. We should remember that beyond a certain point, additional throw-weight provides diminishing returns. With technological advances and miniaturization, massive throw-weight is not necessary to secure potent forces. For this reason, informed analysts conclude that the totality of MIRVed missile forces is a far greater concern than the MIRV potential of the super-heavy missiles. Accordingly, a ceiling on MIRVed ICBMs is at least as great an achievement as tight reins on the MIRVing of heavy ICBMs —which are limited in total numbers now and will stay limited.

As to the reported 2,500-kilometer range limitation on air-launched cruise missiles, critics are now charging that this prevents complete coverage of Soviet targets, if the cruise missiles are fired from stand-off bombers outside Soviet airspace. This criticism seems founded on the assumption that not only must each leg of the triad (bombers, ICBMs, and submarine-launched missiles) *in itself* be capable of saturating the Soviet target system, but that even each *component* of each *leg* of the triad must be capable of doing so. Here we have another case of holding the emerging agreement up to a false and irrelevant standard and then finding it wanting on the basis of such a standard.

Regarding the issue of the Soviet Backfire bomber, it is ridiculous that this has been allowed to play such a central role in the debate. Funda-mentally it is irrelevant to the strategic balance and has been from the moment it was brought up. My inclination is to say: "Yes, on a straight-line, high altitude, subsonic mission, this small payload plane could hit targets in the United States—and so what." Compared to a Soviet strategic force of 2,500 missiles and heavy bombers with some 4,500 warheads, the addition of a couple of hundred Backfires arriving a few hours after the exchange serves only, as Winston Churchill said, "to make the rubble bounce."

We must puncture the notion that SALT is, as the games theorists say, a "zero-sum" game in which the gains of one side are precisely proportional to the other side's losses. Nothing could be further from the truth. Our security will benefit from a SALT agreement, so will the Soviet Union's, and so will world security.

Finally, we must understand the dangers to our nation of a failure to achieve a new SALT agreement. We must combat the idea that the world will be a safer place if there is no SALT agreement. To do this, we must describe the consequences of no SALT treaty.

Briefly, and without speculating too much, the failure to sign or ratify an acceptable accord could have any or all of the following out-comes: It could call into question and perhaps lead to termination of the very useful strategic arms dialogue we have been conducting with the Soviets for a decade. It could engender a strategic arms race more furious than we have seen to date, producing more provocative and destabilizing weapons. It could stimulate the spread of nuclear weapons to countries about to cross the nuclear threshold if they conclude from the Soviet-American example that nuclear weapons *do* increase usable military power and diplomatic leverage without accompanying disadvantages and penalties. It could jeopardize the continuance of existing arms control agreements related to outer space, the seabed, ballistic missile defenses and nuclear weapons tests, some of which are already under pressure from technological innovation. It could increase the mathematical probability of nuclear war, whether or not such a war is planned or desired. It could reduce the opportunity for verifiable strategic arms control agreements, as technology carries the arms race more and more in the direction of so-called "gray-area-systems" which are difficult to locate, count and evaluate with the present verification techniques. It could increase the burden of defense spending in our own and other countries. It could eliminate the possibility of mutually controlling dangerous new weapons technologies. It could cast an added pall over the already difficult problem of Soviet-American relations, perhaps eventuating in a return to the confrontations of the high cold war period. And finally, it could reduce or remove the possibility of success in other arms control efforts, such as chemical weapons control, a comprehensive test ban treaty, or the Mutual and Balanced Force Reduction talks, where the cooperation of the two superpowers is essential to progress.

However, I do not believe this dark picture will be realized. The advocates of strategic arms limitation have learned that, however good, these measures do not *sell* themselves in a climate of opinion still partly paranoid or at best ambivalent, where simplistic and narrow attacks on SALT can successfully exploit long-standing fears. We have learned that to support arms control effectively means much more than a reasonable discussion among reasonable people, but requires a recognition of— and a willingness to join in—the frankly political nature of the ratification process.

We have seen that we cannot confine ourselves to a definition of national security restricted to military and hardware issues but instead must broaden the debate to include all of the factors that influence our security and the security of the world we inhabit. We have realized how important it is to demonstrate that strategic arms controls *are* in our best national security interest, that the threat of open-ended arms racing constitutes a real threat to the continuation of civilization as we know it, and that nuclear arms control is not softheaded, foolish or weak, but realistic, necessary and wise.

The challenge to SALT has been presented, and, as we have seen today, there are sound and realistic answers to those challenges. We know that there are inherent weaknesses in the arguments of the SALT critics and that there are considerable strengths to our arguments that

SALT has clear national security advantages. We know further that the alternative to SALT II—no SALT—is untenable. We have a solid and supportable case. Now, we must go out and make that case.

(December 1977)

The Direct Payoff in SALT II   *Thomas J. Downey*

Those who support SALT II (Strategic Arms Limitation Talks) in the current debate have generally found themselves employing some combination of four basic arguments. First, that SALT II is the "son of SALT I," preserving and somewhat tightening SALT I's numerical limitations which would otherwise be abandoned. Second, that SALT II is the "father of SALT III" which we hope will be of far-reaching benefit and which is probably unachievable if the arms control process were to be stopped by failure of SALT II. Third, that the alarmist objections raised by SALT opponents are invalid. Fourth, that SALT II establishes, for the first time, equal aggregates of strategic weapons for the two sides.

Having repeatedly used these arguments myself and being firmly convinced that any reasonable person should be persuaded by them, nevertheless I find them to have certain limitations. The first two support an ongoing SALT process but do not find virtue in the particular treaty at hand. The third argument must be made to set the record straight, but while it eliminates the negatives it creates no positive reason to support SALT. The fourth does address a specific virtue of SALT II, but it is a virtue which contributes neither to stability (i.e., war prevention) nor to budget reduction; aggregate number of missiles is such a poor measure of capability that we must recognize it as political window dressing necessary to impress the impressionable. In short, a run through the standard arguments may leave the listener convinced we are better off with SALT II than without, but it will not raise his enthusiasm for SALT II, as distinguished from the general SALT process, as high as it should.

The fact is that SALT II, as publicly reported, offers at least one specific concrete benefit which has been generally overlooked. Consider the following passage from Paul Nitze's November 1, 1977, attack on SALT:

> A ban on testing or deployment of new SLBMs [sea-launched ballistic missiles] except for Trident I and SSNX-18 (new Soviet SLBM with a range said to be

as great as that of our projected Trident II missile, the
testing of which would be prohibited) will be included.

If in fact this provision does emerge in the final treaty, it will constitute arms control's first major contribution to strategic stability, and
will be, by a wide margin, the treaty's most significant provision. In
itself, it will mandate approval of the treaty in the interest of U.S.
military security. The reasoning behind this claim is somewhat complex; let us consider it.

As a result of the previous administration's failure to comprehend
the need for *qualitative* strategic arms controls, particularly relating to
such developments as MIRV (multiple independently-targetable re-
entry vehicles) and ballistic-missile accuracy (where the United States
holds a substantial but useless lead), it is now a foregone conclusion
that the Soviet Union will, sometime in the 1980s, deploy ICBMs (intercontinental ballistic missiles) with accuracy and striking power sufficient, at least on paper, to destroy on the order of 70-80 percent of
the United States' ICBM silos in a first strike. While tight qualitative
controls on ICBMs, including a *total* test ban, might deny the Soviets a
high-confidence countersilo capability if implemented in the near future,
this is probably not a realistic political possibility within the time
available.

But while it would be preferable not have to do so, we *can* live with
any degree of Soviet ICBM capability, just as they can live with any
degree of American ICBM capability. The concern over Soviet ICBMs,
which has claimed so many headlines in recent months, overlooks the
fact that *no* ICBM—no matter how large, accurate, or reliable—can
conduct a preemptive strike against bombers. ICBM flight time is
simply too long; its half-hour warning would insure that our penetrating
bombers and cruise missile launchers would be "flushed" safely airborne.

Manned aircraft on the ground are, of course, extremely "soft" and
can be attacked by enemy SLBMs, which offer less warning time than
ICBMs, particularly if the submarines fire from close offshore and use
depressed trajectories. But, through the next decade, SLBMs will lack
the accuracy needed to destroy hard ICBM silos.

Therefore, there is no *single* weapon capable of attacking more than
one arm of our land-based deterrent. Moreover, it is impossible for the
aggressor to increase his effectiveness by coordinating an ICBM attack
on missile silos with an SLBM attack on bombers. This is evident if we
consider the two possible forms of such an attack.

1) The attacker could launch his ICBMs and SLBMs *simultaneously*.
Approximately ten minutes later, the President would receive word that
U.S. bomber bases had been destroyed and that thousands of Soviet

warheads were on their way to our ICBM silos, with impact expected in 15-20 minutes. Given this unequivocal and undeniable warning, the President would have reason to empty our silos, sending our ICBM fleet toward Soviet political and economic targets and leaving behind worthless empty silos for the Soviets to strike. Would he actually do so? His response would probably depend greatly on his assessment of the security of his missile submarines. Nobody can say, but the latest Defense Department Annual Report warns in the most explicit terms that launch-under-attack is an available option. Only the most reckless and foolhardy Soviet leader could risk his nation's survival on the assumption that we would *not* launch-under-attack. And the tradition and history of Russian foreign policy are of caution, not recklessness.

2) The attacker could launch his ICBMs *earlier* than his SLBMs, adjusting his timing for simultaneous arrival on target. This would gain nothing over a straight ICBM attack, however, since the victim's bombers would have sufficient warning to escape.

(A third strategy has been suggested in which some SLBMs would attack bomber bases while others would maintain a barrage above ICBM fields. The barrage, though incapable of destroying silos, would prevent the launch of the victim's ICBMs for a time sufficient to permit the attacker's silo-killing ICBMs to arrive in a second wave. This, however, is not practical: the megatonnage requirement is prohibitively high.)

Thus, the most the Soviets can hope to achieve in the mid-1980s is destruction of one of our three deterrent arms—we wouldn't know which one, but we would know it could be *only* one—leaving us with two arms, which is one more than we really need for deterrence or retaliation.

Now consider the impact of an SLBM with silo-killing accuracy, a weapon probably achievable by the United States within ten years and by the Soviets within five to ten years thereafter. Using these SLBMs alone, it would be possible for an attacker to strike *both* bombers and silos simultaneously, leaving warning time too short for U.S. bombers to escape and decision time too short—and evidence too scanty—for a presidential order to launch U.S. ICBMs before they were hit. Thus, the Soviets would be able to eliminate *two* of our three deterrent arms in a first strike.

This is the situation which SALT II, if the Nitze report of November 1977 is correct, would positively *prevent*. None of the SLBMs permitted (SSNX-18 and Trident I) would be capable of silo-killing, and more advanced SLBMs would be prohibited. True, the protocol runs for only three years and the treaty runs only until 1985. But this is the kind of provision which, unlike cruise missile range limitations, may become permanent once accepted on an interim basis.

Paul Nitze and others may contend that cutting off SLBM improvements at the level of the SSNX-18 and Trident I missiles places us at a disadvantage. It does not require a great deal of thought to discover four flaws in this argment, any one of which is sufficient for its rejection. First, since SLBMs do not engage each other, there is no significance in comparing U.S. and Soviet SLBM ranges. Second, the purpose of a long SLBM range is to enable the submarine to evade enemy anti-submarine warfare techniques. Since our anti-submarine warfare force is far more capable than the Soviets', they need a longer SLBM range than we do. Third, a long SLBM range is stabilizing for both sides, since it not only increases submarine survivability but also increases the warning time if these missiles are used. We would be *more* secure if the Soviets were to *double* the range of all their SLBMs. Last but not least, Mr. Nitze appears to be misinformed. The Navy's only unclassified statement on the SSNX-18 range describes it as "similar to that of the SSN-8" which in turn is, with a typical payload, similar to that of Trident I (about 4000-4500 nautical miles). Moreover, a modest reduction in payload enables Trident I to achieve the range (about 6000 nautical miles) advertised for Trident II. Even with this reduced load, Trident I retains more damage capability than the SSNX-18.

It may also be argued that the possible destruction of two U.S. deterrent arms would be meaningless, since our surviving SLBMs alone are sufficient for deterrence. This is true as long as we are absolutely confident of SLBM security, but there is a significant advantage in hedging against technological breakthrough by placing our deterrent eggs in more than one basket.

More to the point, consider that Minuteman vulnerability will be one of the key arguments raised against SALT II, even though the rejection of SALT II would in no way ameliorate this vulnerability. Those who are concerned about *combined* Minuteman *and* bomber vulnerability should, therefore, be the strongest supporters of SALT II.   *(March 1978)*

SALT: Through the Looking Glass
Marshall D. Shulman

This article was adapted from a paper presented at the 1975 annual meeting of the American Association for the Advancement of Science.

SALT (Strategic Arms Limitation Talks) involves three sets of negotiations: one is between the Soviet Union and the United States, and the other two are internal negotiations within each of the two countries. Until the internal negotiations within the Soviet Union and the United States move to the point where the political leadership of both countries strongly articulates a security interest in stabilizing the military competition and overrides the parochial interests that are now driving it upwards, we are unlikely to make substantial progress in the negotiations between the two countries.

In the arms control negotiations between the two countries, one of the limiting factors is the difference in perception between Moscow and Washington of the present arms balance and the means by which military competition can be restrained. A better understanding of this "perception gap" can help to improve the prospect for arms control.

It is striking how differently the central strategic balance is perceived from Washington and from Moscow. In this country, one reads almost daily warnings from our military planners that the balance of military power is rapidly shifting in an adverse direction; that the Soviet lead in missile megatonnage and in numbers of missile launchers could give the Soviet Union a decisive advantage; that the MIRVing (adding multiple independently-targetable re-entry vehicles) of Soviet heavy missiles could, given anticipated improvements in accuracy, give the Soviet Union the capability to destroy all or most of the United States' fixed-site land-based missiles. Large-scale Soviet testing since the first SALT agreement and the beginning deployments of a new series of Soviet missile systems are viewed with alarm as possible harbingers of a Soviet drive toward strategic superiority. From Moscow, however, the Soviet lead in missile throw-weight, in numbers of missile launchers, and in access to raw materials are seen as far less advantageous than the U.S. lead in numbers of warheads and accuracy, and particularly in technology, as well as access to bases abroad and freedom from hostile neighbors. Despite strenuous Soviet efforts since the early 1960s to overcome the strategic inferiority under which the Soviet Union has lived since the end of World War II, it appears in Moscow that the American technological lead has continued to lengthen. The fact that each country perceives the other as having decisive advantages is a major source of dynamism in the arms competition, which is likely to persist so long as these marginal advantages are thought to have military or political significance.

There is also a difference between the American approach to arms control and the Soviet approach to disarmament. Apart from the initial Soviet suspicions over the word "control," which in Russian carries the connotations of "regulation" or "inspection," and which now appear to be largely dispelled, other differences persist. From the Soviet point of view, disarmament is a much simpler matter than is represented in Western arms control literature, which the Soviets tend to regard as intellectual calisthenics, abstract from life, intended to evade real issues if not to deceive. In negotiations, Soviet representatives are markedly uninterested in concepts, beyond the elementary principle of "equal security." The general way in which the concept of deterrence is applied in the Soviet Union differs in major ways from the much more differentiated meanings it has come to have in Western usage. In Russian, the terms used to express "deterrence" would translate literally as "containment by means of intimidation," and Soviet writings do not emphasize the distinctions to be found in American strategic theory between "deterrence" and "defense" or "war-fighting" capabilities; between "countervalue" and "counterforce" targeting; between "minimum," "limited," "finite" or "graduated" deterrence. Although the recent blurring of the line between "deterrence" and "counterforce" in the posture statement of the American secretary of defense was greeted with alarm in Moscow, it does in some measure bring American strategic doctrine into closer congruence with Soviet doctrinal writings. Whether it is in our interest to move in the Soviet direction on this point, rather than to encourage the Soviet Union to move toward an acceptance of a moderate-level deterrent balance, is another question.

The Soviet decision-making process on SALT matters is quite different from that in the United States. There is no Soviet analogue to the U.S. Arms Control and Disarmament Agency; no precise analogue to the National Security Council and its staff; and no circulation of defense scientists in and out of government, as in the United States, to provide an independent lobby and public debates on arms control issues. The Supreme Soviet, the legislative arm of government, does have standing commissions on foreign policy, which approved the first SALT treaty, but in the Soviet system there is no equivalent to congressional committee hearings, which are independent of and often critical of the administration's position during the period when decisions are being made. In the Soviet Union, the military play a larger role in originating positions on SALT than in the United States. The main locus of work on the preparation of positions for SALT is to be found in the Soviet Ministry of Defense, which has a section charged with this responsibility under the General Staff. Although the Soviet Ministry of Foreign Affairs is involved in the process, its role is largely limited to the diplomatic and political aspects of the negotiations, and it is kept out of the technical hardware details of arms limitation problems. Between the Ministry of Defense and the Party leadership are a number of important mechanisms for coordinating military policy with political and economic considerations, including the Military Council, on which Secretary Leonid Brezhnev sits as chairman, and the Military Industrial Commission, which oversees the Soviet armament industry. The Soviet penchant for extreme secrecy on military matters has restricted technical information on arms control issues to a small circle within the Soviet military establishment, although the effects of summit meetings on SALT may have widened the circle of Party and government officials who are informed and involved in arms limitation matters.

Despite these and other perceptual differences, however, both countries have shown an awareness that strategic military competition operates in a context of political competition between the two countries for influence and for power. As a consequence, although both countries are beginning to appreciate that militarily significant superiority is not possible for either country, military competition continues because of a mistaken belief in the political advantage to be gained by having an edge over the adversary in one weapons characteristic or another. This myth of the rational political utility of strategic nuclear weapons above a deterrent level must be punctured if military competition is to be stabilized at more reasonable levels.

Nevertheless, despite this propensity, both countries have shown an increasing recognition that SALT negotiations should be insulated as much as possible from the rise and fall of tensions in their political relationship. This compartmentalization rests upon the objective interest in both countries in reducing the danger of nuclear war, whether or not detente experiences setbacks on trade or other issues.

This attitude is reflected in recent Soviet commentaries on the Vladivostok agreement, which have hailed the agreement in positive terms and have expressed determination to carry forward negotiations at Geneva to translate the agreement into treaty form despite the disappointing but, one hopes, temporary collapse of the trade agreement.

Soviet commentators have expressed puzzlement over American criticism of the Vladivostok agreement and find it difficult to distinguish between critics who would, they feel, oppose any arms control agreement on whatever pretext and those who genuinely desire more substantial arms limitations. To the latter, Soviet commentators reaffirm the Soviet commitment to negotiate reductions in weapons levels, but they argue that the present agreement, which establishes a simple measure of equality in delivery vehicles, was a necessary first step before the complicated process of reductions could be negotiated. Implied in the Soviet commentaries is concern that the qualitative aspects of military competition need to be brought under control, but here lies the Soviet dilemma: the desire to control the qualitative arms race conflicts with their perception of inferiority in advanced military technology and their desire to avoid an agreement which would freeze them in that position of technological inferiority.

This dilemma is less likely to be resolved in a time of weak political leadership, for the most important requirement, if arms control is to succeed, is for a clear and strong recognition by the political leadership of both countries that their security depends upon stabilization of a strategic military equilibrium at a fraction of present levels. This is one perception the two countries should have in common. *(February 1975)*

New Challenges for SALT   *George Rathjens*

Dr. Rathjens's 1974 prediction that a SALT II (Strategic Arms Limitation Talks) agreement would not be forthcoming has proved sadly correct. The aspects of U.S. defense policy which he highlights here—the move away from a strategy of assured destruction, the momentum of weapons systems, and the need to "buy" support for SALT with new strategic programs—continue to complicate the arms control process.

A year ago President Nixon and Secretary Leonid Brezhnev all but promised that a permanent agreement limiting strategic offensive weapons would be concluded this year. Now though, as Nixon goes to meet with Brezhnev again, there is little expectation that last year's hopes will be realized or that there will be significant progress in other areas relating to strategic arms. It is a measure of how poor the prospects are that on the eve of this year's summit meeting the only agreements that seemed possible were a threshold test ban or a limitation on ABM (anti-ballistic missile) sites to one for each country. Neither would have a significant effect on Soviet or American weapons programs. It is clear that both Nixon and Brezhnev have been pushed in an effort to convey an impression of continuing arms control momentum and, in the President's case at least, to divert attention from his domestic difficulties.

These very difficulties are a major impediment to progress in SALT II. Watergate means that the President goes to Moscow with virtually no flexibility. With his oft-noted sensitivity to the concerns of the political right enhanced by his need to hold conservative support in the event of impeachment, about the only kind of deal he would dare bring back would be a Jackson-type agreement,* one that would require near equivalence in offensive force levels by all measures, and which would not involve any offsets for American superiority in technology and access to foreign bases.

There possibly was a time when a decision might have been made in the Politburo that advantages of other kinds—increased access to American technology, credits on favorable terms, and later, substantial trade—would be sufficient to justify acceptance of a strategic arms limitation agreement that would leave the United States with some net advantage. At least proponents of detente within the Soviet establishment could plausibly have argued such a case. But after the wheat deal, the war in the Near East, and the energy crisis, the situation is changed.

---

* The resolution offered by Sen. Henry Jackson at the time SALT I was ratified and subsequent negotiating proposals advanced by the Washington Democrat have stressed the need for precise equality in U.S. and Soviet forces by each of the static standards of comparison, such as numbers, payload, etc.

The United States' becoming dependent on Soviet oil and gas on a large scale is not in the cards. And the possibility of an extension of massive long-term credits to the USSR at concessionary rates for the development of these resources or for other purposes is much diminished, especially because of linkage with the questions of Jewish emigration and repression of intellectuals in the USSR. In the present climate, the President cannot deliver on improved trade arrangements, so it is hard to see any *quid pro quo* for Soviet willingness to "rectify" the Interim Offensive Arms Agreement.

From the several "state of the world" messages, from more recent statements by Secretary of Defense James Schlesinger, and from congressional reactions to SALT I and to administration budget requests it is clear that the major tenets of arms control orthodoxy which initially underlay the U.S. approach to SALT I are not accepted by this administration nor by the majority in the Congress. Deterrence through the threat of devastating retaliation against industry and population—the concept of an "assured destruction" capability—even as a rationale, let alone as a determinant of strategic force postures, is now widely questioned, as is the view that nuclear weapons are of very limited utility. Thus, Secretary Schlesinger finds substantial support for improvements in missile accuracy that would be irrelevant to "assured destruction," for new weapons and doctrine for using strategic weapons with flexibility against varieties of targets including adversary weapons, and for claims that one side can derive political advantage by having more force and a broader range of options available to it than its adversary. Acceptance of these views means that it is impossible to define a level of weapons that is "enough."

One of the other basic tenets of arms control orthodoxy—belief in Secretary of Defense Robert McNamara's "action-reaction" theory of the arms race—has also suffered erosion in the last several years. It is still true that one of the more powerful arguments that can be used to generate support for a new weapon is a claim that it is needed as a response to an adversary program, real or imagined; but it is now clear that, when needed, other arguments will be adduced, and may suffice, to sell new weapons. Thus, the offensive weapons programs of the Soviet Union and the United States seem to be going ahead with undiminished vigor notwithstanding the fact that with the conclusion of the ABM Treaty the "action-reaction" incentive for them is much reduced. The hope of the orthodox arms control community that the weapons acquisition chain can be broken by imposing constraints in a few key areas has been pretty well dashed.

This, coupled with a resurgence in the United States of the belief that "more" is better when it comes to strategic weapons—there has never been any evidence that a contrary view ever carried much weight in the Soviet Union—means that the framework for approaching the limitation of strategic arms is significantly altered. It is now clear that at least for some time the strategic arms question will have to be approached very much as one would approach the question of limiting conventional arms. Constraining one area of development or procurement is simply likely to mean intensified efforts in others. Thus, the challenge for SALT II is to slow or halt the strategic arms competition *across the board,* and then to produce reductions.

Regrettably, there is not the slightest evidence that either power is presently prepared to take the initiative along these lines.

Under the circumstances, a question must be raised as to whether continuing with SALT is desirable. A really comprehensive agreement could be very advantageous, but it is at best a distant possibility that must be weighed against the costs implicit in prolonged negotiations.

It is now clear that arms control negotiations have become a major factor in the weapons acquisition process. In a negotiating situation there are enhanced incentives to acquire new weapons. *First,* the fact that there are ongoing negotiations has probably been a decisive argument in securing congressional support for at least one or two American strategic programs. *Second,* with agreements in prospect, there will be pressure to make as much progress as is possible in those areas to which proscription may be applied. *Third,* because agreements based on symmetry in force structure are likely to be more easily reached and less severely criticized than those involving major asymmetries, there will be a propensity during the negotiating process to acquire the weapons of the adversary, even if they would be eschewed in a unilateral decision-making context. And if agreements are reached which permit symmetry in each of several areas, there will be incentives to exploit all of the opportunities they permit. *Finally,* to secure domestic support for an agreement, commitments may be made to proceed with new weapons which otherwise would not be developed and procured.

It can be plausibly argued, then, that continuing negotiations, even if punctuated occasionally by limited agreements, may be an exacerbating factor in the Soviet-American arms competition.

Particularly in the present circumstances, when the President is in no position to exercise leadership on the arms control front and when there is substantial internal debate about strategic doctrine, consideration should be given to a moratorium on SALT. Priority should now be given to getting our own house in order. *(June 1974)*

The Status of SALT: A Perspective
Lawrence Weiler

Written after the conclusion of the 1974 Vladivostok agreement, this article reviews the contentious issues that led up to it and highlights the continuing difficulties in reaching agreement between two nations whose strategic forces are differently structured.

Vladivostok, Secretary of State Henry Kissinger believes, produced a conceptual breakthrough, laying down guidelines for negotiation of an eight-year agreement on strategic offensive arms. Kissinger seems optimistic that the "technical" issues remaining can be resolved and an agreement can be ready for signature in 1975. Prudence, however, suggests some caution in this regard. A comparable guideline agreement in the first Strategic Arms Limitation agreement (SALT I) was the May 20, 1971, statement of agreed principles. At that time Kissinger also said there remained "technical" questions to be resolved. These happened to include such issues as the level of anti-ballistic missile (ABM) limitations, the offensive forces to be limited and the level of limitations to be applied. Still, the areas of agreement resulting from Vladivostok seem more specific than those of 1971 and both governments have strong political motivations to reach an accord; thus, if a Middle East war does not poison the climate and preoccupy the energies of officials, chances are that an agreement will be ready for congressional consideration during 1975.

The final nature of that agreement and congressional reception of it will be influenced by the coming period of internal debate in Washington. This will come at a time of considerable disenchantment among many in the arms control community with the SALT process as it has been used by the Nixon and Ford administrations, and also serious misgivings within the defense community about Kissinger's current efforts.

Thus it may be useful to address, even in a brief and incomplete way, the status of SALT. This requires both speculative consideration of the prospects for SALT in light of what has and has not been accomplished so far, and what considerations should be applied to future efforts.

The central result of SALT I was the ABM Treaty, which took care of probably the more important of the two strategic developments—the other being the multiple warheads known as MIRVs (multiple independently-targetable re-entry vehicles)—that threatened to upset a sense of strategic stability and further stimulate the strategic arms race. The ABM Treaty assures the continued effectiveness of surviving missile forces on both sides, an essential element of deterrence and strategic stability. (Also, those concerned with the allocation of public resources should not forget that, however technically and strategically misguided

U.S.-USSR Strategic Weapons (July 1978)

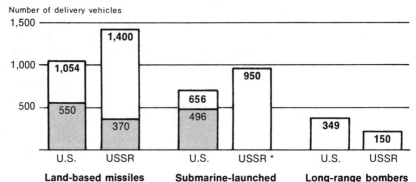

Number of delivery vehicles

Shaded sections reflect the current levels of operational multiple independently-targetable re-entry vehicles (MIRV). This graph adopts the SALT counting convention that any missile that has been tested as a MIRV will be counted as a MIRVed missile.

*—In calculating the number of Soviet MIRVed missiles the SS-NX-18, a Soviet MIRVed SLBM in the process of deployment, has been excluded due to the unavailability of data. Another recently developed Soviet SLBM, the SS-NX-17, has been excluded due to uncertainty about its MIRV capabilities.

it was, the full Safeguard ABM program would have been the most expensive single construction project in human history.) This achievement has been reinforced by the one arms control agreement so far in SALT II, the Protocol reducing permitted ABM sites from two to one, which has the effect of precluding concerns about an expanded radar base that might have developed had either side exercised its second-site option.

If SALT I produced a significant step forward with the ABM Treaty, it failed to achieve any real restraint on the competition in strategic offensive arms, even though the effect of the ABM Treaty was to make that competition relatively less meaningful in a strategic sense. The detailed, technical provisions of the Interim Agreement on Offensive Weapons (which came about because of U.S. insistence) can be misleading. That undertaking was, essentially, a temporary standstill agreement on additional launcher construction that permitted both sides to continue with other planned programs and postponed efforts to achieve real curbs on offensive arms.

The determinant offensive arms issue of SALT was, and is, what to do about MIRVs, a fact that the Nixon administration was slow to recognize, in part because MIRVing our ICBM (intercontinental ballistic missile) and SLBM (submarine-launched ballistic missile) forces *was* the planned U.S. five-year offensive arms program. The Nixon administration's "MIRV ban" proposal was constructed in a manner that assured it would not be accepted. The proposal precluded the Soviets from attainment of a MIRV technology through a MIRV ban—then considered essential for U.S. assurance that no Soviet MIRVs would be deployed. Furthermore, the proposal allowed the United States to manufacture and stockpile MIRVs although it was not permitted to deploy them. Added to this were requirements for the on-site inspection of missiles and of ABM sites. Contrary to published accounts, the Soviets, while never accepting—nor specifically rejecting—a MIRV test ban, continued to advocate a MIRV production and deployment ban during SALT I.

Early in SALT I when the United States proposed abandoning efforts to achieve qualitative limitations on offensive arms, the die was cast on the nature of the offensive arms agreement that would result. While a struggle was carried on within the bureaucracy in Washington, and perhaps in Moscow, to get a serious MIRV negotiation started, it did not succeed. The existing problems were predictable consequences of that failure. Faced with a U.S. proposal that involved no restriction on any planned U.S. programs, the Soviets immediately lost interest in offensive arms limitations. In order to get the ABM Treaty, Moscow agreed to some offensive arms limitations although they made sure these limitations did not interfere with their programs.

The first year and a half of SALT II were sterile as far as efforts to achieve offensive limitations were concerned. In part this was a consequence of Watergate; the Nixon administration was preoccupied with its survival and unwilling to make hard decisions while the Kremlin, uncertain of Nixon's staying power, reverted to its traditional holding tactic of presenting clearly unacceptable proposals.

There was a brief period at the start of SALT II that might have offered an opportunity to hold new programs in check while the two sides reassessed the postponed issues on offensive limitations. The Soviets proposed a freeze on new strategic programs, directing their attention at the U.S. B-1 bomber, Trident submarine and strategic cruise missile programs. No effort was made to see if a temporary halt on new programs could have been used as a negotiating basis (by holding in check new Soviet missile programs designed to carry MIRVs) for either a MIRV ban or a serious restriction on MIRVed forces. So much for use of "bargaining chips"!

Then came Watergate and the upheaval in the executive branch arms control community with its clear message to the rest of the bureaucracy

U.S.-USSR Targetable Warhead Levels
(excluding cruise missiles)

Number of targetable warheads (in thousands)

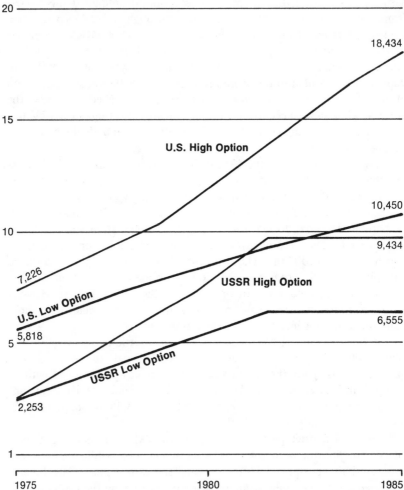

This graph illustrates future nuclear warhead levels for the U.S. and Soviet
Union which are possible under the Vladivostok ceilings of 1,320 strategic
launchers with MIRVs, and a 2,400 limit on the total number of strategic delivery
vehicles. The graph reflects the results of current programs and projects these
programs in order to maximize force levels under the Vladivostok ceilings. Not
included in the projections are future U.S. bomber levels, strategic cruise
missiles, a possible U.S. Trident II missile, or changes in current Defense
Department estimates of the likely MIRV capabilities of the new Soviet ICBMs.

that put Kissinger on the exposed left in the internal SALT debate. As was to be expected, the Soviets initiated new programs of their own, but on such a scale and with a pace that disturbed even some who had been prone to view U.S. programs as the principal catalyst of the arms race.

The nature of the Soviet MIRV program had two effects—one good and one bad. Contrary to earlier expectations that the Soviets would MIRV their SS-11s and SS-9s, their MIRV testing was with new, much larger missiles which require modifications of existing silos that are verifiable by national means; thus the possibility of MIRV controls, even after Soviet MIRV testing, was held open. However, this important development, and the associated Soviet cold-launch technique, had the effect of increasing concern in Washington about ICBM throw-weight asymmetry.*

With these clouds hanging over SALT II, serious efforts, within the context of stringent and balanced MIRV curbs, to overcome the increased asymmetries between the two sides brought about by MIRVs never seemed to have got off the ground.

U.S. concern was focused on limiting the Soviet throw-weight advantages for MIRVed ICBMs. To gain time, an initial U.S. suggestion was apparently made to freeze MIRV testing and deployment. Since this would have halted Soviet MIRV development during a period when the U.S. possessed an already massive MIRVed force, it was rejected. There then seems to have been a U.S. proposal to add to an extended Interim Agreement a limitation of equal throw-weight for MIRVed ICBMs. Soviet rejection of this presumably was based on the fact that, given their larger missiles, they would have been allowed fewer MIRVed ICBMs than the United States while the United States would in addition have had a large MIRVed SLBM force. The Soviet counterproposal reportedly was an equal limit on the total number of MIRVed missiles, while maintaining the unequal missile totals of the Interim Agreement. Apparently, unsuccessful efforts were then made, in the context of an extended interim agreement, to balance off the larger Soviet missile numbers with a MIRVed missile limitation that would allow the United States more than the USSR—and with sublimits on the Soviet SS-18s.

Two of the problems that made SALT II difficult are the size of existing U.S. MIRVed missile forces and the differing view of the two sides on the relative importance of missile throw-weight in counterforce capability. The Nixon and Ford administrations have, in effect, wanted to keep U.S. MIRVed forces close to programmed levels. With the massive size of those levels, particularly in nuclear warheads or re-entry vehicles, this position has made the objective of severe limitations on

---

* The cold-launch technique uses compressed air to "pop up" or elevate the missile before ignition of its engine. This launching method allows a larger missile to be placed in a silo of a given size.

Soviet MIRVs almost impossible. While the United States focused on limitations on land-based MIRVs, the only current area of Soviet MIRV programs, the USSR had its eyes on the 5,000 MIRVs in the U.S. missile submarine force. There apparently has been no U.S. attempt to resolve asymmetries through stringent limitations on MIRVed forces involving significant reductions in U.S. MIRV numbers. Related to this asymmetry have been the differences over throw-weight. The U.S. concern is that the larger Soviet ICBMs will not only confer an advantage in numbers of land-based MIRVs but will also permit warheads of greater explosive power. The Soviet concern has been with the U.S. technological advantage, including accuracy, a factor in a MIRVed world that is next to impossible to measure specifically in any arms agreement. In a recent Soviet article arguing that the United States had attempted to reduce the qualitative balance to a "single arbitrarily chosen parameter," Genrik Trofimenko must have thought it a nice twist to cite Albert Wchlstetter to make his point that a tenfold increase in warhead accuracy equals a thousandfold increase in its explosive power.

The asymmetries of a MIRVed world and the unwillingness to address MIRV controls in a bold fashion have resulted in the Vladivostok accord. That accord appears to represent a decision to let the current strategic generations go and attempt to put a cap on following generations. (This is a philosophy Kissinger used in justifying the proposed Threshold Test Ban Treaty.) Much is still unclear, but the proposed arrangement contains a few pluses and a number of disturbing features.

Agreement on equal aggregates for central systems is not unimportant. For many, SALT II involved as much a matter of appearance as substance, and, because of program asymmetries, agreement on a cutoff point for stopping has always been the most difficult problem. Equal aggregates and MIRV launcher totals may also afford a base for future reductions. Equal aggregates may also have overcome the forward base systems (FBS) issue, though it appears this has been accomplished by making launcher totals so high that FBS is subsumed in the difference between 2,400 and current U.S. levels. There will probably be *de facto* limits (the importance of which is debatable) on Soviet MIRVed ICBMs. Freedom-to-mix gives the United States the "right" to have equal numbers of missiles. And some will see a prospect that, in living with the rough balance struck here, we will reassess the significance of ICBM vulnerability, give heavier weight to the rediscovered "fratricide" problem, and not worry about the concerns of some strategic analysts.*

---

* The possibility that during a nuclear attack the detonation of the initial warheads may degrade the accuracy and effectiveness of following warheads is known as the "fratricide" problem.

Others may hope the ABM Treaty precedent will be followed and future agreements will lower the projected permitted levels.

There are, however, reasons for serious concern with the envisioned agreement. It could have the effect of "legislating" strategic programs desired by the military on both sides. Pressures for U.S. weapon increases to reach 2,400 launchers will exist. The MIRV "limitations" will authorize a large-scale Soviet MIRVing program and, for the United States, not only completion of current Minuteman III and Poseidon submarine missile programs, but a full 10-boat Trident program with 34 launchers to spare. With no restrictions on accuracy improvements and the large Soviet MIRVed ICBM throw-weight capability, strong pressures to move to a replacement for the Minuteman ICBM force will result. The agreement to permit mobile ICBMs—the direct result of the MIRV levels—contains future verification problems whenever reductions are considered. Since whatever promise this agreement may hold lies in future efforts within its framework, it is disturbing that the obligation to start such efforts is relegated to 1980-81. Why not 1977 when an elected U.S. administration will be in office? Finally, this agreement will be regarded by many as a U.S.-Soviet failure to meet their obligations under Article VI of the Non-Proliferation Treaty, the instrument directed at a problem that may pose more real threats to world stability than the current U.S.-Soviet strategic balance.

The status of SALT? Success on defensive arms and limited failure on offensive arms. The limited failure calls for a serious hearing of those concerned with improving the process. In this regard, we should recognize that the status of SALT includes a continuation of the secrecy that has excluded the public and, more than they have realized, the Congress from effective participation in decision making in the process; an examination of this issue might explain a good part of why in one case there was success and in another limited failure. And since the potential for good or ill in the Vladivostok accord lies in the future, a stock-taking in this regard should be part of any ratification of the proposed agreement.

(December 1974)

Verification Guidelines for SALT II   *Walter Slocombe*

The controversy over Soviet compliance with the terms of the 1972 Strategic Arms Limitation Talks (SALT I) agreement continues unabated. From that dispute have emerged some guidelines for the development—and the debate—of any new agreement.

The growing catalog of allegations of Soviet actions inconsistent with the terms or spirit of the SALT I agreements covers a wide range. At the one extreme is the almost absurdly comic flap in which an explosion near a Soviet natural gas pipeline was denounced in the periodical *Aviation Week & Space Technology* as a laser attack on a U.S. sensor satellite. At the other extreme are the tests of Soviet anti-aircraft missiles and radars that apparently ceased only after strong U.S. representations concerning the prohibitions against testing such weapons "in an ABM [anti-ballistic missile] mode." In between—and the focus of much of the controversy—is a series of Soviet actions consistent with a strict reading of the 1972 SALT I agreements but inconsistent with the U.S. interpretation of those agreements expressed at that time. These include the construction of an ABM radar at a test range other than the one the United States identified in 1972 as the sole existing Soviet test range and the deployment of the SS-19 missile which has a volume about 40-50 percent larger than a "light" missile as defined by the United States in a unilateral statement.

This is not the occasion to review the merits of all the allegations or the Soviet responses to those the administration has raised as issues of compliance. Nonetheless, and subject to many qualifications, it is appropriate to conclude that the USSR has pressed the 1972 SALT I agreements to the limit of legalistic interpretation. That was only to be expected. But it is surprising that the Nixon administration has put itself in a position of accepting Soviet actions which can be squared with those agreements only by abandonment of the assurances it gave to the Congress and the American people—and thereby clearly signalled to the USSR as its view—when the agreements were under consideration. This unsatisfactory experience with "unilateral statements" has led to demands that any new SALT agreement be free of ambiguity, provide against all loopholes, and be one in which the United States does not interpret any provision as any more restrictive than the USSR has explicitly agreed it to be.

These supposed lessons of the current compliance flap will have some impact on the negotiations, because they can hardly be entirely ignored by either side. To the extent that a tighter, clearer agreement results, the benefit is clear. However, whatever the substantive and verification terms of a new SALT pact, the shadow of the SALT I compliance controversy will clearly affect the ensuing debate in the United States. Indeed, discussion of verification may dominate the new debate, especially if the agreement comes before the Congress in the midst of an election year, and at a time when detente and "trusting" the USSR have again become politically and publicly disreputable. It therefore seems useful to suggest several general propositions—beyond the somewhat utopian call for comprehensive and unambiguous treaties—which can be derived from the debate and which may serve as guidelines in considering potential verification and compliance issues under a new SALT agreement.

No agreement is acceptable on strategic—and still less on political— grounds which is highly sensitive to cheating. One unfortunate effect of the legalistic turn to the debate is that we lose perspective: Only the most alarmist observers can regard any of the allegations of Soviet cheating, even if wholly true, as materially affecting the assumptions about the strategic balance underlying the 1972 SALT I agreements. The unfortunate fact of the Soviet attitude toward compliance, on which renewed attention has been focused by the latest episodes, means that we cannot risk an agreement in which real dangers to our security might follow from significant violations.

Any agreement must be seen to be verifiable. Especially in a climate sensitized to the issues of verification, an important criterion of political viability of an arms control agreement in the United States is not only that it can be verified but that the military and intelligence communities also share that belief and are willing to say so.

An agreement, once operational, must also be "seen" to be verifiable in the literal sense. The process of checking compliance must take place in a sufficiently public way as to generate the confidence of the American people. To have information about alleged violations dribbled out by critics of the agreement is the worst possible way to maintain public confidence in an agreement in the face of concern about possible Soviet cheating. Here, as in so many other areas, secrecy has corrosive side effects. And it is an inadequate answer to say that the USSR prefers to deal with these issues in private. One Soviet countercharge of American SALT violations is that information about alleged Soviet cheating, and about Soviet responses to U.S. questions, became public! While there is certainly a place for confidential exchanges, it must be made clear to the USSR in the course of the negotiations that, in order to maintain public support for the SALT process, the United States government will have to make full and complete public reports on compliance, on the details of actions which are alleged to violate the agreement, and on the details of Soviet assurances that there is no violation.

Deliberate ambiguity buttressed by unilateral assertion can be a highly useful negotiating device and should not be rejected entirely in the SALT context. There are some key subjects on which the parties will not be able to agree explicitly, but which can usefully be handled by a tacit understanding or even by a clearly asserted "unaccepted" unilateral interpretation. However, in contrast to the apparent practice in 1972, any such unilateral statements of interpretations should be identified clearly to the Soviet negotiators as propositions that the United States will treat as equivalent to agreed provisions and should not be *post hoc* rationalizations for Congress.

The Standing Consultative Commission

The primary purpose of the Standing Consultative Commission is to provide the United States and the USSR with a mechanism for facilitating the implementation of the provisions of the SALT agreement as well as the 1971 Accident Measures Agreement. The latter agreement commits the United States and the Soviet Union to notify each other in the event of any accident or other incident which could create a risk of nuclear war. Although the value of such a commission was discussed as early as the initial SALT negotiations in 1969, U.S. and Soviet disagreement over such issues as the charter and composition of the commission delayed its establishment until December 21, 1972.

One of the primary functions of the Standing Consultative Commission is the formulation of procedures for the replacement of older strategic delivery vehicles as well as procedures for the dismantling or destruction of strategic weapon launchers as required by SALT I. The other major function is to provide a forum for the discussion of questions concerning compliance with the SALT I agreements. The commission is also authorized to consider amendments to the agreements and even proposals concerning further limitations. Some observers hope that the Standing Consultative Commission will some day encourage and institutionalize the strategic dialogue between the two countries.

Each government is represented by a commissioner and a deputy commissioner who are assisted by their staffs. All proceedings of the commission are in private; between sessions the commissioners may communicate through the regular diplomatic channels. The Standing Consultative Commission is required to meet at least twice a year.

Contractual tightness and clarity of expression are not the prime factors that enforce international agreements. Although it may be easy enough to find pretexts for denouncing an international treaty for nonperformance by another party once the treaty is no longer felt to be advantageous, it is never easy to "call" a violation of an agreement that is still regarded as useful and viable in general. Indeed, it may be questioned whether the reaction of the United States to most of the alleged Soviet violations would have been much easier to decide upon had they explicitly been either permitted or forbidden in the agreement. Ultimately, the only sanction against violations is the willingness to renounce a hard-won and still useful agreement or exact costs in other aspects of the Soviet-U.S. relationship. If we expect agreements to be observed, however, we must be prepared to run such risks—and we must make it clear that we will do so.

Verification has been the bugaboo of arms control for a long time. The debate on the 1972 SALT agreements was focused to a remarkable degree not on potential cheating but on the actual substance of the agreement. Proponents of arms control will have no such luck this time. Verification and the potential for violations will be major issues. A "soft" approach to them is no way to advance the long-term prospects for arms control—but neither is accepting the proposition that an agreement can be so clear that the Soviets could advance no conceivable defense of a violation. *(February 1976)*

Editors' Perspective
A Review of the Charges of Soviet SALT Violations

Beginning in late 1974 a number of allegations were made publicly which questioned the Soviet Union's compliance with the basic provisions of the Strategic Arms Limitation agreements—the ABM Treaty and the Interim Agreement Limiting Strategic Offensive Arms. Many of these charges were subsequently raised by the United States with the USSR in the Standing Consultative Commission, a forum which was established by the SALT accords. Some of these questions were quickly resolved; others underwent examination and negotiation with the USSR. The following is a summary of the major charges of Soviet violations and a review of the Ford administration's statements concerning these allegations.

The III-X Silos: During 1973, U.S. reconnaissance satellites detected a large number of new silos (about 150) under construction in the ICBM (intercontinental ballistic missile) complexes in western Russia. The silos were designated "III-X" by U.S. intelligence. If these silos are capable of launching ICBMs, then they are in violation of the provisions of the Interim Agreement which prohibits new missile silo construction.

When the United States raised the issue with the USSR, the USSR explained that these were command and control silos and that this would be increasingly evident as the construction continued. Even though the U.S. intelligence community is said to agree that the intended purpose of these silos is for launch control, what actually concerns the United States is the possibility that these silos might be easily converted to launch ICBMs. This concern arises from the similarity of the new Soviet silos to regular ICBM silos. Defense Secretary James Schlesinger stated in March 1975 congressional testimony that the United States was pressing the USSR to make "design changes that would clearly prevent the facilities from being used to circumvent the agreement." Although it is not apparent from the public record whether the USSR eventually agreed to make these alterations, the issue no longer appears to be under active negotiation between the two countries. Following a long period of discussion with the USSR concerning the need for criteria which would assure the United States that these were indeed command and control silos, Secretary of State Henry Kissinger stated on December 9, 1975, that "we have been given criteria which seem to us for the time being adequate . . . though we will be vigilant in making certain that any unusual construction activity at these silos would raise profound questions."

SA-5 Mobile Radar: One of the most important of the alleged Soviet violations concerns the charge that the USSR may have tested a mobile version of the SA-5 air defense radar in an "ABM mode." The ABM Treaty prohibits the development, testing, or deployment of any mobile ABM system as well as the development of an ABM capability for non-ABM weapons such as air defense systems. The clarity of these prohibitions was reduced by a "common understanding" to the ABM Treaty which permits non-phased array radars for range safety or instrumentation purposes to be located outside of the ABM test ranges. This provision was added to the treaty at the insistence of the United States.

Soviet testing of the SA-5 radar during 1973 and 1974 led to U.S. concern that the radar might be tracking incoming ballistic missile warheads. After a period of internal deliberation, the U.S. government raised this issue with the USSR in February 1975. Shortly thereafter the Soviet testing ceased and the issue appears to be closed. In light of the previous number of tests, the question remains whether the USSR ceased operation as a result of U.S. expressions of concern or whether it was merely part of their planned program.

USSR Laser Interference: During October and November 1975 the infrared sensors upon certain U.S. early warning and communication satellites experienced incidences of strong infrared illumination from unknown sources in western Russia. An article appearing in *Aviation Week & Space Technology* reported these occurrences and concluded that the energy levels of the illumination were too high to be the result of natural causes or ICBM launches. One possible explanation offered was that the USSR was using a laser radar to track high-altitude U.S. military satellites. Another, more serious explanation detailed by the article speculated that the USSR might have been experimenting with ground-based lasers with the aim of blinding the infrared sensors on U.S. early warning satellites.

These incidents did not actually concern the ABM Treaty since it only prohibits interference with photo-reconnaissance satellites used for verification purposes and not the other types of satellites which were involved in the incidents. Yet the concern was expressed that if the USSR did have such a laser capability it might be used against low-altitude reconnaissance satellites.

A few weeks later a *Washington Post* story reported that U.S. photo-reconnaissance revealed the source of the incidents as fires from ruptures in an above-ground natural gas transmission line in western Russia. James Wade, Director of the Defense Department's SALT Task Force, has also suggested in recent congressional testimony that this was the most likely explanation. He stated that the issue was being overblown by the press and further revealed that these incidents had occurred in other parts of the world including one in the Middle East. Finally, Dr. Wade provided for the record the following statement:

> Analysis of these events essentially eliminates initial concerns that lasers were being used against the satellite system. Instead the events are believed to have occurred as a result of several large fires along Soviet natural gas pipelines. These events were local in nature and did not reduce the satellite system's ability to provide early warning of ballistic missile launches.

"Light" versus "Heavy" Missiles: Strategically the most significant allegation of Soviet noncompliance with the SALT provisions concerns the limitations on the deployment of "heavy" missiles. During the SALT I negotiations, the United States was anxious to achieve some type of limits upon the deployment of Soviet SS-9 ICBMs in order to mitigate the threat these large or "heavy" missiles pose to the U.S. land-based missile force. Although the United States was able to gain Soviet agreement to a provision which would prohibit a "significant increase"* in the dimensions of existing ICBM launcher silos, it was less successful in negotiating limits on the deployment of "heavy" missiles.

In Article II of the Interim Agreement Limiting Strategic Offensive Arms the United States and USSR agreed not to convert "light" ICBM launcher silos or "older" ICBM launcher silos into "land-based launchers for heavy ICBMs."** Despite this provision, great difficulty still remained in the formulation of a meaningful definition of the limit between "light" and "heavy" missiles. Since the USSR was not willing to agree on a common definition of a "heavy" missile, the United States was compelled to make a unilateral statement to the effect that it would "consider any ICBM having a volume significantly greater [meaning 10-15 percent] than that of the largest light ICBM now operational on either side to be a heavy ICBM." This meant that since the largest "light" ICBM in 1972 (the Soviet SS-11) had a volume of about 65 cubic meters, the United States would define a "heavy" ICBM as one with a volume of about 80 cubic meters or more.

During congressional testimony on the SALT agreement in 1972 U.S. officials gave Congress strong assurances that new Soviet ICBMs would

---

*According to the U.S. unilateral statement this meant that an increase could not be greater than 10-15 percent of the present silo dimensions.

**Light launchers include the U.S. Minutemen ICBMs and the Soviet SS-11 and SS-13 ICBMs. "Older" launchers include the U.S. Titan II ICBMs and Soviet SS-7 and SS-8 ICBMs.

be constrained by the unilaterally-declared U.S. limit. In particular, Defense Secretary Melvin Laird stated that he would interpret this provision to limit new "light" missiles to an increase of no more than 30 percent in volume.

Since 1972 the USSR has developed a replacement for its SS-11 ICBMs which reportedly has a volume about 50 percent larger than the SS-11. This new missile, known as the SS-19, has achieved its greater volume by means of the more efficient use of silo space and better missile propellant, and consequently does not require a "significant increase" in the size of the launcher silo. While this is in compliance with the agreement's common understanding concerning silo limits, the SS-19 is a direct contradiction of the unilateral, though legally nonbinding, U.S. statement with respect to the limit between "light" and "heavy" ICBMs.

The lesson drawn from this episode by U.S. officials is the need for explicit and precise acknowledgement by the USSR on even the technical details of these issues. As Defense Secretary Schlesinger commented:

> If we want to preclude [the USSR from] doing something, we have to be fairly precise. I think the issue of the deployment of the heavier throw-weight missiles replacing the SS-11 is an issue of this sort. If one reads the words of the agreement, the Soviets are doing something that is not precluded. It is inconsistent, quite clearly, I think, with our understanding of our own unilateral statement. That is an area that calls for much greater precision in the future.

This issue was initially raised in the Standing Consultative Commission, but now has been shifted back into the current SALT II negotiations.

Kamchatka ABM radar: The most recent charge of Soviet cheating involves the Soviet deployment of a modern phased-array radar for testing ABM systems in the Kamchatka peninsula in northeastern Russia. Article IV of the ABM Treaty limited both nations to the ABM test ranges which were already in existence or were "additionally agreed" to by both sides. Since the USSR refused to discuss the location of its test ranges, the United States made a formal statement identifying current ABM test ranges at White Sands, New Mexico, and the Kwajalein Atoll in the Pacific for the United States; and near Sary Shagan in Kazakhstan for the USSR. In response, the Soviet delegation stated that "there was a common understanding on what ABM test ranges were, . . . that the reference in Article IV to 'additionally agreed' test ranges was sufficiently clear, and that national means permitted identifying current test ranges."

In light of these provisions, some individuals such as retired Admiral Elmo Zumwalt have charged that the Soviet Kamchatka ABM radar is in violation of the ABM Treaty. In contrast, administration officials state that it is not a violation. Both Secretary Kissinger and Dr. Wade, the Defense Department's spokesman, have emphasized that this is primarily a "technical issue," and another lesson concerning the need for more specificity in agreements with the USSR. They point out that since the USSR never explicitly provided information on the location of its ABM test ranges, the Kamchatka ABM radar can not be proven a violation of the treaty, especially since the USSR has reportedly always maintained some type of radar capability in Kamchatka. Finally, the significance of this new radar, according to Dr. Wade, is not its effect on the SALT agreements but its value for Soviet ICBM testing.

Other Issues: Both the United States and USSR have charged the other with interference of their national means of verification by means of concealment. There have also been allegations that the USSR has been jamming U.S. electronic intelligence surveillance. *(February 1976)*

The Verification of Arms Control Agreements
George Rathjens

In the summer of 1977 both houses of Congress passed legislation amending the Arms Control and Disarmament Act to include a new section relating to verification of arms control agreements. This legislation, as well as some of the questioning of Paul Warnke during hearings on his confirmation as director of the Arms Control and Disarmament Agency, and the criticism that attended his abolishment of the Verification Bureau in a reorganization of the Arms Control and Disarmament Agency have to be seen as a reflection of renascent and, in my view, exaggerated and potentially disadvantageous concern with the verification question. The current emphasis no doubt has its origins, at least in part, in dissatisfaction with the SALT I (Strategic Arms Limitation Talks) agreements and current Soviet programs which some have seen as evidence of Soviet non-compliance, or in any case, bad faith, and in the general deterioration of Soviet-American relations, now that the bloom of detente is a bit wilted.

Senator Dick Clark (D-Iowa), in discussing the new legislation, wisely observed that "there is a point where the search for perfect verification becomes its own end, and agreements which can be adequately verified are lost in the argumentation over how to attain complete, 100-percent compliance." Too much emphasis on verification, Clark went on, "tends to focus the eye on only one aspect of a highly complex subject, where risks must be balanced against advantages and where in the end we must ask ourselves whether, in the absence of perfection, an agreement which provides adequate limitations, adequate safeguards, and adequate verifications, is still better than none at all." I would warn additionally against another problem: the possibility that excessive emphasis on verification (e.g., insistence on measures that are patently unacceptable to an adversary) can be used to insure that an agreement will not be reached when the real reasons for resistance are otherwise, and perhaps less defensible in the court of world, or domestic, public opinion. This has happened in the past. Examples have been the U.S. insistence in recent years upon on-site inspection as a condition for a comprehensive nuclear test ban treaty and for a ban on multiple independently-targetable re-entry vehicles (MIRVs). With the current emphasis on verification (and interest in a new test ban treaty) it is perhaps instructive to consider these two instances further.

It will be recalled that a comprehensive test ban could have been negotiated at virtually any time during the 1960s but for American insistence on, and Soviet resistance to, on-site inspection as a means of verifying that remotely observed, suspicious signals had their origins in earthquakes rather than in clandestine underground weapons tests. Would the United States have been worse off than we are now had we accepted a comprehensive test ban treaty without on-site inspection? It is extremely unlikely that the Soviet Union would have carried out as comprehensive a program of tests as the one that has ensued, but even if it had, and the United States had conducted no tests, the strategic and tactical nuclear weapons balances would not be noticeably different than they are now, much less critically different. It is much more likely that the Soviets would have complied with the treaty or at least foregone tests in the range above, say, 100 kilotons, where detection and identification capabilities are quite good. In that event, we would surely be less concerned than we are now about the current Soviet ICBM (intercontinental ballistic missile) programs and their potential impact on the strategic balance.

Doubtless, many of those who opposed a comprehensive test ban in the early 1960s unless it had a substantial number of on-site inspections did so because of a genuine belief that the inspection rights were necessary as a deterrent to Soviet cheating which might endanger U.S. security. Now, the situation is somewhat different. Detection, and particularly identification, capabilities have been improved; and weapons design is a mature technology, so that there is less to be learned from further testing than there was a few years ago. Whatever changes in nuclear capabilities we can look forward to are much more likely to be a consequence of improvements in delivery vehicles and in command and control than in warheads. Yet there continues to be opposition to the comprehensive test ban, now apparently grounded more in concern about the United States' being prevented from testing than about Soviet non-compliance. The fact that the limit in the Threshold Test Ban Treaty was set at 150 kilotons when the threshold for detection and identification by remote seismic means was several times lower reflects this desire to go on testing. In this context, arguments that we need on-site inspection if we are to have a comprehensive test ban must be seen as an effort more to gull the public, frustrate agreement, and satisfy the weaponeers, than to protect legitimate security interests.

The test ban experience provides another illuminating lesson that helps put verification problems in perspective. It is now widely known that both the United States and the Soviet Union have been guilty of technical violations of the limited treaty: both have carried out underground nuclear explosions that have resulted in radioactive debris being carried beyond their borders. There was no problem of verification in these instances: there was a problem of how to respond, a problem which has also arisen in connection with SALT.

The case of a ban on MIRVs is very different from that of the comprehensive test ban, but equally as instructive. It seems unlikely that we could have had a MIRV ban even had the United States not insisted upon on-site inspection. In retrospect, however, we certainly should have tried, for even though the United States would have given up a lot, most of us would probably now agree that both the United States and the Soviet Union would be better off in a MIRV-free world. But the fact remains that we did raise the on-site inspection issue as a condition for a ban, even though there was little reason to believe that it would be either acceptable or very useful as a means for the verification of compliance, the important means of control in that case being limitation on testing, something we could verify with unilateral means.

Some of the agreements that were concluded prior to SALT I provide lessons of a different kind: that some arms control agreements may be acceptable even when there is little or no capability for verification of compliance. Certainly, there was virtually none in the case of the biological warfare and seabed treaties and probably not much more in the case of the space treaty. They were approved because it was widely understood that violations would have little impact: none, if not detected or announced; and, if disclosed, an effect that would be mainly political rather than military and probably at least as likely to redound to the disadvantage as to the advantage of the violator. (Note, the treaties were written so as *not* to proscribe useful military activities: the use of reconnaissance and communications satellites in the case of the space treaty and deployment of weapons in the sea, that is in submarines, as distinct from on the seabed.) Verification was simply put aside and the agreements were concluded because it seemed politically useful to do so. How could any arms control agreement that was risk free be other than desirable? At least that was the feeling at that time. And, most people would probably still argue that, on balance, they were desirable, if not very significant.

Yet, the deemphasis on verification in these treaties is inconsistent with at least the House version of the amending language to the Arms Control Act, which states that "it is the sense of the Congress that effective verification of compliance should be an indispensable part of any international arms control agreement," and for that matter with Paul Warnke's statement that "an unverifiable agreement is worse than none at all." (The Senate wisely modified the House language by replacing the word "effective" with the word "adequate" before the word "verification" in the House's language, and then made it clear in debate that it considered no capability at all "adequate" in cases such as these! And, in fairness, it must be noted that Warnke's remark, and one made about a possible need for on-site inspection, were made in a context of what he characterized as "genuine arms control" and an "effective arms control regime." Obviously, he had in mind agreements with much greater military impact than the biological warfare, space, and seabed agreements or, for that matter, the SALT I agreements.)

This brings us to the lessons to be learned from SALT. There has been a lot of dissatisfaction in the United States, particularly with the Interim Offensive Agreement: unhappiness about the asymmetry in numbers of missile launchers allowed and about the asymmetry in "throw-weight," as well as about Soviet activities since the negotiation of the agreements, at least some of which are clearly inconsistent with U.S. "unilateral interpretations" that were offered with respect to them. And, there have, of course, been problems with the Vladivostok understandings, the major ones relating to the Backfire bomber and cruise missile.

It is of great interest that these problems have their origins in sloppy drafting (especially in the case of the Vladivostok Accords), in the nature of the balance agreed to (in the Interim Offensive Agreements), in exaggerated claims made in defense of the agreements which involved treating the unilateral interpretations as if they were part of the agreements, in the way in which we should respond to "violations" of our unilateral interpretations, and, in some cases, the way in which we should respond to clear violations of agreements or Soviet actions which could plausibly be so interpreted—the Soviet launching of missile-carrying submarines prior to dismantling the required number of old ICBM launchers, the covering of mobile missiles and submarine facilities with canvas, and the jamming of our interception of Soviet radar tests. But with the exception of the last two instances, the problems *have not* been related to verification; and in these instances not to verification capabilities but rather to whether the Soviet Union was complying with agreements relating to non-interference with verification.

As we turn to SALT II (and III, IV . . .) probably *the* critical question that will underlie, if not dominate, debate will be that of the role of nuclear weapons in world affairs. Depending on one's view, this will have important implications with regard to verification requirements.* If one believes in the credibility of limited options—in "nuclear war-fighting"—then numbers and performance characteristics of nuclear delivery systems, and defenses, may be important. In that case, one would want good capabilities to verify compliance with agreements that affect these qualities, or in the absence of agreements, good intelligence capabilities for determining what the adversary is doing. On the other hand, to the degree that one believes that the strategic balance is very stable and that limited or nuclear war-fighting scenarios are not credible —or to be more precise, that the weapons which might be affected by agreements have no credible nuclear war-fighting role—the situation is very different. Violations of agreements will not make much difference and therefore there is not much of a direct case for good verification capabilities. But if one accepts this view of the balance, one has to wonder what SALT is all about. A SALT II agreement may have political utility even if it is nearly meaningless in terms of military impact, but to the degree that this is true, the verification question ought to be considered mainly from a political perspective: Are the arrangements for verification and the possibility of verifying compliance or disclosing of non-compliance, which will depend on verification capabilities, likely to have important and favorable effects on Soviet-American relations, including

---

*The possibility of future agreements that may be meaningful from a military perspective raises the issue of precedent. At one time there were those who saw in Soviet-American arms control and disarmament efforts the possibility of a linked series of agreements, with the balance becoming increasingly unstable to perturbations such as clandestine production of a small number of additional nuclear-capable weapons systems. Recall, for example, the three-stage U.S. proposal of 1962 leading to general and complete disarmament. From such a perspective, one could argue the necessity for increasingly effective—and intrusive—verification arrangements, and that there was some danger of getting on a slippery slope where verification capabilities might lag behind the pace of arms control and disarmament. The precedent question no longer seems much of a problem, considering that it is now widely accepted that getting to levels where strategic balance will be qualitatively different will be possible only in the event of major changes in political relationships, and that, in the view of many, SALT II (or III, IV, V . . .) will do little more than legitimate a continuing competition in strategic arms.

Political Aspects of Verification and Response

While considering how to respond to treaty violations, one is led to ask whether one needs better capabilities for observing and assessing adversary actions with an agreement than without one. The answer will vary from case to case, but there are general arguments on both sides of the issue.

On the one hand, the very existence of an agreement commits a state and generally the leadership that negotiated the agreement to a maintenance of the treaty regime. Unless there are very large advantages to be realized, there will be a disposition to comply with the agreement or at least to avoid any significant risk of a verifiable charge of noncompliance. Actions that might lead to such a charge which in the absence of a treaty would be taken on the basis of low-level decisions will commonly either be eschewed or most carefully considered at a political level before being undertaken. Thus, even quite imperfect verification capability may have a powerful inhibiting effect, given a treaty, and one can plausibly argue that the verification capability need not be as good as related intelligence capability in the absence of a treaty.

But there is the other side of the coin: a nation can take actions to compensate for possible adversary moves often at a modest cost in the absence of a treaty, whereas the cost may be high if a treaty is in effect and the response jeopardizes the viability of the treaty. Thus a treaty may inhibit *response* to ambiguous indicators of adversary action and if that is so, there will be a case for a higher standard of intelligence capability than in the absence of a treaty.

There is also the related point: in the absence of a treaty, a response can be initiated without full disclosure of the intelligence capabilities on which it is based, whereas if a treaty is in effect, and the logical response is proscribed by it, a decision may have to be made between, on the one hand, no response at all, and on the other hand, disclosure of capabilities to justify a response.

All of this is to emphasize that the question of what is desirable from a verification perspective cannot be rationally separated from the question of response.

---

the prospects for later agreements that may be more meaningful from a military perspective?

One concludes that consideration of verification must be inextricably linked to—and to a large degree depends on and must follow—discussion of the objectives of agreements and the role seen for the weapons affected. With its amendment to the Arms Control and Disarmament Act, the Congress (with some significant exceptions) seems to be getting the cart before the horse or at least to be looking at the verification problem myopically. There is a danger that the present concern about the adequacy of verification capabilities may divert us from more serious problems with respect to future agreements, and it may lead to our not concluding agreements that would be advantageous. As we look to the future it is worth bearing in mind three main points:

—We have missed at least one opportunity, and possibly more, to improve our security because of excessive concern or misplaced emphasis on verification;

—There appear to have been no instances where we have agreed to anything and had reason to be sorry later because of a failure of verification (although there has been dissatisfaction for other reasons with agreements concluded);

—We have had agreements which have been widely seen as desirable when verification capabilities were nil or nearly so. *(July/August 1977)*

Most of us are exposed to arms control issues through the arguments about weapons systems which we hear briefly on television or read in the newspaper. These arguments often seem to be about simple "yes or no" questions: Should we build the B-1? Do we need the cruise missile? Should we go ahead with the MX? Anyone making a serious attempt to answer these questions, however, comes to realize that they are more complicated than they seem and involve a technical understanding of a weapon's characteristics, an evaluation of its cost effectiveness, and judgments about its role in our nuclear strategy and possible impact on arms control. These latter judgments are the most important and usually the most difficult because they must rest, in part, on speculations about what the Soviets are up to. This section provides an introduction to the kinds of arguments used in the difficult decisions on the shape of American strategic forces.

The first group of articles focuses on U.S. nuclear strategy. Since the acquisition by both superpowers of intercontinental strategic forces, there has been a continuing debate in the West about what its strategy should be. One school of thought has argued that limited nuclear wars are possible and that—after any nuclear war—there will be a victor and a vanquished. Therefore, our strategy must emphasize the capability to fight and win nuclear wars. Such a strategy, it is argued, requires American strategic forces which possess a significant hard-target-kill capability, that is, weapons which can destroy the enemy's weapons, even if they are in hardened silos. The other school of thought rejects these arguments, holding instead that the emphasis in our strategy should continue to be on deterring nuclear war. Hard-target-kill weapons are not necessary to such a strategy and may, in fact, destabilize the nuclear relationship in a crisis by obliging each side to attempt to strike first.

The second group of articles focuses more directly on the weapons systems themselves. Each leg of the Triad—as the American strategic nuclear force of bombers, submarines, and land-based missiles is called—is reviewed and Soviet views on nuclear war are examined to help determine the nature of a Soviet threat and what kinds of weapons and strategy would best meet it without increasing the risks or costs of conflict.

Nuclear Strategy & Weapons

Flexibility: The Imminent Debate   *John C. Baker*

In this article, written at the time of the announcement of the new Schlesinger doctrine of limited nuclear war, John Baker outlines the case against the development of an effective "silo-killing" counterforce capability. Although the doctrine is four years old, the debate on counterforce continues.

In his 1970 "state of the world" message President Nixon asked, "Should a President, in the event of a nuclear attack, be left with the single option of ordering the mass destruction of enemy civilians, in the face of the certainty that it would be followed by the mass slaughter of Americans?" While it was obvious that the President believed that he needed greater flexibility in the employment of nuclear weapons, the specific implications of this remark for American nuclear strategy and strategic weapon programs were unclear at the time, and remained so for the next four years. It is expected that the missing details at last will be spelled out in the President's 1974 "state of the world" message and in Secretary of Defense James Schlesinger's defense budget report.

Congress and the American people would do well to scrutinize these documents closely because it is very likely they will raise fundamental questions for the nation concerning what type of nuclear doctrine it should adopt. Furthermore, the choice of nuclear doctrines will have obvious consequences for American political relations, arms control efforts, and weapon procurement policies. Most importantly, the issue will not be whether the United States *should or should not* adopt greater strategic flexibility in the employment of its nuclear weapons, as some would imply, but rather *what kinds of actions* in the name of strategic flexibility would most contribute to American security—and what kinds would most detract from it.

While "strategic flexibility" is a concept which does not lend itself readily to definition, former Defense Secretary Richardson explained it last year in congressional testimony as "having the plans, procedures, forces, and command and control capabilities necessary to enable the United States to select and carry out the response appropriate to the nature and level of the provocation." Even more recently, Secretary Schlesinger stated that a change in the "targeting strategy" of the American strategic forces has taken place and therefore the United States now has "targeting options which are more selective and which do not necessarily involve major mass destruction on the other side."

These statements imply—erroneously—that the previous American doctrine of "assured destruction" lacked the capacity for flexible options. The implication that new types and numbers of strategic weapons are required is similarly groundless. In the October 1973 issue of *Foreign Affairs* Wolfgang K. H. Panofsky pointed out that there is no inherent technical reason that prevents existing American retaliatory forces from being employed in a limited manner. Similarly, as Schlesinger himself recently reaffirmed, the United States does have strategic weapons which could be used in a "limited counter-force role." Furthermore, the United States has maintained such a capability for some time: Alain C. Enthoven and K. Wayne Smith in their 1971 work, *How Much Is Enough?* (New York: Harper and Row), noted that even with the "assured destruction" doctrine, American strategic weapons could be used to perform "limited and controlled retaliation."

What neither the United States nor the Soviet Union has today is an *efficient* counterforce capability against *hard targets* or *hardened missile silos.** This type of counterforce capability would be comprised of a substantial number of nuclear weapons, each with a high probability of destroying a hardened missile silo. For example, the United States could at present destroy some of the Soviet missile silos with a high degree of confidence, but only "inefficiently"—by means of targeting three or four Minuteman missiles on each Soviet silo. With an "efficient" counterforce capability the number of missiles required to be targeted at each silo might be reduced to the more favorable ratio of one or two Minuteman missiles per Soviet missile silo.

In sum, the doctrine of mutual assured destruction characterized as inflexible by President Nixon and other critics is not inflexible at all.

Several events during the first term of the Nixon administration have fundamentally increased the degree of strategic flexibility available to the United States and should not be overlooked. For one thing, the ABM

---

* Hard or hardened targets are those facilities, usually military, where special construction techniques have been employed to protect the facilities against the blast and radiation effects of nuclear detonations. Generally speaking, no facility can be hardened to withstand fully the effects of a direct hit from a medium- to high-yield nuclear weapon, but protection from near misses or lower-yield weapons is possible.

(Anti-Ballistic Missile) Treaty has significantly enhanced the ability to respond at a low level since every small attack does not have to overwhelm the adversary's defenses. In addition, noteworthy advances in command and control capabilities can now make available to the President an unlimited number of strategic targeting options for the American missile forces. One example of this is the current deployment of a computerized retargeting system which vastly reduces the amount of time required to change the target selections of each missile. Therefore, it is clear that not only did the previous American forces contain a substantial degree of flexibility, but present American forces have acquired even more in recent years. If the present nuclear force structure is already inherently flexible, then what further capabilities could the President and Defense Department desire? Although it is likely that certain improvements could be made in U.S. command and control capabilities to increase flexibility, the only step which remains to be taken in the area of counterforce capabilities is the development of an efficient "silo-killing" counterforce capability. While at the present time the Nixon administration has not explicitly stated that the development of such a capability is an American strategic objective, Secretary Schlesinger in recent weeks has implied that the capability to destroy Soviet military targets, including missile silos, would be one way of enhancing American "strategic flexibility." The forthcoming foreign policy message and defense report are expected to provide the details.

In my opinion the development of such a capability would be not only unwarranted but also dangerous. Moving to a counterforce doctrine would also represent a major policy shift since in the past President Nixon and other top officials have frequently assured the Congress and American public that the United States would neither develop a counterforce capability nor any weapons "which the Soviets could construe as having a first-strike potential." While it is possible to argue that "technically" a hard-target counterforce capability does not constitute a *disarming* first-strike potential since both sides will maintain relatively invulnerable sea-based missiles and bombers, the fact remains that both nations will *perceive* such a capability as an attempt to obtain a first-strike potential and therefore highly provocative, regardless of what is "technically" correct. It is difficult to believe that those Americans who for years have been most concerned about the vulnerability of the U.S. ICBM (intercontinental ballistic missile) force to a Soviet MIRV (multiple independently-targetable re-entry vehicle) attack will not be able to comprehend that even a "limited" U.S. counterforce potential can generate uncertainties in Soviet eyes about our intentions, create instabilities in the strategic balance, and foster suspicions between the two nations.

The acquisition of such counterforce capabilities would increase the likelihood of nuclear war and the potential for crisis instability. The likelihood of nuclear war will be increased since a counterforce doctrine and related capabilities will make nuclear weapons seem more "useable" in addition to making their attractiveness as a viable policy option superficially greater. Crisis stability will be decreased since with hard-target counterforce capabilities and vulnerable land-based forces each side will perceive in a crisis situation the incentive of even a limited first strike upon its adversary's missile force. The attractiveness of counterforce targets in a second-strike attack could never equal those of a first-strike attack. Consequently, an incentive will exist for the side which seizes the initiative to strike first. Yet, any benefits gained from such a first-strike attack would be only short-sighted and illusory since each nation will still retain more than enough nuclear weapons ultimately to destroy the cities of the other. In addition, the development of a hard-target counterforce capability will only promote further strategic arms competition between the United States and the Soviet Union, while impeding progress in arms control efforts such as the SALT II (Strategic Arms Limitation Talks) negotiations and the Comprehensive Test Ban.

In light of the disadvantages of such a capability, the United States should make the basic choice to increase strategic flexibility through further improvements in command and control capabilities rather than by the development of a provocative hard-target counterforce capability.

Finally, the ultimate solution to the problem of an increasingly vulnerable land-based missile force will be found, not in the development of more efficient "silo-killing" weapons but rather in the negotiation of mutual limitations on MIRV flight-testing and deployment as a preface to the eventual reduction of the land-based missiles on both sides.

(January 1974)

"First Use" of Nuclear Weapons   *Herbert Scoville, Jr.*

Since the acquisition of large numbers of nuclear weapons by the superpowers, there has been a continuing debate on the role of these weapons in a "limited" war. In this 1975 article, Dr. Scoville argues against the claim that nuclear war, once initiated, could be contained.

The post-Vietnam-Mayaguez syndrome is now taking a new and very dangerous turn. Seemingly, to demonstrate our manhood and to reassure our allies of our support, the United States is flexing its nuclear muscles by threatening the "first use" of nuclear weapons in a wide variety of situations. The setback in Vietnam will force us to adopt a "stern and abrasive" foreign policy, Secretary of State Henry Kissinger is reported to have said in the final days of that debacle. Apparently, the Ford administration has decided that nuclear saber rattling is an appropriate diplomatic tool for this purpose.

Ever since the initial development of the atomic bomb, the first use of nuclear weapons has been the subject of intense debate. Even now, some thirty years later, it is an unresolved question as to whether the United States should or should not have dropped the bombs on Hiroshima and Nagasaki. In 1953, President Eisenhower discreetly warned the Chinese, Russians, and North Koreans that unless progress was made in the armistice talks, the United States would feel free to use any type of weapons at its disposal (meaning nuclear) and would not confine hostilities to the Korean Peninsula. All during the 1950s, nuclear weapons were brandished by Secretary of State John Foster Dulles and others as the counter to Sino-Soviet aggression with larger conventional forces. During this period the implicit threat of first use of nuclear weapons was a fundamental element of our foreign and national security policies.

As the Soviet Union procured an H-bomb capability of its own, the threat of a U.S. nuclear attack became less and less credible. During the Kennedy administration, defense officials increasingly realized that conventional attacks must be deterred or resisted by conventional forces. Nuclear weapons were primarily regarded as useful to deter a nuclear attack or to be employed only as a last resort when all conventional means had failed. The United States still maintained large nuclear forces in Europe and somewhat smaller ones in Korea to discourage large-scale aggression, but agreement on plans for their use was never satisfactorily worked out. America's European allies had little stomach for becoming the battlefield for a nuclear conflict, although they welcomed the deterrent effect of the presence of tactical nuclear weapons which they hoped would be associated in Soviet minds with the risk of escalation to the strategic level.

Meanwhile, the "firebreak" * between conventional and nuclear weapons became stronger as the years passed without their use. Even during the long and difficult years of involvement in Vietnam, the United States never seriously considered dipping into its atomic stockpile—an option which was becoming less viable each day. When the United States signed Protocol II of the Latin American Nuclear-free Zone Treaty in 1968,

---

* A "firebreak" is a strip of cleared, burned, or plowed land used to stop the spread of a fire. In military usage, it describes the concentration of firepower to prevent movement by the enemy and is also used figuratively to denote distinctions between classes of weaponry, such as between conventional weapons and tactical nuclear weapons, between tactical nuclear weapons and strategic nuclear weapons, or between conventional weapons and nuclear weapons of any type; it refers particularly to inhibitions presumably involved in a decision to employ a more lethal class of weapons, thereby escalating a conflict.

it agreed not to use nuclear weapons against contracting parties to that treaty. Thus, the U.S. cold war policy of maintaining the freedom of action to use nuclear weapons whenever it saw fit was gradually becoming eroded by custom and even by formal treaty commitment.

Now, however, there is evidence of a major reversal of this trend. Instead of just being reluctant to commit itself to a no-first-use policy, the United States has apparently started on a campaign of atomic threats. In March 1975, retired General William Westmoreland mused that "the use of several small-yield nuclear weapons conceivably could have put an end to the whole [Vietnam conflict]." Later, in June, President Ford stated that one lesson America learned from the Vietnam war was how to prosecute such a military engagement. Apparently, the President agreed that controlled escalation with conventional weapons was an unsatisfactory military tactic. Furthermore, ever since the public relations "coup" of the Mayaguez incident, the public has witnessed a barrage of official statements concerning the possibility of U.S. nuclear responses to aggression in many corners of the world.

In May, a highly placed U.S. military officer in Seoul was quoted as warning that the nuclear option would be most seriously considered if war broke out on the Korean Peninsula; Secretary of Defense James Schlesinger more modestly declared that while this would be carefully considered, the ground balance in the Korean Peninsula was not unsatisfactory. On May 29, 1975, Schlesinger released his report to Congress on our nuclear force posture in Europe, in which he simultaneously sought to raise the nuclear threshold by urging improved conventional capabilities and endorsed the use of nuclear weapons even in response to Soviet conventional attacks. At the same time, it was leaked that Strategic Air Command (SAC) crews were being trained for limited nuclear strikes. President Ford, when queried on first use at his June news conference, avoided a direct response but admitted that in the previous eighteen months U.S. security policy had been changed to provide maximum flexibility for such use of nuclear weapons as our national interest might require.

This brandishing of nuclear weapons peaked on July 1 when Defense Secretary Schlesinger stated at a press breakfast that first use could conceivably involve strategic forces possibly in a "selective" strike at the Soviet Union. He attempted to differentiate between a "selective" and a "disarming" first strike, the latter not being achievable because of the invulnerability of submarine missile forces. The improved counterforce capability which Schlesinger is seeking through greater accuracy and higher-yield MIRV (multiple independently-targetable re-entry vehicle) warheads will, however, threaten the Soviet fixed, land-based ICBM (intercontinental ballistic missile) force—a capability which his predecessor, Secretary Melvin Laird, said the United States should never seek. Soviet planners cannot avoid thinking that our military is prepared to initiate a nuclear strike against their ICBM force, apparently what Schlesinger wishes them to believe. Since Schlesinger, in testimony before the Senate Foreign Relations Committee in September 1974, characterized a similar Soviet attack against our Minuteman and bomber forces with several thousand megaton-yield weapons as "limited," the Russians may not be reassured by Schlesinger's term "selective strike." He has stated that they should not worry since they can adopt a "launch-on-warning" posture. If the Russians follow his advice and launch-on-warning, then his "selective" strike will only destroy empty silos while their warheads will be killing millions of Americans.

To allay fears over initiating the use of nuclear weapons, Secretary Schlesinger argues that breaching the "firebreak" between conventional and nuclear weapons by a selective strike would not run a high risk of escalation to a major nuclear conflict. He believes that logic would override psychological pressures on decision makers for such escalation, which would require a conscious policy choice. He further asks why, since conventional escalation was controlled in Vietnam, similar control could not be exercised in the nuclear case. Such arguments ignore the fact that the time available for making decisions is much shorter in a nuclear conflict. And even Secretary Schlesinger has admitted that "Soviet military doctrine does not subscribe to a strategy of graduated nuclear response," so escalation may be inevitable regardless of any U.S. restraint. Finally, since the fate of mankind may depend on the result, can we afford the risk that Schlesinger's judgment might be wrong?

The procurement of new counterforce weapons generates pressures for escalation since both sides know that, unless they preempt, a major element of their force could be wiped out. While it might be possible to limit a conflict if nuclear weapons were used only in a battlefield situation, it would seem very unlikely, if not impossible, for a conflict to be controlled once even a few strategic weapons were exploded on the homeland of either the United States or the Soviet Union. Even a limited nuclear strike would result in millions of casualties, and the pressure to retaliate would be tremendous. A flexible strategic capability only makes it easier to pull the nuclear trigger.

Secretary Schlesinger's objective of raising the nuclear threshold by maintaining sufficient conventional capabilities to cope with non-nuclear aggression is commendable. However, this goal is being undercut by his nuclear saber rattling. The more America threatens to use nuclear weapons as a response to a conventional provocation, the less the United States or its allies will remain prepared to deal with such aggression by non-nuclear means. The forward deployment of tactical nuclear weapons in Europe and Korea can lead the United States to be inadvertently embroiled in a nuclear conflict. Presidential permission to use nuclear weapons will be difficult to deny when forward-deployed nuclear forces are in the process of being overrun. Tactical nuclear weapons should be available only as a last resort after careful presidential and allied review of all the consequences. Redeployment of nuclear weapons to rear areas would be a sounder method of raising the nuclear threshold than threatening a "selective" strategic attack. The use of strategic weapons should be decoupled from tactical situations to reduce the risk of a local conflict escalating to a worldwide holocaust.

Furthermore, this crescendo of nuclear threats is undercutting efforts to prevent the proliferation of nuclear weapons. The more nuclear weapons appear to have political or military usefulness, the more countries without nuclear weapons will become convinced that they too must take advantage of these benefits. While the United States and other nuclear weapons countries are asking non-nuclear states to forego the option of acquiring nuclear weapons, they themselves are unwilling to make a commitment not to use nuclear weapons, even against non-nuclear countries. The United States should make a declaration that it will not use or threaten to use nuclear weapons on non-nuclear weapons states, who are parties to the Non-Proliferation Treaty (NPT). This does not mean that the United States must renounce its "nuclear umbrella" or that allies of the United States would be unprotected against aggression by other nuclear states. Furthermore, to the extent that other nuclear nations make similar pledges, the nuclear threat to these countries is further reduced, providing an added incentive for nations to become parties to the NPT. Unless the spread of nuclear weapons can be halted, they will soon be considered as another conventional weapon. American security will then be greatly decreased, since nuclear weapons are the great leveler, and the United States will become vulnerable to devastation by small nations or even subnational groups.

Apparently, the lesson the administration learned from Vietnam is that the United States must never again be involved in a controlled-response, conventional war. Instead, it must be prepared to move rapidly with nuclear shock tactics to deter further aggression or wipe out the opposition. The groundwork is being laid for public acceptance of such a policy, which is the logical culmination of the goal of acquiring a flexible nuclear response. The warnings of the critics that this would increase the likelihood of a nuclear conflict are now coming true. Escalation to a nuclear level is now being considered less dangerous than a prolonged conventional stalemate. We are trying to find a way of making our nuclear weapons serve some political or military purpose, ignoring the catastrophic destruction that would result if these weapons are ever actually used.

We can't afford the dangerous luxury of using nuclear threats to demonstrate our resolve in the post-Vietnam climate. Actions taken now to restore our national ego could irrevocably lead to our ultimate devastation. *(July/August 1975)*

The View from the Pentagon   *William H. Kincade*

> The long-term and quite well-known factor is that over many years the Soviets have been steadily closing the gap in nuclear capabilities between them and us.
> —James R. Schlesinger, March 1974

> The Soviet Union, whatever its purposes, is without question engaged in a serious, steady and sustained effort which, in the absence of a U.S. response, could make it the dominant military power in the world.
> —Donald H. Rumsfeld, January 1977

> In particular, we should make no mistake about one fact: the Soviet Union is in the process of acquiring military power comparable to that of the United States.
> —Harold Brown, September 1977

That the current secretary of defense and his two immediate predecessors agree on the growth of Soviet military forces, particularly over the last decade, comes as no surprise. This judgment is shared not only by American officials but also by independent Western analysts and, indeed, by Soviet leaders themselves.

Of greater significance is how secretaries of defense have interpreted this long-term development, and what they propose by way of an American response. Analysis of the annual reports, congressional testimony, and major speeches of Schlesinger, Rumsfeld, and Brown over the past several years discloses unanimity, diversity, and subtle differences of emphasis across a range of issues that influence American strategic nuclear policy. These congruences and contrasts illuminate the past course and possible future direction of American strategy, as well as the meaning of various programmatic choices.

A recurrent theme in the public statements of former Defense Secretary James Schlesinger was the "breadth and depth" of Soviet strategic weapons programs, especially in terms of their implications for the strategic balance in the future and for Soviet nuclear strategy. Stopping short of imputing to the Soviets an inclination to fight nuclear wars, Schlesinger nevertheless suggested that this might become a temptation in future years and recommended a series of U.S. actions to prepare for the possible failure of nuclear deterrence. Among them were: (1) increased flexibility in the nature and use of strategic nuclear weapons, (2) adoption of a "limited nuclear war" doctrine designed to deflect nuclear war away from major industrial and population centers, and (3) increased emphasis on American civil defense programs.

His successor, Donald Rumsfeld, repeated many of the themes articulated by Schlesinger but lent his own perspective to some of them. While also emphasizing the "scope and vigor" of Soviet weapons programs, Rumsfeld stressed in particular the need for the United States to have a "counterforce capability" against hardened Soviet military targets, a direction which Schlesinger had said was undesirable for both powers but pursued as unavoidable because Soviet programs were not restrained. Rumsfeld went farther than Schlesinger in crediting the Soviet Union with a nuclear warfighting or counterforce strategy and force posture:

> Soviet programs do not reflect an interest in deterrence
> by massive retaliation alone; their strategic nuclear pos-
> ture is developing a war-fighting capability.

On the existence of this warfighting posture. Rumsfeld predicated the need for "hard-target" or "silo-killing" weapons.

Whereas Schlesinger emphasized potential Soviet nuclear strength, a major motif in Rumsfeld's annual reports were apparent increases in Soviet defense *spending*, which were contrasted sharply with what he viewed as the relative decline in American military expenditures and its debilitating effect on the posture of the United States.

In another variation on Schlesinger's perspective, Rumsfeld indicated that, while new information on Soviet civil defense programs could require the expansion of American *offensive* weapons programs, increased expenditures on American civil defense programs are unnecessary for the present.

In the main, however, the public declarations of Schlesinger and Rumsfeld reveal a basic agreement that defense policies are predicted primarily on the *military* capacity of the Soviet Union and on the need to prepare for a breakdown in nuclear war deterrence by expanding the numbers and capabilities of American strategic weapons.

The assessment made by Harold Brown in his September 1977 speech to the National Security Industrial Association is explicitly based on a wider range of factors. Saying that "it would be a mistake to focus all our attention on this [Soviet-American] rivalry or on its military components," Brown listed both the American advantages and the Soviet weaknesses in their continuing competition. In an equally sharp contrast, Brown took pains to emphasize that the system of nuclear deterrence continues to operate effectively and that maintaining this system is America's "most fundamental defense objective."

Brown did not downgrade the Soviet strategic weapons development programs and, indeed, highlighted some of them. Yet neither did he suggest that the USSR is seeking strategic superiority or a nuclear counterforce capability. In his assessment of the future, Brown, like his predecessors, has conceded the existence of uncertainties about the direction and motivation of Soviet programs. Rather than rendering these unknowables in dire colors, however, his speech reflected assurance about the capacity of American forces to deal with Soviet strategic developments in a satisfactory way. More oriented to technology than his predecessors, Brown has especially emphasized the American ability to exploit its lead in this area.

Describing the missions of U.S. strategic forces, Secretary Brown provided for some flexibility in American nuclear options (in his words, "to control escalation, limit damage insofar as feasible and end an exchange on the most favorable terms possible"). Yet he did not call for a major war-fighting capability, impute one to the Soviet Union, or suggest that either power could "win" in a nuclear exchange. Indeed, Brown has consistently stressed the very devastating impact of nuclear war on *both* the United States and the Soviet Union under any scenario, while his immediate predecessors, Rumsfeld in particular, tended to stress American weaknesses and vulnerability to nuclear attack. As to the implications of civil defense programs for the strategic balance, Brown has been skeptical of the utility of these programs for either superpower and confident of the ability of the United States to overcome Soviet civil defense measures through retargeting and similar expedients.

Varying appreciations of Soviet capabilities stem from and at the same time reinforce different assessments of Soviet intentions. While noting that the Soviet Union has historically acted prudently, both Schlesinger and Rumsfeld took the position that this prudence could not necessarily be guaranteed into the future, in view of the expansion of Soviet military forces, which they regarded as the central fact about the Soviet Union. The public utterances of Harold Brown, on the other hand, plainly eschew the more speculative scenarios. They evince a belief that various political, economic, and military factors constrain the Soviet leaders to a prudent nuclear course now and in the future, providing that the United States offers neither strong temptation nor strong provocation.

The perspectives of the three secretaries of defense differ on other issues, such as first-strike incentives and the probability of nuclear war. James Schlesinger rated the likelihood of nuclear war "very low" and

Harold Brown has called it "the least likely contingency we face," while Donald Rumsfeld declared a nuclear attack "first among the dangers" confronting the United States.

Agreement is highest among the three secretaries on the issues of the strategic arms limitation talks (SALT), the perceptual or diplomatic value of strategic nuclear weapons and on the need to hedge against what Harold Brown termed "unexpected evolutions."

In their official declarations, Schlesinger, Rumsfeld, and Brown have all expressed the desire that SALT might curb the rivalry in strategic weapons, with Rumsfeld appearing the least hopeful. In all three cases, this hope seems to be restricted primarily to limitations on Soviet development and deployment programs. All three secretaries have pledged themselves to vigorous efforts in terms of American strategic weapons, if no progress is forthcoming in SALT. How much of this combined hopefulness and determination is directed to a Soviet audience it is difficult to say. Equally difficult to assess is the effect of secretarial pronouncements on the atmospherics surrounding the SALT negotiations, although Brown's less ominous reading of Soviet strength may help produce a calmer climate.

Hedging involves preparing to meet a "higher than expected threat." Viewed with especial seriousness are threats arising from technological breakthroughs in anti-submarine warfare and anti-ballistic missile systems that would jeopardize the effectiveness of two of the three components of America's deterrent Triad—intercontinental ballistic missiles and strategic nuclear submarines.

Although the counsel of prudence in military planning always favors some hedging in weapons development programs, there are different perspectives on the probability of a greater than expected threat and, hence, on the degree of hedging that may be indicated. Former defense secretaries Schlesinger and Rumsfeld considered Soviet development programs sufficiently menacing to require a variety of hedges in American weapons development and deployment. According to Schlesinger:

> Force diversification is also essential to hedge against
> the unforeseeable risks, such as technological break-
> throughs by the other side and unanticipated weak-
> nesses in one or more of our own systems.

Although Secretary Brown's precise views on the extent of hedging necessary will be seen more clearly when he presents his first complete posture statement early in 1978, a clue to his perspective may be found in his August 1977 testimony before the House Armed Services Committee on the supplemental defense authorization bill, when he said:

The possibility that such unexpected evolutions [break-throughs in anti-submarine warfare and anti-ballistic missile systems] could happen in a very short time, in terms of development and massive deployment, is small. However, we cannot exclude it absolutely, and the consequences would be so serious that we cannot ignore it.

Neither Schlesinger nor Rumsfeld was willing to characterize the likelihood of such breakthroughs as "small." Equally significant is the absence in Brown's remarks of the concept of force diversification which Schlesinger considered so necessary to break out of the "canonical logic of the Triad" and to provide additional options for dealing with hypothetical eventualities "across the entire spectrum of risk." By contrast, Brown's public statements reveal him as far more comfortable with the primary deterrent Triad of air-, sea-, and land-based weapons and more concerned with preserving each of these systems in a viable form than with developing new types.

Much greater agreement exists among the three secretaries on the controversial issue of the diplomatic utility of strategic nuclear weapons. Viewing nuclear deterrence as basically a matter of psychology and perception, Schlesinger, Rumsfeld and Brown strongly endorse the proposition that a perceived imbalance or weakness in strategic forces would reduce the credibility of these forces for allies and adversaries alike, with negative consequences foreseen for the nation which appeared to be in an inferior position. The United States, they hold, must therefore maintain a position of "essential equivalence" with the Soviet Union, even at the expense of enlarging nuclear arsenals. While additional increments of weaponry may not add significantly to military power, they are considered necessary to prevent a perception of relative weakness that could tempt foes or dishearten friends.

Again, however, there is some latitude in how essential equivalence is defined and what indicators are used to measure it. While Schlesinger, Rumsfeld and Brown are alike in predicting possible force asymmetries perceived as favorable to the Soviet Union in the 1980s, Brown's public declarations reveal greater confidence in the ability of the United States to prevent or meet such a development. This is shown in the following quotations, the first from Rumsfeld's 1977 assessment and the second, cautionary quotation from the recent speech by Secretary Brown:

Our nation simply cannot allow Soviet capabilities to continue expanding and U.S. capabilities to retrench—as they have over the past decade—without inviting an imbalance and, ultimately a major crisis. (Rumsfeld)

My own conclusion, in reviewing our defense posture, is that no antagonist should believe that he could bully or coerce us by the threat or selective use of force against the United States or its allies. No enemy should be so reckless as to think that the United States could be confronted with a choice between surrender and annihilation. (Brown)

A comparative reading of the statements of recent defense secretaries suggests an incumbent who views the Soviet Union as less threatening than his predecessors believed and who has a stronger faith in American ability to meet whatever challenges the Soviet Union may represent. This perspective is apparently shared by other officials around President Carter. Secretary Brown characterized his remarks to the National Security Industrial Association as a summary of Presidential Review Memorandum Number 10 or "how this Administration sees the world . . . and the evolving relationship between the United States and the Soviet Union in particular."

As analysis of the declarations of Kremlin leaders has shown, however, words are not a precise guide to deeds. Brown's ability to put flesh on this conceptual skeleton will be strongly influenced by factors which also affected Schlesinger and Rumsfeld before him—primarily (1) the legacy of long-term programs initiated by his predecessors, (2) institutional pressures, and (3) the need imposed by SALT to "talk tough" while negotiations are in progress. These pressures can lead to the production and deployment of new weapons systems now incubating, whether or not SALT ultimately proves successful in limiting or reducing strategic nuclear arsenals. Secretary Brown also faces a pressure less familiar to his immediate forerunners—the need to prevent a "perceptual gap" between his assessment of Soviet capabilities and intentions and more pessimistic American evaluations. If he is unconvincing in presenting his perspective, he may spend most of his time defending the Carter administration against charges of "softness."

Perhaps because of these factors, the programmatic implications of Brown's declared position remain somewhat cloudy. Though the B-1 bomber program (which Brown initially supported because of its more stabilizing, second-strike characteristics) was cancelled by the administration, this did not mean, as some hoped, the beginning of the end for the manned, penetrating bomber. It may yet be built in the form of a modified FB-111, along with still another aircraft to act as a cruise missile carrier. Likewise, the development of the experimental mobile missile (MX) was slowed down by Brown when he took office but earlier this month received his tentative approval for full-scale development.

While less enthusiastic than former Secretary Rumsfeld about the increased-yield warhead (Mk 12A) and a more accurate guidance system for Minuteman missiles, Brown has not said a final no to the deployment of these "silo-killing" counterforce weapons. Both the Minuteman improvements and the MX are viewed by some as undermining rather than enhancing deterrence.

How these will be squared with Brown's less ominous perception of the Soviet-American balance and with his overriding desire to preserve nuclear war deterrence remains to be seen. Such seeming contradictions may be clarified when he defends the military budget for fiscal year 1979. Nevertheless, it is certain that, in terms of the net assessment of Soviet and American power, Brown differs substantially from former secretaries of defense and, in time, these differences will give a new shape to military programs. *(October 1977)*

Counterforce and the Defense Budget
Jeffrey D. Porro

When Defense Secretary Harold Brown took office early in 1977, the fiscal year 1979 defense budget—the first to be prepared solely at Dr. Brown's direction—was anticipated with real interest. It was expected that the new budget would provide a clear indication of Brown's stand on the most important strategic issue of the decade: whether or not U.S. strategic nuclear forces require a significant "counterforce" capability, i.e., the ability to destroy missile silos or other hardened targets. Many hoped that Brown would reverse the policies of his two immediate predecessors by moving U.S. strategic policy away from a reliance on counterforce.

A close look at the new budget, which appeared in early February, reveals a mixed picture. The decisions on strategic weapons funding are somewhat reassuring to those who oppose a larger counterforce component. Compared to fiscal year 1978 funding, the strategic portion of the budget has been increased less than the defense budget overall, rising 5.3 percent in total obligational authority as opposed to 9.4 percent for the entire defense budget. More important, Secretary Brown has reduced the funding for five counterforce weapons systems below the recommendations in former Defense Secretary Rumsfeld's last budget. The most significant cuts hit the two systems seen as having the greatest potential for destabilizing the strategic balance—the new mobile, hard-target missile (MX) and the hard-target Trident II missile.

Funding for Counterforce Programs
(In millions of dollars)

System	FY 78		FY 79	
	Rumsfeld	Brown *	Rumsfeld	Brown
Minuteman improvements	338	113.9	146	122.8
(Mark 12A)			22	22
Advanced ICBM (MX)	294	134.4	1,533	158.2
Advanced ballistic missile re-entry system	109	98.9	125	105
Trident II	5	5	110	16
Improved accuracy	110	109.9	98	102.3

* Totals as modified by congressional action

However, key elements of Brown's thinking on nuclear strategy, spelled out in his annual report to the Congress, closely parallel the rhetoric of former defense secretaries Schlesinger and Rumsfeld, both of whom advocated increases in American capacity for counterforce attacks.

In his presentation to Congress of the defense budget for fiscal year 1975, then-Defense Secretary James Schlesinger announced a new strategic targeting doctrine. According to Schlesinger, the new doctrine was designed to give the President, in the case of a nuclear attack, a range of options for responding which would free him from having to launch a full-scale second-strike attack against the urban-industrial base of the Soviet Union. Schlesinger argued that such options were needed to deter a limited Soviet nuclear attack, especially against U.S. missile silos, or to fight a limited nuclear war if deterrence should fail. Schlesinger worried that, in case of a limited Soviet nuclear attack,

> if the United States were to strike at the urban industrial base of the Soviet Union, the Soviet Union could and presumably would fire back destroying the urban industrial base of the United States. Consequently, the Soviet Union, under those circumstances, might believe that the United States would be self-deterred from making use of its strategic forces. Thus, they might regard themselves as relatively risk-free if our deterrent doctrine, our targeting doctrine, were to stress only going against cities.

Schlesinger, however, was cautious about the implications of his selective targeting doctrine. He took care to stress that the new targeting options did *not* themselves require a change in the size of the U.S. nuclear force. Most important, while he argued that a hard-target counterforce capability would enhance strategic options and should be pursued because of Soviet counterforce capabilities, he repeatedly stated that his new doctrine did not *require* the development of highly accurate counterforce weapons.

When Donald Rumsfeld succeeded Schlesinger, however, he abandoned such caution. Rumsfeld echoed Schlesinger's call for more options but asserted that the Soviets were clearly preparing to fight and win a nuclear war. As a result, he said, it was imperative that the United States be able successfully to wage nuclear war. This required significant increases in U.S. hard-target counterforce capability. Rumsfeld gave a major boost to counterforce programs such as the silo-killing MX missile.

When Jimmy Carter selected Harold Brown to be secretary of defense in December 1976, many who considered counterforce dangerous, and its rationale unproven, hoped that the new head of the Pentagon would reverse or drastically revise the strategic policies of Schlesinger and Rumsfeld. While accepting the idea that a president needed a range of options for responding to nuclear attack, critics of counterforce pointed out that, since the time of Secretary McNamara, presidents had had such options. They argued that the likelihood of a limited nuclear war breaking out and remaining limited was extremely small and did not justify a major re-orientation of U.S. forces towards a hard-target-kill capability.

Moreover, U.S. counterforce weapons with the capacity to destroy a significant portion of Soviet silos would have to appear to a cautious Soviet planner as an American first-strike threat. The Soviets would have to respond, at the very least, by building new systems. The result would be a new, tremendously expensive round in the strategic arms race.

An enlarged U.S. counterforce capability could also drastically increase crisis instability. In a crisis situation, the Soviets, knowing the United States possessed a first-strike potential, would be faced with a choice of using their land-based missiles (which constitute 75 percent of their strategic power) or losing them. Instead of deterring the Soviets, this would give them a strong incentive to preempt or strike first. As one opponent of counterforce, Senator Thomas McIntyre (D-N.H.), put it: "This would put a hair trigger on nuclear war."

The hopes of some for a change of policy by Secretary Brown were not based on wishful thinking. While Brown's record on strategic issues was mixed, there were a number of signs that he might be skeptical of the views of Schlesinger and Rumsfeld on counterforce. Brown had served under McNamara, a secretary of defense who—after briefly flirting with the idea of a counterforce in a "damage limiting policy"—had rejected the concept in favor of a policy emphasizing mutual deterrence through assured destruction. In addition, before being chosen secretary of defense and during his confirmation hearings before the Senate Armed Services Committee, Brown was skeptical about the likelihood that a nuclear war would remain limited. Finally, in a March 1975 speech before the Soviet Institute of the United States and Canada in Moscow, he seemed to criticize indirectly the Schlesinger-Rumsfeld approach. Brown drew a clear distinction between deterrence and nuclear war-fighting, warning that the latter could erode the former:

> Providing that no one is deceived into thinking that the existence of forces, options, and plans for a strategic countermilitary exchange makes survival of either the United States or the USSR in a nuclear war at all likely, or into forgetting that the fatal and almost certain outcome is the explosion on cities of both countries of nuclear weapons, the existence of such plans and the development of such forces is an acceptable idea. However, to the extent that it erodes deterrence, this contingency planning could increase the likelihood of catastrophe. For that reason, it ought to be severely limited.

In his first year as secretary of defense, Brown took a number of actions which indicated that he might view the U.S.-Soviet relationship differently from his predecessors. When questioned, he continued to downplay the likelihood of limited nuclear war. He was also much more skeptical than his predecessors about the damage-limiting capacity of Soviet civil defense. He continued to be much more bullish about U.S. nuclear forces.

Perhaps his most important departure from Schlesinger and Rumsfeld occurred in the aftermath of the B-1 decision, when he conceded that decisions on U.S. strategic weapons programs should not be made in a vacuum. Possible Soviet responses, and their effect on strategic stability, should be taken into account. In reviewing options for future U.S. strategic forces after the cancellation of the B-1, he called attention to "how the Soviets might perceive the threat to them of a U.S. preemptive strike."

> They may calculate that a U.S. first strike would result in a ratio adverse to them, just as we calculate that a Soviet first strike would result in a ratio adverse to us. To the extent that this is so, either side will, during the next decade, have a so-called "advantage" in firing first. I do not consider this a tempting advantage, nor do I think this situation *per se* would lead to preemption: the consequences of such an exchange, whichever side

goes first, would in my judgment be catastrophic for both sides because of the forces on each side that would survive preemption and strike back. But a so-called "advantage" in striking first is a trend in the wrong direction, and we should not aggravate it unnecessarily.

Yet these indications of differences between Brown and his predecessors were only hints. In the newly released *Annual Defense Department Report,* Brown for the first time has detailed his own decisions as secretary of defense on the future shape of U.S. strategic forces.

While restating his skepticism about the possibility of a nuclear war remaining limited, Brown soon makes clear that this does *not* mean the United States should eschew a major effort to have a nuclear war-fighting capacity. He argues that what we believe is not important. It is what we think the Soviets believe which must guide our actions. As he puts it, "the issue is how to make it clear to the Soviets that they cannot gain any military or political advantage from their strategic forces." The solution is to maintain "essential equivalence" which "guards against the danger that the Soviets might be seen as superior—even if the perception is not technically justified."

In defending "essential equivalence," which is the centerpiece of his discussion of nuclear strategy, Brown closely follows Schlesinger and Rumsfeld. He begins by rejecting his earlier differentiation between deterrence and war-fighting in language reminiscent of his predecessors.

In other words, we cannot afford to make a complete distinction between deterrent forces and what are so awkwardly called war-fighting forces. Nor should we continue to plan the force structure on one basis and our employment policies on another—as we could when Soviet strategic forces were more modest. Only if we have the capability to respond realistically and effectively to an attack at a variety of levels can we achieve essential equivalence and have the confidence necessary to a credible deterrent. Credibility cannot be maintained, especially in a crisis, with a combination of inflexible forces (however destructive) and a purely retaliatory counter-urban industrial strategy that frightens us as much as the opponent.

Brown also makes clear, like Rumsfeld, that targeting options require a hard-target counterforce capability. "If control and selective targeting are to be more than an abstraction, sufficient numbers of both missiles and bombers must be designed to deliver both high-yield and low-yield nuclear weapons with great accuracy. And these weapons must be effective against a wide range of targets, including some very hard targets."

Such an embrace of counterforce appears to require that Brown abandon his earlier concern about possible Soviet reactions. Brown now dismisses arguments he earlier took seriously about the destabilizing effects of the MX:

> The technologies which bring increased missile retaliatory effectiveness are a cause of concern to some, who argue that a large throwweight ICBM (intercontinental ballistic missile) would be destabilizing—that it would so threaten Soviet ICBMs that Soviet leadership in a crisis might be tempted to strike first, calculating worse consequences if it did not. To the extent that such a characteristic is a concern, it should be noted that the Soviets will have that capability against our silo-based missiles in the early to mid-1980s (though our silo-based missiles are a smaller fraction of our strategic force). Concerns about instability are thus not eliminated by failure of the United States to improve the hard target kill capability of its ICBM force.

In sum, at the Pentagon there has as yet been no decisive break with the counterforce policy of the last four years. Brown's decisions on funding levels for counterforce weapons do offer hints that he may not be proceeding as rapidly as his predecessor towards counterforce. But there are few signs of a fundamental re-thinking of the Schlesinger and Rumsfeld views. *(February 1978)*

Preserving the Sea-Based Deterrent   *Walter Slocombe*

The United States and the Soviet Union have increasingly come to rely on nuclear submarines carrying ballistic missiles (SSBNs) to deter strategic nuclear war, as increased missile accuracies make fixed, land-based missiles more vulnerable. Although there are presently no known effective means of detecting, continually tracking, and destroying submarine missile forces, the prospect of a breakthrough in antisubmarine warfare demolishing their present invulnerability is always theoretically possible. Consequently, it can be argued, as long as the two nuclear superpowers continue to rely on strategic deterrence for their safety, it should be in both their interests to agree on arms control measures which would insure against the vulnerability of their submarine forces, and thus prolong the life of their sea-based deterrent.

Arms control measures to limit antisubmarine warfare aimed at SSBNs clearly face obstacles formidable even by the standards of the arms control field. Submarine operations against merchant and naval shipping, and measures to protect against such attacks, are central *conventional* missions for all the major navies of the world. Moreover, the inter-relationship of strategic and tactical antisubmarine warfare is political as well as technical and military. The *strategic* submarine problem is essentially one between the two superpowers, but third countries cannot be ignored in the tactical submarine and antisubmarine field. Particularly in the case of the NATO navies, the tactical antisubmarine warfare capabilities of third countries taken together are substantial even in relation to the submarine forces of the superpowers.

Arms control may, however, be both more feasible and more effective as a countermeasure to the one clear potential threat to patrolling missile submarines—"active trailing." High confidence detection and passive (i.e., covert) trailing of submarines by "hunter-killer" attack submarines is feasible only if the hunter is no more than a few miles away— a range making counter-detection and evasion by the quarry relatively easy. The picture changes, however, if the hunter foregoes stealth for an unconcealed pursuit using a powerful active sonar, not merely listening to the emitted noise of the quarry SSBN, but sending out a strong signal of its own and detecting the echo. With a sufficient number of pursuit submarines, trail, once established—presumably as the SSBN left harbor or passed through restricted waters—could be maintained even over a large force for an essentially indefinite period.

The active trail problem should therefore be a prime focus for both weapons system planning and arms control.

Arms control possibilities begin with a ban on active trailing of missile submarines by a formal treaty creating a new rule of international law of the sea. In addition, there could be constraints (numerical or qualitative) on the development of the small, fast, but not particularly quiet, special purpose "hunter-killer" attack submarines necessary to make an active trailing program feasible on a massive scale. These measures could be supplemented by controls on operations and deployments. For example, acquiring initial trail could be made more difficult by barring foreign submarines from operating within several hundred miles of missile submarine bases.

Measures to ban active trailing not only address the most immediate threat but also focus on an area where the interaction with tactical "conventional" antisubmarine warfare and, accordingly, third-country forces would be minimal. Active trailing is of limited utility for wartime tactical antisubmarine purposes, for the central concern of strategic anti-

The first launch of the Trident submarine-launched ballistic missile occurred at Cape Canaveral on January 18, 1977. The United States plans to build 240 of the Trident I missiles for service in ten new submarines. Each missile can carry eight nuclear warheads and has an estimated range of 4,000 nautical miles.

Source: Department of Defense

submarine warfare—the ability to destroy a large force at sea simultaneously—does not exist. In wartime, there is little point—and indeed, much danger—in delaying the attack once initial, overt contact has been made with a hostile submarine. Similarly, submarines designed to maintain active trailing of SSBNs are less suitable for tactical antisubmarine warfare and are likely to be readily distinguishable from other types.

Moreover, limits on active trailing may be more negotiable than many arms control ideas. Verification problems, by definition, do not exist. Neither side seems to engage in active trailing now, nor to have under way any program to develop submarines particularly configured for the trailing tactic. Restrictions on operations, although much more complicated, would have the effect of excluding foreign submarines only from limited areas, generally close to the national territory of superpowers, and so would present far less serious difficulties than attempts to create large open-ocean sanctuaries.

Some precedent, however limited, for such a control on a particular peacetime tactic appears to be presented by the U.S.-Soviet agreement of 1972 dealing with avoidance of incidents at sea arising from mutual surveillance activities of the two navies.

The uncertainties of the still-distant threat to missile-carrying submarines makes most arms control analyses of what is desirable (even without concern for what is negotiable) extremely difficult in this area. It has even been argued that opening antisubmarine warfare up in the negotiating process would set off a "bargaining chip arms race" as each side sought to accumulate antisubmarine forces, purportedly so as to be able to negotiate them away later.

Nonetheless, neither side is yet committed to development of active trailing, despite its grave potential danger. This suggests the wisdom of prompt proposals in the area—during, not after, the effort to reach a new SALT (strategic arms limitation talks) agreement on offensive systems. Banning active trailing seems to be a step which combines considerable arms control effectiveness with relatively reduced negotiating difficulties. That combination is rare in the arms control field, and the opportunity presented should be taken up energetically.

(September 1974)

The MX ICBM Debate *John C. Baker*

Recent events have set the stage for a fundamental debate over U.S. strategic doctrine and weapons posture. One of the main focuses of this debate is the Air Force's plan for advance development of its MX ICBM (missile experimental-intercontinental ballistic missile) program. This program will produce a larger, more accurate ICBM which will carry about ten to twelve warheads (multiple independently-targetable re-entry vehicles or MIRVs) and is intended to replace some or all of the present Minuteman III ICBM force during the 1980s. The Air Force argues that the MX missile is necessary because the present Minuteman ICBM force will not provide sufficient numbers of large, highly accurate warheads to cover the Soviet target system projected for the 1980s.

The requirement for a new, more powerful ICBM also flowed from the unprecedented announcement last month of a U.S. nuclear warfighting philosophy in out-going Defense Secretary Donald Rumsfeld's *Annual Defense Department Report* for the 1978 fiscal year. This new shift in U.S. targeting requirements went far beyond the development of the previous flexible strategic options concept, and would require the United States to have enough weapons to prevent the USSR from being able to recover from a nuclear war more rapidly than the United States. The departing Ford administration also sought to accelerate the MX ICBM toward a deployment date of 1983.

In his first official press conference, Carter's new secretary of defense, Harold Brown, rejected this war-fighting philosophy for planning U.S. strategic forces and instead suggested that the United States should seek what it needs for a "retaliatory capability sufficient to deter under any reasonably expectable scenario." In a budget amendment the Carter administration also reduced the Air Force's MX request for $294 million to $130 million in order to delay the decision for full-scale development of the MX for one year while it considers the missile's basing schemes more fully. Clearly, the scene is now set for a debate over U.S. strategic policy between those who give priority to deterrence, strategic arms limitations, and force survivability, and those who give priority to force matching and developing a greater U.S. nuclear war-fighting capability.

During the next decade fixed-silo ICBMs are expected to become increasingly vulnerable; consequently Defense Department officials emphasize that the MX will be deployed in a mobile basing system in order to enhance its survivability. The development of multiple warheads (MIRVs) in 1968, combined with the prospect for dramatic improvements in missile accuracy, have convinced defense analysts that eventually even the most hardened missile silo will become vulnerable to a missile attack and that a more mobile basing system is needed to maintain ICBM survivability.

After examining a variety of air-mobile basing options, defense planners first concluded that the "buried trench" concept was the most viable mobile basing option. In this mode, the MX missile was to have been transported in a cannister (somewhat like a subway car) hori-

An artist's conception of a launching of the new U.S. MX intercontinental ballistic missile. The controversial MX missile is considered a counterforce or hard-target weapon because the combination of accuracy and warhead yield (350 kilotons) enable it to destroy hardened missile silos.

Source: U.S. Air Force

zontally through a hardened tube or buried trench ten to twenty miles long. Testing, however, revealed that trench basing would not be cost effective.

Current plans are to deploy the MX missile in a "multiple aim point" (MAP) mode. In this MAP basing system, MX missiles would be protected by a kind of "shell game." Several silos, perhaps as many as ten, would be built for each MX. Each missile would be housed in a vertical launch cannister and moved periodically from one of its silos to another. In order to prevent the Soviets from observing which silo contained an MX, dummy cannisters would also be moved from silo to silo. The

Soviets would, thus, be unable to locate and destroy our land-based ICBMs.

One way Air Force officials have sought to reduce the expense of deploying the MX missile, which is estimated to be as high as $30-35 billion, is by urging that it be initially deployed in the existing missile silos until the Soviet threat becomes severe. This plan not only drew sharp criticism from the Senate Armed Services Committee, which pressured the Air Force to consider only the more survivable mobile basing modes for the MX development, but also has been an issue of contention within the Defense Department. The enormous cost of the mobile basing systems has led the Air Force to push to keep the land-based ICBM in the relatively inexpensive fixed silos as long as possible.

The debate over the issues raised by the MX ICBM and the future of the land-based ICBM force is likely to be the most crucial arms control issue to be examined during the next five years. The MX ICBM system has profound arms control implications for strategic stability. Deployments of more potent counterforce weapons such as the MX and the Soviet SS-18 ICBM only compound the problem of crisis instability which would exist if both countries felt under intense pressure during a crisis situation to launch a preemptive counterforce strike. The side which unleashed the counterforce strike first would gain an advantage, and large, improved counterforce ICBMs would add to this instability by increasing the advantage of striking first over striking second. Furthermore, if these new ICBMs were deployed in the increasingly vulnerable fixed silos then even more tempting targets for a first strike would be created. Maintenance of a large, increasingly vulnerable land-based ICBM force would also reduce the stability of the U.S.-USSR strategic balance by increasing the interest of the military planners in adopting a dangerous "launch-on-warning" missile strategy. (A "launch-on-warning" doctrine would try to prevent the destruction of the ICBM force by launching the missiles upon receipt of satellite and radar warning that the enemy had initiated a first-strike attack.) Some top U.S. defense officials have already urged the United States to consider adopting such a strategy.

In addition to its effect upon strategic stability, the ICBM system has serious implications for the ongoing SALT (Strategic Arms Limitation Talks) negotiations. Since the essence of the MX ground-mobile basing system is the deception of the enemy concerning the actual deployment of the ICBM, difficult verification questions will be created for the SALT negotiations. To date each nation has relied on its own surveillance satellites in order accurately to verify the number of ICBM silos constructed by the other side. With the deployment of deceptive ICBM basing systems how will each nation confidently verify that the other side has deployed only one missile in each complex as it claims?

Deceptive ICBM basing systems such as the MX either require each side to accept on faith the other's claim that each huge, concealed basing system contains only one ICBM, not two or more; or alternatively, force the United States and the USSR to negotiate very complex verification procedures. "Blind faith" is an inadequate basis for any arms limitation agreement, and the SALT I and Threshold Test Ban Treaty experiences to date suggest that it may be impossible to negotiate complex verification procedures in the relatively short time remaining before both sides become committed to deploying various mobile and deceptive ICBM basing modes.

While the strategic and arms control problems created by the existence of vulnerable land-based ICBMs are becoming increasingly clear, the solution to these problems is not. Many of the proposed solutions are inadequate and some are downright dangerous. What follows is a survey and an analysis of the currently suggested solutions to the problem of ICBM vulnerability.

The present Defense Department plan: The Defense Department appears to be disposed at present to deploy about 300 MX ICBMs, which will ultimately—if not initially—be deployed in the "buried trench" deceptive basing mode. This core of survivable MX ICBMs would be supplemented by the older, less survivable silo-based missiles consisting of over 500 single-warhead ICBMs and possibly some MIRVed Minuteman IIIs.

The MX ICBM program presents the United States with an arms control dilemma. On the one hand, if the ground-mobile MX system is deployed in large numbers, SALT verification problems are created which could lead to the stalemate and breakdown of SALT II. On the other hand, while a small deployment of ground-mobile MXs would reduce the SALT verification problem, it would not solve the problems of ICBM vulnerability and crisis instability since many missiles would remain in vulnerable silos and the pressure to adopt a "launch-on-warning" doctrine would increase. Furthermore, the MX development policy inherited from the Ford administration is a contradictory one (similar to U.S. policy on the strategic cruise missile) in which a significant new weapon program, which will create verification problems, is allowed to *race* toward deployment while simultaneously U.S. and Soviet arms negotiators *creep* toward negotiating verifiable arms limitations.

Adoption of a "launch-on-warning" missile strategy: U.S. and Soviet adoption of a "launch-on-warning" doctrine would needlessly increase the risk of nuclear war. It is not likely that an American president would ever knowingly adopt such a dangerous policy. What is more likely is that this option may be "incidentally" created for him by defense planners. The operational concepts for a "launch-on-warning" strategy can be easily formulated; and the necessary warning, attack assessment and command systems are currently being developed and deployed. The Carter administration must make it clear to the defense planners that "launch-on-warning" is not an acceptable option.

Strategic arms limitations: Many look to the ongoing strategic arms limitation negotiations to provide a solution to this problem of vulnerable ICBM forces, but the unfortunate fact is that at this point no politically conceivable SALT agreement can halt the trend toward mutually-vulnerable land-based missile forces. At one time during 1969 SALT might have been used to prevent this problem, but the opportunity to negotiate a ban on the deployment of multiple warheads (MIRVs) was foreclosed when the Nixon administration failed to pursue serious negotiations with the USSR concerning a ban on MIRV flight testing.

To admit that SALT is not a panacea is not to say that it has not been beneficial or should not be continued. On the contrary, the May 1972 Anti-Ballistic Missile (ABM) Treaty has prevented both countries from engaging in a dangerous and wasteful competition to deploy ABM systems, and the continuing SALT negotiations hold some prospects for eventual force reductions. During a recent press conference President Carter raised the possibility that the United States would seek Soviet agreement to a ban on mobile missiles, and, according to one press report, the United States did receive indications of Soviet interest in banning mobile ICBMs back in 1975. While a ban on mobile ICBMs would reduce the verification problems facing any new SALT agreement, it would unfortunately do very little in itself to solve the ICBM vulnerability problem.

ABM defense of the ICBM force: The amended 1972 ABM Treaty restricts both the U.S. and the USSR to the deployment of only one ABM site of 100 ABM launchers. In recent years there have been suggestions that the United States consider either abrogating or amending the ABM Treaty in order to allow itself to deploy an extensive ABM site defense system which would attempt to protect the vulnerable ICBM force. However in light of the political capital each nation has invested in the ABM Treaty and the fierce debate which preceded U.S. ABM deployment, it is unlikely that this would be a simple task for U.S. leaders. More important, even the deployment of ABM systems limited to the defense of the ICBM force would create terrible uncertainties for each country as to whether the other side had the ABM capability for city defense as well as ICBM defense. Consequently, while a constituency exists for deploying an ABM defense, its prospects are not very high.

Large numbers of small ICBMs: One of the recent proposals to solve the ICBM vulnerability problem is that both the United States and the

USSR should deploy substantial numbers of ICBMs so small that they could not carry multiple warheads (MIRVs). While academically interesting, this proposal fails to show what would lead the United States and the Soviet Union to undertake the expensive and difficult task of destroying their nearly 2,500 existing ICBMs and dismantling their silos, while replacing them with many more thousands of very small ICBMs.

Restructuring the U.S. deterrent: MX mobile basing systems, "launch-on-warning" strategies, and even the hope that the problem of nuclear warhead "fratricide"* will save the land-based ICBM force all miss the essential point that the ICBM force is already lost. Nuclear deterrence is not based upon the esoteric calculations of ICBM survivability by strategic analysts, but rather upon the political perceptions of the national leadership of each country. A strategic weapon is of little value if the chief decision-maker does not have confidence in it as a survivable deterrent weapon, and this erosion of confidence concerning the land-based ICBM will continue regardless of what is done in the future.

The general solution to the ICBM vulnerability problem is surprisingly simple—land-based missiles must be replaced by other, more survivable strategic forces such as nuclear missile submarines and strategic bombers. Given the various strategic arguments and political obstacles against a total phase-out of the ICBM force, the more realistic course is gradually to phase-down the present U.S. land-based missile force from the total of 1,054 ICBMs to only 200-300 ICBMs. This would mean increasing the reliance of the United States upon the bomber and missile submarine portions of the strategic deterrent and might even result in greater expenditures in order to maintain a high-quality bomber and submarine force.

The benefits which would accrue from restructuring the U.S. strategic force this way would be numerous. Strategic stability would be maintained by minimizing the development of a situation of mutually-vulnerable ICBM forces; the confidence of the national leadership in the American strategic deterrent would be preserved; and a serious obstacle to progress in the SALT negotiations would be avoided. In addition, the phase-down of U.S. land-based missiles would rob the USSR of any political advantage it may have gained by deploying large, new missiles which threaten the U.S. ICBM force. Consequently, the Soviet Union would find itself the sole possessor of an expensive and potentially vulnerable ICBM force which would be of decreasing political and strategic

---

*Some analysts contend that a large-scale attack upon hardened ICBM silos would be nearly impossible due to the "fratricide" problem in which the detonation of the initial warheads during a nuclear attack could degrade the accuracy and effectiveness of the following warheads.

utility. The USSR would be left to worry over whether the United States might eventually deploy new submarine-launched ballistic missiles armed with extremely accurate, terminal-guidance warheads, thereby threatening the survivability of the Soviet ICBM force.

By proposing to maintain some portion of the ICBM force, many of the standard objections can be avoided since the strategic Triad concept will continue to exist. Therefore, while the reduced ICBM force of 200-300 ICBMs is too small to be strategically provocative, it is too large to be ignored by an attacker. The maintenance of this modest ICBM force would also provide the highly responsive force which some strategists argue is necessary to deter the threat of limited nuclear war.

The course sought by the Defense Department is clearly inadequate and unwise. The present MX ICBM program is primarily motivated by the Air Force's search for a new, improved war-fighting weapon rather than by an attempt to enhance the survivability of the U.S. deterrent. Even if deployed in a mobile basing mode, the MX ICBM will still leave large numbers of ICBMs deployed in vulnerable silos and will create pressures to adopt a "launch-on-warning" doctrine. The presently favored "buried trench" system will also create serious verification problems for the SALT negotiations.

Restructuring the U.S. deterrent is the only alternative which will both increase strategic stability and avoid creating difficult verification problems for SALT II. While SALT can no longer directly reduce the problem of ICBM vulnerability, a new SALT proposal could be a useful complement if it sought significant mutual reductions in the present 1,320 MIRVed launcher ceiling envisioned in the Vladivostok accord. This would force the United States and the Soviet Union to begin to set strategic force level priorities and would set in motion the difficult process for reductions in the land-based MIRVed ICBM force.

Given the shortcomings of the MX ICBM concept, the Carter administration was wise not to allow the MX to be accelerated into advanced development. As the Carter administration evaluates the problem of land-based missile vulnerability and the option of the MX ICBM, it should give serious consideration to the advantages of restructuring the U.S. deterrent.´ *(February 1977)*

The Bomber Debate: Is There a B-2 in Our Future?
Ronald L. Tammen

As this article indicates, the future of the manned bomber is by no means settled. The B-1 was finally killed in February 1978 by votes in both houses of Congress after last ditch efforts to save the bomber failed. But there are indications that the Joint Chiefs of Staff may insist on an FB-111H production commitment as one price for their support of SALT II.

"The B-1 seems to have a life of its own," President Carter is quoted as saying during a strategy meeting with congressional leaders. And so it did. It required a presidential declaration, fifteen separate votes in Congress, a nationwide grassroots campaign, and the evolution of the cruise missile to halt development of the B-1. Even then, the margin was razor thin at every step, and support continues to run high for another manned, strategic, penetrating bomber program to replace B-52s.

The key to stopping the B-1 was forged by Senator John Culver (D-Ia.)—the delay amendment. Anticipating a Democratic victory in the 1976 presidential campaign, Culver succeeded in convincing a majority of the Senate to delay full-scale production of the B-1 until

---

Comparing Strategic Bombers

Characteristics	B52G/H	B-1	FB-111H
Length (feet)	159	151	88
Width (feet)	185	70–137	45–70
		(swing wing)	
Maximum takeoff gross weight (pounds)	488,000	395,000	140,000
Crew size	6	4	2
Internal nuclear payload	12	24	4
External nuclear payload	12	—	10
Cruise missile capability (internal and external)	20	24	10–14
Low altitude penetration (Mach)	.53–.55	.85	.85
Penetration altitude (feet)	400	200	200
Maximum high altitude (Mach)	.90	1.6	1.6
High altitude cruise (Mach)	.77	.70	.75
Ferry range—high altitude unrefueled (nautical miles)	c. 8,000	c. 7,000	c. 6,000
Total program cost (billions of inflated dollars)	—	24	7
Program unit cost (millions of inflated dollars)	—	102	45

B52G/H   B-1   FB-111H

February of 1977. Although his proposal was not accepted by the House of Representatives, a similar amendment by Senator William Proxmire (D-Wis.) was signed into law as part of the military appropriations bill.

With the election of President Carter, the Air Force decided to delay the B-1 production decision even further, until the summer of 1977. Then, on June 30, despite widespread expectation of B-1 approval, the President chose the B-52s and the cruise missile as alternatives to the $24 billion B-1 program. The Air Force suffered a severe shock but recovered quickly and set in motion a number of back-up strategies.

But the President's announcement did not end the congressional debate. The Senate voted overwhelmingly for cancellation. The House, which on June 28 had supported the B-1, later narrowly rejected it by a vote of 202 to 199. But the House Appropriations Committee refused to allow the President to stop spending $462 million in "prior-year" funds for two more B-1 aircraft. To further confuse the issue, another "new" manned penetrating bomber emerged as an alternative to the B-1. The President's decision seemed in danger of reversal.

When the President cancelled the B-1, he cited the cruise missile and the improved B-52 as the near-term replacement, with cruise missile carriers (an aircraft designed to carry the new air-launched cruise missile) as a possible future option. Yet he did not completely rule out either the B-1 or another manned, penetrating bomber. This ambiguity led to three perhaps unanticipated responses. First, it gave hope to B-1 supporters that, given a fortuitous event, the program could be resurrected. Second, it encouraged the Air Force and defense contractors to pursue other manned bomber alternatives. Third, and perhaps most important, it raised once again, but in new circumstances, the entire question of the future of the bomber portion of the Triad of strategic deterrent forces.

Several schools of thought have emerged. Some advocate a pure "stand-off" force of aircraft armed with cruise missiles to replace the B-52 fleet, while others argue for a predominantly "penetrating" force of new bombers. Still a third view is that the bomber force should be mixed, so as to complicate further an adversary's air defense problem. Adherents of this approach differ, however, over whether this mixed bomber fleet can be achieved by modifying existing aircraft or whether it requires new planes. The administration favors the former option, calling for B-52 modifications and improvements while examining the long-term potential of the cruise missile carrier. Believing that the bomber force provides insurance against "unexpected breakthroughs" in antisubmarine warfare and antiballistic missile technology, but without provocative first-strike implications, the administration wants to preserve this so-called "air-breathing" component of the deterrent force

The American B-1 bomber in flight. Production of this costly penetrating bomber was cancelled in favor of converting the slower B-52 aircraft into stand-off bombers armed with nuclear-tipped cruise missiles which they were capable of launching from beyond the range of air defense systems.

Source: U.S. Air Force

(as contrasted with the submarine- and land-launched ballistic missiles). It calculates that the improved B-52 followed later by a cruise missile carrier will permit a survivable, retaliatory (second-strike) capacity that will match or exceed projected Soviet strategic growth in warheads, megatonnage, throw-weight, and hardened target destruction capability through at least 1986 *without* the B-1 or other new bomber and *without* the new MX mobile missile. This approach, moreover, would save $10 billion in constant fiscal year 1978 dollars, as compared to the cost of a moderate force of 150 B-1 bombers.

The administration backed up its position by sending Congress a $449 million supplemental military authorization bill requesting funds for upgrading the B-52s, for accelerating development of the cruise missile and for early testing of a cruise missile carrier. No funds were sought for a new, manned, penetrating bomber. Nonetheless, a contender was waiting, the FB-111H. Proposed as early as 1973 by its prime contractor, General Dynamics, the FB-111H is a cousin to the

F-111 fighter and the FB-111A medium bomber, with which it shares a 43 percent common structure. Though similar to the FB-111A, the new "H" model would be twelve feet longer, have a more restricted wing arc, use B-1 engines and electronics, and carry a modified tail section.

The Air Force enthusiastically embraced the FB-111H. No longer the unmentionable stepchild of the B-1, the FB-111H was widely praised and its supporters recommended a full development plan to Secretary of Defense Harold Brown, who initially refused to make a for-or-against decision.

At the same time, the cruise missile carrier was coming under attack. The military supplemental bill contained a request for $90 million to purchase and test a cruise missile carrier. Under scrutiny by B-1 supporters in the House and Senate Armed Services Committees, the administration's plan was found to be almost non-existent. There was no specific spending plan for the $90 million, soon revised downward to $50 million; there were none of the timetables, cost estimates, or performance indicators essential for a go-ahead decision.

Though denigrated by some, the cruise missile carrier concept is popular with other congressmen because of its cost-effectiveness. A force of 50 cruise missile carriers could be deployed with about 3,000 cruise missiles at a cost of $5.8 billion for the aircraft and $3.4 billion for the missiles. A fleet of 100 carriers with 6,000 missiles would cost $16.5 billion. This compares to a 240-aircraft B-1 program cost of $24 billion. The roughly 5,000 nuclear "loadings" of the B-1 force, including short-range attack missiles, would account for another $4-5 billion.

Rockwell International, the B-1 prime contractor, sought to capitalize on Washington's renewed interest in the bomber issue. It was already making a major effort to retain manufacturing capability for the B-1 until 1981 by encouraging the House of Representatives to deny the President's rescission of fiscal year 1977 B-1 funds, thereby allowing production of two more aircraft. Noting congressional and Air Force interest in the FB-111H, Rockwell designed two lower-cost versions of the B-1. A fixed-wing cruise missile carrier option was proposed to compete with the FB-111H by carrying sixteen internal and fourteen external missiles at about two-thirds the B-1 cost. A higher-cost, combined penetrator/cruise missile carrier was also conceived. This proliferation of options and arguments encouraged bomber enthusiasts and brightened prospects for some form of new manned, strategic bomber.

While it appeared that the House of Representatives might simply either resurrect the B-1 or fund the FB-111H, a more comprehensive plan emerged in the Senate Armed Services Subcommittee on Research and Development.

First, the Administration's poor showing in justifying the cruise missile carrier program was used to support a cut in requested funds from $50 million to $5 million for a "definition study." Rejecting a plea from Secretary Brown that this option was "extremely important particularly because it would allow us to expand our strategic capability rapidly," the subcommittee held that a "costly aircraft flight demonstration" is unnecessary due to a "lack of urgency."

While the subcommittee cut monies for the cruise missile carrier, it funded the FB-111H at a level of $20 million. Since no funds for the FB-111H had been requested by the administration, Chairman John Stennis (D-Miss.) would not include this item in the supplemental military authorization bill until formal approval could be obtained from the Defense Department. After a personal conversation, a letter was received from Secretary Brown indicating that he would agree to $20 million for preliminary development work as a "prudent step."

The third element was the subcommittee's addition of a special $5 million authorization for a study of another manned, penetrating bomber called the BX. Again, this was not requested by the administration.

The letter from Secretary Brown to Senator Stennis on the FB-111H touched off a protest in the House from B-1 advocates and critics alike. B-1 advocates decried the FB-111H funding as not cost-effective. Critics saw the aircraft as the "Son of B-1." This unusual coalition struck the FB-111H funding recommended by the House Armed Services Committee in the supplemental military authorization bill. The Senate, however, restored the money in the Conference Committee on the authorization measure.

When House B-1 supporters attempted to resurrect the entire program through the supplemental appropriation bill, only a plea for party unity by Speaker Thomas O'Neill (D-Mass.) and a strong lecture on deterrence by Appropriations Chairman George Mahon (D-Tex.) defeated the amendment to restore $1.4 billion for full-scale production. The administration, in contrast to its earlier efforts, also mounted an effective lobbying campaign. With that vote, the B-1 issue seemed to be settled, with only the "prior-year" funding question remaining to be decided in late November.

A compromise on the cruise missile carrier was reached when the Senate agreed to fund a study at the level of $15 million, higher than the $5 million recommended by the Senate Armed Services Committee but less than the revised administration request for $50 million. The House agreed to the $15 million figure. Ultimately, the unrequested funds for study of the new BX strategic bomber were deleted entirely.

Finally, the unsought FB-111H option was knocked out of the supplemental appropriations bill in the Conference Committee by House conferees, who were adamantly against it. The FB-111H proposal is not entirely dead, however. The conferees agreed that the deletion of the

FB-111H funds was done "without prejudice to the program" and that they would consider any official request this year or next for more funds. For the FB-111H supporters this invitation may prove irresistible, now that the complicating issue of the B-1 appears settled.

If one assumes a need to extend the life of the bomber force, the FB-111H seems a poor candidate in the 1980s. In terms of basic capability, it cannot compete with the B-52 fleet. Current plans call for a mixed force of about 300 B-52s, with 150 B-52Gs as stand-off cruise missile carriers and about 150 D and H models as penetrators. The modifications recently approved by Congress will extend the life of the B-52 into the 1990s, allowing a mixed force for penetrating and stand-off missions for the next ten to fifteen years without producing a new bomber.

The FB-111H has about half the cruise missile capability of the B-52 and less range regardless of the assigned mission. Its radar cross-section and infrared signature provide improved protection against air defenses, but it remains much more vulnerable than a 19-foot cruise missile. If the B-1 is not cost-effective, there is no calculation that can make the FB-111H cost-effective for the same mission. A force of 165 FB-111Hs would have a twenty-year life cycle cost of $17 billion compared to an equal alert force of 61 B-1s at $11.5 billion. The production cost for modifying 65 FB-111s and manufacturing 100 FB-111Hs by 1985 would total $7.02 billion, barring future cost growth. There would be no competitive bidding for the airframe or engines for this aircraft, which are manufactured by General Dynamics (with a sole-source contract) and General Electric, respectively.

Two major strategic bomber studies have, in recent years, analyzed the FB-111H. In commenting on the Joint Strategic Bomber Study during the Ford administration, one defense official noted that the FB-111H is "markedly cost-ineffective compared to all other forces" and deficient in range, payload and electronic countermeasures. According to Secretary Brown, whose B-1 study resulted in the cancellation of that program: "We eliminated the FB-111H. Our analysis showed no significant advantage in cost or effectiveness over the B-1." He also concluded that the BX recommended by the Senate Research and Development Subcommittee could not save money and would take too long to develop.

It appears that the B-1 as such is dead. Nevertheless, the bomber debate is not dead, and it could, given past support in the Congress and the Air Force, still lead to another manned, penetrating bomber.

(November 1977)

Strategic Cruise Missiles and the Future of SALT
Lawrence Weiler

At a few critical points during the post-war period new weapons developments have carried unusually serious implications for the future, as distinct from their immediate effects on the strategic balance. In each case there was a danger of consequent greater insecurity for both sides and increased problems for future arms control efforts. At such times, arms control efforts have been presented with unusual challenges. This was the case with ICBMs, ABMs, and MIRVs.

The half-hearted effort in the late 1950s to stop intercontinental ballistic missiles (ICBMs) was unsuccessful. ICBMs carried not only the future prospect of a major shift in the strategic relationship between the United States and the USSR but also increased tension and the danger of a nuclear holocaust through accident or miscalculation. More recently however, the mutual perception of the role that anti-ballistic missiles (ABMs) could play as a catalyst of strategic arms competition helped produce the one case where the challenge was met—through the ABM Treaty.

In the third and most instructive case, multiple independently-targetable re-entry vehicles (MIRVs), the challenge was not met. In the late 1960s, a fascination with the short-term advantages afforded by the United States' lead in new MIRV technology outweighed interest in halting MIRVs in the SALT I negotiations. As a result both sides now wrestle inexorably with a perceived increased threat to land-based ICBMs and a quantum jump in the numbers of deliverable warheads. The resulting instabilities and increased asymmetries in the two sides' strategic programs, together with the momentum of on-going MIRV programs, produced the artificially high MIRV levels set at Vladivostok.

We are now at a similarly critical turning point: the decision concerning strategic cruise missiles. Unlike ballistic missiles, these aerodynamic vehicles are continuously powered and travel at subsonic speeds within the atmosphere at low altitudes, which makes detection difficult. They require continuous guidance because of requirements for trajectory changes, differing weather conditions, and variations in performance of the propulsion system. Let us here look at the basic features of this system and how they affect the future of strategic arms control.

Developments in long-range cruise missiles are part of a broader technological revolution that affects this class of weapons generally. Cruise missiles are an old weapons system, which in the past were considered marginal or ineffective. In the initial strategic arms negotiations

(SALT I), the United States made a brief effort to limit the number of short-range Soviet naval cruise missiles but did not press the issue since they were considered marginal in importance and at least as questionable as "strategic systems" as U.S. forward-based systems.*

Numerous technological advances have, rather suddenly, changed all this. Improvements in propulsion systems have made it possible to produce missiles of extended ranges with relatively less space required for the propulsion system, leaving more room for guidance systems and warheads. Of much greater significance, the guidance systems themselves have been revolutionized by micro-miniaturization of sensors, logic circuits, memory banks, and communication systems. Such systems opened the way for developing the planned long-range (1,400-2,000 nautical mile), inexpensive cruise missile that, using a terrain matching and recognition terminal guidance system, will have greater accuracy than current ICBMs.

Cruise missiles have become the weapons developer's latest dream. The current U.S. program involves an air-launched and a sea-launched version. The air-launched cruise missiles will be carried by strategic bombers. A critical feature of the current sea-launched program is that the missile, with its 21-inch diameter, will fit into a standard torpedo tube—the Navy's planned primary launch platform.** With the requirements given the weapons designers, this was a logical decision. For the future of strategic arms limitation, however, it is a potential disaster, since all submarines would become potential launcher platforms, with no way of verifying how many strategic nuclear launchers in submarines exist. Moreover, the torpedo tube launchers would be quickly reloadable. There would be no way, as is the case with ICBMs and sea-launched ballistic missiles, of, in effect, equating missile numbers with launcher numbers.

Many factors lay behind the 1972 decision to proceed with the strategic cruise missile program. It was part of the price, together with the Trident program, paid to gain support of the military for the SALT I Interim Offensive Arms Agreement. It also was regarded as a "hedge" or insurance against future Soviet programs or a breakdown of the SALT II negotiations. Some in Washington also viewed it as a SALT "bargaining chip." All this was before the technical developments had become clear to policy makers—and before the arms control implica-

---

*Forward-based systems are United States' aircraft and other weapons primarily based in Europe which are capable of delivering nuclear attacks upon portions of the USSR although their primary mission is to support NATO ground forces.

**The U.S. sea-launched cruise missile is being designed to be capable of launch from a variety of platforms including surface ships, aircraft, and even ground vehicles.

tions of cruise missiles were recognized. Yet, to this day, no persuasive military requirement for strategic cruise missiles has been offered by government spokesmen.

At SALT, the Ford administration argued that strategic cruise missile launchers are not part of the 2,400 strategic launcher maximum agreed upon at Vladivostok. Also, the United States claimed that the Vladivostok accord limiting air-launched missiles to 600 kilometers applies only to ballistic missiles and not to cruise missiles. Thus, a debate within the executive branch concerning the U.S. position began and has continued in the Carter administration. The implications of this debate for the future of arms control should be clearly understood. Were we to continue with an unrestricted cruise missile program, the result would be to create another weapon system that would complicate efforts to place equal limits on each side's total strategic launchers— much as U.S. forward-based systems have done in past SALT negotiations. The forward-based systems issue has not yet been resolved but merely put aside in light of the high levels of the Vladivostok accord; and the Soviets have given notice that it will resurface whenever future reductions are considered. Adding cruise missiles to the unresolved problem of forward-based systems would make it an issue in spades, and would result in a possibly insurmountable barrier to future SALT agreements—and certainly to any reductions.

At the most fundamental level, the present sea-launched cruise missile program would thwart all verification of future strategic launcher levels. Should the Soviets follow suit—and the MIRV experience should teach us that in time they can and probably will—each side would be able to point to potential strategic launchers in all attack submarines, the numbers of which could not be verified unless all torpedo tubes were counted as strategic launchers. (The United States now has sixty-five nuclear-powered attack submarines with a total of 260—reloadable—torpedo tubes, and the Soviets have about seventy-eight nuclear-powered attack and cruise missile submarines with at least as many cruise missile launchers.) The result would be inability to reach agreement—and because of this we would witness uncontrolled strategic arms competition in all strategic forces. The "inexpensive" strategic cruise missile thus could well become one of the most expensive programs ever undertaken.

Despite the technical ingenuity which these new missiles reflect, there is no real need for them in the strategic forces of either side. It is important at this time that we place this issue in a larger perspective and that we look beyond the next five years.

Limiting strategic cruise missiles will present some verification problems, and acceptance of some uncertainties in terms of exact range limitations will likely be necessary. But if the problem is viewed in its larger context of the marginal need for these systems and their effect upon the future of strategic arms limitation, solutions can be found. The acceptable quality of verification should be judged in the context of the limited strategic importance of these weapons.

The starting point must be a prohibition on development of cruise missiles that can be fired from launchers other than those that are clearly verifiable as strategic launchers. The peg that has made verification by national means of strategic arms limitations possible has been to count launchers, not missiles (as was attempted in the mid-sixties). This ability must be retained. This means that under a SALT II agreement strategic cruise missiles capable of using torpedo tubes for launchers must not be permitted. The question of what to do about surface-launched naval cruise missiles is another matter that will have to be addressed. Air-launched cruise missiles present less of a problem since their launchers, the strategic bombers, can be counted. I would further argue for placing some agreed limitations on ranges for air- and sea-launched cruise missiles. This would be a somewhat loose restriction since range can be extended by trading off warhead and airframe space for enlarged fuel capacity, but a restriction with some "give" in it would be better than no restriction on range. Surface ship-launched missiles should be limited to a tactical range of around 300 to 400 kilometers. A permitted range of less than 1,000 kilometers for air-launched cruise missiles would appear to be adequate to redress the asymmetry presented by the large, unrestricted Soviet air defense system.

The exact nature of the specific limitations will involve considerable technical analysis, but we must not allow solvable technical questions to obscure the over-all interest the United States and the USSR have in preventing strategic cruise missiles from foreclosing the future of the SALT process. So vital is this issue that its resolution must come within a broad, informed consensus, not in secrecy or by default.

(October 1975)

Cruise Missiles: Different Missions, Different Arms Control Impact   *Robert S. Metzger*

Originally justified as a dispensable bargaining chip of little military value, the small, pilotless, low-flying winged aircraft known as the cruise missile has emerged in recent years as one of the most controversial weapon systems under development by the United States. Both the critics and advocates of the cruise missile have tended to overlook important distinctions between the air-launched cruise missile (ALCM),

An extended air-launched cruise missile is shown to the left of a standard air-launched cruise missile. Other configurations are being tested for launching from air, land, or sea. Cruise missiles can carry conventional or nuclear explosives. Slower than ballistic missiles, they are nevertheless very accurate. The wings unfold from the fuselage after launching.

Source: U.S. Air Force

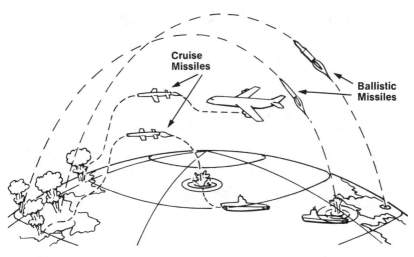

A cruise missile is essentially a pilotless bomber; a ballistic missile, a high altitude rocket whose trajectory is determined in the first minutes after launch.

A capsule containing a sea-launched cruise missile breaks the surface in a Pacific Ocean test launch. After leaving the water, the capsule falls away and the cruise missile begins its flight to the target. Sea-launched cruise missiles can be fired from torpedo tubes.

Source: U.S. Navy

on the one hand, and ground- and sea-launched cruise missiles (GLCM and SLCM), on the other. In particular, there are key differences in mission, effectiveness, and in the impact development and deployment of the systems would have on the prospects for arms control.

The ALCM

Mission. The ALCM is a *strategic* weapon as its mission is to attack targets within the Soviet Union after launch from a manned aircraft. Ultimately, the value of the air-launched cruise missile is itself a function of the value assigned to continuing a strategic bomber force. If the need for a bomber force is accepted, ALCM can be argued for to improve the capability of the so-called "air-breathing" or bomber leg of the Triad of U.S. nuclear deterrent forces. ALCM will assist in insuring the future ability of U.S. bombers to deliver a second strike against Soviet targets even in the face of anticipated improvements in Soviet air defenses. Since the ALCM can fly 1,500 nautical miles to deliver a warhead on a target with extreme accuracy, it increases the target coverage of existing aircraft and will allow U.S. bombers to "stand off" from the Soviet Union, launching attacks without penetrating Soviet air space.

Military Effectiveness. The strategic ALCM is expected to be effective in its assigned role because experts believe it would have an extremely high probability of surviving Soviet strategic air defenses. To defeat a mixed force of penetrating bombers and ALCM-carrying aircraft, the Soviets would have to spend an estimated $10 to $50 billion to develop new weapons, including new long-range interceptor aircraft to attack ALCM carriers, a sophisticated look-down radar able to distinguish low-flying cruise missiles and bombers from ground clutter, and a vast array of terminal defenses using numerous ground-control radars, low-altitude surface-to-air missiles (SAMs), and radar-directed rapid firing anti-aircraft artillery. Even if the difficult technical barriers were overcome, the number of alternative bomber and ALCM penetration routes appears to be large enough to make the task of defense close to impossible.

Arms Control Impact. While the development and deployment of the strategic ALCM does pose some new problems to arms control, on the whole the ALCM's arms control impact could be a positive one since it contributes to greater strategic stability. SALT II (Strategic Arms Limitation Talks) negotiating experience to date indicates that agreements can be reached on limiting the ALCM. The emerging SALT II agreement reportedly limits the number of ALCM-equipped aircraft by counting them in the sub-limits on strategic delivery vehicles with multiple independently-targetable vehicles (MIRVs). While the reported range limitation of 2,500 kilometers (1,553 miles) contained in the three-year protocol is subject to considerable ambiguity, the significance of the ambiguity is slight, as Soviet acceptance of the protocol indicates its willingness to accept imprecision in range verification.

In addition, while the ALCM does have the accuracy and yield combination necessary to destroy heavily hardened targets, the system cannot be perceived as a first-strike weapon against Soviet land-based missiles because of the slow speed of the cruise missile and its carrier aircraft.

ALCM may have a positive arms control effect in that, by assuring the continued effectiveness of the bomber force, the system contributes to the overall capability of U.S. strategic forces. In particular, ALCM helps alleviate concern for the theoretical vulnerability of land-based ICBMs (intercontinental ballistic missiles). Without limitations on the quantitative and qualitative growth of Soviet offensive systems more comprehensive than those reportedly contained in the joint draft text of SALT II, by the end of the next decade the Soviet Union may be able to place at risk a large percentage of our land-based Minuteman force.* While the preferred response to this perceived trend in ICBM vulnerability is pursuit of further stabilizing limitations in SALT III, deployment of standoff bombers equipped with ALCM assures that, at most, only one "leg" of the Triad is at risk, in fact or in theory.

With two survivable retaliatory forces—bombers and submarines—able to maintain target coverage and penetration capability, the justification for proceeding with new ICBMs, such as the mobile MX, is sharply reduced. Reducing the perceived need for the MX would be an important arms control contribution because deployment of the costly MX in the numbers now envisioned (300) and with the capacity presently expected (eight to ten re-entry vehicles per missile, each with hard-target kill capability) could greatly increase crisis instability. MX could appear to the Soviets to constitute a credible first-strike threat against their land-based missiles, which are the backbone of Soviet strategic forces. Potential Soviet responses to the MX are disturbing. At worst, in a crisis they might be tempted to launch a pre-emptive strike. Or the Soviets could adopt a launch-on-warning policy, thus increasing the chance of accidental nuclear conflict, or a launch-under-attack policy, which could lead to expansion of a limited exchange. At the least, the MX would spur further Soviet initiatives to expand and improve their strategic forces. In contrast to the MX, the ALCM permits force modernization while

---

*Concern for this contingency is sometimes overstated by those who focus on potential Soviet increases in MIRVs and in MIRV accuracy while neglecting other requirements for a successful "disarming" attack, e.g., near-perfect operational reliability, near-perfect surprise, near-perfect attack sequencing, and avoidance of re-entry vehicle "fratricide" or other electromagnetic effects. Both powers, moreover, elected to accept ICBM vulnerability when they signed the ABM Treaty but did not prevent the deployment of MIRVed missiles.

Modern Cruise Missiles

	U.S.				USSR	
	ALCM (AGM-86B)	**GLCM**	**Tomahawk land-attack**	**Tomahawk anti-ship**	**SS-N-3**	**SS-N-12**
Range	1500 nm.	2000 nm.	2000 nm.	300 nm.	250 nm.	250 + nm.
Warhead type yield	nuclear 200 kt.	nuclear 200 kt.	nuclear 200 kt.	high explosive	nuclear 1 mt.	nuclear 1 mt.
Guidance	TERCOM*	TERCOM	TERCOM	radar homing	radio command	radio command and radar homing
Hard-target capacity	yes	yes	yes	N/A	no	no
Deployment mode	air: B-52 or cruise missile carriers	ground: mobile cannister	sea: attack subs and surface ships	sea: surface ships	sea: subs and ships	sea: Kiev-class carrier
Mission primary	strategic (USSR targets)	theater	theater	tactical	tactical	tactical (anti-ship)
secondary	N/A	strategic	strategic	N/A	strategic	strategic (U.S. targets)

* Terrain contour matching

enhancing crisis stability, at a cost considerably less than that of the cancelled B-1 bomber.

A Soviet counterpart to the U.S. ALCM, if developed, would extend the target coverage of the Backfire medium-range bomber, providing the Soviet Union with a more sophisticated bomber capability than it has possessed for some years. While not an insignificant possibility, the importance of such a development should not be overstated. Counting an ALCM-equipped Backfire bomber in SALT as a "heavy bomber" within the ceiling on strategic nuclear delivery vehicles would be one approach to easing the arms control disadvantage of a counterpart Soviet ALCM. This approach would require the Soviet Union to reduce its MIRVed ICBMs in proportion to the number of ALCM-equipped Backfire bombers it deployed, thereby replacing a more threatening system with a more stable one and further enhancing the overall stability of the balance of strategic nuclear forces.

GLCM and SLCM

Mission. The primary mission of the proposed GLCM and land-attack SLCM in current U.S. defense planning is against targets in the European theater. The cautious Soviet planner, however, cannot overlook the fact that the 2,000 nautical mile range of these weapons makes them "dual capable" systems, i.e., they could also be directed against *strategic* targets within the Soviet Union. Indeed, one of the initial justifications for the submarine-launched cruise missile was as a strategic weapon.

Military Effectiveness. A recent study by the Los Alamos Nuclear Weapons Laboratory raises a number of questions which have not hitherto received public attention about the utility of cruise missiles in Europe. Essentially, the study casts doubt on the ability of cruise missiles to penetrate to their assigned theater target. The study indicates that, if the altitude at which the missile flies is too low, the probability of crashing into the varied terrain of central Europe—called "ground clobber"—rises beyond an acceptable level. At altitudes where ground clobber is not a problem, the task of radar detection and tracking is eased and the missile is much more likely to be shot down.

Cruise missile penetration to target in Europe is also critically influenced by the degree to which air defense sites are selected to minimize "masking" of defense radars by surrounding terrain features. Earlier studies unrealistically assumed random distribution of air defense sites without regard to masking angles. Yet the Los Alamos data indicates that, as the number of air defense radars located on optimum sites increases, the probability that the defense will destroy the cruise missile rises remarkably. Similarly, though one Defense Intelligence Agency study reportedly found the probability of cruise missile target penetration high, this was based on the assumption that only 5 percent of the Soviet defense sites were active at the time of attempted penetration. The Los Alamos analysis, by contrast, shows that penetration or success rates for the cruise missile fall dramatically when more realistic assumptions are made.

While theater cruise missiles do have a cost-effectiveness advantage over other types of theater nuclear delivery systems against certain types of targets, the theater cruise missile should not be viewed as a universal weapon. It can be used against only a subset of the targets against which tactical aircraft can be used and, because of its slow speed and inflexibility once launched, obviously is of little value against moving and time-urgent targets. Against fixed targets at ranges within about 500 miles, theater cruise missiles compare unfavorably with tactical· ballistic missiles, e.g., the Pershing II, which is much faster and virtually invulnerable to terminal defenses.

The view of many analysts that theater cruise missiles are more vulnerable to defenses than the strategic ALCM reflects a number of factors. The number of bomber launch points and alternative ALCM penetration routes, as well as the number of probable ALCM targets, exceed the comparable figures for theater cruise missiles. And, at present at least, the Soviet Union has deployed the bulk of its low-altitude capable air defense assets with Soviet ground forces (which operate in Europe) and not with PVO-Strany, the Soviet strategic air defense organization.

Arms Control Impact. Theater cruise missiles, ground-launched or sea-launched, pose major difficulties for arms limitation negotiations on both strategic "central systems" and theater nuclear forces. Force level assessment, a critical preliminary to successful negotiations, and verification of any agreement reached become murky propositions at best, due to the very military advantages which cruise missiles possess: mobility, dispersal and concealment of launchers, and flexibility in range, warhead choice and target selection.

The dual strategic *and* tactical *capability* of GLCMs and SLCMs could jeopardize the concepts and structures which underlie contemporary approaches to negotiated arms limitations. Classification of weapons as "strategic" or "tactical" has facilitated separation of issues between SALT and MBFR (Mutual and Balanced Force Reductions talks). But theater cruise missiles resist such classification not only because of their long range but also because of their perceived effectiveness in either role. GLCM and SLCM cut across, and hence blur, distinctions between "strategic" and "tactical." In addition, because any limitation of such weapons in one forum would directly affect the military balances at issue in the other, GLCM and SLCM undermine the existing structure of negotiations by striking at the bilateral basis of discussion between the United States and the USSR which has enabled SALT to proceed independent of MBFR. A precipitous commitment to theater cruise missiles by either the United States or its NATO allies would seriously damage the current basis for arms control negotiations before new structures and new approaches can be fashioned for future negotiations.

Whether U.S. or NATO deployment of ground-launched and sea-launched theater cruise missiles would lead to parallel Soviet systems is not clear, in view of the ability of existing Soviet IRBMs (intermediate-range ballistic missiles) to attack targets throughout Europe with greater certainty of penetration than could be achieved with cruise missiles. Still, the past pattern of Soviet response to American technological accomplishments suggests that a new Soviet GLCM or improved SLCM is not improbable. Even if adding only marginally to Soviet theater nuclear forces, deployment of cruise missiles would further exacerbate force level assessment and verification problems, already exceedingly complicated by the initial Soviet deployment of the mobile SS-20 IRBM.

While a verification scheme has been developed to allow ALCM agreement at SALT II which makes use of each side's ability to verify the number of aircraft which could carry cruise missiles, no analogous approach is available to facilitate verification of theater cruise missiles. GLCMs in particular resist assessment and verification, as the launchers are small, mobile, and may easily be reloaded. While SLCMs could be counted by assuming a certain number of SLCMs to be mounted on ships or subs of particular classes, the ambiguity of such an approach renders it unsatisfactory, given the large number of missiles which could be carried but not detected.

NATO officials repeatedly have voiced opposition to U.S.-Soviet agreement, in a reported protocol to SALT II, to ban deployment (but not development) of GLCMs and SLCMs with a range in excess of 600 kilometers (350 miles). They fear the protocol eventually will be extended to ban completely deployment and transfer of U.S. cruise missile technology to Europe. Underlying these objections is European concern that the cruise missile option should not be abandoned unless coupled with redress of the imbalance in theater nuclear delivery systems which at present distinctly favors the Soviets because of their large medium- and intermediate-range ballistic missile force. At the same time, unless the United States agrees to some limitation on cruise missile technology transfer, further progress at SALT may be in jeopardy.

This is a dilemma without an easy resolution. Certainly the NATO concern over Soviet theater nuclear forces deserves recognition by U.S. planners. Yet recognition of the merit in the European position does not require opposition to the protocol. The three-year protocol does not prevent the United States and NATO from using the eventual deployment decision on GLCMs and SLCMs to encourage Soviet interest in new efforts to negotiate limits on theater nuclear delivery systems. Theater cruise missiles are bargaining chips which both sides should want to avoid. While not without risk, it may be that the present U.S. advantage in cruise missiles can provide leverage to obtain limitation of theater nuclear delivery systems (particularly IRBMs), a subject which to date the Soviets have refused even to discuss at MBFR, as the IRBMs are based in the Soviet Union and hence are outside the scope of MBFR negotiations.

The protocol provides the United States and NATO with breathing space in which three critical tasks must be addressed. First, the United States and NATO should carefully assess whether the doubtful military benefits of ground- and sea-launched cruise missiles justify the virtually certain foreclosure of arms control opportunities still available. Second, the United States and NATO must develop new mechanisms for intra-alliance consultation and coordination to assure more thorough European participation in policy and negotiating decisions which affect theater military balances. Finally, the United States must look beyond the current round of negotiations toward SALT III, when issues of theater nuclear and "dual-capable" or "grey area" systems can no longer be deferred, and with the Soviet Union begin the process of creating new structures for arms control negotiations and new concepts about which to order future arms limitation agreements. *(January 1978)*

Justifying the Defense Budget: Questionable Threats, Irrelevant Responses   *Herbert Scoville, Jr.*

In this article, focusing on the 1977 fiscal year defense budget, Dr. Scoville examines a number of weapons and strategy issues which continue to dominate the U.S. defense debate.

Secretary of Defense Donald Rumsfeld has proclaimed a desire for a U.S.-USSR strategic arms limitation (SALT) agreement which would limit competition in nuclear arms and assure strategic stability at lower levels of force. Specifically, he would prefer to forestall any danger to our ICBM (intercontinental ballistic missile) forces by mutual agreement rather than to replace them. But even on the assumption of success in SALT, he proposes a 30 percent increase over last year in funds for strategic forces (from $7.3 to $9.4 billion). In addition, Secretary of

State Henry Kissinger predicted that if SALT fails the United States would further increase its strategic spending by $20 billion over the next five years.

Is there a new Soviet threat which calls for this expansion of U.S. strategic capability? How might SALT contain it? Finally, how do our expanded programs relate to the new situation?

In his *Annual Defense Department Report* for fiscal year 1977, Secretary Rumsfeld lists eight Soviet strategic programs which cause him concern. Four involve offensive weapons—new ICBMs with multiple warheads (multiple independently-targetable re-entry vehicles or MIRVs), new submarine ballistic missiles, the Backfire bomber, and cruise missiles—and four defensive programs—antiballistic missiles (ABMs), air defense, anti-submarine warfare, and civilian defense.

The most serious threat listed by Secretary Rumsfeld is the development of four new-generation, large throw-weight ICBMs. Three of these ICBMs have been flight-tested with MIRVs. The Soviet deployment of MIRVed missiles, which finally began in 1975, some five years after the initial U.S. deployment of MIRVs, is used to justify the development of a replacement (the mobile missile MX) for our current Minuteman ICBMs in a program which could eventually cost $20 to $30 billion. Yet only a year ago Defense Secretary James Schlesinger stated that even if these same new missiles were deployed in quantity in the 1980s the Russians could never count on being able to destroy our entire Minuteman force.

For some reason the parallel development of four different ICBMs is made to appear very threatening, but shouldn't we really be more alarmed if only one or at the most two were in the program? Such a wasteful and duplicatory development—typical of many in the Soviet Union—could account in part for their large military expenditures. It is a partial explanation of why former Central Intelligence Agency Director William Colby and former Defense Intelligence Agency Director General Daniel Graham testified last year that dollar figures for the Soviet defense budget are one of the biggest bear traps to objective intelligence. Yet the administration still uses such comparisons to justify higher budgets.

Even a successful SALT negotiation will not prevent the deployment of these new-generation MIRVed missiles at below threatening levels. In fact, the U.S. insistence at Vladivostok of setting a ceiling of MIRVed delivery vehicles at 1,320 assures that the Russians can eventually have sufficient warheads to significantly threaten our Minuteman force. Since there are no proposed restraints on qualitative improvements, such as accuracy, the Russians can eventually have an effective counterforce capability. If the military is so worried about the vulnerability of the Minuteman ICBM force, then why have they been so short-sighted about controlling MIRVs in SALT?

Major Military Spenders: Their Rank in Economic-Social Indicators, 1975

RANK AMONG 140 NATIONS

	Military Expenditures US $	Rank Among 140 Nations	ECONOMIC-SOCIAL STANDING Avg. Rank	GNP Per Capita	GNP Public Expend. per Capita	Education School-Age Population per Teacher	Education School-Age Population in School	Education Women in Total University Enrollment	Education Literacy Rate	Health Public Expend. per Capita	Health Population per Physician	Health Population per Hospital Bed	Health Infant Mortality Rate	Health Life Expectancy
USSR	94,000	1	17	27	25	23	46	7	1	27	1	6	34	29
United States	90,948	2	6	6	7	12	4	22	1	13	18	33	13	7
China	18,000	3	79	103	97	56	43	7	26	97	93	117	51	56
West Germany	15,299	4	9	9	15	30	28	45	1	3	9	4	21	18
France	13,093	5	4	11	15	12	23	15	1	6	23	17	8	10
United Kingdom	11,477	6	16	23	18	8	5	61	16	15	26	20	13	10
Iran	7,742	7	65	44	46	71	92	78	85	46	69	105	106	77
Egypt	5,368	8	88	100	82	90	96	70	80	76	52	78	71	84
Italy	4,656	9	24	28	29	23	41	37	30	18	11	14	26	10
Japan	4,640	10	24	21	21	44	20	92	1	16	33	16	2	3
Saudi Arabia	4,260	11	63	20	3	79	117	112	114	31	72	102	113	104
Israel	3,517	12	22	25	24	2	41	22	37	24	2	40	25	10
Canada	3,074	13	4	10	4	8	3	27	26	4	19	21	13	7
India	3,008	14	111	125	121	90	100	78	86	118	83	132	95	88
Netherlands	2,869	15	15	15	5	39	43	74	16	7	22	4	2	1
East Germany	2,644	16	13	24	26	17	32	17	1	23	13	11	13	18
Poland	2,384	17	28	31	35	41	66	12	16	26	17	29	29	29
Sweden	2,344	18	1	4	2	1	10	37	1	1	20	1	1	1
Spain	2,200	19	31	30	48	39	32	53	32	25	25	44	10	10
Turkey	1,971	20	70	59	72	83	85	94	72	79	59	79	83	70

Source: World Military and Social Expenditures 1978, Ruth Leger Sivard, 1978.

Growth of World Military Power (1960-1977)

Strategic nuclear warheads*

Thousands

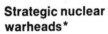
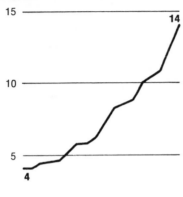

*U.S. and USSR

Arms trade with the third world

Billion dollars

Constant 1975 dollars

Military expenditures

Billion dollars

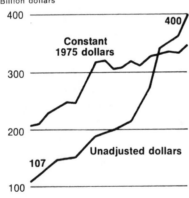

Constant 1975 dollars

Unadjusted dollars

Armed forces

Millions

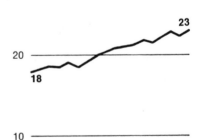

Source: *World Military and Social Expenditures 1978*, Ruth Leger Sivard, 1978.

Moreover, a large part of the proposed expansion of strategic weapons programs does nothing about this potential threat. The development of improved counterforce weapons with the higher yield, more accurate Minuteman ICBMs or the highly accurate, larger throw-weight MX actually makes the Soviet developments more dangerous by increasing the likelihood of a nuclear exchange.

The recent deployment of a new Soviet 4,200 nautical mile submarine-launched ballistic missile (SLBM) is not a threat since it reduces the risk that the United States might become involved in a nuclear conflict. Submarine missiles are primarily deterrent weapons; the longer the range the less the likelihood of their use in a close-in surprise attack against our bomber bases. SALT quite properly does not place any limits on the range of SLBMs, and the Trident I (C-4) missile deployment in Poseidon submarines is a good hedge against a possible future Soviet breakthrough in anti-submarine warfare.

The Backfire bomber is hardly an increase in the strategic threat requiring a U.S. response. Unlike the older Soviet bombers, it can only reach the United States on one-way missions or on refueled two-way missions from Arctic bases. Even then, it could not fly supersonically, its major technological advance over previous aircraft. In any case, since the conclusion of the ABM Treaty, which barred missile defense, we have properly decided to forego defenses against Russian strategic bomber attacks.

SALT could be useful in reducing any uncertainties about the role of the Backfire either by including it in the delivery-vehicle ceiling, by banning its deployment in a mode which gives it an intercontinental capability (i.e., by prohibiting an inflight refueling capability, Arctic basing, or equipping it with long-range missiles), or by reducing the delivery-vehicle ceiling but excluding the Backfire. The latter, proposed by the Russians to Secretary of State Henry Kissinger in January 1976, would have the advantage of forcing the USSR to cut back its delivery vehicles to our current level and of not jeopardizing the Soviet concession to exclude our forward-based bombers from the ceiling.

The final offensive weapon threat cited is the cruise missile. The only thing new here is Secretary Rumsfeld's description of the present Soviet cruise missiles as a *strategic* threat. Such a description is unusual because Soviet cruise missiles were first deployed in 1960, are short-range, and have never been considered anything but anti-ship weapons. Furthermore, Secretary Rumsfeld says there is no evidence that the Soviets possess the technology to pursue over the near term a strategic cruise missile program, and General Graham claims that the United States is at least ten years ahead of the USSR in this field. Soviet cruise missiles can hardly be used to justify major new U.S. weapons programs.

Military Research and Development (1960-1977)

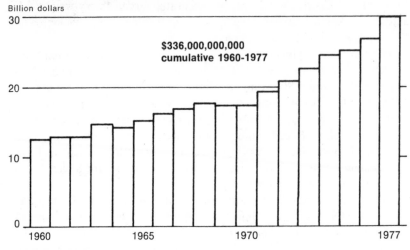

Billion dollars

$336,000,000,000 cumulative 1960-1977

Source: *World Military and Social Expenditures 1978*, Ruth Leger Sivard, 1978.

Cruise missiles are a contentious issue in SALT. If the United States agrees to ban all cruise missiles, then any worries of Soviet procurement of long-range, truly strategic missiles could be alleviated. Why then does the Pentagon oppose this?

A close analysis of the new Soviet offensive weapons shows that only the MIRVed ICBMs appear to pose any real danger, and their development is many years behind schedule. In light of the fact that, during the last five years, the United States has increased its total strategic force loadings (warheads and bombs) by 5,000 while the USSR has added only 800, Secretary Rumsfeld's argument of unilateral American restraint is not very convincing. The United States now has 8,800 such weapons while the Russians have 3,300.

In the defensive area, the threats are even more ephemeral. After an eight-year halt, the USSR may be increasing the number of ABM launchers around Moscow from 64 to the 100 allowed by the ABM Treaty. And although the Russians are also developing new radars which have an apparent ABM capability, these are hardly a justification for new U.S. programs. American security is most effectively insured by the continuance of the ABM Treaty which solidifies the current state of mutual deterrence.

In air defense, the Soviets have always had very strong capabilities, but they have yet to develop airborne radars that permit shooting down low-flying bombers. If, as is expected, the Soviets solve this technical problem, then there will be a strong argument against our going ahead with the procurement of the expensive supersonic B-1 bomber. Instead, the United States should equip the current B-52 bombers with missiles which can penetrate air defenses and thus avoid exposure of the plane and crew. Secretary Rumsfeld now admits this would be an appropriate mission for B-52s through the 1990s; so there need be no rush to replace them. If and when the United States needs a new plane, then one which can launch missiles from outside the Soviet Union would be far superior to the B-1 which must, in any case, fly subsonically when over the USSR. The recent SALT proposal that air-launched cruise missiles not be counted as delivery vehicles but that the aircraft carrying them be considered as MIRVed delivery vehicles would allow this alternative to the B-1 but still keep some restraint against unlimited cruise missile deployments.

In the field of anti-submarine warfare Secretary Rumsfeld concedes that although there is no threat to our present Poseidon force, the United States still should "watch with great care evolutionary improvements in sensor technology." This is hardly any great cause for alarm or justification for a crash Trident submarine program. At the moment there is no discussion of anti-submarine warfare controls in SALT.

Finally, we have the new threat of the year—Soviet civilian defense. Secretary Rumsfeld emphasized Soviet plans to evacuate urban populations—shades of 1962! Malcolm Currie, Director of Research and Engineering, Department of Defense, expressed concern that the Soviets are preparing to sandbag their industrial machinery to protect it against a nuclear strike. And former Deputy Director of Defense Paul Nitze views these actions as proof of Soviet intentions to achieve a nuclear war-winning capability. All of them believe that Soviet leaders would risk nuclear war because civil defense would permit them to survive a U.S. retaliatory strike from the thousands of nuclear warheads which would be left over after any Russian surprise attack. It is time for some of these defense experts to go back to basic training and recall what happened at Hiroshima, Nagasaki, and Bikini and re-learn the realities of nuclear explosions. Civil defense is not a subject which calls for serious arms control negotiations.

This is the sum total of all of the strategic threats which the Defense Department has been able to conjure up to justify dramatic increases in our strategic weapons programs. None justifies spending additional billions on more Trident submarines, the B-1 bomber, or sea-launched strategic cruise missiles. The development of improved counterforce ICBMs—such as the MX or the high-yield, more accurate Minuteman MK-12A warhead—is the wrong answer to Soviet MIRVed missile deployment. Such weapon deployments can only increase the risk of nuclear war.

In conclusion, the Defense Department's case for skyrocketing expenditures on new strategic weapons is very, very shaky indeed. Far greater security would be obtained by seriously negotiating real limitations on strategic arms. *(March 1976)*

Soviet Civil Defense: Myth and Reality *Les Aspin*

Civil defense, a dormant topic since the early 1960s, has suddenly reappeared in the 1976 debate over the defense budget. The focus is no longer on our own shelters and plans, but on the program of the Soviet Union and on its implications for our nuclear retaliatory capability. Claims about the great extent and effectiveness of Russian civil defense abound, but most are exaggerated or unsupported.

Three assertions are offered as evidence of the effectiveness of the Soviet civil defense program. Let us examine them one by one. First, some analysts claim that the USSR has reduced its vulnerability to nuclear attack by avoiding urban and industrial concentrations through a program of geographical dispersal.

As early as 1931, the Soviets had adopted a policy of prohibiting construction, with certain exceptions, of new industrial plants in large cities. Since then the policy has frequently been reaffirmed. The most recent five-year plans support "the policy of restricting the growth of large cities" by prohibiting construction of new industrial plants. The primary consideration behind these moves has been economic, such as a desire to locate industry closer to sources of raw materials.

However, the announced Soviet policies have not been very successful. Large Soviet urban areas continue to expand. For example, the fifty-eight Russian cities having more than 250,000 people in 1959 grew by 30.5 percent between the 1959 census and the 1970 census while the total population grew by only 15.8 percent. Even the three cities with over a million people in 1959 grew by 20.8 percent, faster than the total population.

The major part of Soviet industry remains concentrated in European Russia and associated with major cities. Even where the dispersal program resulted in new towns being built, these towns often provide inviting targets for nuclear weapons. For example, the Kama River Truck Plant, the largest truck manufacturer in the world, is located in the "new town" of Naberezhnyye Chelny; one-fifth of the total output of trucks

Civilian Fatalities in a Limited Nuclear War

Type of attack	Estimated North American Fatalities
All strategic forces: 57-60 percent destruction of U.S. missile silos (1054), bomber bases (46), and strategic submarine bases (2)	3,200,000 to 16,300,000
ICBM Silos Only:	
42 percent missile silo destruction	5,600,000
80 percent missile silo destruction	18,300,000

These Department of Defense estimates were reported in July 1975 to the Senate Foreign Relations Committee and published in their report, *Analyses of Effects of Limited Nuclear War.* The range of estimates results from inclusion of Canadian fatalities and use of different assumptions about burst modes of weapons, civil defense posture, and pattern of attacks.

in the Soviet Union is concentrated in this plant. Similarly, the new town of Bratsk in Siberia boasts the largest aluminum plant and the largest timber-cellulose plant in the world.

Finally, while the United States is more urbanized than the USSR, the population within large Soviet cities is much more concentrated than in the United States. Indeed, there are more than twice as many people per square mile in the fifty largest Soviet cities compared to the fifty largest U.S. cities.*

Another prevalent assertion is that the Soviets are spending at least $1 billion annually on civil defense, roughly ten times more than we are. Dr. Malcolm Currie, director of defense research and engineering, Department of Defense, even told a Senate subcommittee that the billion dollar figure was an intelligence community estimate.

This is not the case. The $1 billion figure was not prepared by and is not supported by the intelligence community. Rather, the figure comes from Professor Eugene Wigner, a proponent of a large U.S. civil defense program, who, working on his own, made a rough, back-of-the-envelope conjecture.

Leon Goure, who has spent his career studying the Soviet civil defense program and who often cites the $1 billion figure, acknowledged

---

* In 1970, the fifty largest Soviet cities held 45.5 million people while the fifty largest American cities held 40.7 million people. But, those fifty Russian cities covered about 4,000 square miles (a density of over 11,000 people per square mile) as opposed to 9,100 square miles for the American cities (roughly 4,600 people per square mile).

before a House panel earlier this year that the estimate was "all guess-work." The only derivation Goure provided for the number was that it equalled the amount it would have cost a U.S. manufacturer back in 1962 "to take 20 million people and provide them with gas masks and protective clothing, rubberized and so on."

Even if a credible estimate of Soviet civil defense spending were available, it would not tell us much. The Pentagon spent $6 billion on the ABM (anti-ballistic missile) but we are no safer because of that expenditure. Throwing money at an effort does not necessarily make it effective. Soviet civil defense capabilities—not budgets—should be the focus of concern.

The most dramatic claim about the Soviet program is that the USSR has a massive evacuation plan which would limit casualties to 5-8 percent of the urban population (3-4 percent of the total population) in the event of a full-scale nuclear war.

The only source for the 5-8 percent casualty figure was a single sentence in a 352-page Soviet civil defense manual published in 1969. There is no explanation of how the percentage was calculated, although the previous sentence in the manual indicating that "a nuclear attack on an unprotected large city may result in a loss of life of as much as 90 percent of the population" was based on statements "in the foreign press."

The 1969 manual was intended for use by the faculties of agricultural institutes and was authorized by the Ministry of Agriculture—hardly a preserve for military planners. All subsequent manuals, including the basic Soviet text for secondary school students published in 1974, make no such claims.

The figure is not very meaningful in any case since it covers only the casualties that would result from the direct effects of nuclear weapons. It does not include deaths from radioactive fallout or from hunger, disease, and other threats to the post-attack survivors.

Nor is there any evidence that the Soviets have a viable evacuation capability. Mass evacuations have not been practiced and most ordinary citizens do not know where to go in a crisis or how to survive once there. If nothing else, cold weather would seem to prohibit any evacuation and survival in required "hasty shelters" for about half the year.

Regardless of the alleged effectiveness of evacuation, both the Defense Intelligence Agency and the Central Intelligence Agency say that the Soviets no longer emphasize such a procedure. Instead, the USSR is focusing on building shelters within large cities, apparently with the goal of protecting essential cadres and key industrial personnel. Yet even those most worried about Soviet civil defense have argued that 80 million people will die in the Soviet Union if urban shelters are relied on.

This drawing from a recent Soviet civil defense manual shows how to tunnel into a blast shelter after a nuclear attack has sealed the entrance with rubble. Soviet texts reflect a sober appreciation of the destructive effects of nuclear weapons.

Source: Defense Civil Preparedness Agency, Department of Defense

Key claims about Russian civil defense are based on suspect evidence. Dr. Conrad Chester of the Oak Ridge National Laboratory has testified that "much of the analysis of the Soviet program, and planning for U.S. capabilities, is based on these [Soviet civil defense] manuals."

The problem with these handbooks is that they are no more reliable as indicators of capability than our own publications. In the early 1960s the United States produced a multitude of civil defense manuals (including 25 million copies of "Fallout Protection—What to Know and Do About a Nuclear Attack"). Yet no one would maintain that we had an effective program then.

In 1974, the Defense Civil Preparedness Agency (DCPA) put out a 64-page catalogue merely listing the hundreds of civil defense manuals available from the government. The 1974 report of the agency lists identified shelter capacity as about 227 million persons and "Community Shelter Plan" spaces are said to be available for 182.7 million people. The agency has established 1,200 warning points across the country and has distributed 200,000 sets to monitor fallout.

The Defense Civil Preparedness Agency has even reported that it has found space for 6 million people in 2,000 mine shafts. Researchers say there is a potential for 50 million places in shafts. A study in Pennsylvania says that all of Pittsburgh can be sheltered in mines within 70 miles of the city. Feasibility studies are under way.

Based on a reading of such literature, the Soviets might conclude that we are trying to develop a "war-winning" capability. Yet our own defense planners say we would lose about 100 million people in a full-scale attack. The fact is that rumblings of a bureaucracy do not constitute an effective program.

The lesson here is not that we can ignore Soviet civil defense. The Soviets do put a higher priority on defensive measures than we do. They have also undertaken more elaborate measures to protect certain war-related industries and their nation's leaders. But our nuclear deterrent is hardly in jeopardy. And we should not overlook the enormous gap between the rhetoric about Soviet civil defense efforts and their actual capabilities. *(September 1976)*

Editors' Perspective
Senate Committee Inquiry on "Limited" Nuclear War

From September 1974 to September 1975, the Senate Foreign Relations Committee undertook a little-noticed inquiry into the subject of limited nuclear war. The committee's broad focus was to examine the feasibility of the concept of "limited" strategic nuclear war which was first publicly espoused by then Defense Secretary James Schlesinger in January 1974.

The inquiry began with a classified briefing by Secretary Schlesinger on September 11, 1974, before the committee's Subcommittee on Arms Control, International Law and Organization, chaired by Senator Edmund Muskie (D-Maine). The hearing was prompted by the request of Senator Clifford Case (R-N.J.), who had urged the committee to seek to determine what Defense Secretary Schlesinger meant when he stated in the annual defense report that a Soviet strategic nuclear weapons attack upon U.S. military installations (i.e., a counterforce attack) would result in only "relatively few civilian casualties." Senator Case also suggested that if this assumption proved to be incorrect, as some experts had argued, then the rationale for a new family of nuclear counterforce weapons could be "called into serious question."

In his testimony before the subcommittee, Secretary Schlesinger argued that while a massive nuclear weapons strike would result in U.S. fatalities on the order of 95-100 million, a limited nuclear attack upon only U.S. strategic military forces would result in a total of only 6.7 million fatalities and 5.1 million nonfatal casualties. This scenario assumed that the USSR would detonate a nuclear warhead over each of the forty-six strategic bomber bases and the two strategic missile submarine bases as well as two warheads on each of the 1,054 ICBM (intercontinental ballistic missile) silos. Furthermore, he stated that an attack limited solely to the 1,054 ICBM silos would result in only about 800,000 U.S. fatalities. The estimates presented by Secretary Schlesinger were clearly at odds with the estimates of many other experts in the arms control community. These experts had argued that even limited nuclear exchanges would result in large numbers of American casualties which would be clearly unacceptable.

In light of this controversy over the Department of Defense estimates, the Foreign Relations Committee asked the newly-formed congressional Office of Technology Assessment to conduct a critical evaluation of the Defense Department's analyses. The Office of Technology Assessment responded by convening a panel of outside experts to review the Defense estimates.* One of the major conclusions of the panel was that the Defense Department's analyses "were substantially too low for the attacks in question as a result of a lack of attention to intermediate and long-term [nuclear weapons] effects," and that the analyses did not adequately reflect the "large uncertainties inherent in any attempt to determine the civilian damage which might result from a nuclear attack." The panel also questioned whether the specific type of Soviet attack postulated by the Defense Department was realistic since it assumed that the USSR was willing to reduce the military effectiveness of its attacks in order to minimize U.S. civilian casualties—in particular, that it would attack missile silos with air bursts rather than with fallout-producing ground bursts. Based on their evaluation, the Office of Technology Assessment panel recommended that the committee request the Defense Department to redo its analyses by using more realistic assumptions such as the use of higher-yield weapons, lower civil defense effectiveness, the "assumption of at least one ground burst in any attack on ICBM silos, and a more plausible pattern attack around U.S. bomber bases."

Following the panel report, the Defense Department submitted a new, more detailed set of estimates to the committee. This analysis examined the range of variability which existed for the figures initially presented by Secretary Schlesinger due to possible differences in wind conditions, civil defense effectiveness, and manner of Soviet attack. Among other things, the new analyses attempted to illustrate the possible range of U.S. fatalities from a Soviet counterforce attack by presenting three different

---

* The initial members of the OTA Ad Hoc Panel on Nuclear Effects included: Jerome B. Wiesner (chairman), Harold Brown, Sidney Drell, Richard Garwin, Spurgeon Keeny, Gordon MacDonald, Gerald Miller, James Neel, and Arch Wood. Charles Townes later replaced Harold Brown and J. P. Ruina later replaced Jerome B. Wiesner as chairman.

sets of assumptions for a "comprehensive" counterforce attack. According to the Defense Department, the case made by Secretary Schlesinger is the "most representative scenario which balances military effectiveness, potential restraint on the part of the Soviets to minimize collateral damage, and the physical uncertainties that could exist at the time of such a postulated attack." Nonetheless, how representative Secretary Schlesinger's 6.7 million figure is can still be questioned. A closer examination of the assumptions underpinning the three cases seems to indicate that by selecting only air burst attacks (which would produce the fewest fatalities) Secretary Schlesinger's scenario tends to minimize U.S. fatalities more than a "representative" case should and relies heavily upon the "potential restraint" of the Soviet military planners.

In spite of this question, the new Defense Department analyses revealed two very important points. The first point is that the persistent inquiry of a congressional committee resulted in the Defense Department's admission that U.S. fatalities from a Soviet counterforce attack could range nearly three times as high as the estimate initially suggested by Defense Secretary Schlesinger. In this sense, the committee's action was a good example of the active role that congressional committees can play in keeping the executive branch "honest" on arms control and defense issues. Second, the new analyses revealed a critical flaw in the Defense Department's argument that a limited nuclear war could result in a relatively small number of casualties. In all of the Soviet attacks postulated by the Defense Department a substantial number of U.S. ICBMs survived. In Secretary Schlesinger's own senario, for example, 40 percent of the U.S. ICBM force (over 400 missiles) was expected to survive the Soviet attack. The fact that such attacks would make no military sense raises serious questions about the credibility of the Defense Department's presentation and the feasibility of the concept of "limited nuclear war."

Although the Senate Foreign Relations Committee did score a success through its critical evaluation of the Defense Department's casualty estimates, it unfortunately failed to continue its evaluation of the larger, more important issues as the Office of Technology Assessment panel had recommended. Consequently, many important questions were only superficially raised, such as whether a limited nuclear war would escalate into a general nuclear war and whether a strategy of limited nuclear war raises or lowers the nuclear threshold. The replacement of Defense Secretary Schlesinger by the less doctrine-oriented Donald Rumsfeld accounts to some degree for the committee's lack of follow-up on this issue.

On September 18, 1975, the committee's inquiry came to a close. On that date the committee received the testimony of three members of the Office of Technology Assessment panel: Dr. Richard Garwin, Dr. Sidney

Drell and Dr. James Neel. These witnesses presented the Foreign Relations Committee with a detailed report of the panel's final analysis and conclusions. *(September 1976)*

Soviet Military Doctrine: The Political Dimension
Christopher D. Jones

Until the early 1970s, American policy-makers had an ethnocentric assurance that the only valid approaches to the questions of arms control and to modern military strategy were the American approaches. Although the U.S. government translated a great deal of Soviet military literature, including major book-length studies, national security experts dismissed this literature with something close to contempt. In the early 1970s, however, the continued failure of Soviet military planners to behave in a manner consistent with American logic led a number of U.S. analysts to look again at Soviet military writing. This second look revealed a formidable intellectual achievement that attempted to integrate the components of Soviet military policy into a consistent military doctrine. It also revealed a connection between certain elements of Soviet military thought and the development of various service branches of the Soviet armed forces. It even led some analysts to conclude that Soviet texts "proved" that the Soviets were seeking military superiority over the United States and were preparing to take military action once they achieved the necessary superiority. But, while the participants in the national debates over SALT II and the NATO-Warsaw Pact balance have begun citing Soviet military scriptures to suit their purposes, a systematic effort to read and decode the whole corpus of Soviet military writing has really only begun, and much of the discussion to date has been oversimplified.

The Soviets make elaborate distinctions among various types of military writing on military doctrine. *The Soviet Military Encyclopedia* defines a government's military doctrine as "a system of views on the ends and character of a possible war, on the preparation of the country and its armed forces for war and on the means for conducting it." The encyclopedia goes on to say that, "in military doctrine there are two closely-linked and mutually dependent sides—the political side and the military-technical side, with the former playing the leading role. . . . The political side includes the questions concerning the political goals and character of a war." In the Soviet view, military doctrine is not a rigid logical structure but a flexible "system of views" that studies the evolving relationships among the dynamic subfields of military doctrine.

One of these subfields is what the Soviets call "military science," a discipline that examines the "objective laws" governing armed combat. The subfields of Soviet military science include several "theories": those of "military art," "troop training and education," "military economics and logistics," and "military construction" (the latter is defined as "the system of economic, sociopolitical and purely military measures of states carried out for purposes of increasing their military might"). The Soviets define "military art" as the theory and practice of combat operations. In turn, the theory of military art has three subfields: strategy, operation art, and tactics.

Both the "military-technical side" and the "political side" of Soviet military doctrine address the question of the rational use of Soviet military power. Many Western analysts, reading only the writings on the "military-technical side," risk developing an incomplete understanding of the Soviet view of war as an instrument of policy. Examination of the "political side" of Soviet military doctrine reveals great Soviet concern with avoiding the kinds of military engagements that could jeopardize the stability of the political systems of the Soviet Union and of the communist states closely linked to the USSR. Soviet military-political doctrine also reveals keen Soviet appreciation of the diplomatic uses of military power and an equally keen appreciation of the utility of negotiation for pursuing both political goals and military security.

Soviet military-political doctrine (the "political side" of Soviet military doctrine) declares that the political objective of a war determines every aspect of military operations: diplomatic alignments, belligerents, theater, weaponry, strategy, tactics, logistics, and the "moral-political factor." The moral-political factor is of special concern to the Soviet military theorists. It is the degree to which soldiers and civilians on both sides of the battlefield support the war efforts of their governments. Among the components of the moral-political factor are the popular legitimacy of a government at the time war breaks out and the esteem in which a nation holds its professional military.

Soviet military writers argue that when a government asks its citizens to sacrifice their well-being and their lives for the sake of the state's military objectives, it is, in effect, calling for a popular referendum on the regime. The Soviets label a war in which a government can count on popular support a "just war." "Just wars" are usually seen as either defensive wars against foreign invaders or wars of national liberation against colonial regimes. According to Soviet analysts, the questions of who started the war or where it is being fought are irrelevant: the critical question is whether the citizens of a state view the government's war as a just one in defense of national sovereignty. The Soviets do not claim that an army fighting a just war will necessarily be victorious; they only say that it will fight courageously with maximum support from its civilians. The outcome of war, according to the Soviets, depends on the interaction of the moral-political factor with other factors: the diplomatic alignments that develop before and during the course of the conflict, the economic bases of the belligerents, technological superiority in weaponry, and the professional qualities of the armies in combat. The choice of the political objective of the war will strongly influence the interplay of these factors, but, the Soviets caution, the outcome of any military struggle is always uncertain. Soviet writers frequently cite the maxim that once war has begun, "politics exchanges the pen for the sword."

Soviet military-political doctrine warns that the course of military conflict can exercise a "reverse effect" on the political systems of states at war. Citing Lenin's assessments of the relationships between military defeats and domestic disorders in Tsarist Russia and citing similar experiences of several Western states (particularly that of the United States during the war in Vietnam), Soviet military writers declare that military setbacks often exacerbate tensions in domestic politics and undermine the legitimacy of the government in power. Such "reverse effects" of war on politics in turn affect the ability of a government to recover from its military defeats; further deterioration of the military situation further aggravates domestic tensions. Colonel Y. Rybkin, a leading Soviet military analyst, declares in no uncertain terms that a ruling communist party must base its decision on whether to wage a war according to the likely influence of the war on its own society. Other Soviet military theorists claim that the "reverse effect" is likely to be greatest in states where there are sharp social divisions and/or antagonisms among different ethnic groups. This latter consideration is of some importance in the Soviet Union, a state consisting of several major national groups and dozens of smaller ones. The Soviets write that the possibility of a "reverse effect" undermining the war effort of a multinational state can be avoided if the state's government sends its soldiers to fight only in "just wars" of national defense.

Soviet military writers claim that the other armies of the Warsaw Treaty Organization have similar predispositions for fighting only just wars in defense of socialist fatherlands and of the "socialist commonwealth" as a whole. They also claim that the Warsaw Pact states share the Soviet view on the role of the moral-political factor in war. The logical but unspoken extension of the Soviet argument on just wars to the armies of the Warsaw Pact leads to the conclusion that the socialist commonwealth is subject to the laws governing the "reverse effect" of war on politics. That is, nationality antagonisms could erupt both within the Warsaw Pact and in the Soviet Union if the peoples of the socialist commonwealth concluded that the Warsaw Pact was fighting an unjust war and then saw Pact armies suffer military setbacks.

Soviet military theorists assert that even nuclear war will not eclipse the importance of the moral-political factor. In fact, according to the claims of Soviet military writers, since nuclear war will obliterate the traditional distinction between front and rear, the role of the moral-political factor will become even greater. They argue that the continued economic functioning of a state in nuclear war will depend not only on civil defense measures, but also on a society's moral-political condition.

The implications for Soviet military-political doctrine and the historical experience from which it is drawn are profound. They suggest that the Soviets would not resort to the use of military power against Western Europe or North America except in the circumstances in which the Soviets have previously resorted to armed force: defensive responses to military attacks or military assistance to local communist parties calling for aid in a struggle to expel a foreign occupier. This is not to deny that Soviet writings raise the possibility of strategic and tactical war. However, such writings indicate the kind of normal military technical contingency planning expected of a general staff determined never again to be caught unprepared as it was in 1941. The question of whether such planning is offensive or deterrent in nature is a question for the "political side" of Soviet doctrine. Soviet military-political writing strongly suggests that discussions of nuclear war-fighting fall into the "theory of military art" category rather than the "military-political goals" category, which is determined by the political side. This is not to say that the Soviets ignore the political importance of war-fighting capabilities. Soviet military-political writing suggests that Soviet leaders believe that having the capacity to fight nuclear wars against Europe and America is of supreme importance in determining the "correlation of forces" between East and West. The Soviet military press almost daily repeats that detente in all its manifestations would not have been possible if the military might of the Soviet Union had not compelled the United States and its NATO allies to come to a sober recognition of the military necessity for political detente. Soviet military-political analysts also claim that the correlation of forces in the East-West balance decisively affects the outcome of just wars of national liberation in the Third World.

Soviet military-political doctrine further suggests that the concern with nuclear war-fighting in Soviet military science and military art serves to unify the Warsaw Treaty Organization around the Soviet Union. According to Soviet texts, the Warsaw Pact members agree (1) that the only possible military defense for small socialist countries in Europe threatened by the NATO imperialists armed with nuclear weapons is to form a socialist military coalition led by the Soviet Union, which alone possesses the nuclear weaponry to hold the NATO aggressors at bay; (2) that in order for the Warsaw Pact states to coordinate their joint military defense they must have a complete "unity of views" on the questions of military doctrine, military science, and military art; (3) that Soviet military doctrine, Soviet military science, and Soviet military art must be the basis of the "unity of views" in the Warsaw Pact because the Soviet armed forces have resolved the problems of conducting a nuclear war; and (4) that each Warsaw Treaty Organization army must thoroughly study and master Soviet military doctrine and the "leading experience" of the Soviet armed forces.

Application of the principle of the "unity of views" leads either to direct Soviet control or at least to close Soviet monitoring of the other Pact armies, except Rumania's, which plans for the defense of Rumania with conventional weapons without direct support from other Pact members.

Thus, discussions of Soviet military doctrine must pay close attention to the distinction between the "political" side and the "military-technical" side of Soviet writing. Failure to do so can lead to oversimplification and unjustified alarm. *(October 1978)*

Soviet Views on Nuclear War   *Robert L. Arnett*

In the West, there are those currently arguing that the Soviet military leaders believe their nation could survive and win a nuclear war. If this is true, then the nuclear deterrent of the United States is in jeopardy and there is an increased possibility that the Soviets might initiate, or threaten to initiate, a nuclear war. Thus, it is necessary that we understand what the Soviets think about nuclear war and the strategic capability of the United States. This can be accomplished by reviewing what Soviet military writers have been saying about the possibility of victory in a nuclear war, nuclear war as an instrument of policy, and the consequences of a nuclear war.

Some Western analysts conclude that the Soviet advocacy of war as a continuation of politics means that the Soviets believe that war, even nuclear war, can still be used as a practical instrument of policy. Harvard history professor Richard Pipes, for example, states that the Soviets believe "thermonuclear war is not suicidal; it can be fought and won and thus resort to war must not be ruled out." To support his claim, Pipes cites Marshal Sokolovskiy's 1962 book *Voyennaya Strategiya* ("Military Strategy") which states, "It is well known that the essential nature of war as a continuation of politics does not change with changing technology and armament." Pipes also states, "As long as the Russians persist in adhering to the Clausewitzian maxim* on the function of war, mutual deterrence does not really exist."

A careful review of Soviet writings, however, suggests that such an inference is incorrect. To the Soviets, there is an important difference between defending the thesis that "war is a continuation of politics" and arguing that "war is an instrument of policy." They continue to argue that war is a continuation of politics because it is a basic tenet of Marxism-Leninism which helps to explain their theory of the causes, nature and essence of war. That theory, in brief, contends that wars don't just happen. Wars are caused by the existence of classes within a nation pursuing by violent means certain political objectives which they could not achieve by peaceful means. Thus, every war is a continuation of politics.

In this context, it is evident that when the Soviets defend the dictum that war is a continuation of policy as valid even in the nuclear age, they are not suggesting, as some Westerners contend they are, that nuclear weapons can or should be used as practical instruments of policy. Instead, the Soviet spokesmen are arguing that the Marxist-Leninist theory of war is still valid and that, if a nuclear war does start, it too will occur because certain classes within a nation are pursuing a policy by violent means. The Soviets have been pointing out for over a decade that to argue that "war is a continuation of politics even in the nuclear era" is not the same as to argue that nuclear war can serve as a practical instrument of policy. Colonel T. R. Kondratkov wrote in 1974, "Considering the essence [class nature] of a possible nuclear war, Marxist-Leninists do not confuse it with another question close but not identical with it—the question of the admissibility of nuclear war."

Soviet military spokesmen have not said that nuclear war could serve as a practical instrument of policy. In fact, they have said just the opposite. In October 1973, Colonel Y. Rybkin stated that "a total nuclear war is not acceptable as a means of achieving a political goal," and that nuclear weapons had made "such a war an infeasible means of policy." In 1976, Kondratkov noted that nuclear weapons had transformed war into an "exceptionally dangerous means for politics."

Those in the West who argue that the Soviets believe they could win and survive a nuclear war generally ignore what Soviet military spokesmen have been saying about the consequences of a nuclear war. The strongest statements on this subject have been made by General-Lieutenant P. A. Zhilin, the chief of the Institute of Military History of the Ministry of Defense. Zhilin's writings suggest that he believes that

*Clausewitz's maxim characterizes war as an extension of diplomacy.

both the United States and the Soviet Union have an assured destruction capability. In 1973, he wrote, "The contemporary revolution in means of conducting war . . . has led to a situation where both combatants can not only destroy each other, but can also considerably undermine the conditions for the existence of mankind." Zhilin made similar statements in 1975 and again in 1976. His view does not appear to be the exception within the military.

A. A. Grechko, the late Politburo member, Minister of Defense, and Marshal of the Soviet Union, wrote in his book *Vooruzhennye Sily Sovetskogo Gosudarstva* ("The Armed Forces of the Soviet State") in 1975 that in the event of a nuclear war, hundreds of millions would die, the earth's surface would be contaminated, entire countries would be destroyed, causing an enormous disaster for mankind. He expressed these same views in two other publications several years earlier. He wrote in *Kommunist* that a nuclear war "will assume a particularly destructive nature," and in *Pravda* that it would be a "deadly threat to the future of mankind." Another member of the Institute of Military History, Colonel Rybkin, wrote in 1977 that the rejection of nuclear war is dictated by the realities of the era. He stated that enough weapons had been stockpiled to destroy all life several times over. Five years earlier, in a book written for military personnel, Rybkin noted that in a nuclear war hundreds of millions would be destroyed and the earth's surface and atmosphere would be contaminated.

Another military spokesman who has given a dire assessment of the capabilities of the nuclear arsenals of the United States and the Soviet Union is General-Major R. G. Simonyan. While arguing that adding weapons could not give either side a military or political advantage, he stated in 1977, "Both sides possess weapons which are capable of annihilating all life on earth many times over." Other military writers have commented on the consequences of a nuclear war in the prestigious journal of the Main Political Directorate of the Soviet armed forces, *Kommunist Vooruzhennykh Sil* ("Communist of the Armed Forces"). In 1972, Kondratkov wrote that a nuclear war would have "exceptionally dangerous consequences." After mentioning the tremendous human and material losses suffered in World War I and World War II, he stated that World War III "will wreak unprecedented destruction on entire countries." In July 1975, Colonel A. Dmitriyev wrote, "A nuclear war will bring immeasurable disasters and suffering to the masses of working people and make it more difficult to achieve the goals of socialist building." Several months later, Colonel S. Tyushkevich, also from the Institute of Military History, wrote that World War III would result in much greater losses and destruction than had been suffered in World War I and World War II combined. He said, "The two World Wars took over 70 million human lives and wiped out thousands of prosperous cities and villages off the face of the earth. A world war involving the use of nuclear missile weapons would lead to even greater losses."

Another pessimistic assessment of the consequences of a nuclear war was made in the 1972 edition of a book written "for the attention of Soviet officers, generals, and admirals." The book, *Marxism-Leninism on War and the Army,* written by faculty members of Soviet military-educational institutions, stated that a nuclear war would cause unprecedented destruction, kill hundreds of millions of people, lay entire countries to waste, inflict irretrievable losses to material and spiritual culture, and throw mankind back many decades.

This review of what Soviet military spokesmen have said about the consequences of a nuclear war explains why they do not consider it to be a practical means of policy. Why then do they still talk about being victorious in such a conflict?

Soviet spokesmen frequently refer to the possibility of Soviet victory in a nuclear war, presumably instigated by capitalism in its death throes. They insist that socialism will emerge from such a conflict victorious and that imperialism will be crushed. In addition, certain Soviet spokesmen who have argued that victory is not possible in a nuclear war have been denounced by other Soviet spokesmen. In 1973, for example, General-Major A. Milovidov attacked those who concluded that no victory is possible in a nuclear war. Milovidov argued that these authors had made errors in calculating the consequences of a nuclear war because they relied solely on quantitative measures which exaggerated war's destructiveness. Eight months later, Rear Admiral V. V. Shelyag also argued that certain authors erred in estimating the consequences of a nuclear war because their analyses were "strictly quantitative." It is interesting to note that Khalipov, Milovidov, and Shelyag were among the leaders of the Lenin Military Political Academy.

Statements such as these have been presented as evidence by some Western analysts that the Soviet military leaders believe they can survive and win a nuclear war and therefore that they do not believe the United States has an assured destruction capability. In evaluating such declarations by Soviet military spokesmen, however, several factors must be taken into consideration. First, there are strong ideological reasons, especially for members of the Military Political Academy, to argue against statements suggesting that in a nuclear war victory would not be possible and that fatalities would be unacceptably high. It is the job of political officers to insure that military writings contain the proper ideological positions and that high morale is maintained within the armed forces. The view that Marxist-Leninist victory is not possible in a nuclear war is not considered proper ideologically, at least by the ideologues. Likewise, to keep up morale, political officers can be expected to criticize those who talk of high casualty rates, the death of civilization, or the impossibility of obtaining victory in a nuclear war. In evaluating the statements of Khalipov, Milovidov, and Shelyag, confusing statements of goals must be distinguished from statements of realistic expectations. These men might believe that the Soviet Union should *try* to win and survive a nuclear war, which is the objective of any military institution, but this does not necessarily mean that they believe such an objective is possible or likely under current conditions.

Although Khalipov, Milovidov and Shelyag appear to believe that it should be a *goal* of the Soviet Union to prepare to win and survive a nuclear war if it should be necessary, at least Khalipov and Shelyag have expressed doubts about Soviet chances for survival and meaningful victory in such a war. Khalipov states that such a war could lead to "unprecedented destruction to entire countries" and could destroy "entire peoples" and "inhibit the advance of the revolutionary process." He also admits that losses may be extremely high but claims that that "depends on the activeness of the masses." Shelyag wrote that the proper "Marxist-Leninist view is not one of futility and pessimism" although he admits that a nuclear war would be extraordinarily dangerous. Statements such as these are attacks on the demoralizing notion that no one could survive a nuclear war and are not meant to suggest that a meaningful victory is possible or that the Soviet Union could avoid unprecedented damage.

In the 1972 edition of *Marxism-Leninism on War and the Army,* the authors talk not only about victory, which they say is determined by the objective laws of history, but also about the balance of forces, which they suggest now favors the Soviet Union. Thus there is some indication that they actually believe it is conceivable the Soviet Union might emerge relatively less damaged from a conflict. However, they also talk about the dire consequences of a nuclear war and state that there would be unprecedented destruction. Such a contradiction leads one to question what kind of victory Soviet military writers are referring to. On the latter question, we should remember that there are many meanings for the term "victory." At one extreme there is absolute victory, in which one nation totally defeats another and incurs little or no damage. At the other extreme is a victory in the sense of just barely coming out ahead of a totally defeated enemy, but with one's own economic, social and political system in shambles. Between these extremes, there are many degrees of victory. In evaluating what outcome the Soviets expect, we should keep in mind the fact that when Soviet military spokesmen consider the contingency of an attack by U.S. strategic nuclear forces, they vigorously proclaim that the imperialist forces would be crushed and the socialist nations would emerge victorious. This is clearly necessary to keep up morale at home and to maintain the credibility of Soviet nuclear forces. Yet, when the Soviets discuss the practical consequences of a nuclear war, they admit that there would be unprecedented damage. Thus, Soviet military spokesmen seem to expect that in a nuclear war they could obtain, at best, only a pyrrhic victory.

This review of what Soviet spokesmen have been saying about nuclear war does not support the claims of various Western analysts who argue that the Soviets believe they can win and survive a nuclear war— especially the notion that they can survive such a war with fewer losses than they incurred in World War II. The Soviets do not believe that nuclear war can serve as a practical instrument of policy nor do they believe that their system could avoid unprecedented, perhaps fatal, injury in such a conflict. Thus, although it may be true that the Soviets believe it is necessary to prepare for the worst case, they have few illusions as to the consequences of initiating nuclear war or the threat posed by U.S. nuclear forces. *(October 1978)*

The distinction between tactical and strategic nuclear weapons is, in a certain sense, an arbitrary one. In theory, tactical nuclear weapons are designed to "win the battle," while strategic weapons are designed to "win the war." Thus, tactical nuclear weapons are those intended to be used in a limited geographic area, the battlefield, against targets (armies, airfields, supply depots, etc.) whose destruction will directly affect the outcome of a battle. Strategic nuclear weapons, on the other hand, can be used across intercontinental distances and are targeted against the enemy's political and economic infrastructure.

In actual practice, however, these neat distinctions break down. Some nuclear weapons, like those carried by the Soviet SS-20 missile or the U.S. F-111 bomber, though generally labeled "tactical," are larger than strategic weapons and are targeted against strategic cities and economic assets. Some "strategic" weapons are targeted against tactical targets, as part of the warfighting capability of both superpowers. And a growing problem for arms control are theater or "gray-area" weapons, like the Soviet Backfire bomber and the U.S. cruise missile, which—to a greater or lesser degree— are "dual capable," able to carry conventional or nuclear weapons, and "dual mission," performing in either strategic or tactical roles.

Perhaps the most useful way to describe tactical nuclear weapons is to say that they do not, *under realistic conditions, have the capability to destroy significant targets in the homeland of one superpower from beyond its borders.*

The most important U.S. tactical nuclear weapons are those deployed in the European theater. Their primary purpose is to deter a massive Soviet attack against our NATO allies. While most analysts and decision-makers in the United States and Europe agree that this should be the purpose of tactical nuclear weapons, many disagree vehemently on how this purpose is best served. Two related questions, dealt with here, are at the heart of these disagreements: What role can and should different kinds of tactical nuclear weapons play in deterring a conventional attack or defending against one if it occurs; and how tight should the linkage be between tactical nuclear weapons and strategic weapons?

3

Tactical Nuclear Weapons

U.S. Tactical Nuclear Weapons in Europe: 7,000
Warheads in Search of a Rationale   *Jeffrey Record*

In an era of strategic arms limitation and of continuing efforts to reduce opposing conventional forces on the European continent, the U.S. deployment of tactical nuclear weapons in that area has so far remained undisturbed. Yet that deployment constitutes one of the most destabilizing elements in the European military balance largely because there exists no credible scenario for the use of tactical nuclear weapons. Moreover, pressures are mounting to refashion the character of that deployment in a direction that could only serve to magnify its present weaknesses.

U.S. tactical nuclear weapons—so designated because their use is not contemplated against strategic targets—were first introduced in Europe in the mid-1950s by a budget-conscious Eisenhower administration convinced that comparatively cheap tactical nuclear weapons could be substituted for more costly conventional forces. These weapons, it was argued, not only permitted the maintenance of fewer U.S. troops on the continent but also provided the only means whereby NATO could offset what was then perceived as overwhelming communist superiority in conventional arms.

These rationales were compelling at a time when the USSR possessed neither tactical nuclear weapons nor a credible strategic deterrent. However, Soviet development and deployment of tactical nuclear weapons in the late 1950s and early 1960s eliminated the prospect of a one-sided tactical nuclear war in Europe and, with it, the assumption that possession of tactical nuclear weapons conferred upon NATO a distinct military advantage over the Warsaw Pact. A two-sided tactical nuclear exchange involving, almost inevitably, the employment of large numbers of comparatively indiscriminate Soviet tactical nuclear weapons against numerous targets in densely populated Western Europe promises a level of collateral damage that would make a mockery of any pretense of meaningful defense. In addition, as many studies have shown, more conventional forces would be required in a tactical nuclear war than in a non-nuclear conflict because of the certainty of higher losses.

The Kennedy administration realized that the warfighting credibility of tactical nuclear weapons was declining and was convinced that "inevitably, the use of small nuclear armaments will lead to larger and larger nuclear armaments on both sides, until the world-wide holocaust has begun."* Yet, despite this allegiance to the "fire-break" theory of nuclear escalation, as well as a growing recognition that the conventional military balance in Europe was not nearly as unfavorable to the West as had been previously assumed, the Kennedy administration both doubled the number of U.S. tactical nuclear weapons in Europe and established, via a strategy of graduated response, a set of relatively detailed prescriptions governing their use. The rationale offered for these developments was that the presence of U.S. tactical nuclear weapons in Europe, however high might be the risks attending their actual employment, nonetheless enhanced the credibility of America's strategic deterrent by providing a link between possible failure of conventional defense and U.S. willingness to use that deterrent on behalf of its European allies. This line of reasoning, if at one time convincing, is now less so, because the emergence of rough strategic parity between the United States and the USSR has raised justifiable doubts as to whether America would ever launch its strategic weapons in circumstances short of a direct attack on its own territory.

The end result of these historical developments is a U.S. deployment in Europe of over 7,000 tactical nuclear weapons—accurately labelled by former Assistant Secretary of Defense Paul C. Warnke as "dangerously excessive"—based on a hodgepodge of justifications that are at best questionable and at worst illusory. Although Secretary of Defense James R. Schlesinger acknowledged in his *Annual Defense Department Report* that "it is not clear under what conditions the United States and its allies would possess a comparative military advantage in a tactical nuclear exchange" in Europe, he continued to offer the classic albeit tattered argument that this U.S. presence must remain "as long as opposing forces maintain similar capabilities." This kind of logic, of course, drove the USSR to develop its own tactical nuclear weapons and, in so doing, to erase whatever military benefits their unilateral possession had previously bestowed on NATO.

Even more disturbing are present proposals, apparently under serious consideration by Pentagon officials, to develop miniaturized tactical

*John F. Kennedy, *The Strategy of Peace* (New York: Harper & Row, 1960), p. 185.

U.S. and NATO Tactical Nuclear Weapons In Europe

Type of tactical nuclear weapon	Number of weapons or delivery vehicles	Number of weapons (warheads or bombs) [1]	Maximum range of weapon
Atomic demolition munitions: atomic mines	300	300	N/A
Artillery: M-109 155 mm. and M-110 203 mm.	1010	3030	10 to 18 miles
Surface-to-surface missiles: Honest John and Sergeant to be replaced by Lance	175	175	25 to 85 miles
Pershing	108	324 [2]	variable: 60-450 miles
Tactical aircraft [3] U.S. aircraft: F-4 and F-111	316	1020	500 to 1000 mile combat radius
Other NATO aircraft	612	1224	420 to 600 mile combat radius
Surface-to-air missiles	720	720	60 miles
Land-based anti-submarine warfare aircraft	380	380	1800 mile-combat radius
Totals	3621	7173 [4]	

[1] All weapons are in low-kiloton/high-kiloton range, except for some air-deliverable bombs in the low megaton range.
[2] The United States maintains approximately 216 of these in reserve.
[3] These do not include 98 nuclear-capable aircraft on the two U.S. aircraft carriers regularly stationed in the Mediterranean Sea.
[4] Total number is based upon the assumption that the maximum capability of each weapon will be utilized. Some weapons such as aircraft have flexibility to carry a range of payloads. Of the total number of tactical nuclear weapons approximately 150 are British and over 7,000 are American. France also maintains about 100 tactical nuclear weapons in Europe in the form of aircraft and Pluton surface-to-surface missiles.

nuclear weapons or "mini-nukes" whose destructive effects would resemble those of large conventional munitions. Such weapons admittedly would possess greater battlefield "utility" than present tactical nuclear weapons and perhaps would be, in the words of one proponent, "clearly not escalatory." Yet, a new family of "mini-nukes"—the cost of which is currently estimated in the billions of dollars—would provide NATO with no net military edge over Warsaw Pact forces. Indeed, "mini-nukes" would drastically lower the nuclear threshold, if not obliterate altogether the crucial ability to separate nuclear from non-nuclear defense. Moreover, it is highly unlikely that the Soviet Union would accept nuclear devices of even the smallest caliber as simply "improved" conventional ordnance. Longstanding Soviet disinclination to reduce the relatively large yields of its own tactical nuclear weapons suggests an image of tactical nuclear conflict at great variance with the selective, controlled use of discrete tactical nuclear weapons envisaged by U.S. strategists. In fact, Soviet military doctrine not only emphasizes the necessity for "mass employment of nuclear weapons" in a major European conflict, but also uniformly contends that "the side which first employs nuclear weapons with surprise can predetermine the outcome of the battle in his favor." In such circumstances even the most discriminating NATO nuclear riposte would make little difference in either the final outcome of conflict or in the resulting aggregate level of collateral damage. Is the United States therefore to develop a new and expensive set of weapons in the mere hope that the USSR will obligingly discard its established nuclear posture to suit our use of those weapons? *(April 1974)*

Editors' Perspective
U.S. Tactical Nuclear Weapons

It is generally known that the United States and its NATO allies maintain some 7,000 tactical nuclear weapons in Western Europe. These weapons include a wide variety of different types of delivery systems, many of which carry or fire more than one nuclear bomb. Often overlooked is the fact that, while slated for battlefield use, many tactical nuclear weapons have very large yields or warheads. For example, the Pershing missile can field a 400 kiloton warhead which is twenty times larger than the Hiroshima bomb and four times larger than a Poseidon missile warhead. The costs of maintaining American tactical nuclear weapons and supporting forces in Europe alone is estimated at over $500,000,000 annually. The United States also has regularly assigned about three Polaris/Poseidon missile submarines to the NATO targeting plan known as the General Strike Plan. A portion of U.S. and NATO tactical nuclear weapons, such as tactical aircraft, are kept loaded with nuclear warheads and ready to go at all times on quick reaction alert. Some experts are concerned that the vulnerability of such systems may create an incentive for an enemy pre-emptive attack.

In addition, the United States maintains a number of aircraft capable of carrying tactical nuclear weapons aboard two aircraft carriers in the Mediterranean Sea. These aircraft, as well as other nuclear-capable aircraft in Europe, are known as forward-based systems. They have been a point of contention between the United States and USSR in the SALT (Strategic Arms Limitation Talks) negotiations. The USSR charges that since these weapons are capable of reaching Russian territory they should be included in the SALT negotiations. On the other hand, the United States claims that these aircraft are limited to tactical missions in the European theater and therefore should be discussed in the Mutual and Balanced Force Reduction talks (MBFR).

On the other side, the USSR is reported to have somewhat less than 3,500 tactical nuclear weapons in the form of aircraft and surface-to-surface missiles. The USSR also has 600 SS-4 and SS-5 intermediate-range ballistic missiles deployed in western Russia which are aimed toward Europe.

Outside of Europe the United States has deployed three to four thousand tactical nuclear weapons in the Far East, primarily in such locations as Guam and South Korea. Often overlooked is the fact that the United States does maintain many more thousands of tactical nuclear weapons on its own mainland in addition to those in Western Europe and the Far East. *(April 1976)*

Neutron Weapons: A West German Perspective
Hans Günter Brauch

A great deal has been written about the "neutron bomb," or enhanced radiation warhead as it is more formally known, since it first came to public attention last summer. Most recently, President Carter's April 1978 decision to defer its production sparked front-page stories in major newspapers and national periodicals. Most of these analyses, however, have paid little attention to the attitudes toward the neutron bomb of West Germany, the nation on whose soil these weapons would be deployed. Yet an analysis of the West German policy debate on the enhanced radiation warhead is essential to the understanding of the national security and arms control implications of this weapon. Moreover, such an analysis can tell us a great deal about the current state of United States-NATO relations concerning tactical nuclear weapons.

The general attitude of West German policymakers toward tactical nuclear weapons was aptly summarized by Charles N. Davidson, a scientific adviser to the U.S. Army Nuclear Agency, who wrote, "these weapons are welcomed by the Germans solely as an additional deterrent, and should that fail, only in the forlorn hope that their use will quickly escalate the conflict to a U.S.-Soviet strategic exchange, thus sparing the Federal Republic of Germany further destruction." This general attitude has led the West Germans to pursue three specific, somewhat contradictory, policy goals: a West German role in the decision to employ tactical nuclear weapons; the limiting, as much as possible, of collateral damage from tactical nuclear weapons; and a tight coupling of the U.S. strategic deterrent to U.S. tactical nuclear forces in Europe.

The trigger question. Two major concerns have been raised by West German policymakers and military leaders: Will the West German government be consulted in any decision by an American president to use tactical nuclear weapons on or from the territory of West Germany? Conversely, do the present release procedures allow an efficient use of nuclear weapons if deterrence fails?

The first concern was allayed partially by the formation of NATO's Nuclear Planning Group in late 1966, which provided a permanent forum for consultation on the use of nuclear weapons. But some German military thinkers still fear that tactical nuclear weapons may not be released in time to be of any use. A group of strategists, including the highly respected retired Bundeswehr General Graf von Kielmannsegg, at the Stiftung Wissenschaft und Politik, the think-tank of the Federal government, suggested in 1974 that "certain already existing small nuclear weapons as well as the new ones to come must be extracted from the current nuclear philosophy" allowing them to be used without a cumbersome political decision. They concluded that otherwise "selective use will come too late and that the aggressor will not be stopped effectively." Despite these fears, the dominant West German view remains that all nuclear weapons should continue under political control. Leaders of all the parties in the West German parliament, the Bundestag, rejected the suggestions of the Kielmannsegg group.

Collateral damage. The West German fear of extensive collateral damage as a result of a nuclear war on German territory was expressed in the West Germans' 1970 Defense White Paper which warned that "in Central Europe . . . a large-scale tactical nuclear war would have the same devastating effects as a strategic nuclear conflict." Chancellor Helmut Schmidt, a former defense minister, writing in the 1960s also expressed this concern. "Even if the use of tactical weapons did not lead to extremes of escalation . . . it would nevertheless lead to the most extensive devastation of Europe and to the most extensive loss of life amongst its people. Those who believe that Europe can be defended by the massed use of such weapons will not defend Europe but destroy it."

Coupling. The issue of coupling between European tactical nuclear weapons and the U.S. strategic forces is the most important one to the West Germans, and the most complicated one in terms of U.S.-West German relations. Since the development of Soviet intercontinental ballistic missiles, there has been a basic conflict of interest between the United States and West Germany which has not yet been resolved. It is in the American national interest to prevent, unless absolutely necessary, any nuclear escalation to the strategic level that might endanger the American homeland. Thus, American experts on tactical nuclear weapons have tended to argue that the use of tactical nuclear weapons in Europe would not necessarily lead to a general strategic exchange. There are, they argue, several nuclear thresholds, so a nuclear war might be confined to Europe.

A few West German military analysts have begun to accept at least some aspects of the American view. But the dominant German view was articulated by Chancellor Schmidt when he wrote in the early 1960s, "it is utopian to hope for a mutually acceptable distinction between levels of nuclear conflict that would be sustained throughout a war."

West German political and military decision-makers continue to believe that tight linkage must be maintained. The attitude of the ruling Social Democrat/Liberal coalition, for example, was summed up in a 1972 Defense Ministry report which stated, "Only this inseparable connection between tactical and strategic deterrence is capable of equating the conventional superiority of the Warsaw Pact." Opposition conservative coalition spokesmen are in basic agreement. Manfred Wörner, Chairman of the Defense Committee of the Bundestag and the Conservatives' spokesman on defense, stated recently,

> It is the European interest that the risk for the aggressor be heightened by the prospect of a relatively quick escalation of the battle and its consequent endowment with new qualitative and geographical dimensions. . . . The territory of the USSR cannot be allowed . . . to become a sanctuary in the nuclear phase of a conflict in Europe. The Soviet Union cannot be invited to contemplate a war limited exclusively to Western Europe, or even to German territory.

It is against this background that the public debate on the enhanced radiation warhead took place.

The discussion of the neutron bomb did not remain confined to military experts in West Germany. For the first time since the initial debate on the deployment of nuclear weapons in the 1950s and early 1960s, wide public attention was focused on a theater nuclear weapon. As a result, the debate involved political, as well as narrowly military arguments on both sides.

Egon Bahr, the intellectual architect of detente under Chancellor Willy Brandt, started the controversy when he denounced the neutron bomb as "a symbol of mental perversion" in July 1977. While much of the public's opposition to the enhanced radiation warhead which developed throughout the summer was emotional, focusing on the fact that the bomb "killed people and spared buildings," the military utility of the neutron warhead was also criticized.

Theo Summer, the respected editor of *Die Zeit,* focused on the triggering problem in raising questions about the enhanced radiation warhead. "Is it not possible," he wrote in July 1977, "that the need for the weapons to be in forward positions, and for any early decision to be taken regarding their use, will undermine the strict control of events at the highest political levels in Washington?" A number of retired generals became involved in the debate. In an appearance on national television in August 1977, former Luftwaffe Chief of Staff General Steinhoff focused on the coupling issue in his criticism:

> I am in favor of retaining nuclear weapons as political tools, but not permitting them to become battlefield weapons. I am not opposed to the strategic employment of these weapons, however, I am firmly opposed to their tactical use on our soil. I cannot favor a nuclear war on German territory while the two superpowers observe safely at a distance.

A supposedly "cleaner," more "usable" weapon such as the neutron warhead might make nuclear warfare "more manageable" and therefore more likely.

Retired Army General Wolf Graf Baudissin, a former head of the NATO Defense College, voiced doubts that deployment of the enhanced radiation warhead could be restricted to merely tactical purposes or that it could enhance the security of West Germany. Baudissin foresaw the weapon's negative effects on detente and on-going arms control negotiations. He pointed out that the Soviet Union might not agree to a complete test ban treaty unless it also possessed neutron weapons. The Soviets, he argued, might compensate for the absence of enhanced radiation warheads by beefing up their conventional capabilities further. Either development would postpone arms limitation treaties and stimulate a qualitative arms race.

Opposition also came from the rank and file of the Social Democrats. During a September 1977 debate on defense policy in the Bundestag, Hans Koschnick—the mayor of Bremen and deputy chairman of the Social Democratic Party, as well as chairman of its national security policy committee—stated that the deployment of the neutron warhead would lower the nuclear threshold, thereby making deterrence less credible. Alfons Pawelczyk, the Social Democrat's chairman of the arms control subcommittee of the Bundestag, pointed out the negative effects the enhanced radiation warhead might have on on-going arms control negotiations. In November 1977 more than twenty resolutions calling for an open rejection by the West German government of the deployment of enhanced radiation warheads were submitted to the Social Democrat Party Convention. The membership of the ruling coalition's minority partner also seemed split on the neutron bomb.

But the enhanced radiation warhead gained some significant support. The conservative dailies *Die Welt* and *Frankfurter Allgemeine Zeitung,* as well as many journals close to military circles, called for the development of the neutron bomb. A number of former generals also came out in support. Perhaps most importantly, the neutron warhead was supported by a large majority of the conservative opposition parties. Their parliamentary spokesman, Manfred Wörner, was a consistent spokesman for the warhead. In February 1978, the Christian Democrats formally passed a resolution supporting the stationing of neutron bombs in West Germany.

Throughout the debate, Chancellor Schmidt tried cautiously to mute controversy and keep his government's options open. Government spokesmen stayed out of the heated emotional arguments which raged during the summer. During the September 1977 Bundestag debate on defense policy, Defense Minister Leber said only, "The neutron weapon has to be looked at as to whether it has any value as an additional means of deterrence strategy as a means to prevent a war." Another government spokesman, Conrad Ahlers, went a bit further saying, "We would have to learn to live with the neutron weapon and to include it in our defense concept," but he also made some critical comments.

At the Social Democratic Party convention in November 1977, government officials worked for a compromise resolution designed to prevent an outright rejection of the neutron weapon. The resolution which emerged left the Schmidt government some leeway by calling on it to "arrange its security and disarmament policies so that neutron weapon deployment on West German territory would not be necessary."

Schmidt's caution was probably due to several factors. Schmidt himself, while ambivalent about the enhanced radiation warhead, did not want to give away what he believed was a possible bargaining chip which might be used to achieve conventional arms reductions. Moreover, the Carter administration was pressing him to request the neutron bomb. Yet he had to take into consideration the majority opinion within his own party which opposed the neutron bomb, especially since four important state elections were taking place in 1978.

The public position finally arrived at by Schmidt was that the decision on production of the neutron bomb was solely an American one, and that a decision on its deployment in Germany should be made taking arms control considerations into account.

As Schmidt said in his Alastair Buchan Memorial Lecture to the International Institute of Strategic Studies on October 28, 1977:

> Until we see real progress on MBFR [Mutual and Balanced Force Reduction], we shall have to rely on the effectiveness of deterrence. It is this context and no other that the public discussion in all member states of the Western Alliance about the "neutron weapon" has to be seen. We have to consider whether the "neutron weapon" is of value to the Alliance as an additional element of the deterrence strategy, as a means of preventing war. But we should not limit ourselves to that examination. We should also examine what relevance and weight this weapon has in our efforts to achieve arms control.

Informally, it appears that Schmidt indicated to the Carter administration that he would agree to neutron bomb deployment in West Germany, provided that one other continental power also accepted neutron bombs on its soil.

President Carter's policy on the enhanced radiation warhead seemed to fluctuate between four positions: 1) to go ahead with production unilaterally, irrespective of future deployment in other NATO countries; 2) to forego the mission unilaterally; 3) to postpone a final decision in order to obtain a response from the NATO allies; 4) to use enhanced radiation warheads as a bargaining chip in arms control negotiations.

In his letter to Senator John C. Stennis (D-Miss.) of July 11, 1977, Carter "urged Congress to approve the current funding request" for development of the neutron bomb (option 1). However, once the opposition mounted both within the United States and in Western Europe, he postponed a final decision on production in order to obtain a public endorsement for his production decision (option 3). At the October 1977 meeting of the Nuclear Planning Group in Bari, Washington's position was that the decision on production would depend on a prior commitment by NATO's European allies to deploy enhanced radiation warheads. That strategy failed. Not one NATO government asked President Carter publicly to deploy neutron bombs on its territory, though West Germany apparently gave some private assurances. In fact, European opposition began to mount.

Not having received a firm commitment on deployment by the NATO allies, during the weekend of March 18-19, 1978, President Carter tentatively decided to forego the mission unilaterally (option 2). But when a *New York Times* article of April 4 stated that "Aides Report Carter Bans Neutron Bomb," and a major domestic and transatlantic controversy flared anew, President Carter announced on April 7, 1978:

> I have decided to defer production of weapons with enhanced radiation effects. The ultimate decision regarding the incorporation of enhanced radiation features into our modernized battlefield weapons will be made later, and will be influenced by the degree to which the Soviet Union shows restraint in its conventional and nuclear arms programs and force deployments affecting the security of the United States and Western Europe. . . . The United States is consulting with its partners in the North Atlantic Alliance on this decision and will continue to discuss with them appropriate arms-control measures to be pursued with the Soviet Union.

In his final position, President Carter made production of enhanced radiation warheads a bargaining factor in arms control negotiations (option 4).

Although the way in which it was made has unquestionably produced criticism, Carter's final decision seems to be in several respects a prudent compromise. It somewhat neutralizes the negative reaction in the U.S. Congress that may jeopardize SALT II (Strategic Arms Limitation Talks), while simultaneously mollifying the pro-arms control forces in the Senate. It also reflects the recommendations of the West Germans that the neutron bomb be dealt with in an arms control framework; and it avoids the paradoxical arms multiplication aspects of the bargaining chip approach since production is indefinitely postponed. The decision also signals to the Soviets President Carter's continued willingness to come to arms limitation agreements. Further, it may enhance the credibility of President Carter's commitment to arms control and disarmament at a time when world public opinion is focussed on the United Nations Special Session on Disarmament.

Though President Carter's decision-making process relating to the neutron warhead caused confusion, uneasiness, and harsh criticism in the West European and West German press, his final decision was publicly supported by the West German government. A government spokesman declared on April 7, 1978,

> This government stresses the American President's conviction that the technological possibilities of the West must continue to be maintained and should be used to maximum advantage in compensating for existing disparities. As before, this government continues to attach major significance to the utilization of the possibilities with regard to arms control, so as to reduce power disparities—especially as to the medium-range potential and to tanks. Accordingly, the planned Alliance consultations on utilizing existing possibilities to advance arms control policies have particular weight for this government. . . . We welcome and share the U.S. President's determination with regard to modernizing the NATO weapons system and to strengthening the joint forward defense.

On April 13, 1978, Chancellor Helmut Schmidt in a speech to the Bundestag backed President Carter's decision to defer production of the weapons. The debate ended with the adoption of a pro-Government resolution by a vote of 240 to 224. The resolution favored President Carter's decision to bring up the neutron warhead at the arms control talks and in the meantime deferring a decision to produce or deploy in Europe.

President Carter has decided to use the decision on producing the neutron warhead as a bargaining chip in arms control agreements. The key question for the future of this weapon is, therefore, how this might best be done. Two possibilities seem especially attractive:

The United States and the Soviet Union are in the process of negotiating a comprehensive test ban treaty. A decision by the President (perhaps announced at the United Nations Special Session on Disarmament) stopping further testing of the neutron bomb and linking its production with the achievement of a comprehensive ban on testing, might speed the negotiations.

Alternatively, weapons with enhanced radiation effects could be dealt with in the framework of gray-area systems, i.e., new weapons technologies which do not fall neatly into either SALT II or Mutual Balanced Force Reduction. Within a broader framework, perhaps a third forum of tactical arms limitation talks, complex package deals might be worked out. For example, mutual agreement on non-deployment of neutron bombs might be linked to limited deployment of mobile medium-range ballistic missiles (SS-20s) or to a mutual agreement not to use chemical weapons in Europe. This would be a step towards a complete ban on chemical warfare.

Whatever finally emerges, one of the most important outcomes of the debate on the neutron bomb in the United States and West Germany is that a weapons procurement and deployment decision has been clearly placed within an arms control framework. *(June 1978)*

Neutron Weapons: A Military Perspective
Arthur S. Collins, Jr.

President Carter presented a profile in courage when he delayed the production decision on the neutron bomb. In the debate of the past few weeks the President's reported and actual decisions were branded as "frightening," "feckless," "ominous," "truly scary," and as signs of buckling under to the "flaky left" or, worse yet, the Russians.

The case made for the neutron bomb—which is a missile warhead rather than a bomb—is that it would correct the dangerous imbalance in conventional forces between the Warsaw Pact and NATO. Many believe that if the Russians launch a massed-tank attack in Central Europe the neutron weapon is the only hope for stopping it; many believe the weapon would make nuclear war less likely; others describe NATO nations as anxious to get this new weapon.

The number of uncritical and emotional assertions about the benefits the neutron bomb will bring us are surprising. Articles and editorials are way off target when they say "there are no serious arguments against the deployment of this weapon" and that the President's decision is "a significant step backward in European defense." This new weapons system would at best add little to NATO's defense, at worst it could lead to disaster.

Outside of the United States, there is no great enthusiasm for this weapon in NATO. While the Netherlands has been the only nation to renounce it publicly, the lack of clear NATO support indicates other nations have reservations. NATO military commanders no doubt endorse the neutron bomb, but the silence of NATO's European national leaders suggests they anticipate problems with the public and their respective governing bodies if they endorse it. It appears our NATO allies want to look the other way and let President Carter take the heat for the decision.

Failure to produce the neutron bomb is not a step backward in the defense of Europe. On the contrary, it might make Europe more secure. The defensive nature of this weapon leads some to hope the neutron bomb might be used without triggering nuclear retaliation. That view is generally expressed by civilian nuclear theorists in the United States, and it is supported by some in responsible positions. Senator Sam Nunn's (D-Ga.) statements indicate he is so inclined. But few military commanders consider this even a remote possibility.

Proponents of tactical nuclear warfare are prone to stress weapons' effects on the enemy. These proponents are not nearly as objective or explicit about nuclear effects on their own forces. NATO use of neutron weapons developed for limited employment, discrete fire techniques, and pinpoint accuracy in defense of NATO is going to draw a Soviet response with tactical nuclear weapons; there should be no fuzzy thinking on that point.

The asymmetry between Soviet nuclear weapons and the neutron bomb would be so great that the larger and less accurate Soviet weapons would be devastating to NATO forces using the small weapons. War games and studies have repeatedly shown that where there is careful and discrete first use of nuclear weapons, the side that initiated the nuclear attack is overwhelmed by a sudden and massive enemy nuclear response. Ask any U.S. commander what he would do if his units were hit by a few small nuclear weapons. The response would be a request for all the nuclear firepower he could get. Are the Russians likely to be more restrained in similar circumstances? Soviet military doctrine gives little evidence of concern for collateral damage, especially on hostile soil. The most likely result of NATO first use of neutron bombs would be for NATO to lose faster.

An emotional editorial in the *Wall Street Journal* said that the new weapon "annoys the Soviet Union." This may be true, but don't put too much stock in that; the Kremlin is easily annoyed by what the United States does. It is doubtful the Soviet military planners are concerned about a small neutron weapon, which to them is just another nuclear weapon. If they believed NATO might break the nuclear barrier with small neutron bombs, it is conceivable they could see a military advantage for them and this might encourage them to recommend a military attack.

The perceptions of the Warsaw Pact nations other than Russia are important, too. They will be less inclined to support a Russian attack on NATO if the threat of nuclear damage to their homeland and forces is great. If these nations perceive the neutron bomb as a nuclear weapon that will pose no great damage to them, they might be more willing to support a Russian attack. Then the uncertainty about what might happen after war comes and the nuclear barrier is broken could lead to the catastrophe no one wants to have happen. The neutron warhead could pose a threat to the security of Europe because it blurs the distinction between conventional and nuclear war for us, but not for the Russians.

The cost of the neutron bomb from development to placement in operational storage sites would be close to a billion dollars, maybe more. Since the new weapons raise the cost of defense without adding to the defense now in place, why not leave the weapons which have been an effective deterrent where they are? Then, if conventional defense of NATO is the real concern, use some of that billion dollars to provide forces in Central Europe with more of the very effective anti-tank missiles that have been developed. NATO would then be able to put up a better conventional defense and retain its current capability for a nuclear defense.

A conventional defense of NATO's Central Sector would not be easy, but with the right emphasis it could be made credible. The lessons of the last Arab-Israeli war indicate that, with new anti-tank weapons, tanks can be destroyed in large numbers and quickly. Surely NATO has done its homework based on that short, violent war in October 1973.

In times past the countries of Western Europe have had effective reserve and mobilization systems. This was especially true of Germany. Each year more men are completing their military training and passing into the territorial forces. If these troops are properly equipped and trained for a defensive war in their own local areas, every farm, town, village, and forest of Western Europe would provide defensive strong-points to slow down any advance. With the conventional weapons now available, what can be seen can be hit; what can be hit can be destroyed. There are costs involved, but they are not nearly as great as those which the employment of tactical nuclear weapons would entail. NATO nations in Central Europe could survive a conventional defense; there would not be much left after a tactical nuclear war in that area.

President Carter has said that the ultimate objective with respect to nuclear weapons is to negotiate for their eventual elimination. In the years ahead, some combination of national leaders may be able to make progress to that end. This will never be easy for a U.S. president because so many members of Congress, officials in government agencies, and columnists view reluctance to approve a new nuclear weapons system as surrender to the Russians. The history of the neutron bomb would be a good case study for all; it might make some people wonder how failure to produce that weapon could be branded "ominous" and a capitulation to the Russians.

From a military point of view the President's decision was not a retreat from reality, but a facing up to reality. It was militarily sound and in the long run may prove to be the same politically. *(June 1978)*

In the 1970s, a number of events took place which disappointed earlier hopes that, if we could gain adherents to the Limited Test Ban and the Non-Proliferation Treaties and negotiate a ban on underground nuclear tests, significant barriers to the testing and spread of nuclear weapons would be provided. Various technical advances combined to increase the number of potential nuclear weapons states. Existing nuclear powers refused to sign the Non-Proliferation Treaty or to halt atmospheric tests. Rising fuel costs increased interest in nuclear power, especially in fuel-saving technologies which also produce weapons-grade materials. India's detonation of a nuclear device—fabricated in part from materials supplied for research—called attention to the potential danger of peaceful nuclear exports and to loopholes in restrictions on them.

While concern about the problems of nuclear proliferation and testing grew, solutions proposed proved highly contentious—energy-poor countries decrying the double standard restrictions imposed or threatened by exporters through the Non-Proliferation Treaty, the Nuclear Suppliers Group and the U.S. Non-Proliferation Act of 1978. The exporters, with lucrative contracts at stake, were unable to agree on a single strategy for preventing nuclear proliferation.

To provide a breathing spell and to review thoroughly the options available for the safe pursuit of nuclear power technology, in 1978 a large, representative group of nations began an International Nuclear Fuel Cycle Evaluation (INFCE). It was hoped that fundamental technical agreement on proliferation-resistant measures could be reached by the end of the evaluation process in 1980 so that the atmosphere for the 1980 Non-Proliferation Treaty Review Conference would be improved.

In addition, prospects for conclusion of a limited-duration comprehensive test ban—one banning underground tests—appeared somewhat brighter in 1979, following limited Soviet concessions in 1977 and despite last-minute U.S. military calls for exceptions to permit low-yield reliability tests of existing weapons. Domestic and international pressure for a comprehensive ban remained strong, for it would force the nuclear superpowers to carry out their obligations under the Limited Test Ban and to show their good faith in restraining the proliferation of nuclear weapons.

Nuclear Proliferation & Testing

The Spread of Nuclear Weapons—Is the Dam About to Burst? *Thomas A. Halsted*

In two articles—this one written before the May 1975 Non-Proliferation Treaty Review Conference, the following one shortly thereafter— Halsted reviews some of the obstacles to controls on proliferation. Developments since 1975 have tended to bear out his rather gloomy prognosis. India continues to refuse to agree to International Atomic Energy Agency safeguards; of the important near-nuclear powers, only Japan has adhered to the treaty; and the pressures for the use of plutonium as a fuel source are increasing.

"If we had known in 1968 how little the nuclear powers would do over the next six years to meet their end of the NPT bargain by controlling their arms race, I would have advised my government not to sign the treaty."

Thus spoke a distinguished former diplomat from a still non-nuclear country at a recent conference held by the Arms Control Association to discuss issues likely to dominate the May 1975 Review Conference required by Article VIII of the Treaty on the Non-Proliferation of Nuclear Weapons (the "NPT").

The NPT resulted from a consensus between nuclear and non-nuclear countries that the birth of more nuclear powers would lead inevitably to greater risks of nuclear war and that therefore it would be in the mutual interest of all to devise a regime which would prevent the spread of nuclear weapons without denying anyone the potential peaceful benefits of nuclear energy. Thus the treaty, which was drawn up in 1968 and took effect in 1970, is a compact between the nuclear powers, which committed themselves to end their arms race and work toward nuclear disarmament, and the non-nuclear powers, which, in exchange for foregoing acquisition of nuclear weapons, could look forward to reaping the benefits of the peaceful uses of nuclear energy.

Concern about the continued arms race between the nuclear super-powers is only one reason the NPT is in trouble today. Blame for the fragile condition of the treaty can be laid in many directions:

—First, on the enormous worldwide appetite for nuclear-generated electric power, which brings with it vastly expanded opportunities for the diversion of plutonium and highly enriched uranium from peaceful purposes to the manufacture of weapons, both by irresponsible governments and by nongovernmental terrorist or criminal groups. The world-wide energy crisis has added greatly to this appetite for nuclear power, while tending to minimize concerns about its attendant risks.

—Second, on the persistent notion that nuclear weapons bring greater security, a delusion held by non-nuclear as well as nuclear powers;

—Third, on exaggerated claims for the potential benefits of nuclear explosions for peaceful purposes.

All of these factors have combined to provide incentives, or at least excuses, for a numerically small but important group of nations to stop short of ratifying the NPT.

Six months ago many observers had reason to believe that the NPT had come of age, and that the Review Conference was likely to be un-eventful. Almost ten years had passed without the addition of another nuclear power, eighty-three countries had acceded to the treaty, and, with the apparent resolution of problems that had delayed their accep-tance of International Atomic Energy Agency safeguards on peaceful nuclear programs, it appeared only a matter of time before a number of important holdouts (West Germany, Italy, the Benelux countries, and Japan) would complete the ratification process. This optimism was, unhappily, premature. A series of events which took place over only a few weeks' span have provided a sharp reminder of the fragility of the NPT regime.

The Indian Nuclear Test: On May 18, 1974, India detonated its first nuclear "device," a 15-kiloton explosive set off under the Rajasthan Desert of Northwest India. Indian spokesmen insisted to the world that it was for peaceful purposes, and that India would never develop nuclear weapons. The test produced almost universal acclaim in India itself and grave concern and undoubtedly a reappraisal of nuclear options in Paki-stan. But elsewhere there was sharp criticism only in Japan, Sweden, and Canada (which had provided the reactors which supplied the nuclear fuel for the Indian test), general approval or at least no criticism from China and the USSR, and only mild clucks of disapproval from the United States. What political leverage the United States might have exercised to discourage the Indian nuclear program all but evaporated in Secretary of State Henry Kissinger's visit there last month. In an October 28,

Annual Production of Plutonium (1972-2000)

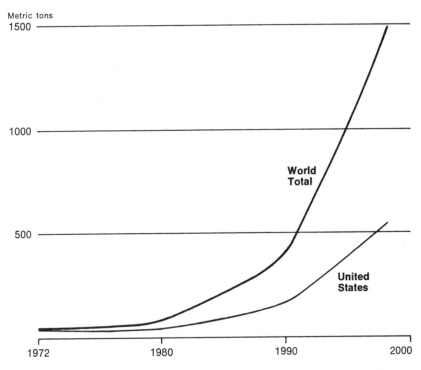

By the end of this century world plutonium production could reach over 1,500 metric tons (1.5 million kilograms) per year. Only a few kilograms are needed to make a weapon the size of the bomb that destroyed Hiroshima.

Source: *Nuclear Theft: Risks and Safeguards*, Mason Willrich and Theodore B. Taylor (Cambridge: Ballinger Publishing Co., 1974).

1974, speech to the Indian Council on World Affairs in New Delhi, he seemed to give further official U.S. blessing to India's new status by calling on India to act responsibly in considering the export of nuclear technology. Aside from demonstrating that it could safely run the risk of momentary international disapproval, India gave renewed credibility to arguments in such countries as Argentina and Brazil that peaceful nuclear explosives have a promising future.

The Middle East Reactors: In June 1974 the Nixon administration announced that it had offered to sell Egypt and Israel each a 600 megawatt reactor to produce electric power. The announcement was coupled with the assurance that stringent safeguards would be attached to the sales agreements, probably to include a requirement that the plutonium produced in the reactors would be returned to the United States for re-processing, to prevent its possible diversion to weapons production. For the first time since the Non-Proliferation Treaty was signed, a nuclear power, party to the treaty, had undertaken to supply to non-parties equipment capable of producing nuclear weapons materials in significant amounts. The treaty does not prohibit such transactions, and American defenders of the deals are quick to point out the extra stringency of the safeguards provisions (applied, however, only to the reactors and the materials provided under this transaction, but not to any other nuclear facilities in the recipient countries). Nevertheless, the sales agreements have been strongly criticized by many who view the infusion of major additions to nuclear technology in the Middle East as extremely danger-ous and by others who see them as not in keeping with the spirit of the NPT, or even as an outright breach of its provisions. In any event, it is difficult for a non-nuclear party to the NPT not to consider the transac-tions to be discriminatory if Egypt and Israel, both non-parties, are asked to put only these particular installations under safeguards, while non-nuclear parties to the treaty must place *all* nuclear facilities under safeguard.

The Moscow Summit: Finally, the arms control agreements between the United States and the Soviet Union announced on July 3, 1974, in Moscow were seen by many non-nuclear parties as a slap in the face. The bilateral Threshold Test Ban Treaty signed there, allowing both sides to continue testing nuclear weapons underground as large as 150 kilotons (ten times the size of the Hiroshima bomb) after March 31, 1976, and even then permitting the continued testing of "peaceful" explosives of any size, seemed a direct contradiction to the two superpowers' commit-ments to bring their arms race under control and "seek to achieve the discontinuance of all nuclear test explosions for all time."

At the September 1974 Conference which the Arms Control Associa-tion held in Divonne, France, these and many other factors were con-sidered at length by the twenty-five participants that were present from seventeen countries and several international organizations. They con-cluded that the NPT, "while far from perfect, is a useful and workable instrument." They felt that performance under the treaty had suffered more from failure fully to implement its provisions than from weaknesses in the provisions themselves. They made a number of concrete recom-mendations for action which should be taken to strengthen the treaty:

1. The nuclear weapon parties to the treaty should take seriously their obligations to work toward disarmament, in particular by reducing num-bers of nuclear delivery vehicles, limiting further missile flight testing, and negotiating a comprehensive (not a threshold) nuclear test ban

treaty. They viewed the threshold treaty as a "disheartening step backward."

2. To provide better security assurances for non-nuclear powers, nuclear weapons states should pledge themselves not to use or threaten to use nuclear weapons against non-nuclear states party to the treaty; the establishment of nuclear-free zones should be encouraged.

3. The benefits of peaceful nuclear explosives are questionable. A study should be commissioned by the Secretary General of the United Nations of all the implications of such programs, and it was suggested that meanwhile a moratorium on further peaceful nuclear tests should be imposed.

4. Henceforth, provisions of nuclear supplies and technology should be made only to those recipients, whether or not parties to the NPT, which agree to place *all* their nuclear facilities under International Atomic Energy Agency safeguards.

5. Safeguards systems should be strengthened and made universal, with increased attention given to physical security applied to all materials. The problem of diversion of nuclear materials by terrorists, organized criminals, and other non-governmental groups should be given immediate attention.

Over the long run, implementing these recommendations could provide enough glue to hold the NPT together, but to do so will require overturning major obstacles all along the way.

The United States and USSR view complaints about their lack of progress at SALT as exaggerated and clearly think they have bought off objections to their lack of progress in curbing nuclear testing with their dubious threshold test ban. No-first-use agreements have little support from either (although France and China, both non-parties to the NPT, have each offered no-first-use formulations). Nuclear-free zone proposals are being discussed again at the United Nations, but the only one likely to be in existence for some time is in Latin America—and there there are notable holdouts in the case of Cuba, Argentina, and Brazil.

Peaceful nuclear explosions remain a serious stumbling block. The more the nuclear powers discover their uselessness, the more non-nuclear powers declare that the United States and USSR are looking for excuses to duck their NPT obligations to provide peaceful nuclear explosion services when the technology becomes available. And India's example has given a powerful new impetus to peaceful nuclear explosion zealots in other countries considering taking that step.

There is some reason to hope that domestic pressures in the United States will lead this country to adopt a more inclusive sales policy with respect to safeguards, but considerably more thought must be given to safety and security implications as nuclear power installations grow over the coming years in size, number, and geographic distribution. Other potential suppliers of nuclear materials and technology also would do well to consider the long-range security and non-proliferation implications of transactions they might negotiate in the future. There was considerable uneasiness, for example, over the recent announcement that France will sell five large reactors to Iran. Although Iran is a party to the NPT and France, though not a party, has repeatedly stated that it would behave exactly as if it were, the size of the deal provoked serious concern. French sales of reactors or other nuclear facilities to a *nonparty* in the present atmosphere could have grave implications for the future of the treaty.

Time is running out. More constructive action must be taken if more countries, disappointed by lack of progress toward disarmament by the nuclear powers, and seeking new ways to enhance their prestige and security, do not soon follow the Indian example. Otherwise the Review Conference next year may well be more a wake than a celebration. *(November 1974)*

NPT: Report from Geneva *Thomas A. Halsted*

The Non-Proliferation Treaty (NPT) Review Conference, which took place in May 1975 at the Palais des Nations in Geneva, Switzerland, ended the evening of Friday, May 30, after four weeks of debate. The conference was convened in compliance with the treaty's Article VIII, which called on parties to meet five years after the treaty's entry into force to examine whether "the purposes of the Preamble and the provisions of the treaty are being realized." The conferees concluded their discussions by adopting a compromise declaration, drafted by Conference President Inga Thorsson (Sweden) after a drafting committee had failed to reconcile divergent views. The declaration reaffirmed the conferees' support of the treaty's purposes, called on the parties—particularly those possessing nuclear weapons—to do more to meet their treaty obligations, and proposed that a second review conference be convened in 1980. In two hours of discussion which followed the adoption of the resolution, a number of the delegates delivered final statements to the conference, many of them expressing dissatisfaction about the outcome of the talks; it is a foregone conclusion that the disputes aired then and earlier at the review conference will be raised again in other forums in coming months.

Almost on the heels of the conference came the unwelcome news that West Germany (which had just completed ratification of the treaty) was about to conclude a multi-billion dollar deal to provide all the elements of the nuclear fuel cycle (enrichment, reactors, and plutonium fuel separation facilities, adequate to make nuclear weapons if desired) to Brazil, a conspicuous non-party to the NPT. That such a transaction was completely legal under the treaty demonstrated at a most unfortunate time how easily and dramatically its intent could be circumvented.

But even without this depressing punctuation mark, the conference was disappointing. Not that anything really unexpected occurred; I had supposed that there would be a month of fairly inconclusive debate over the rights and obligations of treaty parties, coupled with some progress toward solving some of the more urgent technical obstacles standing in the way of providing the benefits of the peaceful atom to as many consumers as possible. What I and perhaps a few other optimists were less prepared for was the degree of acrimony and discord that permeated much of the discussion, chiefly of the more political problems, and that may in some subtle ways make the NPT regime less stable in the future.

Considering that speaker after speaker at the conference referred to the meeting as the most historic disarmament conference to be held in thirty years, it was remarkably poorly attended and generated almost no attention from the world press. Of the ninety-six nations eligible for full participation only fifty-eight bothered to show up. Before the conference all parties had been invited to attend; several had been unaware of the meeting. One asked if it were a party to the treaty; one eligible party (Iraq) requested and obtained permission to participate as an observer rather than a full party, thereby exempting itself from the obligation to pay a share of the $645,000 budgeted for the month-long session.

In addition to the fifty-eight parties, seven signatories not yet parties attended, and seven additional non-signatories attended as observers.

Was the conference a success? Opinions ranged from the assertion that the fact that over ninety states have ratified the treaty proves the smashing success of the review conference to the charge that if the nuclear superpowers do not immediately negotiate a comprehensive test ban, undertake immediate and major reductions of strategic arms, and vow never to use nuclear weapons against anyone not possessing them, it will have been a catastrophic disaster.

There is some validity in both of these extreme positions. Considering the worst that might have happened in the past seven years, the fact that the review conference took place at all is a plus. That there are as many as ninety-six parties to the treaty is a credit both to the original concept of the treaty and to the confidence that new parties have placed in it, no matter what its apparent shortcomings. That none of the parties that have subscribed to the NPT has subsequently withdrawn from it has probably significantly strengthened the treaty.

It must be remembered, however, that those ninety-six states that have ratified the NPT still do not include in their number the half dozen or so most likely to retain an interest in acquiring nuclear weapons—the problem the treaty was intended to solve in the first place.

The treaty cannot stop proliferation, only make it a little harder to facilitate. The way it has been implemented up to now was reflected in the development of the debate in the two main committees of the review conference—one dealing with disarmament and other security problems, the other with technical issues related to the orderly growth of peaceful nuclear industry. As expected, it turned out easier to come up with promising or at least acceptable solutions to the technical problems than to solve the essentially political ones.

In the technical area, the conference gave renewed stimulus to some promising concepts: to the idea of regional or multi-national fuel cycle centers, for example, and perhaps to a more careful appraisal of the real prospects for and problems of peaceful nuclear explosions. The conference will undoubtedly also help to encourage development of improved safeguards systems, heighten concern about security of nuclear materials and facilities, and, one hopes, lead to less discriminatory supplier policies. In short, the conference underscored the fact that for the most part the treaty has been an effective instrument for facilitating access to the peaceful uses of nuclear energy.

Where the treaty—and the review conference—continue to fall short remains in the harder questions of security, chiefly those of implementing Article VI, dealing with the obligations of the nuclear-weapons parties (the United States, Britain, and the USSR) to do more about disarmament and arms control. These problems were made more difficult to grapple with at the conference by the hard-nosed approach the nuclear powers chose to take. No one realistically expected the United States and USSR to "take the pledge" at the review conference and give up the arms race entirely, but neither did it seem reasonable for them to react to criticism of their behavior by asserting that the scope and pace of their bilateral arms control negotiations were nobody's business but their own. A Soviet delegate called such criticism "unacceptable interference."

If non-proliferation means the less nuclear weapons the better, the nuclear powers must set a better example. They can and must do more than they have so far been willing to do, toward ending nuclear tests, reversing the qualitative and quantitative strategic arms race, and adopting some form of commitment not to use nuclear weapons against those who have agreed to forswear them. These are steps they should take even if there were no Non-Proliferation Treaty.

But even if the superpowers took these necessary steps tomorrow, their action would still leave unresolved the immediate security concerns of the potential sixth, seventh, or eighth nuclear-weapons powers, whose decisions to acquire nuclear weapons will not be based on concerns about attack from the United States or Soviet Union but rather from their neighbors. In this area, it is events and undertakings outside the scope of the treaty and beyond the responsibility of the review conference that will most affect the future of nuclear weapons proliferation.

Regional political solutions to regional conflicts, including serious consideration of nuclear-weapon-free zones, in those few areas where they seem feasible, will do far more to remove incentives for "going nuclear" than any imaginative technological fix, however laudable, which might make it more difficult to obtain the means to do so. Furthermore, the suppliers of conventional arms, by continuing to dispense their lethal largesse so abundantly to troubled parts of the world, are certainly not doing their part to alleviate regional tensions or to lessen the likelihood that appetites for nuclear weapons will be diminished. A non-proliferation treaty for conventional arms could do a great deal to bolster the nuclear NPT.

What, then, did the review conference accomplish? That it took place at all, reaffirming a commitment to the treaty, may turn out to have been its most significant achievement. If it also served to underscore the many grave problems nuclear weapons and nuclear power have posed for the world and to stimulate creative thinking toward their solution, it will have been well worth holding. Even the widespread dissatisfaction expressed by many of the non-nuclear powers present could turn out to be beneficial if it finally prodded the nuclear powers to faster and better progress in disarmament. The review conference provided a forum for a careful reassessment of the risks and benefits of the peaceful atom. If some day it would also be possible to start thinking seriously about *fewer* nuclear-weapons powers rather than merely congratulating ourselves that there are no additional ones, the review conference could signal the beginning of a welcome step toward international sanity.

Some of the non-governmental observers present at Geneva felt the conference had been a failure. They apparently saw it as an occasion for the nuclear weapons states, suitably chastised, to get religion, to realize that they had to mend their ways and could no longer set such a bad example.

I take a different view. One could hardly expect in thirty days to bring about solutions that had not been found in five years. The Non-Proliferation Treaty is a complicated instrument—an amalgam of political and technological commitments and half-promises, a bargain between states with very different objectives and approaches, both to their security and to solving the problems facing a world of nuclear energy. The review conference was not a forum for major new developments, only a check point at what—I hope—is an early stage in the life of the NPT and a broader international concern about the many problems of the Nuclear Age. *(June 1975)*

Do Peaceful Nuclear Explosions Have a Future?
Franklin A. Long

The idea of peaceful uses for nuclear explosive devices arose almost simultaneously with the concept of the nuclear explosion itself. It has been a powerful idea in that it soon generated major study efforts in the United States and the USSR and also captured the interest of many developing nations. (Witness, for example, the 1974 explosion by India of a nuclear explosive device as part of what has been announced as a program of peaceful uses.) But in spite of this considerable interest and much expenditure of funds and effort, the expectation that economically viable uses will be found for peaceful nuclear explosions looks even more distant now than when the first studies were initiated. This, at least, is the conclusion of two recent U.S. studies* of the economic feasibility and time scale for application of peaceful nuclear explosions by the United States.

The larger of these two studies was prepared by the Gulf Universities Research Consortium, and dealt particularly with possibilities for use in the United States by 1990 of *contained,* i.e., underground, peaceful nuclear explosions. A recent, briefer analysis by an *ad hoc* panel assesses the implications of the Gulf report, considers other uses for peaceful nuclear explosions, and summarizes the reasons why there is only a small possibility that there will be significant use of them by the United States before the year 2000.

The technical characteristics which led to the expectation that peaceful nuclear explosions would have important applications remain significant today. The energy density of a nuclear explosive device is very high (whether utilizing nuclear fission or nuclear fusion**), a characteristic that has great significance in underground engineering. Furthermore, the devices are comparatively inexpensive. The current best U.S. estimate for the cost of a 100 kiloton nuclear explosive device for peaceful uses is around $700,000—not exactly cheap, but very much less than the cost of 100,000 "equivalent" tons of a chemical explosive like TNT.

---

*The two studies are "PNE (Peaceful Nuclear Explosion) Activity Projections for Arms Control Planning," Gulf Universities Research Consortium, Galveston, Texas, April 1975, and "An Analysis of the Economic Feasibility, Technical Significance, and Time Scale for Application of Peaceful Nuclear Explosions in the U.S., with Special Reference to the GURC Report Thereon," The Program on Science, Technology and Society, Cornell University, Ithaca, New York, April 1975.

**Fission is a nuclear reaction in which an atomic nucleus is split into two equal parts; in fusion, atomic nuclei combine to form a larger nucleus. Both reactions produce a large amount of energy.

Unfortunately, there are also drawbacks to use of peaceful nuclear explosions: production of radioactivity is an inescapable concomitant; underground nuclear explosions generate seismic waves which are similar in character to those from earthquakes and which, like the latter, have potential for damage to buildings and other structures. Since nuclear explosive devices for peaceful uses are similar to those for nuclear weapons, their production is a government monopoly and their transportation, storage, and use is subject to close, often onerous, governmental regulation. If peaceful nuclear explosions are to have a commercial future, the world must locate technological needs where the special virtues of nuclear explosives loom large and where the drawbacks are minimized so that, on balance, the use of peaceful nuclear explosions is attractive.

In the eighteen years from 1956 to 1974, the U.S. Atomic Energy Commission (later the Energy Research and Development Administration) spent about $160 million on peaceful nuclear explosion-related studies, including test explosions. About two-thirds of this went to studies of excavation, i.e., canal-building and the like. However, in recent years, especially after the passage of the Limited Nuclear Test Ban Treaty in 1963, the U.S. emphasis has been on underground or contained applications. The recent analyses have identified three technical applications of particular interest: stimulation of production of natural gas from "tight" formations; *in situ* retorting of oil shale which has been "rubblized" by an underground nuclear explosion; and the use of nuclear explosions to generate underground storage cavities for oil or natural gas. Closely related to the second of these is *in situ* leaching of low-grade copper ores which have been rubblized by nuclear explosions. The results of actual field tests for the first of these applications illustrate the kinds of problems that will probably plague the others.

Effective stimulation of production from the extensive "tight" gas formations of Colorado and Wyoming could contribute importantly to U.S. energy needs. Hence, Atomic Energy Commission-industry collaboration was readily established for three U.S. field tests for gas stimulation. In 1967 a test called Gasbuggy demonstrated that a large vertical "chimney" of rubble could be generated by a nuclear explosion. The 30-kiloton explosive yield for Gasbuggy produced a "chimney" 330 feet high and 160 feet in diameter. Moderate stimulation of gas production was obtained. Two other commercially oriented tests were then accomplished: Rulison in 1969 and Rio Blanco in 1973. Each produced some stimulation but, overall, each was disappointing. These tests also demonstrated some of the drawbacks to use of nuclear explosions. Initial gas temperatures were worrisomely high, as was the radioactivity of the gas. Extensive precautions were required to minimize seismic damage. The tests were delayed by regulatory requirements and by protests from environmental groups. All this discouraged industry sponsors, but of perhaps equal importance in diminishing industry interest in use of nuclear explosions is that a recently developed alternate technique for stimulation, massive hydraulic fracturing, appears to be simpler to use and more cost-effective. Hence, the future appears dim for application of nuclear explosions to gas stimulation.

For virtually all of the other contemplated applications of underground nuclear explosions, the technology for their use is even less explored and even more uncertain than in the above case. Generation of underground storage cavities for oil or gas is a possible exception, but the cost savings do not appear to be sufficient in this case to outweigh the inevitable uncertainties due to regulatory delays, seismic consequences, and other sources. It is for these several reasons that, for the United States at least, significant use of peaceful nuclear explosions by 1990 appears most unlikely. The fact that U.S. funding for experiments with peaceful nuclear explosions has diminished sharply and that no new field tests are currently scheduled underscores this conclusion.

World-wide, the use of nuclear explosions for excavation, canal building, and the like has captured more attention than the underground uses. Here, the prospect of atmospheric radioactive discharges which would violate the 1963 Limited Test Ban Treaty constitutes a formidable barrier to use. But apart from this, the presumed advantages of nuclear explosions for excavation tend to diminish as specific projects are carefully studied. This was dramatically illustrated by the $20 million U.S. study of construction costs for a sea-level replacement to the Panama Canal. Even though two-thirds of this study was devoted to possible use of nuclear explosions, the ultimate recommendation was that conventional methods of excavation were preferable.

The significance to world peace of these pessimistic conclusions on prospects for the use of peaceful nuclear explosions is clear: The likelihood of significant cost savings or other benefits is sufficiently low that provision for their continuing use should not stand in the way of otherwise attractive measures of arms control and disarmament. *(May 1975)*

Why Not a Nuclear Fuel Cartel?   *Steven J. Baker*

The pace of nuclear energy exports has quickened since the end of 1974 as multi-billion dollar agreements have been signed by Iran, Brazil, and most recently by South Korea. These agreements carry with them the risk of further nuclear weapons proliferation because the reactors being exported produce plutonium as a matter of course and because for the first time fuel cycle technologies are to be exported as well as reactors: Iran is interested in a fuel reprocessing plant, Brazil has an option on reprocessing and enrichment facilities, and South Korea has contracted for a reprocessing plant. All of these proposed exports will be covered by international safeguards. However, the crucial fact is that the export of these facilities will, over a period of five to ten years, give these nations independent access to potentially weapons-grade nuclear materials and therefore a nuclear option should they choose to exercise it.

The burgeoning export market in nuclear equipment and know-how is, in large part, a result of the post-October 1973 energy crunch. Nuclear power is for the first time clearly economically competitive with fossil fuel power; the high price of oil, the uncertainty of supplies, and not least the political strings that may be attached to oil supplies have heightened all nations' interest in nuclear energy. While advanced industrial nations all project increased future dependence on nuclear energy, even developing nations are considering ambitious nuclear programs: the International Atomic Energy Agency is now promoting nuclear power in plant sizes as small as 100 megawatts that are fitted to the needs of developing nations. Nuclear exports promise to ease the balance of payments problems of the industrial countries, and nuclear imports will help to make developing countries less dependent on the oil-producing nations by diversifying their sources of energy. As international competition among exporters sharpens, the acquisition of nuclear weapons capabilities by nuclear importers quickens its pace.

The threat of proliferation has not been ignored altogether; it merely has been subordinated to other kinds of economic and political concerns. The conferences that nuclear exporters—the United States, the Soviet Union, Great Britain, Canada, France, Japan and West Germany—have held in London over the last several months are evidence of this concern. But the definition of the problem that seems to have emerged is that nuclear exports *per se* are not the problem—nuclear energy is positively valued and its international spread is seen as both inevitable and profitable to the nuclear exporting nations. The problem is defined as the *competition* among exporters of nuclear energy. It is this competition that erodes the kinds of political controls that the industrial nations might be able to place on this technology, with each being compelled either to under-cut the others in terms of the kinds of safeguards and political conditions attached to exports or to risk losing lucrative export markets. In order to obtain Brazilian reactor contracts for which Westinghouse had the inside track, the West German government was willing to sponsor the export of reprocessing and enrichment facilities as a "sweetener" to clinch the deal. Obviously, others will be tempted to do the same in order to compete in the future.

Remedies for this kind of competition that aim at restricting nuclear energy exports run up against a fundamental dilemma. If the restrictive measures are unilateral, they tend to be self-denying, which makes them politically unpopular with domestic economic groups and, given alternative sources of technology, dubiously effective. If more restrictive measures require international cooperation, they run counter to the established competitive drives that are the main source of the problem. This makes the prospects for a meaningful agreement coming out of the London talks rather doubtful.

The task is to balance the requirements of nonproliferation and nuclear energy exports—of arms control and the commercial promotion of nuclear power. The search should be for a pattern of international competition more suited to slowing the pace of the spread of nuclear weapons capabilities to developing countries while meeting their legitimate nuclear energy needs. The recent success of the Organization of Petroleum Exporting Countries (OPEC) has inspired similar attempts in commodities as various as bauxite and bananas—why not, then, a nuclear fuel cartel?

In principle the nuclear field is well suited for cartelization. Five or six nations dominate the international nuclear market, and the nuclear industries of each are closely controlled and promoted by the governments. Demand for nuclear hardware and services is high, but the capital requirements are so enormous that steady economic returns could be more attractive in the nuclear field than the possibly higher but also more risky returns that might result from less restricted trade. There is no reason in principle why a cartel could not establish a loose international framework that would permit limited economic competition among the industrial nations while reducing the dangers of proliferation inherent in the present pattern of competition.

The motivation behind a nuclear cartel would be political, not economic: the primary objective of such an arrangement would be to limit the spread of nuclear weapons capabilities by, for example, prohibiting the export of fuel cycle technologies. The primacy of this objective suggests a subordination of the cartel members' economic interests to the common political goal if the two should seem irreconcilable. But it might be possible for cartel members to pursue their economic interests without sacrificing their common political goals. The cartel might, for example, provide enrichment and reprocessing services on a commercial basis, guaranteeing a steady return on the members' investment in this field. The individual members would then be free to compete in the reactor export field with fewer worries.

A nuclear fuel cartel among the major industrial nations—with the Soviet Union perhaps acting as if it were a member—would have major advantages for all concerned. 1) It would give advanced industrial nations an opportunity to cooperate on a program that links proliferation with wider economic and political concerns, perhaps providing a basis for institutionalized cooperation among the members on other aspects of energy policy. 2) The cartel members' relations with client-states would be improved by the application of a single set of political and economic standards for dealing with all. By satisfying the world-wide demands for enriched uranium fuels, a cartel based on a political nonproliferation rationale would gain from having a positive economic task. 3) The cartel's formal obligations would serve as a common standard for guiding the policies of the individual members, helping to coordinate and restrain the various bureaucracies and industrial groups involved in nuclear exports.

With cartel membership restricted to advanced industrial nations with demonstrated capabilities in the nuclear field, the discriminatory features of such an arrangement would be a source of resentment in developing nations. But it should be emphasized that such a cartel would represent only a marginal change from the present circumstances: nuclear technology is not yet available free of political restraints. Market forces further limit the access to fuel cycle technologies to those nations that can afford the costly capital investment they require. A cartel would simply add another kind of political condition, and in return provide a positive service that would be available even to those without huge capital resources. If the cartel should resort to price-gouging or the manipulation of fuel contract terms, then the incentives for the development of national fuel cycle facilities outside of the cartel would grow irresistibly. This prospect, especially in a field in which a high rate of technological innovation promises to make fuel facilities of very modest dimensions possible and economically attractive, should restrain the cartel from abusing its position.

The very idea of a cartel is, of course, an anathema to many, especially in the United States. Those who continue to define American interests in terms of maximum international free trade could be expected to oppose a cartel as a matter of principle. The nuclear industry might be expected to oppose a cartel for more practical reasons. It might be argued that such an arrangement would simply subject other nations' industries to the same kind of restrictions under which U.S. industry already operates (e.g., the prohibition against the export of fuel facilities). However, the cartelization of the nuclear fuel cycle would demand a continued close supervision of the nuclear industry. In contrast to President Ford's proposed privatization plan, a nuclear cartel would probably require the continued government ownership and management of the uranium enrichment services.

While there are many other problems that remain to be confronted, the idea of a nuclear cartel deserves serious consideration. This is a form of the multinationalization of the nuclear fuel cycle that may be most compatible with established economic interests and patterns of international interaction. It would help retard the international spread of nuclear weapon capabilities. It may be that a nuclear cartel is an idea whose time has come. *(November 1975)*

U.S. Nuclear Export Policy: A Positive First Step
John Gorham Palfrey

The year 1976 may be the first time in history that a presidential election campaign led to a creative and ultimately bipartisan initiative in pursuit of arms control. Usually, the opposite is the case, as it was this year in terms of strategic arms control. In terms of non-proliferation strategy, however, a major change in course was charted—first by Governor Carter and, at the very last moment, by President Ford. The core of this change of direction is the recommendation of both candidates to defer commercial reprocessing and the recycling of plutonium in current U.S. light-water reactors.

At first blush, the domestic decision to defer reprocessing may not seem to be a momentous step in the evolution of U.S. non-proliferation strategy. In purely domestic terms, such a decision could be justified today, in view of escalating costs of large-scale reprocessing, which, together with unresolved environmental, safeguard, and security considerations, have combined to make reprocessing and plutonium recycle a marginal commercial venture at best—although there is sharp disagreement on this point.

On closer examination, however, the major importance of the decision emerges. It is twofold. For the first time in recent years, the full international implications of U.S. domestic decisions in the nuclear power field were recognized and articulated at the presidential level. Second, as a proposal for action that was more than rhetoric, the United States provided to the world the first hard evidence in many years that henceforth commercial considerations would become the instruments, not the masters, of our efforts to contain the spread of nuclear weapons, while meeting world energy needs.

The most prominent recent example of the U.S. failure to take into account the international implications of its domestic decisions was on the issue of uranium enrichment. For the last six years the U.S. government took note of the increased interest by private industry in the enrichment business and focused its attention on meeting domestic uranium enrichment needs instead of upgrading and expanding its gaseous diffusion plants to meet increasing domestic and foreign demands.

Now, the proposals of both candidates plus the increasing congressional support for government construction of a fourth enrichment plant make it clear that top priority will belatedly be given to a government program to reestablish the United States as an assured supplier of enriched uranium to meet its own and the world's nuclear power needs.

In the case of commercial reprocessing, the most important aspect of the two candidates' positions is a tacit one. What Carter, and then Ford, said in effect was that, even if the proponents of reprocessing and recycling are correct on commercial grounds, the non-proliferation priority against reprocessing must prevail. If necessary, we must sacrifice the benefits of a supplementary source of fuel in the face of rising uranium and enrichment costs and even complicate the time-scale in the development of commercial breeder reactors twenty-five years hence (although this is debatable) in order to buy time to deal with the problem of preventing the worldwide spread of plutonium separation capabilities. Thus, the United States has seemed to have decided to concentrate on extending the life of the current light-water reactors, without reprocessing, for the period ahead. Obviously, an expansion of uranium exploration and extraction and of enrichment capabilities is essential, as is the provision of adequate spent fuel storage facilities.

The deferral of U.S. commercial reprocessing will also strengthen the Non-Proliferation Treaty (NPT) regime by reducing its familiar asymmetries between the undertakings and commitments of nuclear weapons states and of non-nuclear weapons states. Developing non-nuclear weapons states which have ratified the NPT and accepted its nuclear safeguards in expectation of nuclear power benefits may be downright insulted to *then* be told they cannot acquire national reprocessing plants at the same time that all of the advanced countries are actively engaged in such reprocessing.

As to the second point—convincing our major allies and principal competitors that we mean what we say in subordinating commercial profits to non-proliferation objectives in urging a common front against the sale of national reprocessing plants—we have a long road to travel. Our handling of uranium enrichment is but one example of recent behavior which has convinced many Europeans that the opposite is the case.

Central to the U.S. decision on reprocessing is our effort to convince the French and the Germans of the danger of selling national reprocessing plants. We have warned that such plants provide the purchaser with direct access to nuclear explosive materials. This makes such plants extraordinarily difficult to safeguard with assurance against a diversion to build bombs, because, even if safeguards could promptly detect diversion of material, the time interval in which to take effective action to prevent the manufacture of nuclear explosives is so much shorter than it is with diversion in other areas of the nuclear fuel cycle.

For a while, the United States sought alternatives to national plants such as the establishment of a few large multinational fuel centers. To date, the response of suppliers and consumers to this idea has been skeptical. Some suppliers have regarded it as a transparent ploy to block the sale of national plants, and some consumers have regarded it as a device to preserve supplier domination and to limit access to reprocessing technology. Moreover, the United States began recently to realize that such large plants might attract Third World interest in reprocessing that otherwise might not exist because they make more economic and technological sense than national plants. Consequently, the U.S. position is now somewhat ambiguous. While still on record in support of multinational fuel centers, we are placing increased emphasis on International Atomic Energy Agency spent fuel storage facilities, rather than full fuel cycle centers.

Meanwhile, the Europeans are actively engaged in reprocessing in the pursuit of breeder reactors. They are unlikely to stop their own activities just because we do. But by our own restraint, we will reinforce our message to France and Germany: "In any case, do not sell reprocessing plants to Third World nations." The Europeans, however, and particularly the Germans, regard this as a "sour grapes" attitude on our part because we lost out in the competition to sell reactors to Brazil. It is difficult for Americans to realize the depth of cynicism in some European circles about U.S. motivations in its warning on the proliferation dangers from advanced nuclear sales.

What should the United States do about this problem? How tough should we get with Western Europe? I would reject out of hand the approach recommended by Senator Abraham Ribicoff (D-Conn.) which would threaten a cut-off of uranium fuel unless the Europeans do what we want. Such an approach would be both counterproductive and at total odds with President-elect Carter's emphasis on strengthening transatlantic relationships. My personal view is that we should keep up the pressure to obtain consensus at the supplier conferences and hammer out a joint policy and, at the same time, that we have a lot more housecleaning to do at home, carried out in the spirit of deferral proposals.

There are reports in the press that France is engaged in a very high-level reassessment of its own non-proliferation strategy. If the French should move toward the U.S. position on the dangers of national reprocessing, my own view is that the German government would reassess its own position on non-proliferation priorities, if identified as the sole hold-out against a supplier's common front.

Suppose, however, in the period ahead, we are successful in achieving a common front on the export of sensitive technology among the suppliers, as we already have achieved on safeguards; suppose we succeed in limiting supplier competition to the sale of reactors, the major hurdle is still ahead of us: how to convince Third World nations that they can meet their nuclear power needs for the next twenty-five years without the need for reprocessing? How can they be convinced that they are not being deprived of access to technology, and that they are not at the mercy of the commercial whims of the developed world? It is one thing to talk about "guaranteed" long-term supplies of enriched fuel at a reasonable cost, it is another to convince the Third World that they can count on it.

There are a number of possible ways to fortify that perception. One would be a firm commitment of fuel to be funneled through, or distributed by, the International Atomic Energy Agency. Another would be an agreement among suppliers for Third World investment participation in existing and future enrichment facilities in order to strengthen the guarantee of an assured supply. A third could be the formal establishment by international agreement of an international enterprise providing fuel services in a separate body established under the aegis of the International Atomic Energy Agency.

Whether or not a formal international entity is established, existing or future fuel centers could provide the opportunity for Third World countries to return their spent fuel to these centers with the provision, in return, of an equivalent value of enriched uranium to fuel their reactors. Another alternative that could emerge from the current International Atomic Energy Agency study of multinational centers could be the preliminary establishment of centralized spent-fuel storage facilities around the world.

In conclusion, it is my judgment that, before the suppliers engage in further governmental and nongovernmental studies of possible ways to meet the nuclear power needs of Third World countries without national reprocessing, we ought to find out how particular Third World countries with nuclear power programs feel about the matter. One way to find out is for the International Atomic Energy Agency to call a meeting of a group of suppliers to meet with a group of such countries (quite separate from the London suppliers conference). The best solution of all would be for one or more enterprising Third World countries to grapple realistically with the problem of nuclear power and non-proliferation and come up with initiatives of their own. One such example was that of Finland, which proposed that receiving countries deal only with suppliers which require full safeguards on the facilities of the purchasing nations. The ultimate route to the containment of the spread of nuclear weapons is the discovery by nations of the world that proliferation is everybody's problem, and that the best solutions are those that are not imposed by anyone on anyone but are arrived at by general consensus. The time has come to encourage the generation of such a consensus. It might just be that nuclear power could then become a bridge to the Third World, rather than a chasm.   (*November 1976*)

Arms Transfers and Nuclear Proliferation
Steven J. Baker

In the continuing controversy over conventional arms transfers to Israel, Iran, and other countries in the Middle East and Persian Gulf, the relationship between conventional arms and nuclear weapons proliferation should be given careful attention. Some observers who favor limits on conventional arms transfers have expressed concern that such limits could have a negative impact on non-proliferation. There are two inter-related propositions which underlie this concern. The first is the notion that conventional arms supplies reduce the incentives for proliferation. The second proposition concerns the impact of conventional arms transfers on countries which have already or are very close to going nuclear—that by increasing conventional capabilities, the nuclear threshold is raised, making the use of nuclear weapons less likely. If one or both of these propositions is accepted, then the United States and other arms suppliers should continue to supply large quantities of conventional weapons to other countries in order to slow the spread of nuclear weapons and reduce the likelihood that existing nuclear weapons will be used in war. In other words, these propositions imply that limits on conventional arms transfers and nuclear non-proliferation may be incompatible goals. While there are instances in which these propositions seem plausible, we should think carefully before accepting them as a general rule or applying them specifically to the Middle East and Persian Gulf. It seems more convincing to argue that, in general, conventional arms buildups whet the appetite for nuclear weapons and that, in particular, the continuing conventional buildup in the Middle East and the Persian Gulf will both encourage further proliferation and increase the likelihood that existing nuclear weapons in these areas will be used in war.

Before accepting the first proposition, we must ask if conventional weapons are a substitute for nuclear weapons. American strategic doctrine has usually emphasized the reverse, i.e., that nuclear weapons can substitute for conventional capabilities—from strategic air power in the 1950s to tactical nuclear weapons in Europe today. In the past, both the Russians and the Chinese have advocated the superiority of conventional capabilities over nuclear, but both have proceeded to develop their own nuclear weapons. The great powers' own example suggests that militarily conventional forces and nuclear forces are complementary. But perhaps even more important, conventional capabilities do not substitute for the political influence and prestige which are perceived to accrue to possessors of nuclear weapons.

In the Middle East and Persian Gulf, conventional arms transfers have helped to create large, effective military establishments with a dominant claim on the resources of their nations. Trained by the great powers and schooled in the military dogmas of the great powers, these military establishments are likely to see nuclear weapons as a complement to the nuclear-capable delivery systems which they are importing at an increasingly fast rate. These kinds of military establishments are already in power in many of the Middle Eastern countries; in the future, they may come to power in the Persian Gulf and in the process may call into question the political commitments of the nonmilitary regimes they replace, including commitments like membership in the NPT. This is plausible since various Third World countries have argued that foregoing nuclear weapons raises security problems for non-nuclear states which have no superpower nuclear security guarantees and which are faced with nuclear-armed adversaries. However, no amount of conventional

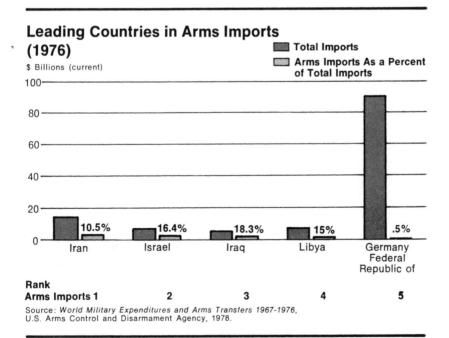

Leading Countries in Arms Imports (1976)

$ Billions (current)

■ Total Imports
☐ Arms Imports As a Percent of Total Imports

Source: *World Military Expenditures and Arms Transfers 1967-1976*, U.S. Arms Control and Disarmament Agency, 1978.

arms aid—however massive—can solve this problem, a case made clear by Egypt and Syria. Therefore, limits on conventional arms shipments to these areas are not in contradiction with non-proliferation policies but are instead a necessary part of a comprehensive, effective non-proliferation policy.

The second proposition, that large levels of conventional arms raise the nuclear threshold, is called into question by the Israeli example. It is widely conceded that Israel may have between five and twenty nuclear weapons. Even those who hesitate to accept this judgment concede that Israel is only a matter of hours away from having nuclear weapons. American and Israeli officials have good reasons for publicly refusing to acknowledge that this is the case, but Israel's potential adversaries cannot ignore this probability nor should analysts of conventional arms supply policies. It is difficult to imagine that any level of conventional arms will succeed in convincing Israel's potential adversaries, Egypt and Syria, that nuclear weapons are not necessary for their national defense and political objectives. Therefore their motivation to go nuclear also increases.

There is an important related question: will continued conventional arms shipments make it less likely that Israel will be forced to use the nuclear weapons it may have acquired? While this seems to be a logical extension of the flexible response kind of thinking, it ignores the assumption that small, primitive nuclear forces are very vulnerable and therefore exceedingly provocative. The existence of such a force in the event of conflict creates strong incentives for early or pre-emptive use of nuclear weapons by Israel or for surprise attack by Israel's enemies in order to knock out the nuclear weapons before they can be used. In either case, the existence of such a force is destabilizing. Providing the conventional military capabilities which enhance a pre-emptive or surprise attack from either side only adds to the instability of the region.

Worst of all is the example set for others by the continued conventional arms shipments to an Israel regarded as armed with nuclear weapons. Far from being a substitute for conventional arms, Israel's bombs in the basement appear to be an effective means for assuring continuing supplies of conventional arms from the United States. Israel is being rewarded either *because of* or *in spite of* the fact that it has gone nuclear. In either case, the lesson will not be lost on Egypt, Iran, and other nations around the world.

As long as American arms supply policy appears to be based on a misleading linkage between conventional arms sales and nuclear proliferation, there will be incentives for other nations in the Middle East and Persian Gulf to go nuclear in order to guarantee conventional arms supplies and to acquire or match the political influence and prestige of adversaries. The primitive characteristics of these nuclear forces make it likely that they will be used in future conflict. These are all additional reasons to impose restrictions on arms transfers in order to implement nonproliferation objectives. (*April 1977*)

Carter's Antiproliferation Strategy   *Robert Brennis*

High worldwide interest in nuclear power and controversy about the nuclear future have meant uneven success for the Carter administration's efforts to prevent the proliferation of nuclear weapons capability. The Carter program for achieving adequate energy without promoting proliferation is a long-range one, however, and time may be on its side. The administration's strategy is to retard the commercial development and spread of breeder reactors and nuclear fuel enrichment or reprocessing plants (all of which produce potential weapons material) while seeking an internationally acceptable nuclear fuel cycle that can easily be safeguarded against diversion of materials for nuclear explosives. Recognizing that the non-proliferation regime for the first generation of nuclear power technology is inadequate for the coming generation of plutonium-fueled fast breeder reactors, the Carter approach is founded on the

---

Carter's Seven-Point Non-Proliferation Program

1. Defer indefinitely commercial reprocessing and recycling of plutonium from U.S. nuclear power programs.
2. Restructure the U.S. breeder reactor program, giving greater priority to alternative breeder designs and deferring the date when the breeder would be put into commercial use.
3. Redirect U.S. nuclear research and development funding to accelerate research into nuclear fuel cycles not involving direct access to material usable in nuclear weapons.
4. Increase U.S. production capacity for enriched uranium to provide an adequate and timely supply of nuclear fuels for domestic and foreign needs.
5. Propose legislation to permit the United States to offer nuclear fuel supply contracts and delivery guarantees to other countries.
6. Continue to embargo the export of U.S. equipment or technology permitting uranium enrichment and chemical reprocessing.
7. Continue discussions with nuclear exporting and importing countries on international frameworks permitting nations to meet their energy objectives while reducing growth in the number of countries which are capable of producing nuclear explosive devices.

---

expectation that the age of the breeder is still some distance in the future, allowing time for alternative technologies to mature, if they begin to receive support now.

The administration approach is faulted by antinuclear and environmental groups, who doubt that nuclear power can be made safe, and by many foreign governments, the nuclear industry, some congressmen and even by officials within the administration, who see rapid commercialization of breeder reactor technology as the solution to energy cost and dependence and who doubt there is a technical answer for the problem of nuclear weapons proliferation. Since President Carter's April 1977 announcement of his seven-point anti-proliferation program, international criticism has been voiced at the Transfer of Nuclear Technology Conference in Iran, the Salzburg Conference on Nuclear Power and Its Fuel Cycle in May and, most recently, at the World Energy Conference held in September in Istanbul.

International resistance to the Carter program may have peaked with the September meeting in London of the two-year-old Nuclear Suppliers Conference. The exporting group, now enlarged to fifteen countries, confirmed its earlier accord on conditions for the sale of current-generation nuclear technology. Also discussed were mutual sanctions against nations which fail to honor these conditions of sale. At the meeting, the United States abandoned as unrealistic Ford administration efforts to achieve agreement on banning the export of uranium enrichment and reprocessing facilities. With the United Kingdom and the Soviet Union, the United States has proposed "full fuel cycle safeguards" or "full scope safeguards" permitting International Atomic Energy Agency inspectors to examine imported nuclear reactors, as well as associated facilities (fuel rod fabrication plants and fuel reprocessing plants)

Nuclear Suppliers Conference: Major Agreed Principles

For any supplied material, the buyer must agree to

—accept the safeguards of the International Atomic Energy Authority,

—forswear using the material supplied for peaceful nuclear explosions,

—demonstrate the ability to safeguard the material against theft or sabotage,

—forgo copying imported facilities in order to evade the safeguard commitments, and

—transfer nuclear facilities or technology to a third country only under the same conditions agreed to by the original importing nation.

whether or not they were imported. France and West Germany have objected to these safeguards, apparently out of concern that they would limit the growth of the nuclear market.

Responding to a perception that its approach is heavy on "denials" and lacks "incentives," the administration has been stressing the International Nuclear Fuel Cycle Evaluation program. Meeting in Washington in October, some thirty-five suppliers and buyers of nuclear technology began a two-year scientific and economic analysis of eight aspects of the nuclear fuel cycle. Officials hope this tour of the technological horizon will reveal nuclear alternatives. At the same time, increasing the efficiency of current nuclear fuel utilization, expanding known uranium reserves, and solving the nuclear waste disposal problem would prolong the use of available thermal reactor technology and reduce interest in rapid commercialization of the breeder technology that exists today.

As the International Nuclear Fuel Cycle Evaluation analysis got under way, President Carter announced two other incentives. To insure an adequate supply of nuclear fuel for responsible consuming nations, the United States will boost enrichment capacity and aid in establishing an international nuclear fuel bank, so that, if there is a temporary breakdown in bilateral supply of nuclear fuel, a reservoir will exist to meet a nation's needs. To help foreign and domestic nuclear plants with waste disposal problems, the President also offered to store wastes in the United States until a safe means can be found for their use or disposal. Though this may reduce pressures for nuclear waste reprocessing, the selectivity of this policy and transportation and storage charges may reduce its appeal to foreign and domestic producers.

The administration and its supporters in Congress were unable to secure passage of an anti-proliferation bill in 1977. Although officials believe most administration initiatives can be pursued without legislation,

International Nuclear Fuel Cycle Evaluation: Working Groups

Working Group Title	Number of countries participating
Fuel Availability	29
Enrichment Availability	19
Supply Assurances: Technology, Fuel and Services	32
Reprocessing, Plutonium, and Recycling	22
Faster Breeder Reactors	16
Spent Fuel Management	19
Waste Management and Disposal	27
Advanced Concepts	23

they wanted a bill this year, lest other nations become "reluctant to renegotiate their [nuclear export] agreements with us because they fear that new legislation might suddenly change the terms of cooperation." Among the issues in the bill were stiff provisions for "timely warning" safeguards and banning national nuclear fuel reprocessing centers. The executive did not want its hands tied diplomatically, while the nuclear industry objected to possible constraints on sales.

In November 1977 the President vetoed legislation authorizing the Clinch River breeder reactor, a commercial feasibility demonstration project which the administration calls "inconsistent" with its anti-proliferation program. Although the Congress voted $80 million to keep the project alive, energy officials believe its progress has been substantially slowed, if not halted.

Despite only partial success in dampening pressures for rapid development of breeder and associated technologies, supporters of a strong non-proliferation policy believe an unrestricted plutonium age may be as much as a decade away. The weak state of the nuclear industry domestically and internationally, its limited capacity to produce export hardware, the steady expansion of known uranium reserves, and the time required to build demonstration and then commercial plants may combine to delay the widespread commercialization of breeder technology. This could provide the Carter administration with the time to find—and convince others of the necessity for—a nuclear power technology with adequate safeguards against nuclear weapons proliferation.

(November 1977)

Nuclear Testing: Time for a Halt
Edward M. Kennedy

On May 17, 1974, India exploded a nuclear device, the sixth country to do so. And even if India does not make a true bomb—as it has promised not to do—we must now face with greater urgency the critical issue of a world of many nuclear powers. For that reason among others, I strongly support the negotiation now of a comprehensive ban on all nuclear testing.

The Partial Test Ban Treaty of 1963 is now almost eleven years old. Since then, there has been little progress in extending the ban on testing that was then agreed for the atmosphere, space, and underwater. In the intervening years, the pace of underground testing was actually stepped up periodically by both the United States and the Soviet Union. Now interest has been revived in further limits on nuclear testing. I believe a comprehensive test ban treaty is particularly important and attractive at this time, when the immediate prospects for revising the 1972 Interim Agreement on offensive strategic weapons are so bleak.

A comprehensive test ban has several attractions. *First,* it would complement the agreements reached at SALT I, by making it more difficult for either superpower to make major qualitative improvements in their nuclear arsenals. If all testing were stopped, at least this would dampen fears on either side that the other would gain a high degree of confidence in some new generation of first-strike weapons.

Second, there is the matter of political will itself. The atmosphere surrounding both detente and the possibilities for arms control would be helped if there were some agreement at the forthcoming Moscow summit. I believe that promoting that constructive atmosphere, so hard won, is particularly important at this time, when there is widespread questioning in the United States (and apparently in the Soviet Union, as well) about the real basis for improved Soviet-American relations. In addition to its own merits, therefore, a comprehensive test ban would demonstrate that the United States and the Soviet Union are both still committed to real limits on arms. In fact, it might then be easier to break the log-jam at SALT II on revising the Interim Agreement. This reasoning may explain the strong support for a comprehensive test ban which Soviet leaders expressed to me during my recent trip to Moscow—about which I will say more later.

Third, a comprehensive test ban would reinforce the Non-Proliferation Treaty (NPT), which is due for review next year. Many non-nuclear nations have branded the NPT as unfair to them. They have given up nuclear weapons, along with whatever political and military benefits these weapons seem to confer, while the superpowers forge ahead in their own arms race.

A comprehensive test ban would be a major indicator of the good faith of the major powers, if they are determined to prevent the spread of nuclear weapons. Such a demonstration of good faith is particularly important now that India has become the sixth power to explode a nuclear device. Will there be more? In part, the answer to this question will depend on what the superpowers do to show restraint—whether or not India, China, or other countries continue to test.

The continuation of underground testing also weakens the efforts of the United States and Soviet Union to bring France and China into real discussions on arms control. A comprehensive test ban on its own would not prevent proliferation or lead to broader arms control talks; but it could be a significant step on the way.

Finally, a comprehensive test ban would permit some savings in the nuclear weapons programs of both superpowers, to be applied to other uses, and end the remaining environmental hazards from underground testing. While such hazards are not the overriding reason for banning all tests, about one-fifth of our tests have vented, sending radioactive particles into the air. In addition, the side effects of massive explosions deep within the earth's crust are still not fully known, according to the Pitzer Panel, appointed by the President's Office of Science and Technology.

Many of these arguments for a comprehensive test ban treaty were reflected in talks I had with Soviet leaders in Moscow during April. In these talks, they shifted their position on an important point. They are no longer insisting that France and China join a comprehensive test ban at the outset. Rather they are prepared to reach agreement with us now and then seek the support of other nations. To be sure, Soviet leaders told me they want an escape clause, in the event that France and China do not respond. (Such clauses have become standard in most arms control agreements.) And it is important for us not to allow a comprehensive test ban to be used as a weapon in the diplomatic conflict between the Soviet Union and China. But Soviet leaders also agreed that such a ban could be an important step forward, symbolizing our shared concern to limit the race in nuclear arms.

Yet what assurance is there that the Soviet Union would not test nuclear weapons in secret? To begin with, our ability to detect underground nuclear weapons tests has improved considerably during the past decade (and the Soviet Union has frequently expressed a willingness to rely on national means of verification). In fact, testimony before the Senate Arms Control Subcommittee—from a variety of sources—has supported the conclusion that we have a greater capacity now to detect and identify nuclear explosions through national means alone than we would have had in 1963, even with the seven on-site inspections a year that we then demanded. There is widespread belief that current developments in seismology alone would enable us to detect and identify explosions having a yield of only a few kilotons. And this does not take into account satellite reconnaissance and other techniques to gather information. In addition, the Soviet Union would always be uncertain of our capabilities. And, being uncertain, Soviet leaders would have to calculate the risks—and the consequences—of being caught at cheating. With so much else at stake in arms control and in our bilateral relations, these risks and consequences would weigh heavily on them. This would be especially so since the benefits to be gained from cheating—some improvements in low-yield weapons—are most unlikely to bring any marked advantage in the nuclear arms balance.

I believe, therefore, that the issue of verification no longer need stand in the way of further limits on nuclear testing by the superpowers. Consequently, I have introduced a Senate resolution calling for a mutual moratorium on all nuclear testing by the United States and the Soviet Union, followed by the conclusion of a comprehensive test ban treaty, that I hope will be negotiated in time for the Moscow summit this summer. At the time of writing, this resolution has thirty-six cosponsors, and has been cleared for Senate action by the Foreign Relations Committee.

Press reports on preparations for the forthcoming summit, however, indicate that the administration is seeking only a "threshold" test ban— that is, a limit on tests producing a seismic signal above a given magnitude. Of course, for the political and psychological reasons I have advanced above, even a threshold treaty which genuinely ruled out major changes in strategic weaponry could still be valuable. But even a threshold treaty set at a low level would be less desirable than a complete ban on testing by the superpowers.

First, it is not clear that a threshold treaty would be enough to demonstrate the commitment of the superpowers to end their arms race. Would India have tested a nuclear device if Washington and Moscow had signed a comprehensive test ban treaty? We cannot know, although India long demanded this progress as the price of its own forbearance. Its recent action, therefore, should increase our desire to regulate the superpower arms race—with a *comprehensive*, rather than another *partial*, test ban agreement.

Second, a threshold treaty would be even more difficult to monitor than a comprehensive test ban, since it would require a precision in seismic detection that is not needed when the issue is one of verifying whether or not there has been a nuclear explosion of any size at all. Disagreements on such technicalities could very well lead to more political tension, not less.

Third, the level of the threshold would tend to be set by arms developers rather than by arms controllers. As long as some level of testing is permitted, there will be strong pressures to test up to the limits (as happened with the Partial Test Ban Treaty)—even if quotas were imposed on the number of tests each power could make each year. There would also be a tendency to refine nuclear weapons arsenals even further—especially in the area of tactical weapons. This could lead to a blurring of the distinction between nuclear and non-nuclear weapons.

Finally, will the Soviet Union accept a threshold ban that would be a real improvement on the present Partial Test Ban Treaty? Since the Soviet Union generally tests weapons larger than ours, a threshold ban would tend to favor U.S. weapons developments, and could raise doubts in Soviet minds about our sincerity in wanting to advance mutual interests in this area.

For all these reasons, I believe that a threshold ban would be far from the best answer in the area of controlling nuclear testing. I have urged the administration to pursue a comprehensive test ban to the limits of negotiation, before turning to a less desirable alternative. And I believe that it can be negotiated this year. (*May 1974*)

Why Not a Real Nuclear Test Ban?
Thomas A. Halsted

In May 1976, the Arms Control Association issued a formal statement on two recently negotiated treaties with the Soviet Union—the July 1974 Threshold Test Ban Treaty and the May 1976 treaty on peaceful nuclear explosions. The Arms Control Association criticized both treaties, arguing that, by legitimizing the continued explosion of large nuclear devices, the treaties were a step backward from a comprehensive test ban. The association called on President Ford to reopen negotiations toward a comprehensive test ban treaty. Halsted's article details the Arms Control Association's critique.

On May 28, 1976, in separate ceremonies in Washington, D.C., and Moscow, President Ford and Soviet General Secretary Leonid Brezhnev signed a Treaty on Underground Explosions for Peaceful Purposes (the "PNE" Treaty). It was negotiated as a companion agreement to a Treaty on the Limitation of Underground Nuclear Weapon Tests (the Threshold Test Ban or the "TTB" Treaty). Both treaties are to be submitted to the Senate for ratification. Why can't we quit testing nuclear weapons? In thirty-one years the United States and Soviet Union alone have conducted more than 1,000 nuclear tests between them, yet by agreeing to these two treaties they are declaring that there is a need for still more. Meanwhile a growing number of critics in the United States and abroad are complaining that agreements like the TTB and PNE treaties, in the guise of setting new controls, are really only devices for setting new rules for both sides to continue doing as they please. As the Arms Control Association statement points out, the limits imposed by the treaties are hardly limits at all. (There is even an escape clause in the PNE Treaty—Article III, Paragraph 3, allowing for tests larger than the 150 kiloton ceiling: "The question of carrying out an individual explosion having a yield exceeding [150 kilotons] . . . will be considered by the Parties at an appropriate time to be agreed.") Is it any wonder that some critics of the treaties call them worse than nothing?

The reasons that the Threshold Test Ban and Peaceful Nuclear Explosion Treaties are inadequate are spelled out in the ACA statement. The case for the harder, but only acceptable course—a complete test ban—is not a complicated one.

Simply put, a comprehensive test ban would be a clear and unambiguous signal that the nuclear weapons states were at last willing to take a major step away from the nuclear brink. Since the nuclear weapons age began, only one of the arms control agreements between the nuclear superpowers—the 1972 Anti-Ballistic Missile Treaty—has resulted in stopping nuclear weapons development. After nearly twenty years of negotiations, the failure to achieve a comprehensive nuclear test ban treaty has become a symbol of superpower unwillingness to end a wasteful and destructive arms race which has produced more and more lethal weaponry, but has only diminished world security. Agreeing to a comprehensive test ban would be a positive sign that the United States and the Soviet Union were at last moving away from dependence on nuclear weapons and from the belief that the possession of nuclear weapons is the hallmark of a great power and that nuclear wars are thinkable, fightable, and even winnable.

Three of the six countries that have conducted nuclear tests are parties to the Treaty on the Non-Proliferation of Nuclear Weapons (the NPT). Year after year since that treaty went into effect, and particularly at the 1975 NPT Review Conference, the non-nuclear weapons states party to the treaty have warned the nuclear weapons states that they cannot go on forever building up nuclear arsenals, threatening to use nuclear weapons, and, most of all, continuing to test nuclear weapons while still expecting other nations to agree to forego nuclear weapons of their own. A comprehensive test ban would undeniably be a symbolic gesture towards these critics. By itself it would not end the arms race, but it would be a symbol badly needed if mankind is to avoid almost certain destruction at his own hand.

The Threshold Test Ban, like the Limited Test Ban and the Non-Proliferation Treaty, gives lip service to a commitment to end all nuclear weapons testing, but neither the United States nor the USSR has adopted a public position which would make achievement of a comprehensive test ban treaty realistic. The United States contends that it would be possible for the USSR to conduct militarily significant tests in secret unless the treaty included a provision for on-site inspection to resolve any ambiguities. The USSR asserts that such inspections are unnecessary but insists on the right to conduct peaceful nuclear explosions and further declares that all nuclear weapons states must be party to a comprehensive ban—a condition to which China and France, neither of them a party to the 1963 Limited Test Ban or the Non-Proliferation Treaty, are unlikely to agree.

Both sides' arguments are a smokescreen for a more basic objection to a comprehensive test ban: neither the United States nor the USSR wants to give up the option to conduct nuclear weapons tests. As far as the capability of identifying small nuclear tests is concerned, it is highly improbable that the Soviet Union could confidently conduct clandestine, *militarily important* nuclear tests without detection by a combination of seismic and other intelligence means—chiefly photographic satellites. On-site inspection is no longer necessary. Furthermore, a test ban observed by only the United States and Soviet Union, without the participation of other nuclear weapons states, would not affect the security interests of either superpower for many years, regardless of the amount of testing France or China conducted. The utility of peaceful nuclear explosions is so dubious that further efforts should be made to persuade the USSR to shelve its peaceful nuclear explosion program, as the United States already has. In no event should the unlikely prospect that nuclear explosions might some day prove to be useful be allowed to stand in the way of a ban on all nuclear tests.

A recent Energy Research and Development Administration report (*Funding and Management Alternatives for Energy Research and Development Administration Military Applications and Restricted Data Functions,* Washington, D.C.: Publication No. 97, 1976) provides for the first time some public details of the accomplishments of thirty years of U.S. nuclear testing: seventy-four different types of weapons have been tested, fifty of them accepted in the stockpile at one time or another, twenty-six of them currently in the stockpile in thirty-three different weapons systems. It can be assumed that Soviet weapons development is at a comparable level of diversity. There is hardly any theoretically possible development that has not been explored by now, at least by the two superpowers, and scant reason to expect such developments in the future. To be sure, weapons designers can always come up with new concepts to explore; under a comprehensive test ban treaty, they would have to make do with existing designs. Under the 150 kiloton TTB, in fact, the Energy Research and Development Administration report acknowledges that such adaptation would be necessary for any higher-yield weapons that might be required.

Large and well established bureaucracies exist in the United States and the Soviet Union which have an unavoidable vested interest in the continuation of nuclear weapons programs, including testing. According to the Energy Research and Development report, last year the "weapons complex"—the U.S. weapons laboratories, the Nevada Test Site, and the seven government-owned plants which produce nuclear weapons—"employed more than 40,000 people, had an operating budget of more than a billion dollars, and represented an investment of more than $2.6 billion." In the event of a comprehensive nuclear test ban, many of these individuals, a large number of whom may have devoted their entire lives to nuclear weapons, would need to acquire new skills and seek work elsewhere. They and their supporters in the executive branch and Congress could be expected strongly to oppose a comprehensive test ban. In a recent speech, Lieutenant General Edward B. Giller, director of weapons development for the Energy Research and Development Administration, expressed his concern about this possibility: "Above all we must not allow the nuclear weapons development and production complex to erode. In many respects this complex is unique and some of the assets are unreplaceable. The weapons laboratories represent a combination of trained manpower and physical resources that is available nowhere else in the West." This narrow view—one that has prevailed until now—suggests that ending nuclear testing, because it means foreclosing options to test in the future, is *ipso facto* a bad thing for the United States. But would a comprehensive ban really hinder national security? There are scarcely any new developments "interesting" enough to justify further weapons testing; a test ban would inhibit Soviet as much as U.S. developments. The security issue therefore becomes one of whether the United States is better off in a situation where neither side is testing than in one where both continue to test. Since the present trend in U.S. weapons development is toward more accurate delivery systems rather than higher yields, future concerns lie more in missile guidance developments than in nuclear weapon testing. If there are possible "breakthroughs" ahead, a comprehensive test ban would inhibit their likelihood for both the United States and the USSR.

Finally, it has been suggested that to reject the TTB and PNE Treaties would be damaging to detente, already battered badly out of shape. But would it? Why would it not be more constructive for the United States and USSR to agree to work out a test ban treaty with real arms control significance, rather than a transparent phony? Because the TTB and PNE Treaties are so inadequate, they tend to devalue detente, rather than enhance it, and serve further to erode public support. However, if the two nations, which have been engaged in a devastating nuclear arms race for over thirty years, were instead jointly to take the first meaningful step toward ending that race, that would have more meaning for detente—not only for the two adversaries, but also for the entire world—than any step yet taken.

There is another aspect of the detente/arms control issue to remember: even if there were no detente and relations between the two countries were far worse than they are today, arms control measures would *still* be in our net interest. We can survive with detente in a weakened condition, as long as we are honestly pursuing means of ending the arms race. The reverse is simply not the case.

The Threshold Test Ban and Peaceful Nuclear Explosion Treaties are more likely to prove to be stumbling blocks than stepping stones toward a comprehensive test ban. The TTB is an idea whose time is past; linking the PNE Treaty to it has insured that no comprehensive test ban will be possible as long as the Soviet Union maintains an interest in peaceful nuclear explosions. It is time to put aside peaceful nuclear explosions as a costly and unnecessary obstacle to at last fulfill a thirteen-year-old commitment, first stated in the preamble to the Limited Test Ban Treaty, "to achieve the discontinuance of all test explosions of all nuclear weapons for all time." *(June 1976)*

A Comprehensive Test Ban As a Prelude to SALT II
John B. Rhinelander

We are living in a volatile period of shifting political coalitions—composed of new interest groups, executive bureaucrats, and congressional staffers—which form around policy issues. This iron triangle, with political leadership provided by different members of Congress as issues change, frequently seems, and sometimes is, more potent than presidents, who are unable to exercise coherent leadership with the consistent support of stable voting blocs. Foreign affairs issues are not immune to this debilitating condition.

The Panama Canal Treaties provide an example. While the President and the bipartisan leadership of the Senate worked together and with the near-unanimous support of the foreign policy establishment, they had to scratch hard for the necessary two-thirds votes, compromising the negotiated texts in the process, with changes almost unacceptable to Panama. Some observers have suggested—and many senators accept the notion— that the mass mailing, political fund-raising and similar activities of ad hoc groups have made it possible for affirmative votes on issues like these treaties to threaten a political career.

For all their value in dealing with a long-festering problem, the Panama Canal treaties are a dangerous prelude to congressional review of SALT II (Strategic Arms Limitation Talks), particularly in light of the process of attaching reservations. Senators who voted for the treaties may be politically exposed and under pressure to show their independence and to reassure conservative groups in their constituencies. Moreover, the congressional leadership may well be split on SALT, and the foreign policy establishment is clearly divided.

A crater is visible over the area where an underground atomic detonation has just taken place in this 1969 photo at the Nevada Test Site. This is the first still photograph ever taken of a crater collapse.

Source: Department of Energy and Los Alamos Scientific Laboratory

President Carter was preoccupied with Panama and, like President Ford in January 1976, let SALT slip; this month's trip to Moscow by Secretary of State Cyrus Vance may be too late. The President's defense posture statement and budget, while gaining near unanimous support for augmenting NATO forces, is under vigorous attack from various quarters. Soviet activities first in Angola, and now in the Horn of Africa, when coupled with their overall military buildup, have increased distrust of the Soviets and prompted serious debate among "experts" in and out of government over Soviet intent and U.S. responses. The President's chief SALT negotiator, who is as able, skillful, and articulate as any in Washington, still carries the burden of the forty negative votes from his acrimonious confirmation. The President's credibility, both at home and abroad, has been further harmed by the neutron bomb decision-making process.

Above all, if a SALT II agreement follows soon after the Panama Canal Treaties, senators will again be called upon to vote on a controversial international agreement, involving perceptions of the essence of our national defense, which will have very vocal constituent group opposition. All Senators are now schooled in the art of adding amendments, reservations, and interpretation by a majority vote of the Senate, whether "killer" or not. A clear danger is that a SALT II agreement would be "approved" in principle by the Senate but conditioned with reservations that would be unacceptable to the President, the Soviets, or both.

Some strong advocates of SALT read the political tea leaves differently, arguing that the approval of the Panama Canal Treaties and the lessons learned from that exercise provide an auspicious climate for consideration of SALT II. There are persuasive reasons for believing otherwise and for adopting a different strategy in presenting a SALT agreement to the nation.

A SALT agreement concluded this year and submitted for Senate ratification during 1979 would make SALT, and "trust" of the Soviets, a political issue in the 1978 fall campaigns and frame nuclear arms control in a narrow bilateral context. While it appears true that the Soviets now want a SALT II agreement as much as, if not more than the United States, the political compromises necessary by both sides to reach final agreement are probably unacceptable to a blocking minority in the Senate, who could thwart ratification of a treaty if SALT II stands alone.

One approach which should be considered is to lead with a comprehensive nuclear test ban treaty which is, in fact, comprehensive. This would significantly increase non-proliferation restraints—an objective broadly supported both by the public at large and in the Congress—and also would impose qualitative constraints on the programs of the United

States, the Soviet Union and other nuclear weapons states that become parties. A comprehensive nuclear test ban, if negotiable along the lines of the present U.S. position, would not be without controversy. On the contrary, the issues of reliability testing of fission trigger mechanisms and the ability to verify Soviet compliance are now the focus of an intense and urgent review within the administration. The secretary of defense, with support from the scientific community, will have to recommend, and the President agree, that a complete ban on nuclear testing represents an acceptable risk for the United States which is offset by the non-proliferation gains. Under these circumstances, a comprehensive test ban would be preferable to SALT II as an international agreement for initiating a public debate in the United States over, and Senate consideration of, nuclear weapons control.

To date, the administration and the press appear to be focusing as a first priority on SALT II rather than on a comprehensive test ban. This may reflect a judgment as to which will probably be concluded first rather than a tactical decision to give a lower priority to a test ban treaty. The case for SALT II would be strengthened in the eyes of the public, however, by conclusion and ratification of a comprehensive test ban. This could well be a case of leading from comparative strength with an agreement which is more comprehensible to the general public.

However, there are considerations more compelling than tactical matters for giving a comprehensive test ban treaty a high priority at this time. In signing the Limited Test Ban Treaty (LTBT) in 1963, the United States and the Soviet Union committed themselves to seek "the discontinuance of all test explosions of nuclear weapons for all time," not only in the atmosphere but also underground. While President Eisenhower had even earlier urged this course, fifteen years after the conclusion of the LTBT this goal remains unachieved. Yet, in the intervening period, the technical and political barriers to a treaty prohibiting all nuclear weapons tests have shrunk and the incentives for such a comprehensive test ban have grown significantly. A review of the technical and political factors suggests that it is now in the interest of the U.S. and Soviet governments to pursue the conclusion of a comprehensive test ban as a matter of special priority and not merely as a prelude to SALT II.

Political considerations—both international and domestic—provide numerous incentives for concluding a test ban in the near future. Among the most important of these considerations for the current nuclear weapons states is the problem of nuclear proliferation. The spread of nuclear weapons affects the security of all nations, and especially the current nuclear powers, in direct and fundamental ways. An increasing number of non-nuclear weapons states have approached or crossed the technological and economic thresholds which formerly placed nuclear weapons beyond their reach. The spread of nuclear power technology and, less often noticed, the spread of sophisticated weapons systems, such as new fighter-bombers and precision-guided munitions, have contributed to a situation in which a sizeable number of countries can realistically consider a nuclear weapons option. Since even a nuclear weapons state's security depends not only on its own resources and military capacity but also on the stability of the surrounding international community, the major powers have a vital interest in avoiding a world of additional nuclear weapons states.

The non-nuclear weapons states are less and less constrained to forego the nuclear weapons option as they see the technological, military, and economic obstacles to nuclear weapons dwindle and as they consider the continuing refusal of the nuclear weapons states to forego weapons testing and other reductions in their own arsenals. The attitudes of the nuclear weapons states often appear to provide an incentive for going nuclear by substantiating the apparent political and military importance of nuclear weapons. The double standard explicit in the Non-Proliferation Treaty (NPT) becomes more evident, and forbearance less compelling, to the non-nuclear weapons states.

The effect of the many non-proliferation activities instigated by the nuclear weapons states—the International Nuclear Fuel Cycle Evaluation study, the Nuclear Suppliers Group's safeguards, the multilateral nuclear reactor fuel bank, and similar initiatives—may be vitiated by the failure of the international community to prohibit testing of nuclear weapons, which should be a primary focus of a non-proliferation strategy. The forthcoming United Nations Special Session on Disarmament in May and June 1978 will in large measure be a forum for the non-nuclear weapons states to castigate the superpowers for this failure, which, intentionally or unintentionally, has built an international case for any country which decides to go nuclear. Moreover, while it is far from clear that non-signatories of the LTBT and NPT—France and China in particular—would adhere to a comprehensive testing ban, it is certain that they will not limit their own test programs in the absence of such a total ban.

In short, a comprehensive test ban is now more than ever an indispensable element in any serious and realistic non-proliferation strategy, and a serious non-proliferation strategy is indispensable to American security, as well as the security of the world we inhabit. In addition, both the United States and the Soviet Union have significant domestic incentives—economic and institutional—for giving special attention to a comprehensive test ban treaty at this moment.

As recent studies by the Central Intelligence Agency and the Congressional Research Service document, the strategic nuclear arms race and the comparatively higher cost of defense in the Soviet Union impose burdens on an already faltering Soviet economy and on the leadership's goal of achieving the status of an economic superpower. The seriousness with which the Soviet Union now views horizontal nuclear weapons proliferation among the non-nuclear weapons states (which pose a more serious threat to the Soviet Union than to the United States) is evidenced by the three major concessions the Soviet leadership has recently made to obtain a comprehensive test ban. First, they have given up their long-standing insistence that peaceful nuclear explosions be permitted by agreeing to a moratorium on *all* nuclear explosions, including peaceful ones, until such time as peaceful explosions may prove to be economically or technically feasible. This will permit a truly complete test ban treaty for now, although the duration of the moratorium and the way in which it will be stated is apparently still under negotiation. Second, the Soviets have retreated from their position that, to go into effect, a test ban must have as signatories all nuclear weapons states, including France and China. Finally, the Soviet Union has softened its opposition to on-site inspections. In March 1977, General Secretary Leonid Brezhnev said, "In order to clear the road to agreement, (the USSR) is ready for on-the-spot inspections on a voluntary basis, in the event of any doubts concerning the fulfillment of treaty commitments." Foreign Minister Andrei Gromyko made a similar offer in September 1976, before the United Nations General Assembly. The details of this commitment must, of course, be pursued in actual negotiations. Advances in technology make it possible to detect seismic events—either earthquakes or explosions—and to identify whether they are nuclear or not, so that there would rarely be a need for on-site inspections. Nevertheless, Soviet willingness to submit to on-site inspections in rare cases of ambiguous events greatly increases political confidence in the feasibility of a comprehensive test ban treaty. Provision could be made in the treaty, or in a separate agreement among the nuclear weapons states, for on-site inspection if a doubt as to the character of a seismic event should arise.

Removal of these major roadblocks not only opens the way to conclusion of a meaningful and verifiable agreement, but it also reflects the strength of the Soviet desire to achieve a comprehensive test ban treaty. While the Soviets may be slow in reaching agreements and are "legalistic" with respect to the constraints of nonbinding provisions, their compliance with the SALT I agreements and dialogue over ambiguous events in the Standing Consultative Commission established in SALT I is encouraging, as the recent unclassified report on compliance with those agreements attests.

Similarly, in addition to the continuing national security imperatives of reducing the probability of nuclear war and the spread of nuclear weapons, there are specific political reasons from the U.S. perspective for pursuing a test ban at this juncture.

Conclusion of a test ban should improve the technical setting (and ultimately the political setting) since elimination of nuclear weapons tests by the superpowers will reduce the extremely high confidence levels required for a disarming first strike or surprise attack. Since lower levels of confidence are adequate for a second strike or retaliatory attack, an effective comprehensive test ban should reduce U.S. first-strike fears and perceptions of Soviet incentives. This will not only help stabilize the nuclear balance but also undercut arguments for counterforce weapons.

At the same time, conclusion of a truly "comprehensive" test ban treaty is fully compatible with the President's decision to defer production of the neutron warhead. While a comprehensive test ban would not prohibit production or deployment, it would retard development across the board, both in the United States and in the Soviet Union, of the whole family of enhanced radiation weapons, of which artillery shells with "neutron" warheads are the most prominent example.

Finally, a comprehensive test ban agreed upon by the United States, the United Kingdom and the Soviet Union, and open to all nations to join, might help to regain some of the public support and bipartisan leadership for nuclear arms control as an important element of our national security.

Progress in technology, especially in the area of so-called "national technical means of verification" or satellite, seismic, or other detection mechanisms, has over the years greatly improved the possibilities for the negotiation and implementation of complete test ban and arms control agreements in general. SALT I would not have been acceptable to the United States but for developments in verification. Today, the technological concerns about a comprehensive testing ban which exist in the U.S. scientific community focus on reliability testing of American weapons stockpiles.

The definition of a nuclear explosion in a comprehensive test ban treaty must describe a detonation in such a way as not to prohibit the release of nuclear energy in normal, peaceful scientific experimentation, such as fusion power research. Resolution of this definitional question, however, is not seen in the scientific community as posing any obstacles to conclusion of a nuclear test ban or to fusion research.

Reliability or "proof" testing to assure that existing nuclear weapons are operable and that deterrence remains credible is the key issue. Such testing has rarely been done in the past and nuclear weapons states have continued to be confident of their inventories, so the issue may not be as significant as it first appears. The reasons for not engaging in reliability testing, aside from the cost, are that nuclear warhead design is a mature technology and, after more than one thousand nuclear tests by the superpowers, sufficient data is available to make high-confidence forecasts about the reliability of existing designs. The reasons for electing to forego proof-testing in the past are equally persuasive reasons for accepting a treaty prohibition of such tests in the future.

While current discussions within the administration focus on the need to test the most vital component of a nuclear weapon—its low-yield fission trigger—any attempt to permit this in a "comprehensive" test ban would involve establishing another invidious distinction between the nuclear weapons and the non-nuclear weapons states. Such a double standard is almost certain to be unacceptable to the non-nuclear weapons states, and, even if accepted, would vitiate the beneficial impact on nuclear non-proliferation.

Lastly, the United States must insure that verification of a comprehensive ban is commensurate with the security risks that *undetected* violations by the Soviet Union would pose. In this connection, meaningful nuclear weapons testing involves not a single test but several. The means of evading detection are problematic to begin with and the chances of successfully avoiding detection for an entire series of tests necessary to obtain reliable data are slender. While there is no such thing as ironclad verification of compliance, the advantages of cheating are few and the risk of discovery is high so that a workable treaty should be easier to achieve today than before. At the present, seismic and other verification techniques have become sufficiently sophisticated to permit discrimination between natural and artificial seismic events above a few kilotons. Below this level, national technical means of verification can observe, if not always identify, these events, permitting further investigation of low-order seismic occurrences which may raise doubts as to their origin. For these ambiguous events, on-site inspection would be useful and provide high levels of confidence.

With significant political incentives before them, and with the necessary directives from their capitals, it may be possible for the Soviet, U.S. and British negotiators to agree upon a test ban treaty in Geneva over the near term, if the current review within the executive branch confirms prior policy that a truly comprehensive test ban is in the net U.S. interest. While care must be taken to insure that there are no oversights or ambiguities in the drafting due to haste, the objective should be to complete a text, initial it, and open it for signature by other nations immediately, perhaps during the United Nations Special Session. Given both international pressures and domestic circumstances, where timing will be an important factor, this path would be preferable to the more conventional route of prior consideration of a draft text by the Conference of the Committee on Disarmament in Geneva and then by the General Assembly of the United Nations. This schedule would also make possible Senate hearings on, and ratification of, a comprehensive test ban treaty in 1978. Success on this front can only improve the domestic climate for consideration of a SALT II agreement in 1979.   *(April 1978)*

While modern arms control has tried to deal first with nuclear arms control—the most serious problem— some theorists have hoped that there would be a "spill-over effect" from progress in that one area to negotiations in others. To some extent, this appears to have occurred, at least during the early years of detente. The United States and the Soviet Union concluded SALT I and the Incidents at Sea, "Hot-Line" Modernization, Prevention of Nuclear War, Threshold Test Ban, and Peaceful Nuclear Explosion agreements. Conventions were also signed prohibiting biological weapons and environmental modification techniques.

However, on the debit side, "transference" of the arms competition from one type of military technology or from one geographic sector to another has also occurred. For example, SALT and the ongoing talks on Mutual and Balanced Force Reductions in Europe have increased interest in some quarters in chemical warfare. Many also believe that reductions in nuclear weapons will require larger inventories of conventional weapons to sustain deterrence.

The attenuation of the bipolar confrontation that marked the cold war and the prospect of superpower arms control have increased regional security concerns and led to a world-wide proliferation of conventional weaponry, marked by the burgeoning of country-to-country transfers, the development of new conventional weapons technologies, and the creation of indigenous weapons production capacity.

Efforts to grapple with the problems of controlling non-nuclear weapons have been intermittent and, to date, unproductive, except in the case of biological weapons. The Arms Export Control Act, passed by Congress in 1976, has yielded no significant reversal of planned sales. A U.S. policy announced in 1977 to restrict arms sales was met with an attitude of skepticism by other leading weapon suppliers and followed by an increase in the volume of U.S. sales. Soviet-American talks on limiting chemical weapons and conventional arms transfers have proceeded slowly. Debate continues among supplier and recipient nations as to who should bear the responsibility for the increasing volume of arms transfers. Meanwhile, the size of the powder keg and the number of potential fuses grows larger.

5

Non-Nuclear Arms Control

Have Arms, Will Sell   *Anne H. Cahn*

> Throughout history men have sought peace but suf-
> fered war; all too often deliberate decisions or miscalcu-
> lations have brought violence and destruction to a world
> yearning for tranquility . . .
>
> Secretary of State Henry A. Kissinger
> before the Senate Foreign Relations Committee,
> September 19, 1974.

The arms which have brought not only violence and destruction but death to more than 10 million people since the end of World War II have for the most part been obtained through an international arms trade which has exhibited an exponential growth rate in recent years. From a world expenditure of about $300 million in 1952, world trade in non-nuclear weapons will total about $18 billion this fiscal year, an increase of 6000 percent.

The United States can well be dubbed the "General Motors" of this arms trade, with arms sales for fiscal year 1973 of $8.5 billion and estimated to reach $12 billion this year. This represents an over eight-fold increase since the 1970 fiscal year, when sales were about $1.4 billion. Even correcting for exchange rate differences, the Soviet Union lags far behind in this competition with sales of approximately $5 billion this year.

Looking at the monetary value of the arms trade can easily distort our vision. There are several reasons for this. *First,* the dollar value of arms traded is a slippery concept. Weapons can be given away, they can be sold on credit with variable interest rates and repayment provisions, and the prices charged for the weapons can and do vary from surprisingly low to seemingly outrageous. *Second,* the data usually refer to orders placed, not items delivered. So arms deals negotiated or an-

Leading Countries in Arms Exports (1976)

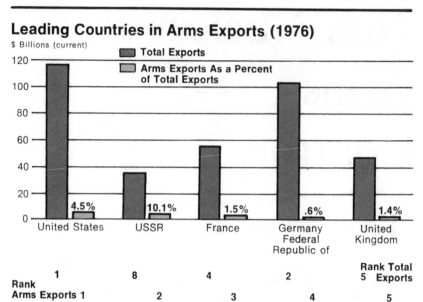

$ Billions (current)

Legend: ■ Total Exports | ▨ Arms Exports As a Percent of Total Exports

	United States	USSR	France	Germany Federal Republic of	United Kingdom
(percent)	4.5%	10.1%	1.5%	.6%	1.4%
Rank Total Exports	1	8	4	2	5
Rank Arms Exports	1	2	3	4	5

Source: *World Military Expenditures and Arms Transfers 1967-1976,*
U.S. Arms Control and Disarmament Agency, 1978.

Major Arms Exporters to the Developing Nations

Billion dollars, cumulative 1970-1976

United States	25.5
USSR	12.2
France	2.4
United Kingdom	2.1
West Germany	1.6
Italy	0.7
China	0.4
All others	3.2

Source: *World Military and Social Expenditures 1978,* Ruth Leger Sivard, 1978.

nounced this year will affect the military balance more in later years. For example, a U.S. agreement to sell Chile eighteen F-5E fighters was agreed to in June 1974 and announced in October; delivery begins in May 1976. *Third,* the data are difficult to obtain and agreement is rare among disparate sources such as the International Institute for Strategic Studies, the Stockholm International Peace Research Institute and the Arms Control and Disarmament Agency. *Finally,* current world-wide inflation may account for a sizable portion of the noted increases.

Consequently, a more meaningful criterion is to examine the quality of the arms traded. Here we find a dramatic increase in the technical sophistication of the weapons. No longer is the world trade in arms confined to second-hand, obsolete weapons. What the supplying nations are offering to their clients now are their most technologically advanced weapons, hot off the design tables. For instance, the Bell AH-1J gunship helicopter, ordered by the Shah of Iran, can fire cannon, rockets and anti-tank missiles and is more advanced than any now used by the U.S. Army. This whirlybird will be delivered to the Iranians at the same time it is introduced into the American armed forces.

Similarly, Egypt and Britain are in the process of negotiating a major arms deal which will most likely include Egyptian purchases of the newest jet fighter being produced in Britain, the Hawker-Siddeley "Hawk." The prototype of this plane (which can be developed as a strike aircraft carrying rockets, bombs, and guns) flew for the first time in September 1974 and is not scheduled for service in the Royal Air Force until 1976. Yet as early as October 1974 the plane was the subject of arms trade negotiations. The Soviet Union also delivered to Syria its MIG-23 swing-wing interceptor aircraft, before making it available to its Warsaw Pact allies.

According to a study prepared for the Congress by the Arms Control and Disarmament Agency, 57 nations each exported at least $500,000 worth of weapons between 1961 and 1971. In addition, 113 countries each imported weapons with a value of at least that amount during the same decade. This brisk and growing international traffic in arms represents governmental decisions because the arms trade today is a government-to-government business. Private arms sales account for less than 5 percent of the total transactions and only a small fraction of these operate without governmental approval.

It is clear that governments buy and sell arms to pursue and further a number of military, economic, social, politico-strategic, and technical objectives. What is not at all clear, however, is any understanding of how well the objectives of either suppliers or recipients are met by any given arms sales agreement. The underlying relationships between the numbers and kinds of weapons traded and the occurrence or deterrence of wars, the interactions with competition for scarce resources, tensions

between suppliers and recipients, the impact of conventional arms transactions upon the proliferation of nuclear weaponry and technology—
these issues are not well understood and, indeed, seldom examined. As
a result, many recent arms sales negotiations seem to be ad hoc and
ad lib, often with unforeseen or unintended consequences.

In the Middle East, each of the superpowers has become a patron,
arming its client and thereby hoping to achieve its objectives through
surrogates. But these acts produce their own escalating demands on the
superpowers who are forced always to increase and intensify their commitment, until finally, according to one observer, it is the superpowers,
not their clients, that are the dogs being wagged by the tail.

In Europe, long-standing alliances are being subjected to an intense
competition for a new lightweight combat aircraft for NATO. Belgium,
Denmark, the Netherlands, and Norway are bidding for a plane to replace the F-104 Starfighters which have been the basic NATO aircraft
for the past decade. Although the four European nations are expected
to order only 350 airplanes, market projections are now being forecast
for at least 2,000 planes, and may reach 3,000 over the lifetime of the
program, due to anticipated third-country sales, with total sales expected
to reach $10-14 billion.

The main contenders now are the French Mirage F-1 and the American Northrop YF-17. In order to win the contract for the Americans,
the Defense Department has alternated between the carrot of red-carpet
treatment for the four visiting defense ministers with cannons booming a
welcome over the Potomac, music by the Navy band, and seats in the
Presidential Box at the Kennedy Center, and the stick of dropping thinly
disguised hints that if the contract is not awarded to the American company, U.S. defense expenditures in Europe will have to be reviewed. A
likely consequence of pushing the NATO allies to purchase the U.S.
planes to help us with our balance of payments is to insure that these
allies will seek compensating military arms sales in Asia, Africa, Latin
America, and the Middle East in order to correct their own payment
imbalances.

France and Britain especially have become heavily dependent upon
export sales for the survival of their defense industries. According to
recent studies, the French aerospace industry exports over 50 percent of
its output while British aerospace companies rely on exports to absorb
over 30 percent of their output. The British Aircraft Corporation now
has a $2 billion order backlog of which 72 percent is for exports. The
U.S. government has designated aerospace as a top priority export
industry and France has lifted its Middle East export ban.

It is disturbing to find that arms trade issues are seldom on the
agenda of either statesmen or scholars. Past attempts to regulate the
international flow of arms have been strenuously resisted by many

(Above) Soviet SA-9 surface-to-air missiles mounted on a mobile launcher. These missiles have been provided to Iran, Hungary, and Poland. (Below) U.S. Hawk surface-to-air missiles on a launcher. An improved version of this air-defense missile was sold in 1976 to Sweden, Iran, Jordan, Saudi Arabia, and Taiwan.

Sources: Department of Defense (above); U.S. Army (below)

The new F-16 (above) and F-15 (below) fighter aircraft are part of a controversial package of arms sales to Israel, Egypt, and Saudi Arabia which the Congress approved in 1978.

Source: U.S. Air Force

recipient nations. Proposals made in the United Nations by Malta in 1965 and Denmark in 1968 for establishing a system of publicity concerning arms transfers were severely criticized by lesser developed countries. Their chief objections were that such proposals for registration should cover production as well as trade and that they should be worldwide. Proposals for regulating the arms trade, rather than just publicizing it, draw even greater ire from recipient nations—their main argument being that the need for arms control and disarmament is among the supplier countries, rather than among the recipient nations.

Proposals to regulate or to limit international transfers of weapons, if they are to overcome such opposition, will first have to deal with such basic questions as: Should the arms trade be controlled? If so, what should be controlled? What can be controlled? Who should control it? How should agreements be implemented and how should they be enforced? If arms trade policies are to be formulated rationally, and if arms control as well as other national objectives are to be attained, then the critical and sustained intellectual probing and policy-oriented analytical efforts previously expended on nuclear arms questions must also be applied to the international flow of non-nuclear arms.

(October 1974)

Does the U.S. Have a Conventional Arms Sales Policy?
Edward C. Luck

The United States is by far the world's leading arms merchant, having exported almost as many defense articles and services during the past decade as all other nations combined. The pace of U.S. arms transfers has more than doubled over the last ten years, while the principal means of financing has shifted from aid to sales, which now constitute more than 95 percent of the total. Foreign orders for arms sales through U.S. government and commercial channels, under $1.5 billion in fiscal year 1970, are expected to exceed $10 billion in fiscal year 1976 for the third fiscal year in succession. Not only has the volume of U.S. arms transfers grown dramatically, but so has the proliferation of sophisticated weapon systems on the international market. Some of the most advanced weapons in the U.S. arsenal, such as F-14 fighters, Lance missiles and Spruance-class destroyers, are being supplied to Third World countries. This trend has particularly dangerous arms control implications.

The massive transfer of armaments to potentially explosive regions of the Third World can exacerbate local tensions and increase the likelihood of armed conflict. In particular, the introduction of innovative and

F-5E fighter aircraft with AIM-9 Sidewinder practice missiles. The F-5 is sold by the United States to many of the developing nations.

Source: U.S. Air Force

highly sophisticated weapons may magnify uncertainties in the perceived military situation, leading to over-confidence or insecurity between local rivals and spurring a qualitative arms race. As the arms inventories of the Middle Eastern adversaries have grown in quantity and, more importantly, in quality, each round of the Arab-Israeli conflict has become more costly in terms of both equipment and manpower. Since perceptions of the military balance are likely to vary considerably from country to country, it is very difficult for outside powers to secure regional military stability through increasing arms shipments to particular nations.

The widespread deployment of certain weapons systems may increase the incentive to strike first. These would include weapons which: 1) are particularly effective in an offensive role; 2) are vulnerable or relatively ineffective for defensive purposes; or 3) reduce the time period necessary to prepare and launch a surprise attack. While no weapon is designed solely for offense or defense, a force posture oriented around tanks, fighter-bombers, surface-to-surface missiles, and forces-in-being might well appear more offensive to a neighboring country than one stressing anti-tank and anti-aircraft missiles, heavily fortified positions and reserve forces.

The large-scale influx of weapons with strategic capabilities into conflict-prone Third World regions could significantly increase the threat of escalation should war occur. Of course the mere possession of strategic weapons does not guarantee their use against cities, but a country faced with major losses on the battlefield may be tempted to resort to selective strategic strikes. The widespread bombing of cities would not only greatly multiply civilian casualties, but would also increase the threat of direct superpower involvement. Once the distinction between tactical and strategic targets has been breached, the escalation from conventional to nuclear weapons may seem less drastic, particularly to local leaders faced with the large-scale conventional bombing of their cities. With the growing danger of nuclear proliferation, the transfer of nuclear-capable delivery systems could raise dangerous ambiguities regarding the intentions and capabilities of the recipient countries, especially in regions, such as South Asia and the Middle East, in which at least one country appears to have access to nuclear weapons.

Despite a policy of not exporting nuclear weapons, the United States has supplied nuclear-capable F-4 Phantoms to several non-NATO nations. Israel has received nuclear-capable Lance missiles and has requested the longer-range Pershing missile as well. Though considered "tactical" when deployed in Europe, these systems have "strategic" implications when transferred to areas such as Korea, the Middle East, and the Persian Gulf. The proposed Pershing sale seems particularly inappropriate from an arms control perspective, since this relatively large missile, with a 450-mile range, was initially designed solely to carry nuclear warheads (though a conventional model is under development).

The United States should declare a moratorium on exports to the Third World of weapons whose primary or exclusive function is either to attack cities or to deliver nuclear warheads. Other suppliers should be encouraged to adopt similar restraints and to consider joint efforts to restrict the shipment of advanced weapons systems to conflict-prone regions such as the Middle East and Persian Gulf.

The dramatic shift from military assistance to sales may reflect a growing emphasis on economic motivations. It is frequently argued that arms sales aid the balance-of-payments and support our domestic arms industry. Yet in the long run, dependence on fluctuating foreign markets could be detrimental to the health of U.S. defense industries.

Massive arms purchases are certainly not the most productive allocation of the limited resources of developing nations, whose arms expenditures have been increasing more rapidly than those of the developed countries. Even the oil-rich Persian Gulf states require major economic development programs to attain long-term economic viability and social progress. Their purchase of large numbers of high technology weapons can be especially costly both in terms of the initial purchase price and the technical support necessary for maintenance. In order to encourage

The E-3A Airborne Warning and Control System (AWACS) aircraft, a modified Boeing 707 with a rotodome mounted forward of the tail. Designed as an information processing and command center, AWACS can be used for both defense and offense, monitoring incoming bombers and directing interceptors against them, assisting friendly forces in an air battle, or directing bombers and attack aircraft against enemy targets. The sale of the costly AWACS to NATO collapsed when the NATO countries chose the less expensive British Nimrod aircraft. In 1978, however, Congress approved the sale of AWACS to Iran.

Source: U.S. Air Force

a reduction in military outlays in developing countries, the United States and other developed countries should take account of the reasonableness of local military expenditures as one factor in determining the level of bilateral and multilateral economic aid programs.

Short-run economic motivations tend to lead to open-ended arms sales programs which may be inconsistent with more important national security, foreign policy, and arms control considerations. The increasing competition for arms sales contracts has led many private arms manufacturing firms to employ foreign agents to promote arms sales, often through unethical means. Congress should vigorously pursue its efforts to open arms sales transactions to public scrutiny, since increased publicity may inhibit the widespread use of large agent fees and bribery of foreign officials to obtain contracts. Moreover, in light of their important national security and foreign policy implications, arms sales through commercial channels should be phased out entirely. Arms transfers should be conducted solely on a government-to-government basis.

Arms transfers are often justified on the grounds that they increase the supplier's influence over the domestic and foreign policies of recipient countries. Yet, the experiences of the Soviet Union in Egypt and of the United States in Vietnam, South Korea, Greece, and Turkey suggest that the political influence gained through arms transfers may prove to be illusory or temporary. At times, it appears that the recipient gains more leverage than the supplier. Through the transfer of armaments and concomitant support programs, the United States can inadvertently become identified or involved with potentially unstable and often unattractive regimes whose policies are largely beyond U.S. control. Moreover, as the Soviets learned in Indonesia and the United States discovered in Vietnam, a change of regime can convert an "asset" to a "liability" overnight.

During recent years, arms transfers have increasingly been employed as a primary instrument of U.S. bilateral diplomacy, especially in our relations with the Persian Gulf and Middle Eastern countries. Secretary Kissinger, in particular, has perceived arms sales as an important factor in counteracting Soviet influence in the Third World. In fact, the major decisions to escalate the quantity and, more importantly, the quality of U.S. arms exports to particular regions have emerged from high level diplomatic discussions, often without review by the relevant U.S. government agencies. These precedent-setting transactions include the transfer of F-4 aircraft to South Korea, F-14 aircraft to Iran, and Lance (and possibly Pershing) missiles to Israel. Once it has been decided to sell arms to a particular friendly and strategically important nation, there appears to be no well-defined quantitative or qualitative limit to the program.

Unless there is a reversal of the administration's perception of arms sales as a major tool of diplomacy, meaningful restraints on U.S. arms exports will be difficult to achieve. Without greater U.S. restraint, effective long-term multilateral limitations on the global conventional arms race cannot be attained. It is high time for the United States, as the dominant arms supplier, to take the first step by adopting unilateral restraints on its arms exports. *(May 1976)*

U.S. Arms Sales to China?
Nancy V. Yinger and Angus Simmons

The fundamental problems in Sino-American relations, dramatized by Secretary of State Cyrus Vance's August 1977 visit to the People's

Republic of China, may be traced both to persistent factors, such as the ambiguous status of Taiwan, and to new policies adopted in Peking and Washington. The resolution of certain of these outstanding issues may be necessary in the near future, irrespective of when the two governments achieve a complete normalization of diplomatic relations. Among them is the matter of how and to what extent the United States will support Chinese efforts to update its technology base, including military technology.

For the United States, the issue is how any initiatives can be made consistent with the administration's broader foreign policy objectives, such as President Carter's intention to reduce the level of American exports of military equipment, as well as with United States security or other commitments to specific countries. In China, the question is whether the new leadership, styling itself pragmatic, will make any significant changes in the former policy toward imports in general, and toward arms imports in particular, in their quest for more rapid modernization.

Though they discussed it unofficially, neither the Chinese government nor the U.S. government appears to have considered the sale of American arms to China seriously in the past. Dedicated to a policy of self-reliance and ideological purity, the Chinese imported little from the West and especially from their second major adversary, the United States. The importation of high technology equipment, military or civilian, was, moreover, too costly for the Chinese. Their priorities lay in agricultural and industrial development. Finally, the Chinese economy was not developed to the point where the Chinese could make efficient use of the most modern equipment. At the same time, the United States continued active military and political support for the Taiwan government while trying to isolate the People's Republic.

The death of Mao Tse-tung in September 1976 and the subsequent resolution of China's succession question have put these issues in a new perspective. China's current leaders—Party Chairman Hua Kuo-feng and Vice Premier Teng Hsiao-ping—are emphasizing accelerated modernization and more pragmatic rather than more ideological solutions to China's development problems.

Evidence on future Chinese priorities is of two kinds: the declaratory policy of the new leadership and trends in Chinese imports. As to the first, in February 1977, the Chinese government held a series of four meetings at which modernization plans were discussed. The "four modernizations" of agriculture, industry, the military, and applied research and development were re-emphasized but with the significant modification that applied research and development would receive top priority.

Chinese imports also reflect an apparent interest in giving greater attention to the development of a more modern technology base. Over the past few years, the Chinese have purchased Japanese Hitachi M170 and M160 computers, American Cyber 172 computers, British Rolls-Royce Spey jet engines, French Super Frelon helicopters with Omera-Segid surveillance radars, and German Messerschmidt-Bolkow-Blown Bo105 helicopters, as well as aluminum which could be used for aircraft production. Further, looking more closely at these past purchases, the Chinese officials who argued in favor of these imports during the extensive internal debates are now the ones making the decisions. The Chinese have also invited several Western observers, such as James Schlesinger and journalist Drew Middleton, to witness military operations in the People's Republic, usually with outdated equipment. The apparent rationale for these invitations was that if visitors reported China to be militarily weak (which they did), then the case for improvements in Chinese military forces would be strengthened.

It is unlikely, however, that the shift in China's import policies will be sudden or dramatic. Despite China's nuclear arsenal of 200 to 300 weapons and its influence in the Third World, the People's Republic is . still a developing country. Its leaders face significant problems in marshaling economic resources to serve a population of 900 million people. Balanced economic development across all sectors simultaneously has been China's approach to these problems. While it would be unrealistic to expect that Chinese military forces would be left out of this process, it would be equally unrealistic to assume that modernization of the military is China's major preoccupation. Instead, Chinese leaders seem to be interested primarily in technology that can be readily diffused through several economic sectors in pursuit of an overall strategy of balanced growth. To achieve this, the Chinese government appears willing to submit to extensive controls in order to obtain the items it requires. For example, the Chinese agreed to on-site inspection of the Cyber 172 computer centers to reassure the United States that these computers are not being used for military purposes.

China's current, high-ranking military leaders supported Hua Kuo-feng in his struggle with the Gang of Four, presumably in part because they agreed with his "pragmatic" modernization policies. Senior military officials are therefore likely to endorse Hua's general approach to modernization and are in a position to insure that the People's Republic's armed forces also benefit from this "pragmatic" approach in terms of more up-to-date equipment and technology. Teng Hsiao-ping's prominence in the new Chinese government, combined with his military background and strong ties to regional military commanders, give further credence to this assumption.

The interest of the new Chinese leadership in military modernization probably does not mean that China will abandon its basically defensive posture or the ideology of a "people's war." For one thing, if the reports of recent U.S. observers are correct, military modernization for China means moving from a 1950s level to a 1960s level of military technology. Moreover, the Chinese have articulated clearly the threat they feel is posed by the Soviet Union, which, according to some Western estimates, directs about 30 percent of its defense budget toward China. The goal of the Chinese nuclear arsenal is to deter a Soviet attack. The population is mobilized by constant reminders of the need to be prepared for external aggression. Civil defense preparations in urban areas, the organization of militia units throughout the country, and the concept of the people's war itself (which hinges on the involvement of the entire population) are additional examples of the defensive, Soviet-oriented strategy of the People's Republic of China.

Nevertheless, despite an apparent willingness to upgrade military forces from the level of Soviet equipment of the 1950s, the Chinese are unlikely to provide a large market, in terms of volume, for U.S. exports, although the sale of specific high-cost, high-technology items may be profitable for individual companies. Typically, the Chinese prefer to purchase a limited number of items as prototypes for copying or adaptation to Chinese needs. While the new government may be putting less stress on self-reliance and more on "making things foreign serve China," they continue to be concerned about becoming dependent on foreign suppliers, not only of weapons but of any high technology equipment.

Additionally, military expenditures in China do not appear to be rising. In early 1977 the government re-issued an earlier declaration of the "ten great relationships" which indicates that military spending should not exceed 20 percent of the annual budget. Since this includes the upkeep of a three-million-man army, and partial support for the militia, there will not be extensive funds available for dramatic increases in arms imports.

The export of arms or related equipment to China involves potential conflicts with other American foreign policy priorities and commitments. Among the major dilemmas for the Carter administration are the effect such sales might have on SALT (Strategic Arms Limitation Talks) and on U.S.-Soviet relations in general, on relations with Taiwan and American allies in Asia and Europe, and on American arms control and technology transfer objectives. Arms sales to China by the United States would be regarded by Taiwan and the Soviet Union as inimical to their interests. Such sales could further retard the already slow progress of

Soviet-American arms negotiations, which the Chinese view as an effort to deny China its nuclear place in the world.

Soviet concern over possible U.S. arms sales to China would be heightened by the fact that the Chinese are interested in advanced technology equipment, such as sophisticated aircraft and electronic equipment (radar and computers), the latter of which could be used to improve the warning, targeting, and guidance systems for China's intermediate-range ballistic missiles. Moreover, the Soviets made a 1975 trade agreement with Britain contingent on British refusal to sell Harrier Mk 50 vertical take-off and landing aircraft to China.

The case of Taiwan is, if anything, more complicated because the island's future is at the heart of Sino-American negotiations on diplomatic recognition. An argument often heard in the United States is that arms sales to the People's Republic would lead to a military threat to Taiwan and, therefore, the United States should forego consideration of these sales. On the other side of the question, however, there is the fact that the ability of the People's Republic to mount an attack on Taiwan is very limited (because of the lack of adequate aircraft, surface combatants, and amphibious and support craft). There is very little evidence to suggest a military build-up on the mainland opposite Taiwan, some 100 miles away, although a naval blockade is conceivable with the People's Republic's fleet of sixty-five attack submarines, eighteen destroyers and frigates and many missile patrol boats.

Furthermore, Taiwan has had almost unlimited access to American technology, civil and military, for many years. Taiwan is, for example, a special exception to the limitation of arms sales to less developed countries under the Foreign Military Sales Act. It has acquired from the United States 15 destroyers, 5 fleet support ships and 2 submarines. Taiwan also has been acquiring 180 Northrop F-5 fighters under a contract with licensing provisions that will permit Taiwan to be self-sufficient in fighter aircraft production when the contract ends in 1978. A system for control and coordination of Taiwan's interceptors and Hawk ground-to-air missiles has been built by Hughes Aircraft Corporation, while Raytheon is installing a new battalion of improved Hawk missile launchers and upgrading an existing battalion. Taiwanese military forces number nearly half a million, with an army of 375,000 (65,000 on the off-shore island of Quemoy), a navy of 32 major surface vessels and 35,000 men, and an air force composed of 85,000 men and 560 jet aircraft.

The current military balance on either side of the Taiwan Straits is perhaps less significant, however, than long-range plans of the People's Republic for resolving what they regard as a purely internal problem. Although they have not absolutely ruled out the use of force, if necessary, the Chinese leadership apparently continues to believe that in time Taiwan will be reintegrated with mainland China.

Arms sales to the People's Republic by the United States would be inconsistent with longstanding American security commitments to Taiwan, commitments which have a symbolic importance to U.S. allies in both Europe and Asia. For the most part, however, America's European and Asian allies are also interested in harmonious relations with the People's Republic of China. The Western European nations, like the United States, want to see a strong and friendly China that could deflect Soviet energy away from Europe by providing a counterweight in Asia. They also have an economic interest in more open trade with China. The NATO countries have a specific voice in the trade issues through the International Coordinating Committee, the allied panel which reviews the sale of strategic items to communist countries. Aside from competitive considerations, they would probably not object to expanded U.S. trade with China, if not specifically in arms, then at least in high technology items that could be adapted by the Chinese. The expanding European arms industry, combined with the continued leniency of the International Coordinating Committee (which did not object to the French and British arms sales cited above), provides opportunities for Chinese access to advanced technology without direct U.S. involvement.

Also to be considered are the arguments heard in connection with the Foreign Military Sales program: that the United States can gain diplomatic leverage by becoming an important supplier of weapons to China; and that, if the United States does not exploit a possibly expanding market in China, other nations will do so, thereby penalizing American manufacturers whose share of the international aerospace market dropped from 86 to 68 percent between 1960 and 1975 while the West European share increased from 11 to 25 percent.

While the United States has an interest in strengthening its ties with the People's Republic and in seeing a strong China to counterbalance the Soviet Union, direct military sales at this point would appear to be more damaging than helpful to the broad range of American interests that would be influenced by such sales. At the same time, expansion of the sale of high technology equipment of the kind that has been exported in the past, such as the Cyber 172 computers, would assist in Chinese modernization programs and hence in normalizing relations with China without seeming overtly threatening to the USSR or Taiwan, especially if these transactions are accompanied by controls on the use of the exported items.

The sale of weapons to China is constrained by the International Security Assistance and Arms Export Control Act of 1976, which restricts weapons sales while providing the President discretionary power for transactions up to $350 million a year, and by President Carter's military export policy which restricts sales to nations in non-favored status, co-production agreements, third country exports and re-transfers, and U.S. introduction of advanced weapons into new regions.

As regards restrictions on transfer of technology, Defense Secretary Harold Brown's Interim Policy on Export Control of U.S. Technology does not appear to create serious obstacles to selling non-military systems to the People's Republic; it provides that: "Defense will normally recommend approval of sales of end products to potential adversaries in those instances where 1) the product's technology content is either difficult, impractical or economically infeasible to extract, 2) the end product in question will not of itself significantly enhance the recipient's military or warmaking capability, either by virtue of its technology content or because of the quantity to be sold, and 3) the product cannot be so analyzed as to reveal U.S. system characteristics and thereby contribute to the development of countermeasures to equivalent U.S. equipment."

It is reasonable to assume, however, that over the long run the current Chinese modernization efforts will succeed in most major respects. In such a case, China would achieve her modernization goals including the development of a modern weapons industry, with or without U.S. technology, arms transfers or other assistance. It is therefore not too early for the American government to think about policies other than how to strengthen China militarily. In the past, the tendency of the People's Republic has been to regard U.S. and other arms control initiatives with suspicion. The advent of new leaders in Peking and Washington, each with an announced commitment to disarmament, suggests that now might be an opportune time to open a dialogue (quite apart from the issue of normalizing diplomatic relations) leading to discussion of practical bilateral or multilateral steps to implement this mutual commitment. *(September 1977)*

New Conventional Weapon Technologies
Richard Burt

Despite the almost constant attention focused on new developments in the realm of strategic nuclear weaponry, until recently little notice has been taken of the profound technological changes under way in the area of conventional weapons. While the United States is by no means the only nation that is actively pursuing new avenues of weapons design, the Department of Defense is at present engaged in over thirty research and

Advanced Conventionally-Armed Missiles in 1978

In Service —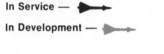

In Development —

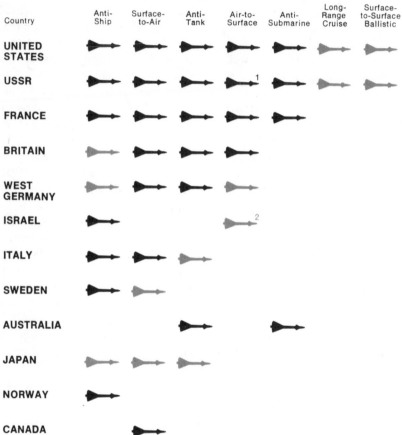

Country	Anti-Ship	Surface-to-Air	Anti-Tank	Air-to-Surface	Anti-Submarine	Long-Range Cruise	Surface-to-Surface Ballistic
UNITED STATES							
USSR				[1]			
FRANCE							
BRITAIN							
WEST GERMANY							
ISRAEL				[2]			
ITALY							
SWEDEN							
AUSTRALIA							
JAPAN							
NORWAY							
CANADA							

These are missiles in service or in development which could be used in roles now assigned to nuclear systems. "Advanced" refers to systems using seeker guidance, precision positioning, correlation guidance and stellar inertial guidance (but not other forms of inertial guidance). Weapons in service but not developed indigenously are not shown.

[1] Includes only long-range, command-guidance missiles, though the AS-5 Kelt may have an active radar-seeker.

[2] A TV-guided missile, the Rafael, is reported to be under development.

Six AIM-54 Phoenix radar-homing, air-to-air missiles slung under the wings and fuselage of a carrier-based F-14 Tomcat fighter. Sidewinder, Sparrow, and Agile missiles can also be carried by this all-weather, air-to-air combat and air-to-surface attack fighter.

Source: U.S. Navy

development programs which incorporate new guidance, sensor, and communication technologies that promise to give future weapons vastly higher accuracies, improved target acquisition capabilities, and the ability to strike at targets at longer ranges with smaller warheads. The implications of these developments for U.S. military doctrine and force level design are not yet clear. For arms control, at least, the new conventional weapons technologies appear to offer some solutions to old problems while raising new ones.

Perhaps the most striking area of improvement in conventional weapons performance is higher accuracies, where so-called *precision-guided munitions* have reduced the circular error probable* of some battlefield weapons to less than ten feet. The "smart" weapons or precision-guided munitions, first unveiled in the closing days of the

---

*Circular error probable is a measure of the accuracy of offensive missile attacks on point targets. It is the radius of a circle around the target within which half of the attacking warheads can be expected to fall. Consequently, the smaller the circular error probable of a missile the more accurate it is.

Vietnam war, are relatively cheap and easy to operate and have begun to enter the U.S. inventory in great numbers—as air defense missiles, anti-tank guided weapons, and air-launched glide bombs. (In 1975 alone, the U.S. Army is purchasing 46,000 light- and medium-weight precision-guided anti-tank missiles.)

To achieve high hit probabilities, precision-guided munitions are usually guided towards targets in their mid-course and terminal phases, utilizing a growing range of sophisticated radar, laser, infrared and/or electro-optical sensor and designation systems. Typical of the weapons now entering or about to enter the U.S. arsenal are the Army's TOW, a wire-guided anti-tank missile, the Air Force's Maverick, an air-launched, TV-guided anti-tank system and the Navy's Condor, a TV-guided anti-ship cruise missile.

Precision-guided munitions now under development for deployment later in the decade include laser-guided artillery shells and multiple independently maneuvering submunitions, a small warhead dispensed from a cluster bomb which would use a terminal guidance system to attack individual targets. Further along, research efforts are concentrating on what may perhaps be the ultimate "smart" bomb—high-powered laser strike weapons.

Developments in this technology coincide with vast improvements on other conventional fronts: the use of remotely piloted vehicles as strike aircraft, improvements in data processing and transmission to upgrade command and control capabilities, the establishment of "real time" reconnaissance systems and the use of advanced communication and sensor systems to enhance target identification and acquisition. Taken together, these developments might presage a qualitative change in the nature of conventional warfare. For example, small mobile land (and sea) forces will have increasing firepower at their disposal. As a result, large and expensive systems—tanks, fighter and bomber aircraft, and aircraft carriers—may become increasingly vulnerable to weapons carried by single soldiers or small units. Also, given the capabilities of the new systems, it could become less desirable to concentrate forces on the battlefield. The ability to move and hide forces will likely be more important, suggesting that the new technologies will be more advantageous to the defender than the attacker. And because of higher accuracies, it may be possible to use smaller warheads against targets and thus reduce the unintended or collateral damage to civilian structures and population during wartime.

If the acquisition of the new weapons does result in such changes, a Pandora's box of new problems and prospects will be opened. For Western forces in Europe, conventional technologies favoring the defender could help right the perceived imbalance in conventional capabilities with the Warsaw Pact states. New conventional systems might also allow NATO to rely less on tactical nuclear weapons to deter and defend against an attack on Europe, which would have the dual advantage of raising the nuclear threshold and delaying the political problem of ordering the use of nuclear weapons. Thus, the use of new conventional weapons for some missions that are now assigned to nuclear arms might enable the United States to withdraw some of the 7,000 nuclear weapons now deployed in Europe. If this were shown to be feasible, it might then be easier to negotiate a more comprehensive agreement on mutual force reductions with the Warsaw Pact in the Vienna talks.

Such reasons compel the exploration of the potential offered by the new family of weapons. But in so doing, some possible problems should also be recognized. Many of the systems developed for conventional use are *dual-capable* and therefore can be easily adapted for delivering nuclear weapons. This will provide new arguments for the deployment of "mini" nuclear weapons in Europe. More generally, the new technologies tend to "blur" the traditional distinctions between conventional, tactical, and strategic weapons, and it may become almost impossible for negotiators to use existing diplomatic forums for arms control without linking the understandings reached in one setting with those in others.

Some possible limitations of the new technologies must also be taken into account. Despite rapid improvements in terminal guidance, during the next decade most precision-guided munitions will need clear daylight to operate effectively, and only now are their vulnerabilities to countermeasures being investigated. Costs and numbers are another consideration. To make a difference on the battlefield, the new weapons will have to be bought in abundant numbers. Is it realistic to assume that, under existing pressures on defense spending, Western nations will be able fully to exploit the new technologies?

Finally, while the new systems have been developed for deployment primarily in Europe, many have already found their way into the Third World. Some analysts have speculated that such arms transfers are stabilizing, because smaller states will become better able to defend themselves. But it is highly unlikely that the proliferation of these weapons will proceed in a balanced manner, and the sudden acquisition by some states of greatly increased military firepower could upset existing regional balances. *(January 1975)*

What Policy for Nerve Gas? *Matthew Meselson*

During World War II Germany produced, but did not use, a new supertoxic class of lethal chemicals, the nerve gases. During the 1950s and 1960s the United States produced thousands of tons of nerve gas and stockpiled nerve gas weapons designed for tactical battlefield use. These are stored mainly in the continental United States, with a lesser quantity deployed in Europe in the Federal Republic of Germany. We have no reliable estimate of the size or the composition of the Soviet poison gas stockpile, although the USSR and a number of other countries could readily produce nerve gas.

Lethal chemicals are generally considered to be weapons of mass destruction. For example, under not uncommon meteorological conditions a single light bomber could deliver enough nerve gas to cause a high percentage of fatalities over a downwind area of several square miles. But despite the potential of nerve gas and certain other lethal chemicals for inflicting mass casualties, quite effective protection can be provided for combat troops, in the form of modern gas masks, protective clothing, vehicle air conditioners, and other equipment. Although an initial resort to nerve gas would inflict heavy casualties on military units if caught off guard, its subsequent use against troops with modern protective equipment would be much less effective, a fact of potential importance for chemical arms control.

The principal treaty dealing with chemical weapons is the Geneva Protocol of 1925. All militarily important nations are parties, including the members of NATO, the Warsaw Pact, and the People's Republic of China. After nearly fifty years of alternating controversy and inattention, the United States has finally become a party to the Protocol, following its ratification by President Ford on January 22, 1975, with the undivided support of the Senate. The Protocol is, in effect, a no-first-use agreement. It *does not* prohibit stockpiling of chemical weapons or reprisal in kind against a violator. However, the United States and USSR, as parties to the Biological Weapons Convention of 1972, have undertaken, under Article IX, to negotiate effective measures for prohibiting the development, production and possession of chemical weapons of war. At Moscow in July 1974, President Nixon and Secretary Leonid Brezhnev declared their agreement to consider a joint initiative at the Conference of the Committee on Disarmament in Geneva to obtain an international convention eliminating the most lethal chemical weapons. This was reaffirmed by President Ford and Secretary Brezhnev at Vladivostok in November 1974. However, no such initiative has yet been made nor has the United States put forward any proposals of its own.

Meanwhile the Department of Defense has renewed its request, voted down in the House of Representatives in 1974, for funds to build a facility to produce a new generation of nerve gas weapons, safer to handle and store, called binaries. Only $8.8 million is being sought for the new facility, but over the course of several years it would cost approximately a billion dollars to produce binary nerve gas weapons to replace the existing stockpile and perhaps three quarters of a billion more

Biological Weapons Disarmament

The unilateral renunciation of biological warfare by the United States in 1969 and the entry into force of the Biological Weapons Convention of 1972 have essentially ended apprehension that the world might be drifting into the military acceptance and possibly even the use of disease as a weapon of war.

During the 1950s and the 1960s, the United States developed and produced anti-personnel biological weapons utilizing disease-causing agents such as anthrax and Venezuelan equine encephalitis and anti-crop agents such as rice blast and wheat rust. Whether other nations have produced or possess such weapons is unknown.

However, after an extensive review prompted in part by public and congressional questioning, President Nixon and his advisors concluded that biological weapons serve no important U.S. military requirement and that their use would risk massive and unpredictable consequences. On November 25, 1969, the President announced that the United States would destroy its biological weapons stockpile and renounce the use of biological weapons. On February 14, 1970, this renunciation was extended to toxins, the toxic substances made by living organisms and the synthetic counterparts of such substances. The U.S. stocks of biological weapons, including toxins, have been destroyed. The biological weapons laboratories at Fort Detrick, Maryland, have been converted to cancer research and the former production plant at Pine Bluff, Arkansas, is now a testing center for the Food and Drug Administration.

On January 22, 1975, President Ford, with unanimous support of the Senate, ratified the Biological Weapons Convention of 1972, a treaty proposed by the United Kingdom and negotiated at the Conference of the Committee on Disarmament at Geneva. The convention prohibits the development, production and stockpiling of biological weapons. Following our example in renouncing biological weapons, more than one hundred countries have signed the convention, which came into force on March 26, 1975, when instruments of ratification were exchanged by the United States, Great Britain and the Soviet Union. Under the terms of the convention all biological agents, weapons and delivery systems are to be destroyed within nine months from this date. Neither France nor the People's Republic of China is among the parties, although France has enacted a domestic law making biological warfare preparations a crime. The parties did not consider it essential to require verification provisions beyond a pledge to cooperate with any investigation the United Nations Security Council may initiate on the basis of a complaint from a party and an undertaking to facilitate scientific exchange in bacteriology and related fields. Still, the renunciation of biological warfare by the United States and the entry into force of the convention would seem to make biological warfare extremely unlikely.

to dispose of the latter. For two years the Defense Department has testified before Congress in favor of binaries, while the director of the U.S. Arms Control and Disarmament Agency has testified against. The case for buying binaries is not that they are more effective on the battlefield—in fact they are not. Rather, the arguments for and against them are largely psychological and political. Advocates consider that their safety features will overcome public opposition to transportation and forward deployment of nerve gas weapons. Critics argue that a major new round of chemical weapons procurement will spoil chances for negotiating a chemical arms control treaty and will stimulate the international proliferation of chemical weapons.

While the dispute over binaries has occupied center stage, the present situation represents a crossroads of a more fundamental nature. Broadly defined, the choice is between (1) replacement of the existing stockpile with binaries or at least the retention of the current inventory, possibly with some modifications to suit newer types of aircraft and artillery, or (2) renunciation of lethal chemical weapons, either through international agreement or unilaterally, seeking a treaty afterwards.

It is not maintained that chemical weapons are needed to deter war itself. Our conventional and nuclear forces serve that role. Neither do senior officials consider that we would have any important incentive to be the first to attack with gas should a major war occur. Stated U.S. policy has long been not to start poison gas warfare, a doctrine further solidified by U.S. ratification of the Geneva Protocol. Rather, it is argued that the prospect of retaliation in kind would contribute importantly to deterring the Soviets from using the nerve gas that they must be assumed to possess and that, if such deterrence fails, our retaliation could enable us to defend Europe without necessitating immediate resort to nuclear weapons. The rationale for these beliefs rests not on the direct casualty-producing capability of nerve gas, which would be minimized by the use of protective equipment, but rather on the reduction in fighting efficiency that results from wearing masks and suits and taking other protective measures. It is contended that the ability to retaliate in kind in the combat zone and in rear support areas would allow us to impose on the Soviets the same protective posture they impose on us, greatly reducing the advantages to them of any protracted use of gas. However, it must be admitted that our retaliatory capability does nothing to reduce the advantage to the Soviets inherent in the initial casualties and confusion that could be inflicted by a surprise gas attack on our forces.

But technical military considerations aside, the case for having nerve gas rests on psychological assumptions that go to the heart of NATO defense doctrine. Would our nerve gas deter Soviet first use or would it instead encourage them to think at a desperate moment that they might use nerve gas to break a battlefield deadlock without provoking a nuclear response? And if NATO is attacked with nerve gas, would our retaliation in kind help to gain time and promote the sanity needed to terminate hostilities? Or would it so complicate the calculations of both sides as to preclude the clarity of analysis and communication needed to stop a war short of an all-out nuclear exchange? Indeed, must not nuclear weapons inevitably come rapidly into play in response to any determined Soviet thrust into Europe, thereby completely overshadowing the question of gas warfare?

It is generally agreed that in addition to the cost in resources, there are other costs of stockpiling nerve gas and having an active nerve gas program. Today, no non-nuclear nation is thought to have stockpiled nerve gas weapons. It is very much in our interest to preserve this situation. Our great wealth allows us to expend enormous quantities of conventional munitions in tactical war and to maintain large strategic and tactical nuclear forces. Very few countries even approach this capability. However, nerve gas weapons have the potential of wide area coverage at relatively low cost. Their proliferation would greatly enhance the capability of smaller countries and perhaps even of dissident paramilitary groups for threat, harassment, and destruction. The United States and the Soviet Union set the pace and direction of military developments throughout the world. The more interest we display in nerve gas weapons, the more we pioneer their technology and invest in them, the more lesser military powers are likely to question their case for refraining from acquiring nerve gas weapons of their own.

On a different level of concern, the rapid and accelerating advancement of biochemistry and the biological sciences is inevitably leading to a profound ability to manipulate life processes for good or ill. Over the long run, it may be very important to create an international consensus that such knowledge is not to be exploited for military purposes. The possession of nerve gas weapons maintains institutional commitments to such exploitation. In contrast, if nerve gas can be eliminated we would be free to create an atmosphere in which our increasing knowledge of life processes is directed solely to man's benefit and in which research is conducted under the more or less open public scrutiny that is probably necessary to insure such beneficial use. *(April 1975)*

In the first years of the 20th century, the Balkan countries of Eastern Europe, a then-remote part of the world, experienced a decade of almost constant war and revolution. All efforts to stabilize the region failed and in 1914 other countries were drawn in; an unparalleled bloody conflict ensued. The origins of World War I illustrate vividly the importance of regional arms control. In an era of massive nuclear arsenals and rapidly evolving technology, the possible consequences of regional conflicts dwarf those of Sarajevo.

There has been some progress toward regional arms control in recent years. The most spectacluar recent example, of course, is the Camp David Framework for Peace in the Middle East. The framework, which followed several years of confidence-building measures such as mutual troop withdrawals, could lead to a demilitarization of the Sinai Desert.

There are other examples. In Latin America over twenty countries have declared themselves part of a nuclear-free zone, and talks are currently under way on the demilitarization of the Indian Ocean. In 1971 the ASEAN countries—Indonesia, Malaysia, the Philippines, Singapore, and Thailand—formally proposed that Southeast Asia become a "zone of peace, freedom and neutrality, free from any form or manner of interference by outside powers." Nothing concrete has yet emerged from this proposal, and, although there is some hope that a regional agreement may yet be signed, there is war again in Southeast Asia. In Europe, the key military powers of both East and West have been engaged for several years in talks aimed at force reductions. Some progress was apparent in early 1978 when the Soviets agreed to a number of Western proposals— most importantly that after troop withdrawals, each side would have a ceiling of 700,000 troops. However, the Soviets refused to accept NATO's contention that the Warsaw Pact countries have 150,000 more men in their ground forces than the 805,000 listed in official Pact figures, and the talks remained deadlocked.

The problem of damping regional conflicts remains a crucial one. Indeed, in a multipolar world, where regional interests are less and less dominated by the superpower confrontation and where detente cannot insure even a fragile peace, regional arms control can make a vital contribution to international security.

6

Regional Arms Control

Prospects for Arms Control in Latin America
John R. Redick

Conventional wisdom in this country often portrays Latin America as prone to violence, military coups, and chronic instability. Such views have an element of truth but overlook the fact that, in comparison to other regions, Latin American countries spend relatively little on military armaments. In addition, no Latin American nation has detonated a nuclear explosive device—although that situation may change in the near future. Latin America is also noted as a region that has produced one partially successful attempt to eliminate nuclear weapons and several conventional arms control proposals, including the recent Declaration of Ayacucho.

The effort to eliminate nuclear weapons in Latin America culminated in the Treaty for the Prohibition of Nuclear Weapons in Latin America (Treaty of Tlatelolco) signed on February 14, 1967, following over three years of intensive negotiations. Negotiations occurred primarily through meetings of the Comisión Preparatoria para la Desnuclearización de la América Latina (COPREDAL) in Mexico City and to a lesser degree at the United Nations. The Tlatelolco Treaty is currently in force for twenty Latin American nations (excluding several important states such as Argentina, Brazil and Chile) and provides for the complete military denuclearization of the Latin American area. The treaty's machinery—the Organization for the Prohibition of Nuclear Weapons (OPANAL) with a small secretariat—permanently resides in Mexico City.

The treaty prohibits the development or production as well as the receipt or installation of nuclear weapons by any Latin American country. The Tlatelolco Treaty restrictions are more extensive than those of the Non-Proliferation Treaty, as Latin American nations pledge not to permit the deployment of nuclear weapons on their territories under the control of foreign nuclear powers (i.e., no nuclear weapons bases). Under the terms of the treaty, the Latin American parties are to negotiate safeguard agreements with the International Atomic Energy Agency. Although progress in some cases has been slow, this regional treaty obligation has been instrumental in facilitating Latin American acceptance of international safeguards.

Two additional protocols to the treaty concerned non-Latin American nations. Protocol I pledges non-Latin American countries with possessions within the treaty zone to place them under the same restrictions as parties to the treaty. Thus far the United States and France have refused to sign this protocol. Protocol II involves a pledge by nuclear weapons states not to use or threaten to use nuclear weapons against parties to the treaty. Four of the five nuclear weapons states (excluding only the USSR) have signed the protocol. This protocol provoked considerable study and some doubt within the U.S. government prior to its ratification since it represents a self-denying obligation which the United States has avoided elsewhere.

However, the current situation as regards the nuclear weapon-free zone treaty is uncertain at best. Gaining full support by all Latin American and nuclear weapons states is of vital importance to the ultimate success of the treaty. The issues are, of course, inter-related—ratification of additional protocols by all five nuclear weapons states will have a bearing on future decisions by Argentina, Brazil and Chile to allow the treaty to enter into force for themselves. Conversely, nuclear weapons states are likely to give greater credence to a nuclear weapon-free zone agreement if supported by all Latin American nations.

For the Tlatelolco Treaty to become a completely effective arms control mechanism, it is essential that there be some degree of accordance among both the states within the zone and significant non-zonal states as to the intent and meaning of the important provisions of the agreement. At present, harmony of views on such issues as "peaceful nuclear explosives" (some Latin American nations interpret the treaty as permitting them while others do not) and the transportation of nuclear weapons through the territory of Latin American nations does not exist. More significantly, however, at least two Latin American nations, Argentina and Brazil, have publicly announced their intention to detonate "peaceful" nuclear explosives and appear to be on the verge of acquiring a capacity to do just that. Nevertheless, twenty Latin American states have formally renounced nuclear weapons and consequently enjoy the pledge of four of the five nuclear weapon states "not to use or threaten to use" nuclear weapons against their territory. Thus, although incomplete, the Latin American nuclear-free zone is an important model for other regions as well as a significant regional step toward general and complete disarmament.

Ayacucho: Controlling Conventional Arms

According to the U.S. Arms Control and Disarmament Agency, twenty-three Latin American nations received a total of about $800 million in armaments in 1976, or considerably less than recent U.S. sales to any one of a number of Middle East nations. In the same year Latin America imported only 6 percent of the world's arms exports, an amount dwarfed by the imports of other regions such as the Middle East, Europe and East Asia. The total amounts of weapons imported into the Latin American region have been and remain miniscule on the world scale. And, as Latin American nations are, at present, almost totally dependent on extra-regional sources for advanced weapons (Brazil is a growing exception), bilateral and multilateral agreements to control weapons can have a major positive impact on the peace and security of the region.

The most recent and interesting Latin American endeavor is the so-called "Declaration of Ayacucho" signed on December 9, 1974, in Lima by Argentina, Bolivia, Chile, Colombia, Ecuador, Panama, Peru and Venezuela. The eight-nation declaration, primarily a nostalgic call for Latin American unity, did include a significant paragraph which stated their intention to "create the conditions which will make possible the effective limitations of armaments and an end to their acquisition for offensive purposes so that all possible resources may be devoted to the economic and social development of every country in Latin America." The declaration which was proposed by Peru's former president, General Juan Valasco Alvarado, drew strong praise from U.S. Assistant Secretary of State for Latin American Affairs William D. Rogers, who declared it "an extraordinary and unprecedented step which could substantially reduce tensions in the hemisphere."

This declaration of principle must be considered in the context of the historical rivalry between Chile and Peru, as well as recent ambitious arms purchases by Peru (including the acquisition of Soviet tanks in 1974 giving Peru apparent military superiority over its southern neighbor). The Peruvian proposal may have been an effort to freeze its advantage, or it may have represented a genuine attempt by an economically strapped military regime sincerely dedicated to promoting national development. Whatever their motivations, Chile and Peru have made significant progress in recent months in defusing their long-standing border controversy.

Obviously, motivating factors impelling the Andes nations to sign the declaration (Brazil has not joined the effort, and Argentina is backing off) were of a mixed nature. The Ayacucho meeting was followed by a meeting of technical delegations of six of the eight signatories which considered such questions as establishing demilitarized zones and monitoring weapons inventories. For Ayacucho, the willingness of all Latin American states to translate noble declarations into concrete agreements is essential. Equally important is a willingness of the major exporting nations to respect the will of Latin American nations when clearly expressed.

While the current situation is extremely fluid, nuclear technology with all its military implications is clearly accelerating in the region. Ambitious nuclear power programs of varying types and sophistication are (or soon will be) producing an unavoidable by-product, plutonium. Although estimates differ, it is generally believed that a 1,000 megawatt power reactor using slightly enriched uranium will produce between 200-300 kilograms of plutonium in a year. Natural uranium reactors produce a far greater quantity of plutonium and the fuel-load may be removed far more easily without a shutdown of the reactor. Approximately five kilograms of plutonium are sufficient for a nuclear device capable of destroying a densely populated portion of a major city such as New York's Wall Street or a similar section of Buenos Aires or Sao Paulo.

Since 1974 Argentina has had an operating 320 megawatt natural uranium power reactor which was supplied by West Germany. A second 600 megawatt natural uranium (CANDU) reactor supplied by Canada will be completed by 1979, and the recent Argentine Nuclear Program 1975-1985, prepared by their national atomic energy agency, calls for three additional CANDU reactors in the early to mid-1980s. A heavy water production plant is to be completed by 1980; construction has begun on an industrial scale fuel fabrication facility, and with French assistance, a chemical reprocessing plant capable of separating a militarily significant portion of plutonium will be constructed to supplement the small pilot plants Argentina has possessed for several years.

The Argentine Nuclear Program with its reliance on natural uranium technology, careful insulation from internal politics, and stress on independence is strikingly similar to the Indian program. In addition, a July 1975 inquiry by Senator Abraham Ribicoff (D-Conn.) revealed the existence of a U.S. intelligence report of a fifty kilogram diversion of plutonium from the Atucha power reactor. Although the U.S. Energy Research and Development Administration has denied that the incident occurred (several influential senators remain unconvinced) it nonetheless illustrates what could and may easily happen—and the limited U.S. response.

Brazil's first nuclear power reactor, a 626 megawatt enriched uranium facility, supplied by the United States, will come into operation in 1977. In a much publicized and highly criticized (in the United States) sale, West Germany agreed in June 1975 to build four 1300 megawatt enriched uranium reactors in Brazil by 1986 and four more by 1990. More significantly, the Germans agreed to supply Brazil with a nuclear package of fuel fabrication, plutonium separation, and a "nozzle" enrichment plant. While the agreement is subject to far-reaching International Atomic Energy Agency safeguards, and Brazil has pledged not to use the equipment received for the production of nuclear explosive devices, there can be no ignoring the fact that an independent and parallel mili-

Regional Growth of Armed Forces and Military Expenditures (1960-1976)

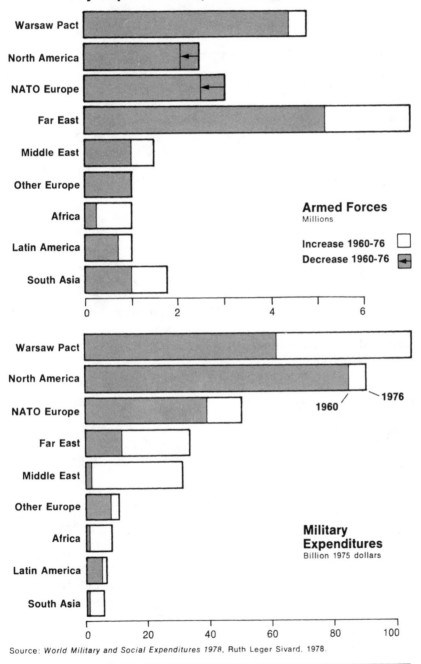

Armed Forces
Millions

Increase 1960-76 □
Decrease 1960-76 ◄■

Warsaw Pact
North America
NATO Europe
Far East
Middle East
Other Europe
Africa
Latin America
South Asia

0   2   4   6

Military Expenditures
Billion 1975 dollars

1960   1976

Warsaw Pact
North America
NATO Europe
Far East
Middle East
Other Europe
Africa
Latin America
South Asia

0   20   40   60   80   100

Source: *World Military and Social Expenditures 1978*, Ruth Leger Sivard. 1978.

Regional Shares of Arms Imports and Military Expenditures

World Arms Imports, 1976
Shares by Regions

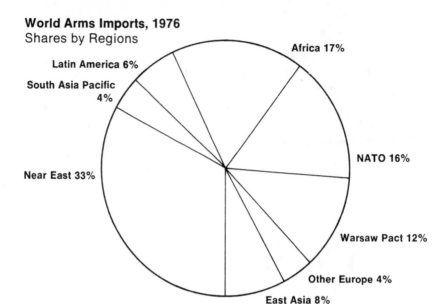

Latin America 6%
South Asia Pacific 4%
Near East 33%
Africa 17%
NATO 16%
Warsaw Pact 12%
Other Europe 4%
East Asia 8%

World Military Expenditures, 1976
Shares by Regions

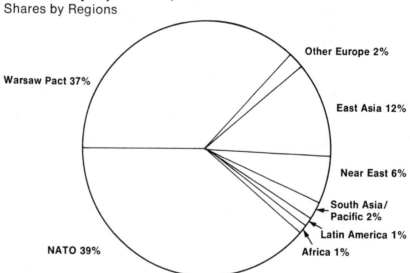

Warsaw Pact 37%
Other Europe 2%
East Asia 12%
Near East 6%
South Asia/Pacific 2%
Latin America 1%
Africa 1%
NATO 39%

Source: *World Military Expenditures and Arms Transfers 1967-1976*, U.S. Arms Control and Disarmament Agency, 1978.

tary program is a clear possibility. This factor, coupled with Brazil's posture concerning peaceful nuclear explosives, opposition to the Tlatelolco and Non-Proliferation Treaties, and the extreme secrecy which cloaks all aspects of the Brazilian nuclear program, lends credence to a military interpretation.

Elsewhere in Latin America the shift toward nuclear power is also apparent. Currently under construction in Mexico are twin 660 megawatt enriched uranium reactors scheduled for completion in 1977 and 1978, and a larger unit is under serious consideration. Venezuela is reportedly negotiating with Canada and European suppliers for a multiple unit natural uranium facility, and Chile will construct a small power reactor by the early 1980s. The Soviet Union has agreed to assist Cuba in constructing two 400-500 megawatt reactors by 1980. (Cuba has announced its intention to construct a total of nine reactors.)

Tlatelolco and Ayacucho—both names have a legacy of violence: the former is the site where the last of the Aztec kings fell before the power of Cortes; the latter is the location of one of the great Latin American revolutionary battles. While neither attempt legally to prohibit nuclear or conventional armaments can be considered fully successful—each is significant if only for its promise. For Tlatelolco to succeed several factors are necessary: 1) the fostering of regional cooperative measures in the nuclear fuel cycle (including joint or multilateral fabrication, reprocessing and possibly enrichment facilities); 2) cooperation between the region's two principal threshold nuclear powers, Argentina and Brazil, as has been suggested recently by a respected Argentine military figure; 3) resolution of the difficult peaceful explosive issue (including perhaps a cooperative peaceful nuclear explosive service between OPANAL and the International Atomic Energy Agency; and, most importantly, 4) a greater degree of cooperation between the principal exporters of nuclear technology. Finally, it is of great importance that Latin American nations continue to develop or perfect all the essential mechanisms and machinery to insure the success of agreements.

Latin America has established an enviable record, compared to other areas, in the regional management of armaments. It is an ongoing process that should be both nurtured and emulated. *(September 1975)*

Demilitarization of the Indian Ocean: A Multilateral Approach Is Essential *Monoranjan Bezboruah*

President Carter's recent call for a "complete demilitarization of the Indian Ocean," strong congressional interest in the matter, and the announcement of plans to establish an American-Soviet joint working group to explore the problem offer hope for a comprehensive Indian Ocean naval arms limitation agreement. Until recently, this great ocean was spared the stresses of the extended superpower arms rivalry taking place in the Atlantic and Pacific. In keeping with its promising emphasis on other arms control matters, the new administration can initiate a process that would return the Indian Ocean to the status of a "peaceful lake," and reduce the possibilities of superpower confrontation in that part of the globe. A demilitarized Indian Ocean is both feasible and desirable. Such a goal conforms well with the overall process of detente.

There has been a strong voice in Congress urging an administration initiative toward an Indian Ocean naval arms limitation agreement. During the deliberations on the proposed expansion of the Diego Garcia facility of the last few years, several congressmen, particularly Senators John Culver (D-Iowa) and Edward Kennedy (D-Mass.) and Representative Lee Hamilton (D-Ind.), clearly expressed their concern about the pitfalls of continued arms rivalry in the Indian Ocean. The Ford administration also expressed the view that, once the Diego Garcia expansion was approved and the so-called asymmetry with the Soviets was corrected, there would be a renewed prospect for such an Indian Ocean naval arms limitation agreement. However, despite approval for Diego Garcia, no initiative was taken. And in the absence of any U.S. initiative, the declared Soviet interest in an Indian Ocean arms control endeavor had political dividends for the Soviets. The Carter administration's initiative in the direction of demilitarization should offer the long needed diplomatic counterpunch to the Soviets.

The present administration is right in treating the Indian Ocean demilitarization issue as part of the overall strategic arms limitation process. The strategic implications of an increasingly volatile Indian Ocean arms race are indeed ominous. Strategically, the Indian Ocean is an attractive deployment area, which will assume increased significance as land-based missiles become more vulnerable to advanced counter-force missiles. In a scenario in which land-based missiles become totally vulnerable, and the United States shifts its nuclear reliance from a triad of systems to a diad of submarine-launched ballistic missiles (SLBMs) and bombers, the Indian Ocean would understandably acquire greater prominence as an additional deployment area. Therefore the loss of the Indian Ocean area as a consequence of a U.S.-initiated demilitarization process might appear as a unilateral abdication of a potentially great advantage. However, there are many dangers inherent in any treatment of the Indian Ocean as a primary site for U.S. strategic deployment. Permanent deployment of SLBMs by the United States in that area would lead to increased Soviet presence in the ocean, and to an intensification of the arms rivalry. Furthermore, a U.S. insistence on such additional deployment (apart from the Mediterranean, the North Atlantic, the Pacific, and the Arctic) might be interpreted in Moscow as a Washington quest for decisive strategic advantage and might stimulate Soviet attempts to catch up. This would mean a vertical proliferation of arms to the detriment of the overall control process.

An intensified strategic arms rivalry in the Indian Ocean might also contribute to horizontal proliferation. Such superpower rivalry would heighten the sense of insecurity among the littoral countries and undoubtedly would stimulate the efforts of potential nuclear powers in the region to acquire nuclear capabilities. Such developments would probably have a domino effect, thus frustrating U.S. hopes for preventing the spread of nuclear weapons.

As an initial step toward demilitarization of the Indian Ocean, a bilateral U.S.-Soviet dialogue appears logical. However, to achieve complete demilitarization, a multilateral approach is essential. An arrangement between the two external superpowers, made without the participation of the area countries, would naturally raise the question of superpower condescension as well as the specter of superpower hegemony over the region. It follows that any naval arms limitation talks for the Indian Ocean must contemplate the participation of the littoral countries, which have regularly expressed their deep concern over the developing external power rivalry in the ocean. Intensely nationalistic, these countries do not subscribe to any notion of an Indian Ocean vacuum to be filled by an external presence. Nor would they appreciate any imposed Indian Ocean order that smacks of superpower condominium.

An emphasis on the multilateral approach, with the participation of the littoral countries such as Sri Lanka and Tanzania—which have expressed an active interest—or regional powers like Iran and India, would offer the negotiating process the legitimacy that successful demilitarization would require. Such a multilateral approach would mend diplomatic fences that were damaged by loose talk about providing "a deterring influence" in the area, or acting as a"policeman on the beat." An active role in the demilitarization process would also be therapeutic for some of the littoral countries. The Shah of Iran, with his accent on fast military build-up, has already staked a claim in the affairs of the Indian Ocean. Through his espoused "gulf security system" and extended Iranian perimeter in the Indian Ocean, the Shah has indicated possible assertion of a patrimonial role in his vicinity. An active incorporation of Iran would, one hopes, offer the Shah a sense of importance and would possibly prevent any Iranian move for unilateral assertion of its emerging prowess. A second example is to provide an active participatory role for India, either in recognition of its status as the most populous, the largest, and the most important country in the region or as a leading advocate of the aspirations of the littoral countries. Constrained by its lack of resources to confront unexpected realities in the ocean, India has a sense of claustrophobia and apprehension because it is only at the receiving end of events in that vital area. A U.S. willingness to bring India into the forum of such naval demilitarization talks would very likely alleviate its reactive and claustrophobic posture. It would also remove New Delhi's nagging feeling that Washington does not accord India due recognition. Over the years, India has seen constant attempts by Washington to neutralize its importance and legitimate standing in pursuit of a policy of three-way detente.

The Nixon statement that "Asian hands must shape the Asian future" notwithstanding, most of the Asian leaders perceive that Washington is still pursuing the old Machiavellian policy of divide and rule toward Asian nations. The U.S. expansion of the Diego Garcia base facility was itself seen as an indication of the continued Washington interest in playing the game of power politics, which has stood in the way of regional cooperation and understanding. A U.S. approach toward a multilateral process, with due participation of the littoral countries, would indeed contribute toward strengthening those countries' ability to withstand pressures from outside—itself a long envisioned goal of the United States.

In addition to the participation of the littoral countries, both the United Kingdom and France must be included, since the presence of these powers in the area is still substantial. A successful demilitarization process should also incorporate Japan, one of the primary users of the ocean, and China, an important interested party. The United Nations, too, should be encouraged to play a role, in the interest of advancing the institutionalization of the arms control process.

President Carter can feel reassured by the fact that the essential framework for realizing his demilitarization goals already exists in the well articulated concept of the Indian Ocean as a zone of peace. First enunciated at the Fourth Summit of Heads of the Nonaligned States at Lusaka (1970), this concept called upon

> all States to consider and respect the Indian Ocean as a
> zone of peace from which great Power rivalries and
> competition, as well as bases conceived in the context
> of such rivalries and competition, either army, navy, or
> air force, would be excluded.

This concept has come to crystalize the hopes and aspirations of the peoples of the area for a peaceful, demilitarized Indian Ocean. The United Nations General Assembly, since its first designation of the

Arms Transfers: Selected Regions And Suppliers
(1967-1976 in millions of unadjusted dollars)

Recipient		Total Arms Transfers	MAJOR SUPPLIERS				
			U.S.	USSR	France	United Kingdom	People's Republic of China
EAST ASIA:	Republic of China	1,785	1,781	—	—	—	—
	North Korea	771	—	480	—	—	280
	Republic of Korea	2,625	2,615	—	5	—	—
	Japan	745	740	—	—	1	—
NEAR EAST:	Egypt	2,801	1	2,365	125	15	5
	Iran	5,271	3,835	611	15	270	—
	Iraq	2,451	—	1,795	95	5	5
	Israel	4,941	4,761	—	105	35	—
	Jordan	650	505	—	55	60	—
	Saudi Arabia	1,440	671	—	225	451	—
	Syria	2,261	5	2,015	5	5	1
SOUTH ASIA:	India	1,680	40	1,365	41	75	—
	Pakistan	831	85	25	265	10	335
AFRICA:	Algeria	445	5	315	5	—	—
	Libya	1,835	65	1,005	325	55	—
	Nigeria	221	31	70	1	50	—
	South Africa	500	30	—	365	10	—
LATIN AMERICA:	Argentina	361	131	—	75	55	—
	Brazil	690	300	—	155	105	—
	Chile	355	110	—	11	145	—
	Peru	655	105	165	111	50	—
	Venezuela	375	105	—	125	45	—

Source: World Military Expenditures and Arms Transfers 1967-1976, U.S. Arms Control and Disarmament Agency, 1978

While public attention tends to focus on nuclear weapons and the superpower military rivalry, there exist grave regional antagonisms and accompanying competitions in weaponry, to which the U.S. and the USSR have contributed as the world's leading arms exporters. To some, these regional arms purchases represent funds diverted from economic development projects.

Indian Ocean as a zone of peace (Resolution 2832 [XXIV] of December 16, 1971), has repeatedly called upon the great powers, the littoral and hinterland states, and the maritime users of the ocean to enter into multilateral consultations for the establishment of a demilitarized regime. The concept of the zone of peace—an increasingly popular idea in the field of arms control and disarmament—seems to aim at exactly the same "complete demilitarization" that President Carter is so rightly striving for.

In order to implement a successful demilitarization agreement a two-tier arrangement is necessary. First, the United States and the Union of Soviet Socialist Republics (through bilateral deliberations) need to agree on the basic demilitarization provisions. Secondly, the two super-powers, acting together, should arrange to bring the other interested parties into the agreement. Such an arrangement would naturally create rights and duties requiring supervision and enforcement. A multilateral supervisory body could be established, with representation from the littoral countries, the United States, the USSR, France, the United Kingdom, Japan, the People's Republic of China, and a member of another region such as Latin America. The supervisory body might be provided with permanent fixtures—a headquarters in a centrally located, non-aligned, Indian Ocean littoral country such as the Seychelles or Mauritius; the necessary international staff; and an adequate budget. To secure the benefits of an institutionalized process, this supervisory body should be closely linked with the United Nations. The demilitarization agreement should be registered with the United Nations Secretariat under Article 102 of the Charter. The United Nations General Assembly should also be allowed to discuss pertinent issues relating to demilitarization under Article 11 of the Charter.

A complete demilitarization of the Indian Ocean is both feasible and desirable. The Carter administration can begin by supporting the idea of an international conference as proposed for several years by the United Nations Ad Hoc Committee on the Indian Ocean. Such U.S. support and eventual participation would undoubtedly contribute to the success of the deliberations, and the administration can find a ready-made platform by affirming its association and identification with the ideal of the zone of peace in the Indian Ocean. *(May 1977)*

MBFR As Arms Control? *Jane M. O. Sharp*

Mutual and balanced force reductions may be desirable, but are they negotiable? Reducing the level of military confrontation in Europe is the declared objective of the current talks between NATO and the Warsaw Pact, but previous arms control experience suggests that pursuit of a formal international treaty could yield quite a different result. With no final agreement in sight in Vienna and the prospect of long drawn out negotiations, it behooves us to re-assess the wisdom of this traditional approach. Chances of successfully codifying a new security system at lower levels of force need to be weighed against the risks, inherent in the adversary bargaining process, of exacerbating international tensions and perhaps even generating pressures for the acquisition of forces which otherwise might not have been procured.

Some general propositions about the likely effects of negotiations on force posture derived from earlier arms control efforts, and the impact of Mutual and Balanced Force Reduction (MBFR) talks since NATO first invited the Pact to negotiate in June 1968, underscore these risks.

The Urge for Symmetry: Force asymmetries are emphasized when former or potential adversaries attempt to negotiate arms control. States become hypersensitive to newly perceived inadequacies and tend to correct them by leveling up to parity in a variety of force categories. Final agreements usually set limits which allow the weak to attain the force levels of the strong; established as force ceilings these limits soon come to be regarded as floors, thereby providing the rationale for increased forces.

The initial MBFR proposal stimulated a wave of reassessments of the European military balance. Western defense analysts began to stress that NATO forces, postured to sustain a protracted conflict, were dangerously inappropriate to counter Warsaw Pact forces poised for a blitzkrieg type of attack. Expressions of considerable equanimity about the balance in the late 1960s gave way to a growing concern with Pact advantages, followed by increasingly alarmist exhortations to correct deficiencies. Recent NATO force improvements focus on increasing combat strength, anti-tank fire power and close-in air support to enhance short war capability. Meanwhile the Pact, apparently acting under a similar imperative, seems to be emphasizing support facilities and long-range air interdiction capabilities to hedge against the possibility of a longer conflict.

The Bargaining Chip Phenomenon: In anticipation of future limitation, parties to an arms control negotiation tend to acquire extra and retain surplus forces as chips to be cashed in later with no real loss of strength. These forces then become immune to critical evaluation on their merits and to the extent they are not cashed in become part of the permanent force structure.

Forces newly deployed as part of routine modernization schedules are sometimes difficult to distinguish from those deployed for bargaining purposes, but the 1,000 Soviet T-62 tanks which were moved into East Germany during 1973 could be regarded as bargaining chips. On the NATO side there seems little doubt that some forces have been retained which in the absence of negotiations would almost certainly have been withdrawn. Senator Mike Mansfield's (D-Mont.) efforts to reduce American force levels in Europe were regularly blocked by invoking MBFR. Similarly, proposals to reduce the dangerously excessive deployment of tactical nuclear weapons in Europe have repeatedly failed because of U.S. State Department sensitivity to the allied negotiating position in Vienna—where tactical nuclear weapons now feature in the latest NATO proposal. As former Defense Secretary James Schlesinger told the Senate Foreign Relations Committee: "There are diplomatic reasons associated with the size of that stockpile."

The Bureaucratic Effect: Negotiations narrowly focused on military forces tend to increase the relative influence of the defense establishment (both military and industrial components) in domestic and alliance decision making.

Since the balance of forces is usually discussed in terms of hypothetical military action and negotiators must consult the military on a technical level, only those items to which the services are not especially attached are likely to be limited. Preventing the use of biological weapons or the deployment of weapons in outer space or Antarctica proved relatively easy, but attempts to control forces-in-being usually meet with considerable resistance. Witness the cancellation of a scheduled reduction of 8,000 U.S. support troops from West Germany last year under pressure from General Frederick Weyand. Moreover, there is the risk that final agreements will be seriously compromised to gain military approval and can easily be exploited afterwards if expectations are disappointed. The kind of MBFR treaty which will satisfy NATO commanders, in terms of retaining their own freedom to move and deploy troops and equipment, is unlikely to constrain either side's forces very effectively.

The Displacement Effect: The possibility of controls in one area tends to divert the force acquisition process into areas unlikely to be proscribed and to stimulate technological innovation to compensate for quantitative limits with qualitative improvements.

This effect has been apparent in the American, British, and West German efforts to compensate for possible numerical limits by increasing combat-to-support ratios among ground troops in the MBFR guidelines area.* NATO is also investing in programs to increase the accuracy of both conventional and nuclear munitions, improving logistics and rein-

---

*The MBFR guidelines area comprises Benelux (Belgium, Netherlands, and Luxembourg) and West Germany, East Germany, Poland and Czechoslovakia.

forcement capabilities and moving towards standardization of both weapons and tactics within the alliance. The ten European members of NATO, whose defense efforts are coordinated through the Eurogroup, have made major contributions of new equipment since 1970. While some of these programs would have occurred under routine modernization, indications are that MBFR provided the impetus for many of them and there is no question that the Vienna talks have been used to justify the extra defense spending involved.

The Regional Effect: The prospect of a regional limitation on forces tends to destabilize those areas contiguous to the control zone.

This can be seen in the anxieties expressed by European neutrals, as well as by northern and southern flank states of NATO, that an agreement confined to the MBFR guidelines area could result in the redeployment of forces into areas which hitherto have been relatively stable. The only kind of MBFR treaty likely to satisfy Norway for example, would be one limiting Soviet forces in the Kola peninsula; likewise the Yugoslavs might feel more sanguine if there were less risk of disturbing the current alignment of Soviet troops, i.e., predominantly facing Northern and Central Europe and the Chinese border.

The Effect on Alliances: Arms control negotiations tend to increase security anxieties of small alliance powers who fear super-power bilateralism at their expense; and to introduce rigidity into force planning as group pressure is exerted to maintain a strong cohesive bargaining position.

Fears of super-power duopoly were more evident in the early stages of MBFR than lately, though there is a constant undercurrent of anxiety among Europeans as they contemplate a Soviet-American deal on theater nuclear forces.

MBFR has had a substantial effect on the force planning of NATO members. Before the search for a formal MBFR agreement became official policy in June 1968, member states adjusted their forces unilaterally, more in accordance with national priorities than alliance commitments—and were able to do so without causing undue alarm. After the 1961 Berlin crisis, NATO governments acted in response to perceptions of a steadily diminishing threat from the East, growing economic pressures, and in several cases, extra-alliance demands on military forces. The trend—except for West Germany—was towards reduced defense budgets and lower force levels in Europe. During the MBFR gestation period 1968-1972, and especially since formal talks began in 1973, this earlier flexibility has given way to a rachet effect in which the only acceptable adjustment is upwards. Unilateral reductions in manpower have been virtually halted and attempts to curtail any aspect of defense activity arouse severe criticism from NATO headquarters.

Britain and the Netherlands have both been under strong domestic pressure to reduce defense spending but have held the line against cuts in the MBFR guidelines area. Britain has reduced its presence in the Mediterranean and its capability to patrol the eastern Atlantic but has actually improved its commitment in West Germany. The Netherlands may be forced to make cuts in the Dutch navy which national priorities indicated should be in the army, because NATO reportedly vetoed any tampering with ground forces, which feature in proposals currently on the table in Vienna.

Canada, the only NATO member unilaterally to cut troops from the guidelines area since June 1968, is now under pressure to increase its forces stationed in Europe; Italy on the other hand, which is not a full participant in the MBFR talks and has no forces stationed in the critical central area, has been able to reduce manpower without recrimination.

The International Effect: Arms control negotiations tend to emphasize the narrow security aspects of international relations at the expense of more cooperative and functional interaction.

Only on rare occasions have arms control agreements served to codify improved relations; more often states in a semi-relaxed relationship enter a negotiation in which each then seeks to increase its own relative security advantage—declarations to the contrary notwithstanding—exacerbating tensions by focusing on the balance of military force and other sensitive issues.

It is sobering to speculate to what extent the current disillusionment with detente might be attributable to the SALT and MBFR negotiations. Certainly there is less talk of force reductions in Vienna than talk of force improvements in Brussels; there the emphasis is on an increase in the Eurogroup contribution to the NATO defense effort, transatlantic standardization, and a revival of interest in a West European defense identity—to the point where even France is considering joining a cooperative armaments procurement agency.

A European defense community dominated by West Germany has been a recurrent bogey for the East since the late 1950s and to resurrect such a concept now, when Chancellor Helmut Schmidt is so unabashed about his leadership potential in both the European Economic Community and NATO, could appear more than a little ominous and is hardly conducive to a more conciliatory attitude at the negotiating table.

To summarize: by focusing on precisely those aspects of division which most Europeans have been patiently trying to erase, the MBFR talks could undermine a decade of effort to improve East-West relations on the old continent. By holding out the attractive prospect of joint reductions and focusing debate on narrow military and technical issues, arms control negotiations fundamentally alter the balance of political forces which surround questions of resource allocation in any given society. The result seems to be a serious weakening of the legislative constraints on defense spending, which in turn leaves the conservative tendencies and appetites of the military relatively unchecked.

It is worth recalling that when Tsar Alexander I suggested negotiated force reductions in Europe after the Napoleonic wars, Lord Castlereagh, the British Foreign Secretary, rejected the idea in the following terms:

> . . . the settlement of a scale of force for so many Powers —under such different circumstances as to their relative means, frontiers, positions and faculties for rearming— presents a very complicated question for negotiation . . . and further, on this as on many subjects of a jealous character, in attempting to do much, difficulties are rather brought into view than made to disappear.

Castlereagh suggested instead that each state should unilaterally reduce its arms to the minimum it considered necessary, and then

> Explain to the Allied and Neighbouring States the extent and nature of its arrangements as a means of dispelling alarm and rendering moderate establishments mutually convenient.

If the history of arms control seems to confirm Castlereagh's premonition about the negative potential of negotiations, perhaps we should pay more attention to his advice: planning our forces unilaterally and flexibly as required, rather than in lockstep with our political adversaries.

(April 1976)

This volume has so far focused on substantive arms control policy questions; in this final section the focus is less on the content of arms control policy decisions than on the way these decisions are made.

In the United States, there is a growing body of scholarly literature which suggests that foreign policy decisions are greatly influenced by the political interplay of the bureaucratic institutions involved. At the highest level, cabinet departments vie for influence over the President, and within each department, bureaucracies try to control the flow of information and ideas to the secretary. While the impact of these bureaucratic struggles should not be exaggerated, it is clear that institutional structures do play an important role.

On the international level, institutional imperatives can also be important, though for somewhat different reasons. Nations generally make arms control policy decisions on the basis of their perception of national interest, but a strong, organized, international consensus for arms control can help push the powers toward agreement. The institutional structure of multilateral arms control negotiations can also influence a nation's decision to join these negotiations. For example, one of the problems with the Geneva Conference of the Committee on Disarmament was that China and France protested that, until 1978, the conference was co-chaired by the USSR and the United States.

Articles here on the 1978 UN Special Session on Disarmament reflect this concern with institutional issues. For some observers, the reform of international institutions for disarmament was the most concrete outcome of this first of a series of special sessions. On the basis of this progress, many hope, a broader effort can be established to solve the problems of arms proliferation.

A U.S. effort to institutionalize improved arms control information in the form of annual Arms Control Impact Statements was frustrated at first but has gained ground in the current administration.

Both institutions and individuals influence policy, however. Perhaps no individual has more impact on arms control policy than the American president. Also reprinted in this section, therefore, are the views of the major party nominees in the 1976 presidential election on major arms control issues, a reflection of the growing significance of arms control for national and international security.

Institutionalizing Arms Control

Strengthening the ACDA   *Thomas A. Halsted*

Each turnover of presidential power has seen opportunities for arms control lost while new weapons developments have been advanced. Incoming presidents, unsure of their footing in the foreign policy field, sensitive to suggestions that they might be found wanting if the Soviets "tested their mettle," and under strong pressure from interests supporting expanded military establishments, have tended to cast a wary eye on proposals to take immediate and positive action on the arms control front, and to neglect opportunities to negotiate with adversaries abroad while avoiding confrontation with cold warriors at home.

Thus in 1961, despite clear evidence that there was no "missile gap," John Kennedy made decisions which led to the expansion of planned U.S. missile forces to 1,000 Minuteman ICBMs (intercontinental ballistic missiles) and 41 Polaris submarines carrying a total of 656 submarine-launched missiles—far more strategic striking power than could plausibly be justified for any military purpose. One consequence of this unwarranted buildup has been a non-stop Soviet effort to match and overmatch the United States by trying to achieve the same astronomical levels of military force.

In 1969 Richard Nixon disregarded the advice of much of the arms control and scientific community, including the prestigious General Advisory Committee on Arms Control and Disarmament, and gave the go-ahead to the MIRV (multiple independently-targetable re-entry vehicle) deployment program. Once again, the Soviet Union followed the U.S. lead. Today some of the same big defense advocates who pressed for MIRV deployment are worrying that Soviet MIRVs could spell an end to stability by threatening the U.S. deterrent. "I wish," said Secretary of State Henry Kissinger in 1974, "that I had thought through the implication of the MIRVed world" when the MIRV program was approved.

Now Jimmy Carter is about to take office at another of these critical decision points. He is under pressure to be tough with the Soviet Union (the intense campaign to return James Schlesinger to the Department of Defense was only a foretaste of what is likely to come), to go slow on arms control, and to approve a number of radically new, and in some cases highly destabilizing, weapons programs. But there are hopeful signs that President Carter will not follow the lead of his predecessors. For one thing, throughout his election campaign he repeatedly expressed his commitment to strategic arms limitation, to preventing nuclear proliferation, to coming to grips with the conventional arms sales problem, and to reducing substantially dependence on nuclear weapons as an instrument for international relations. He also affirmed his readiness to take up the Soviet leadership on its offers to negotiate significant arms control agreements. Additionally, many of Carter's top advisors are intimately familiar both with the issues involved and many of the negotiating problems. There is no need for an excessive period of policy review and study of options before progress can be made. The Carter administration can start out in high gear.

For his arms control programs to succeed, however, much will depend on how his administration is staffed and organized to cope with the sizeable challenges it will face. The nominations of Cyrus Vance and Harold Brown to the State and the Defense Departments are promising signs that the commitment to real progress in arms control that Carter has pledged so far will be matched by key members of his national security and foreign policy team. The pattern of past transitions may have been broken, and new standing and impetus given to arms control and disarmament. But a dedicated and persistent effort in this area will require institutional changes throughout the bureaucracy, and nowhere more critically than in the Arms Control and Disarmament Agency (ACDA).

ACDA, formed in 1961 to develop and support arms control and disarmament policies and negotiations, was effectively gutted in 1973— its budget slashed by a third, its SALT (Strategic Arms Limitation Talks) negotiating role taken away, and many of its most imaginative and effective officials transferred or retired. Morale dropped sharply. With the single exception of efforts to develop nuclear export policies more in line with non-proliferation goals, ACDA relinquished to other agencies, or, more often, to limbo, what leadership it once had in developing U.S. arms control policies.

This process must now be reversed. A greatly strengthened ACDA, with new independence and authority, and the full backing of the President, his secretaries of state and defense, as well as his national security advisor, is needed to fill the policy vacuum that now exists and to translate Carter's good intentions into effective action.

Some conceptual and institutional notions about the future role of ACDA are offered below.

First, ACDA's role is not only to develop plans and policies; it also provides a platform for advocacy; it should be a central focal point for arms control thinking in the executive branch, and a day-to-day proponent, both in private government councils and in a greatly expanded public education role, of the concept that arms control is an essential and inseparable part of national security planning. Thus ACDA and its director must not play the role of promoter or apologist for new weapons programs, but rather should constantly seek to inject arms control perceptions into both the public and the official dialogue on defense and security issues. ACDA should be promoting its cause more vigorously even than some elements in the bureaucracy may be ready to accept, rather than joining in an effort to keep on the brakes.

Public opinion about arms control and disarmament has grown skeptical in recent years. This is in part because *no* government official has effectively rebutted exaggerated charges that the United States is growing weaker and the Soviet threat therefore needs to be met by greater military expenditures. ACDA could play a prominent role in a major public education effort to put the military balance in a more reasonable perspective.

The relationship of ACDA to the rest of the bureaucracy needs reexamination. By statute, the agency is semi-autonomous. Its director serves as "the principal advisor to the secretary of state and the president on arms control and disarmament matters," but with the sole exception of negotiations, which he is to carry out "under the direction of the secretary of state," he is accountable directly to the President. In recent years, however, ACDA's negotiating function on the most critical arms control issue—SALT—as well as the sensitive nuclear "supplier club" negotiations has been turned over entirely to the State Department. ACDA retains responsibility for the Geneva Conference of the Committee on Disarmament and the Mutual and Balanced Force Reduction talks, but otherwise it is given negotiating responsibility only in cases of lower-priority issues, such as the forthcoming review conference on the Seabed Arms Control Treaty.

ACDA should, as a matter of course, reassume the overall responsibility for *all* arms control negotiations, and lead the U.S. delegations to them. This is particularly true with respect to SALT, likely to dominate all other arms control issues in the months ahead. A senior, respected negotiator with broad experience in arms control matters should be appointed to head the SALT delegation, under the direction of the ACDA director and backstopped by the ACDA staff. Quite properly, the conduct of the negotiations should be thoroughly coordinated with the secretary of state, as the statute provides.

Second, consideration should be given to expanding the permanent staff of professional arms controllers. Nearly one-third of the professional staff are foreign service and military officers detailed to ACDA. Many of these latter are competent and dedicated professionals, but their first loyalty must necessarily be to their parent services, and many of them view their ACDA tours as undesirable detours from career patterns in other fields. Expanding the permanent ACDA staff, and transferring to it many of the slots now occupied by these detailed personnel, might help to attract more talented individuals to the arms control profession and stimulate scholarship in the field.

Third, the advantages of physically removing ACDA from the State Department building, where it is at present housed, should be weighed. Aside from perpetuating the impression in other agencies that ACDA is only a *de facto* bureau of the State Department, housing it in the same building has led to the State Department's viewing it as such, involving the agency in the department's clearance procedures and other coordination functions, rather than treating it as the independent agency it is supposed to be. To be sure, there are advantages in the present relationship: the director participates in (and can have some influence on) the secretary of state's staff meetings; access to cable traffic and secure communications facilities are readily available; the State Department motor pool is at the agency's disposal. But these advantages appear to be largely superficial when weighed against the disadvantages of a loss of true independence, and the cost of duplicating necessary facilities should not be a serious obstacle. It is also true, however, that the pros and cons of physically separating the agency from the State Department are likely to be affected significantly by the degree to which the secretary of state views the role of arms control and disarmament in international affairs and is willing to stand up for ACDA.

The arms control impact assessment process, initiated in 1976, has so far been a failure. This new congressionally-mandated process requires the executive branch to provide detailed and careful analysis of the potential impact of new weapons programs or policies on arms control negotiations and programs. The Carter administration will need to look on impact statements not as a proceeding to conceal adverse findings from Congress, nor as a means of finding an arms control justification for otherwise questionable weapons programs, but rather as the law intended: a mechanism for avoiding unwise arms decisions with potentially undesirable or dangerous outcomes. ACDA should play a leading role in this effort.

The ACDA research budget should be increased and imaginative efforts undertaken to increase both in-house and external research on areas now largely untouched. The agency's budget is sufficiently starved at the moment that external research projects are frequently piggybacked on Department of Defense or Central Intelligence Agency contracts, a practice tending to make the contractor's findings consistent with those agencies' views.

Finally, the word "disarmament" seldom crosses a bureaucrat's or politician's lips, and little or no serious thinking on the subject takes place in the government. In 1978 the Eighth Special Session of the United Nations General Assembly will be devoted to disarmament; and preparatory commission meetings for that session begin in March 1977. ACDA should play a prominent role in developing a U.S. position that, one hopes, will help make the Special Session a constructive examination of opportunities for progress in disarmament, rather than a propaganda forum for whipping the superpowers, as some observers fear. Over the longer run, however, ACDA also needs to be better organized to think about disarmament goals and processes. The ACDA director might consider assigning a few talented staff members to think only about long-range arms control and disarmament objectives. President-elect Carter has stated that "the ultimate goal of this nation should be the reduction of nuclear weapons in all nations of the world to zero." Imaginative thinking about means of attaining this goal and related disarmament measures is needed. ACDA should be thinking about disarmament objectives for the next century—not just concentrating on the negotiating problems of the next week or month.

This article has focused on rebuilding and rededicating the Arms Control and Disarmament Agency to equip it better to tackle an imposing array of issues in the months and years ahead. But unless the entire government, both the executive branch and Congress, is committed to the task, no amount of restructuring or strengthening of ACDA will mean much. The Departments of State and Defense, the National Security Council, key regulatory agencies, the Senate, and the House of Representatives must all be willing to make a concerted effort to overcome the many obstacles to progress in ending the debilitating arms race and finding better ways to build and keep a secure and stable society. And the committed leadership of the President, with the full support of the American people, will count most of all. *(December 1976)*

Arms Control Impact Statements: A New Approach to Slowing the Arms Race? *Betty G. Lall*

To date, international negotiation has been the principal means used to try to slow the momentum of the arms race. While some positive results can be cited, e.g., the partial test ban treaty, and the ABM (Anti-Ballistic Missile) Treaty, negotiation clearly has not produced substantial progress. There might be more progress if other methods could be pursued simultaneously.

Among the reasons that negotiation has yielded such limited progress is the manner in which decisions are made to develop and produce new weapons systems. The major nations have built specialized bureaucracies whose principal job is to maintain their defense establishment in a perpetual state of modernization. Consequently, as new weapons systems move from the initial research stage to later stages of development, testing, production, and deployment, they become more difficult to control or eliminate through international disarmament and arms control negotiations. The weapons acquisition process has accumulated an impressive array of vested interests. The enormous investment of funds in a new weapons system and the disruption which would result from its termination cause national political leaders to be reluctant to abandon it once development and procurement have commenced.

Another factor obstructing the efforts to slow the momentum of weapons development is that the people responsible for arms control and disarmament policy and negotiations often have not had up-to-date information about new weapons systems, and particularly about the early research and development activities which may have an important bearing on arms control policy and negotiations. Such research programs often become buried in a maze of defense authorization and appropriations data. For example, although the United States began the serious development of multiple warheads (MIRVs) in the early 1960s, their arms control implications were not really considered until about 1969.

Late in the fall of 1975 the U.S. Congress passed legislation establishing a process for determining the impact of new weapons systems on the arms race. The purpose of this process is to reveal the arms control impact of a weapons system while it is still in an early stage of development. The legislation specifies that programs which may have significant implications for arms control policy and negotiations shall be subject to analysis and assessment. The agency responsible for such weapons programs must furnish the director of the Arms Control and Disarmament Agency (ACDA) "on a continuing basis . . . full and timely access to detailed information" about them. The director of ACDA, "as he deems appropriate, shall assess and analyze each program with respect to its impact on arms control and disarmament policy and negotiations, and shall advise and make recommendations, on the basis of such assessment and analysis, to the National Security Council, the Office of Management and Budget, and the Government agency proposing such program." If the National Security Council decides that the programs have significant arms control implications, then the agency's request to the Congress for funds must be accompanied by "a complete statement analyzing the impact of such program on arms control and disarmament policy and negotiations."

The new legislation also provides that any one of eight different congressional committees may request the advice of the director of ACDA "on the arms control and disarmament implications of any program with respect to which a statement" on the arms control and disarmament impact was submitted as part of the budgetary request. Two of these committees—the House Committee on International Relations and the Senate Committee on Foreign Relations—have established a procedure to evaluate the impact statements submitted to them. Experts of the Congressional Research Service will advise the congressional committees about the adequacy of the impact statements. It is possible that the Congressional Research Service will consider focusing on a few of the programs that appear to have the most significant arms control impact, and, along with the various congressional committees, may eventually develop an independent arms control impact analysis capability.

It is important to note that the legislation stipulates that agencies involved in research, development, testing, and production programs for weapons must furnish the director of ACDA with information on a continuous basis. Thus, one of the difficulties in attempting to control weapons at early stages of development should be removed. All nuclear weapons programs are subject to this information requirement as well as weapons programs with expenditure levels exceeding $50 million annually or $250 million in total costs. Moreover, the information flow can begin for weapon programs or policies even below these levels of expenditures. The House Committee on International Relations pointed out the reason for this provision: "Included in this intent are items of 'seminal' nature, such as major philosophical or doctrinal changes in defense posture or new weapons concepts in various stages of research and development."

The key to the effectiveness of the legislation is the kind of analysis prepared by the director of ACDA, since this will be the basis for any decision by the National Security Council to submit the impact statement with the agency's budgetary requests to Congress.

The legislation does not specify what, if anything, should be done if an ACDA assessment of a weapons program indicates that it would have a negative or countervailing effect on arms control policy or negotiations in process. It might be presumed that a strong ACDA leadership would bring such a finding to the attention of the National Security Council, the secretary of defense, and possibly to the President. Much depends on the character of the ACDA leadership.

If a conflict arose would the weapons system be abandoned, postponed, developed at a slower rate, or, alternatively, would the arms control policy be altered? The answer to this question cannot yet be known because the legislation has not been implemented. The executive branch has stated that the legislation was passed too late to have it applied to the budgetary process which began in January 1976. It was anticipated, however, that impact statements on some twenty to thirty weapons programs for consideration would be prepared this year. Finally in early August, Congress did receive sixteen impact statements concerning Defense Department and Energy Research and Development Administration programs—unhappily, too late to have any impact on congressional consideration of the current defense programs. It is reported that about 100 weapon programs will be assessed for 1977.

ACDA's choice of criteria in making its assessments is crucial to the efficacy of the arms control impact statements as a means of slowing down the arms race and as a contributor to more successful arms control and disarmament negotiations. While the legislation does not require ACDA to reveal its criteria they will undoubtedly become known because Congress is likely to require such information as part of its analysis of the materials submitted to it by the executive branch. Such criteria might include, for example, answering such questions as: At what point in the development of a new weapons system should it become the subject for international negotiation? To what extent should the rate of research and development of a weapons program be slowed in order not to have it complicate already delicate and difficult negotiations? Will there be times when a new weapons program should be delayed altogether pending the outcome of negotiations? Should new weapons programs serve as bargaining chips in negotiations? Should research contracts for verification be let simultaneously with contracts for the weapons themselves so as to assure that means of verification will be available? What are reasonable time periods that should be set to give negotiations time to succeed pending decisions to proceed with a weapons program from one stage of development to another?

It is possible that the impact statements will also affect the formulation of arms control and disarmament policy. This effect could be both positive and negative. It could be positive because the ACDA personnel responsible for formulating policy would have much more information to work with. Similarly, the Congress would also have more data with which to judge the adequacy of the present policies. Policy might become more comprehensive and long range as compared to the present ad hoc and limited approach. Theoretically every weapons system is a candidate for control, reduction, or elimination. However, if the weapons program can be identified by ACDA at an earlier stage, the result could be both a savings of money and a reduction in tension among nations—provided such identification leads to a postponement of the development of that program and its eventual control through international negotiation. In terms of the current arms race, in the overwhelming majority of cases the introduction of new weapons, as well as the deployment of existing weapons in new locations, has been a source of tension and not the reverse. ICBMs (intercontinental ballistic missiles), the intercontinental bomber, MIRVs, and ABMs are examples. A significant exception is the long-range ballistic missile on submarines. However, this legislation is not likely to reach its full potential and effectiveness unless similar approaches are adopted by the other major arms producing countries.

On the negative side, increased pressure could be put on ACDA, the National Security Council, the President, and Congress by weapons-producing agencies either to assess the impact of a weapons system as being of no consequence to the success of arms control policy or negotiations, or, if the impact was considered harmful to arms control efforts, to change the policy itself. For example, in the 1950s and early 1960s military leaders resisted successfully all efforts to include ICBMs as active and serious subjects for reduction and control in international negotiations.

On balance, the concept of arms control impact statements is a promising new development in achieving arms control and disarmament. The effectiveness of this approach would be enhanced if it were adopted in other countries. Since the U.S. legislation is at such an early stage of implementation, it necessitates the scrutiny of arms control observers in order to make certain its intent is being realized. *(July/August 1976)*

The Outlook for the UN Special Session on Disarmament *Michael J. Sullivan III*

The Special Session of the United Nations General Assembly on Disarmament, lasting from May 23 through June 28, 1978, is, in the words of United Nations Secretary-General Kurt Waldheim, the "largest, most representative gathering ever convened" to consider the arms race. The heads of state or government of such military powers as Britain, France, West Germany and India are attending. Scores of non-governmental organizations from throughout the world are mounting a series of demonstrations and other exercises in public education to draw attention to the event.

At least six distinct groups can be identified as having some importance for the special session: (1) the Group of Non-Aligned States; (2) the Soviet Union and some of its Eastern European allies, plus

Mongolia; (3) a group of Western states associated with, but not including, the United States; (4) individual states which have a history of interest in disarmament, but which are not members of the Eastern or Western alliance system and/or of the non-aligned group; (5) the alienated nuclear-weapon-states France and China, and (6) a significant number of states which have not participated in the disarmament debate to any significant degree.

The initial idea for a General Assembly special session was made at the first summit meeting of heads of non-aligned states in Belgrade, Yugoslavia, in 1961. Since that time, the Non-Aligned Group has grown in number from the twenty-five states which met in Yugoslavia to the eighty-two which gathered in Sri Lanka in 1976 for the fifth such summit meeting. This group has played the prime role in nurturing the idea of an all-inclusive world assembly devoted to disarmament.

In the 1960s, the non-aligned states often called for either a special session or a world disarmament conference. One of their goals was to bring China into the world's arms negotiating forums. Since the People's Republic was not a member of the United Nations, an extra-United Nations alternative had to be offered. After Peking's admission to the General Assembly in 1971, the Soviet Union embraced sponsorship of the world disarmament conference, perhaps with an eye to embarrassing the new Chinese delegation which they suspected might be unprepared for any protracted disarmament debate. In addition, the USSR may have assumed there was value in proposing the most sweeping disarmament machinery possible, where the restraining rules of procedure of the General Assembly would not be in force, and "actual decisions on disarmament," as contrasted to mere resolutions, could be made.

In the 1972 General Assembly, the non-aligned states moved to regain the initiative for a world disarmament conference from the Russians by proposing it as a vehicle for "rejuvenating the stalled global arms control effort." This formulation implied a criticism of SALT (Strategic Arms Limitation Talks) and of the Geneva Conference of the Committee on Disarmament (CCD), with its Soviet-American co-chairmanship and cold war blocs of representation (eight Western, eight Eastern, and fifteen non-aligned states). Besides muting the apparently anti-Chinese character of the Soviet proposal, the non-aligned initiative struck a responsive chord in France, which began to participate in the United Nations disarmament debate for the first time in a decade. The General Assembly then moved to commission an ad hoc committee to "study the feasibility of a world disarmament conference."

After three years of little progress in this committee, the Non-Aligned Group, at their 1975 foreign ministers' meeting, began to propose once again the idea of a special General Assembly session as an alternative to a world disarmament conference. At the 1976 summit meeting in Sri

Lanka, they proposed a special session in which the "question of convening a world disarmament conference would be on the agenda." With this compromise wording to meet the anticipated Soviet objections to the abandonment of the world disarmament conference as an imminent goal, the General Assembly endorsed the concept of a special session and established the fifty-four nation preparatory committee which has been working since March 1977.

It is in this preparatory committee that the other four tendencies in the international disarmament debate have emerged, particularly as the committee began to draft the document which will form the framework for the deliberations at the special session. To oversimplify, the six identifiable groups in the debate can be placed along a continuum with respect to the degree of concern with which they view the global arms race and the degree of urgency with which they assert the need for some corrective international machinery.

Significant Individual Participants. The state which apparently regards the arms race with the greatest urgency, when measured by the sheer numbers of papers, speeches, and initiatives presented in the past two decades, is Mexico. Due chiefly to the energy and intelligence of its chief disarmament negotiator, Alfonso Garcia Robles, Mexico led the movement which resulted in the 1967 Treaty of Tlatelolco, declaring Latin America a nuclear-free zone. It has been openly pushing for a reorganization of the Geneva CCD since 1969. Mexico also has the grandest vision of the potential of a special session. Specifically, it envisions the special session as the first of an institutionalized series which will recur regularly in the manner of the United Nations Conference on Trade and Development in the economic field. This first special session could, it is hoped, enumerate certain nuclear disarmament measures to be taken by the two superpowers over the next three years, during which time a reorganized successor to the CCD could negotiate a comprehensive program of disarmament for a Second Special Session of the General Assembly on Disarmament in May 1981.

Mexico's proposals are mentioned first to provide a standard of specificity against which the policies of other states and caucuses can be compared. There are certain other states which might also be categorized with Mexico in a group expressing urgent concern over the arms race, at least as regards certain specific issues. These states, however, have little in common other than their espousal of certain issues and their absence from any of the other groups. Among them are: Sweden, which is interested in controlling weapons of indiscriminate and inhumane slaughter (fragmentation bombs, napalm, etc.) and supports United Nations studies on the comparability of national military budgets; Austria, which goes farthest in asserting the powers of the United Nations Secretariat in the field of disarmament; Rumania, which is most extreme in criticizing military alliances and calls for the prohibition of "multinational military maneuvers or shows of strength" near the frontiers of other states; New Zealand, which espouses the "broadest possible application" of a comprehensive nuclear test ban; Pakistan, which raises the issue of pledges of security guarantees for, or non-use of nuclear weapons against, non-nuclear-weapon states; and Brazil which, along with Pakistan and (non-aligned) Argentina, most frequently counters any demands for strict controls over nuclear-weapons proliferation with an assertion of the "inalienable right of all states" to develop nuclear technology for peaceful purposes.

Non-Aligned States. The Non-Aligned Group, on the other hand, appears more representative of the mainstream of opinion in the General Assembly. It has worked to modify many of the foregoing issues in order to gain wider acceptance for certain basic disarmament concepts. Of the eighty-two non-aligned states at the Sri Lanka summit, twenty-seven are on the preparatory committee. This group's core leadership—Yugoslavia, Sri Lanka, Egypt, India, Algeria, Nigeria, Malaysia, Argentina, and Peru—has lobbied not only among the other non-aligned states, but also among the other nations and factions in the preparatory committee and has become most influential in developing the four main parts of the tentative special session document. These include:

—a *preamble,* which stresses controlling the global arms race (particularly the nuclear arms race) within the framework of the United Nations, especially the General Assembly; and the concept of the special session as the "first" of others in a process of general and complete disarmament which, when attained, will facilitate the achievement of "the new international economic order."

—a *declaration,* divided into a review of the current state of the arms race, a statement of priorities for controlling it, and a list of principles. Nuclear disarmament has the "highest" priority. Among the principles are the following: the United Nations plays the "primary" role in disarmament, non-nuclear-weapons states have certain "rights," there is an "integral link" between disarmament and development, the resources released by ending the arms race should be devoted to the economic and social development "particularly of the developing states," and overseas bases and troops should be withdrawn because "security should not be built upon weapons and alliances."

—a *program of action,* which envisions both a comprehensive program "culminating in" general and complete disarmament, as well as some immediate, short-term measures to get the process started; these latter involve some steps of nuclear disarmament for which the two superpowers bear a particular responsibility and include the "immediate" conclusion of a comprehensive nuclear test ban. Other priority items, ranked in order after nuclear disarmament, include chemical weapons, incendiary weapons, other weapons of mass destruction, conventional weapons, and the reduction of armed forces and military budgets.

—a section on *international disarmament machinery,* in which this comprehensive program is entrusted to a new special committee of the United Nations which should prepare a report for the 1980 General Assembly. The existing bilateral (SALT), regional (Mutual and Balanced Force Reductions talks or MBFR), and multilateral (CCD) negotiating bodies are seen as having made "no progress," and any future disarmament efforts must be "organically linked" to the United Nations General Assembly. The world disarmament conference is deferred "to an appropriate time."

Soviet Group. The final allusion of the Non-Aligned Group's tentative program for the special session is to the favored proposal of the next most identifiable bloc in the preparatory committee, the Soviet Union and its six allies: Bulgaria, Czechoslovakia, Hungary, Poland, East Germany, and Mongolia. As a group, these nations' working papers have tended to advance certain recognizable Soviet policy themes. Peaceful coexistence and detente are constantly invoked as having already been achieved and now in need of "strengthening" by a treaty on the non-use of force (or even its threat) in international affairs and by pledges not to "exacerbate tensions." Nuclear weapons are not mentioned often; the eschewing of force seems to cover the matter. Even the phrase "nuclear-free zone" is rejected in favor of "regional military detente."

In the program of action, these Eastern Bloc states do not want a specific listing of priorities but rather a simple stressing of the "urgency of just measures." Nuclear disarmament is of "primary" (not, the "highest") importance for this group of states; they are more concerned with the production of "new" weapons of mass destruction and the "qualitative improvement" of existing arsenals. They explicitly single out "neutron weapons" for "mutual renunciation." They do not admit a link between disarmament and development; rather, they make two separate statements: (1) they are for economic and social development and (2) they are for assistance to developing states. The world disarmament conference is still seen by this group as the appropriate end result of the special session and steps toward this end should be prepared by a committee of the CCD which is to "continue to be the principal multilateral negotiating body in the field of disarmament." The United Nations has only an "important" role in this field and is to be kept informed "on a voluntary basis" by states taking disarmament measures.

Western Group. In contrast to the Eastern bloc, what is most distinctive about the several joint working papers of certain Western alliance states has been the absence of the participation by the most powerful alliance member, the United States. While it may be assumed that certain American sentiments are reflected in these "Western" papers, the United States has maintained a low profile in the Preparatory Committee, issuing only one working paper in April 1977 and generally not associating itself with any explicit proposals, beyond agreeing to participate in a study of ways to calculate and compare military budgets.

Meanwhile, eleven Western alliance members—Britain, West Germany, Italy, Belgium, the Netherlands, Denmark, Norway, Turkey, Canada, Australia, and Japan—have submitted a joint document on the declaration. Ten of this group (all except Turkey) collaborated on a paper concerning the program of action. There have also been numerous individual working papers by states in the Western alliance—roughly one-third of the first sixty submitted in response to the secretary-general's call for ideas for the special session. Despite great diversity on special issues, certain identifiably "Western" positions nevertheless emerge. While nuclear disarmament is a "high" priority, the special session must be equally concerned with preventing the proliferation of such weapons to states which do not now have them and with the growing arms race in conventional weaponry. The devastation of "all wars," not just nuclear war, is recalled. Alliances and overseas bases are justified by adding to the non-aligned assertion that pacts and foreign bases do not bring security, the modification that security does not come "merely" from weapons or "exclusively" by alliances.

The role of the United Nations is variously characterized by Western states as "important," "central," and "coordinative," but never "primary." The desirability of "a new international economic order" is accepted, but not with the capital letters or the specific "the" of the phraseology used by the non-aligned states. Only a "close relationship" between disarmament and development is admitted and no specific arrangements are suggested for the resources released as a result of disarmament. With respect to international machinery, a second special session is "to be considered" at the 1980 General Assembly. There is a certain amount of disagreement over modifying the CCD. Only six of the group—Britain, West Germany, Denmark, Norway, Canada, and Australia—were able to agree on a working paper which provided for greater participation in the CCD (e.g., by all nuclear-weapon states, by a "limited" increase in size, and by participation on an ad hoc basis for states whose concerns are being debated). But the proposal still retained the Soviet-American co-chairmanship and made the point that many global security problems do not lend themselves to multilateral resolution but would be best handled on a bilateral or regional basis.

France. The CCD co-chairmanship is one of the main reasons France and China have been the two nuclear-weapon states most alienated from the history of disarmament negotiations. France attained its nuclear status in the year the CCD was established (1961) and no provision was made in the embodying arrangements (the McCloy-Zorin principles) to give any preferred status to this nascent nuclear power. As a result, France boycotted the Geneva Conference and refrained from the United Nations disarmament deliberations while it developed its nuclear potential over the next decade. Since the 1972 non-aligned resolution on the world disarmament conference, however, France has followed disarmament matters closely.

In February 1978, France presented to the Preparatory Committee unique proposals for an international observation satellite agency for collecting and organizing all satellite-gathered data affecting security, a semi-autonomous international institute for research and disarmament independent from the United Nations, and an "international fund for disarmament for development." Concerning a more acceptable disarmament negotiating forum, France has proposed that the First Committee of the General Assembly restrict its affairs exclusively to disarmament matters and that it establish a subcommittee for negotiations with a two-year elected chairmanship and thirty to forty members including the full Security Council (hence all five nuclear-weapon-states plus ten rotating seats to insure balanced geographic representation) plus fifteen to twenty-five other members "with a particular interest in questions of disarmament."

China. Like France, China has not been interested in international disarmament talks and probably will not be until it feels more secure militarily vis-à-vis the United States and the USSR. Since its admission to the United Nations in 1971, its official position has been that it will not engage in any disarmament negotiations until the two superpowers fulfill two pre-conditions: (1) that they pledge not to be the first to use nuclear weapons, particularly against non-nuclear-weapon states; and (2) that they withdraw their armed forces and military bases from the territories of other countries. Although both these points speak to issues which are very often raised by the Non-Aligned States, China has not seen any diplomatic advantages to be gained by taking a more active role in the disarmament deliberations. However, it is notable that the General Assembly resolutions establishing the special session and its preparatory committee have been made by consensus; China has thus had numerous opportunities to thwart the effort and has chosen not to do so.

Notable Non-participants/The "Fourth World." Finally, a significant group generally overlooked in most analyses of the disarmament debate are what might be called the "Non-Participants." Approximately fifty states among the 149 in the General Assembly seldom, if ever, take part in the First Committee's deliberations on disarmament and have not responded to the secretary-general's call for suggestions and working papers on the special session. They include several of the world's poorest states, according to the Overseas Development Council's list of "fourth-world countries" (i.e., the world's poorest billion people), whose situation is so desperate they cannot even afford a disarmament delegation at the United Nations.

More importantly, they also include nine of the world's forty-two most significant military powers according to Ruth Sivard's listing in *World Military and Social Expenditures* (WMSE Publications, Leesburg, Virginia). These include four states which are not United Nations members (Switzerland, Taiwan, North Korea, and South Korea—26th, 28th, 29th, and 42nd, respectively, on the list) and five United Nations members which have avoided most General Assembly debate on arms control matters: Israel (15th in military spending), Vietnam (21st), Saudi Arabia (27th), South Africa (32nd), and Portugal (35th). In short, this sixth category of states is significant. Approximately one-third of the world's states, including nine of the forty-two major military powers, have seldom expressed any sustained interest in the international debate over disarmament.

Expectations for the Special Session. Conclusion of actual arms control agreements is not provided for or anticipated at the special session. Instead, it is designed to accelerate the glacial pace of disarmament by developing an agenda, a program of action, and an improved organizational structure and by increasing public awareness and educational efforts globally. In United Nations terminology, disarmament includes *all* measures related to the prevention, limitation, reduction, or elimination of weapons—embracing the entire range of arms control negotiations in which the United States is involved.

Whether the public posturing and the work of the preparatory committee results in any progress toward disarmament hinges chiefly on the attitudes taken by the Soviet Union and the United States. The primary focus of the special session is naturally and intentionally on the largest, costliest, and potentially most dangerous weapons competition in the world today—the superpower arms race. As the world's preeminent producers of nuclear weapons and the nations responsible for two-thirds of all global military expenditures since 1960, their meaningful participation is essential to the success of the special session.

The attitude of the American government is particularly crucial. Not only is it the most significant state from which a bold policy initiative might come, the United States has the mass media with best access to the special session and a public whose opinion is directly relevant to disarmament.

There are many signs that President Carter is sincere about controlling the arms race: the campaign promise to cut the military budget; the inaugural wish for a world without nuclear weapons; announcement of a nuclear non-proliferation program; the cancellation of the B-1 bomber program; institution of a policy to reduce conventional weapons transfers; initiatives toward concluding SALT, comprehensive test ban and chemical weapons treaties; and the initial decision not to produce neutron weapons. Each of these initiatives has occasioned tremors in various sectors of the public and in the Congress. Thus, there have been compensating policy adjustments, e.g., actual increases in the defense budget; inhibitions about the SALT and comprehensive test ban treaties; the decision to build cruise missiles; and the decision to prepare for production of neutron weapons while using them as "bargaining chips."

The President finds himself in a difficult position. The success of the special session in many respects turns on the ability of the United States to make concrete proposals. Yet for President Carter to advance anything of significance, he needs the support of the American public, particularly as it affects the legislative branch. To date, little effort has been made to gain this support. An effective public education program, comparable to what the opponents of SALT and the Panama Canal Treaties have mounted, must be undertaken if the administration is to make the sort of policy initiatives which would contribute to the success of the special session. *(May 1978)*

The UN Special Session: An Evaluation
Ann Hallan Lakhdhir

The Tenth Special Session of the United Nations General Assembly, the first on disarmament, ended in the early hours of July 1, 1978, after a five-week session preceded by five meetings of the preparatory committee stretching over eighteen months. Though it fully satisfied no country and required many compromises in the closing hours, a four-part document was approved with the consent of 148 of the 149 countries in the United Nations—"a diplomatic miracle," according to Ambassador James Leonard of the U. S. Delegation. Much of this miracle was due to very skilled diplomacy by the chairman of the preparatory and ad hoc committees, Ambassador Carlos Ortiz de Rozas of Argentina, and by the "super-coordinator," Ambassador Alfonso Garcia Robles of Mexico. Credit also belongs to the members of other delegations, including the representatives of India, Yugoslavia, and Canada, and to the U.S. Delegation.

The most significant outcome of the special session was changes in the international arms control negotiating machinery. The Conference of the Committee on Disarmament (CCD) in Geneva will be transformed not later than January 1979 into the Committee on Disarmament (CD), which will report annually to the General Assembly and will be composed of thirty-seven to forty states under a rotating chairmanship, instead of the current U.S.-Soviet co-chairmanship. The Committee on Disarmament will operate by consensus, as does the CCD, and its plenary meetings will generally be open to the public. The secretary-general of the United Nations will appoint a secretary of the committee to act as his personal representative, and non-member states may submit written proposals to the CD or participate when issues of particular concern to them are discussed.

Exactly how the present CCD will be dissolved is, in the words of Ambassador Adrian Fisher, "a fine theological point." The uncertainty reflects disagreements as to whether the CD should be clearly the creation of the United Nations General Assembly or the legatee of the CCD, which was not an official United Nations body. There is also uncertainty as to the membership of the CD, though initially the current members of the CCD will participate in the new forum. It was decided at the special session that "the membership of the Committee on Disarmament will be reviewed at regular intervals" by the General Assembly. The French, who had objected to the Soviet-American condominium on the CCD, have indicated that they will be active in the CD. The People's Republic of China has not declared its intentions regarding the reorganized body and may not for some time.

The four-part final document also re-energized the United Nations Disarmament Commission, which has not met since 1965. Composed of all member-states of the United Nations, the Disarmament Commission will be a deliberative body; it is expected to meet for a month in 1979.

The special session also revised the mandate of Committee One of the General Assembly so that it will consider only disarmament and related issues. The special session left to the 33rd General Assembly the determination of the exact date for the next Special Session on Disarmament, but it is expected to be convened in 1981.

The special session also provided fertile ground for a number of proposals, some old and some new, which, though they did not achieve consensus, are likely to be taken up by Committee One of the General Assembly in the fall or in subsequent international disarmament forums. Among the most notable were French President Valery Giscard d'Estaing's proposals for an international satellite monitoring agency (to provide to all states data already available to the United States and USSR), for a disarmament development fund to be capitalized at $1

Economic Aid and Military Expenditures 1960–76

MAJOR DONORS	Economic Aid Given [1]			Military Exp.	
Donor Nations	mil. $	% GNP	An. Avg. $ per cap	% GNP	An. Avg. $ per cap
United States	57,100	0.4	16.8	7.4	347.1
France	19,100	0.7	22.6	4.4	137.8
West Germany	12,100	0.4	11.9	3.7	123.8
USSR	9,200	0.1	2.3	12.7	239.5
United Kingdom	9,100	0.4	9.8	5.4	124.9
Japan	8,200	0.2	4.7	0.9	18.6
Saudi Arabia*	6,100	5.2	52.9	12.8	129.1
Canada	5,400	0.4	15.5	2.5	100.8
China	4,400	0.2	0.3	6.4	11.4
Netherlands	3,600	0.6	16.6	3.6	99.3
Australia	3,400	0.6	16.7	3.4	101.8
Kuwait*	3,000	5.2	194.5	4.0	149.3
United Arab Emirates*	2,900	9.7	433.3	1.2	55.2
Sweden	2,800	0.5	20.6	3.7	155.9
Belgium	2,600	0.5	15.8	3.0	89.8
Other donors	13,000	0.2	2.3	3.2	44.4
TOTAL	162,000	0.3	5.0	6.2	94.6

MAJOR RECIPIENTS	Economic Aid Received [2]			Military Exp.	
Recipient Nations	mil. $	% GNP	An. Avg. $ per cap	% GNP	An. Avg. $ per cap
India	19,500	2.1	2.2	3.4	3.5
Vietnam	10,000	12.0	30.4	16.7	42.2
Pakistan	9,700	7.8	10.0	6.4	8.2
Egypt	7,400	6.2	13.7	18.7	41.2
Indonesia	6,100	4.1	3.0	3.4	2.5
South Korea	4,500	3.2	8.7	4.7	12.9
Turkey	4,300	1.7	7.5	4.9	22.1
Algeria	4,300	4.5	19.4	2.1	9.2
Cuba	4,200	5.4	30.7	5.8	32.8
Brazil	3,400	0.4	2.2	1.8	10.1
Syria	3,200	8.4	31.6	11.1	41.9
Bangladesh	3,000	7.9	2.6	1.0	0.4
Poland	2,700	0.3	4.9	3.0	47.1
Israel	2,600	2.5	53.6	22.6	484.6
Jordan	2,400	20.5	65.2	14.0	44.6
Other recipients	68,800	0.6	2.2	4.2	15.0
TOTAL	156,000 [2]	1.0	3.5	4.3	12.9

Source: *World Military and Social Expenditures 1978,* Ruth Leger Sivard, 1978.
[1] includes loans as well as grants. [2] excludes aid undistributed by recipient. * 1970-76

World Military Expenditures and Economic Aid (cumulative 1960-1976)

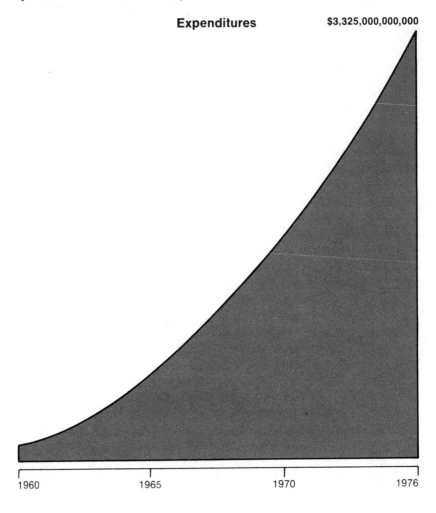

Expenditures $3,325,000,000,000

1960   1965   1970   1976

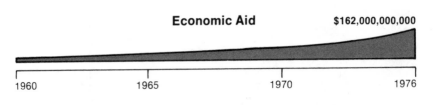

Economic Aid $162,000,000,000

1960   1965   1970   1976

Source: *World Military and Social Expenditures 1978*. Ruth Leger Sivard, 1978.

billion and supplemented by resources released through disarmament measures, and for an international institute for disarmament research. Pierre Trudeau, Canada's prime minister, called for disarmament progress through the "suffocation" of armaments initiatives by means of a nuclear test ban treaty, an agreement banning all flight testing of strategic delivery vehicles, a prohibition of the production of fissionable materials for weapons purposes, and an agreement to reduce military spending on new strategic nuclear weapons. Canada also indicated it would replace its nuclear weapons with conventional arms and thereby become a non-nuclear weapons state. The prime minister of India, Morarji Desai, renounced any further Indian nuclear testing, even for "peaceful" purposes, and any development of Indian nuclear weapons. Ambassador Iqbal Akhund of Pakistan responded that the way is now open for creation of a South Asian nuclear weapon-free zone, an undertaking often proposed by both nations but heretofore stillborn amidst polemics.

Non-governmental organizations were officially involved in the special session when, together with six international peace research organizations, representatives of twenty-five non-governmental organizations addressed the assembly on June 12 and 13. It is hoped that this opening will lead to an expanded role for non-governmental organizations in United Nations disarmament deliberations, especially in the United Nations Center for Disarmament.

At a press conference at the end of the special session, Delegate Averell Harriman summed up the prevailing view of the American role:

> Most of the delegations . . . expected more of the United States in the reduction of nuclear arms and in other steps to reduce the dangers of a nuclear disaster. . . . They expected greater leadership from the United States in this vital direction. . . . I hope as many Americans as possible can understand what other nations expect of us, so that the members of Congress will be less influenced by those who oppose effective action.

No major initiatives were proposed or undertaken by the United States, which confined itself to an expression of support for a standing United Nations peacekeeping force, to a restatement of the highly qualified U.S. policy regarding the non-use of nuclear weapons against non-nuclear states, and an offer of technological aid in developing satellite or ground-based monitoring systems. The United States stopped short of supporting an international agency to conduct these verification efforts.

The weak showing of the United States came despite the preparation of a host of position papers on feasible initiatives by the State Depart-

Public Expenditures Per Capita for Military, Education, and Health, and Distribution of World Population, 1975 (in dollars)

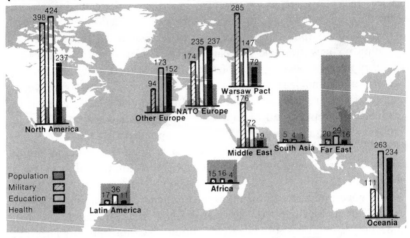

Source: *World Military and Social Expenditures 1978*, Ruth Leger Sivard, 1978

ment and the Arms Control and Disarmament Agency and despite an able and distinguished delegation and staff which included Special Session Coordinator Lawrence Weiler, Ambassadors James Leonard and Adrian Fisher, Representative Charles Whalen, actor Paul Newman, Governor Averell Harriman, Senator George McGovern (D-S.Dak.), and Michael Congdon, John Hirsh, and Charles Floweree from the U.S. Mission and the Arms Control and Disarmament Agency.

The failure of the United States to play a leadership role was felt more keenly because of President Carter's declared desire, expressed in his inaugural address and his 1977 speech to the United Nations, to achieve a world without nuclear weapons and to halve defense expenditures reciprocally. Yet President Carter chose not to address the special session. The speech delivered in New York by Vice President Walter Mondale seemed to revert at times to cold war rhetoric. Emphasizing concern primarily with increases in Soviet forces and expenditures, the speech was obviously addressed to a domestic audience, rather than to the member-states of the United Nations; it revealed the administration's new-found willingness to argue the case laid out by its right-wing critics, instead of seizing the opportunity to change the terms of the arms debate and thus affect the nature of the outcome positively.

Except for the Mondale speech, the cold war was not otherwise much in evidence at the special session. The Soviet Union, like the United

States, played a relatively inactive role; both superpowers were often allies of a sort, resisting pressures on such issues as a moratorium on nuclear testing and the language in the final document regarding the Non-Proliferation Treaty.

An agreement by the USSR and the United States to a moratorium on all nuclear testing pending the conclusion of a Comprehensive Test Ban Treaty (CTBT) would have had the greatest positive impact on the special session. The moratorium was requested by the non-nuclear countries out of dissatisfaction with the lack of superpower progress in SALT (Strategic Arms Limitation Talks) and CTBT negotiations. Pressure on the United States and the USSR will certainly intensify on this issue. Yet the special session ended in considerably better humor than expected, reflecting the many efforts to reach compromises.

If opportunities were lost at the special session through want of leadership and commitment, it nevertheless represented a new beginning—in terms of both reforming international deliberative and negotiating machinery and concentrating serious attention among all countries of the United Nations—to progress toward a world where change is accomplished more peacefully. It is up to us to insure these new opportunities are not squandered. *(August/September 1978)*

The Views of Two Presidents

Six presidents, over a period of a quarter-century, have advocated arms control through negotiated agreements and independent initiatives as a means of improving U.S. and international security. As arms control has become an increasingly important part of the foreign policy agenda, it has naturally assumed an important role in election campaigns. Therefore, in 1976, the Arms Control Association asked President Gerald Ford and Governor Jimmy Carter for their views on a variety of arms control issues. Their answers, provided by their campaign committees, appear below, as they were published in the pre-election issue of Arms Control Today.

Do you support the proposition that arms control and disarmament objectives are central to national security? If so, what would you do in your cabinet appointments and through your policies to implement this view?

Ford: President Ford most definitely feels that continued negotiations with the Soviet Union, in an effort to reduce both the level of tensions between the two nations and the dangerous arms race, are necessary to protect the interests and security of the United States. As he stated in February 1976:

> It is my duty... to do all that I can to reduce the level of danger by diplomatic means. So my policy for national security can be summed up in three words: peace through strength. I believe it is far better to seek negotiations with the Soviet Union . . . (based on strength) . . . than to permit a runaway nuclear arms race and risk a nuclear holocaust.

To implement these views the President has appointed and retained men, dedicated to such policies, both to Cabinet and sub-Cabinet positions: Donald Rumsfeld, formerly our ambassador to NATO, later the President's chief of staff, and now serving in another position of high responsibility as secretary of defense; Secretary of State Henry Kissinger; Brent Scowcroft, assistant to the President for national security affairs; and Fred Ikle, director of the Arms Control and Disarmament Agency.

The President will continue to appoint men of such high quality to these and other positions in the future. Furthermore, the policy of attempting to negotiate with the Russians will continue. Arms control and disarmament efforts in other parts of the world will be continued as well.

Carter: I believe that the mutual balance of terror is an inadequate foundation for a peaceful and stable world order. While maintaining our military strength and the American nuclear deterrent are essential to world order under today's conditions, we also need a positive arms control program as a coordinate element of national security policy. The specific steps I favor in the various major arms control areas are outlined in my answers below.

Do you believe that cessation of the arms race and general nuclear disarmament should be the objective of the United States? If you do, what specific proposals would you put forward?

Ford: While cessation of the arms race and general nuclear disarmament are the ultimate goals of U.S. policy, they cannot be attained easily or quickly. The immediate aim, therefore, of the President's policy of negotiations is the relaxation of tensions and continued steady gains in our relations with the Soviets. The U.S. policy of controlling the strategic arms race has been carried on under five presidents; the agreement at Vladivostok is aimed at quantitative limitations on such weapons. Continuation of our present policy of peaceful negotiations is our best hope for ever attaining nuclear disarmament.

Carter: The international atomic weapons race must stop. I believe that the ultimate goal of this nation should be the reduction of nuclear weapons in all nations of the world to zero. Clearly, this is an ultimate rather than an immediate objective, and it may not occur in my lifetime. But I would work toward ending the world's growing dependence on atomic weapons by specific measures in the areas of SALT (Strategic Arms Limitation Talks), nuclear proliferation, and nuclear testing, as outlined below.

Do you believe that the Arms Control and Disarmament Agency (ACDA) should be strengthened and given a more important role in developing and implementing national security policies? If so, how?

Ford: The Arms Control and Disarmament Agency occupies a prominent position within the decision-making structure of the Ford administration with regard to national security policies, and no change in that position is foreseen. President Ford regards the agency as an important factor in the development of policies in its area. The current director, Dr. Fred Ikle, participates in National Security Council meetings when arms control, disarmament, and arms transfer questions are under consideration, and ACDA also plays a prominent role as a member of the Verification Panel where basic policy discussions in this field are studied. This indicates the esteem in which the President holds the agency and its officers, and the responsibility he is willing to lay upon it in elaborating upon his policies in this complex and crucial policy area.

Carter: An early task of my administration would be reform of the organization of our national security agencies. In such a reform, I would emphasize that arms control considerations must be given a major voice in national security deliberations.

The Republican administration has gutted ACDA, and that is one of the reasons they have made so little real progress in arms control. Its functions must be revitalized.

The exact role of ACDA, or any other agency, would be established in the context of my general review of organizational questions. Certainly I would insure that my administration would abide by the spirit as well as the letter of the Zablocki Amendment, which requires arms control impact statements on major new weapons programs—a requirement which the present administration has slighted.

Do you favor a SALT II Treaty based generally on the 1974 Vladivostok Accords? If not, explain your objections.

Ford: President Ford views SALT II as an extension of SALT I, inasmuch as both are parts of our major, overall arms control objectives. He feels that SALT I was quite successful and deserves to be followed up:

> Those who argue that SALT talks jeopardize the security of the United States are badly mistaken. In Vladivostok we began negotiating an agreement which, if successfully completed, will place equal ceilings on missiles, heavy bombers, and multiheaded missiles. . . . We are continuing the Strategic Arms Limitations Talks with the Soviet Union for the simple but very good reason that these negotiations offer the best hope for sanity in super-power relations.

Carter: The Vladivostok levels are too high. Moreover, despite the ballyhoo, the administration has not been able to produce an acceptable agreement on the Vladivostok guidelines in two years of trying and there still appear to be important issues unresolved. Information on the details of the obstacles have not been made public. Whether next year it would be best, if there is still no agreement, to seek to implement the Vladivostok ceilings and go on from there to agreements on reductions and technological controls, or whether a new approach would be required is a judgment on negotiating policy that I would make only after careful review of where the talks stand in January 1977.

Do you believe the SALT II Treaty should place restrictions on the deployment of strategic cruise missiles?

Ford: Although cruise missiles may eventually have some limitations placed upon them as part of a comprehensive arms control plan, the administration does not favor the imposition of unilateral restrictions on their development prior to firm commitments by the other side. At present the development of a U.S. cruise missile is well advanced over Soviet efforts and is continuing as an essential element in our strategic arsenal.*

*During the October 6, 1976, presidential candidate foreign policy television debate, however, President Ford offered a different view concerning cruise missiles in SALT:

Question (Henry Trewhitt, *Baltimore Sun*): "Let me . . . submit that the cruise missile adds a whole new dimension to the arms competition—and then cite a statement by your office to the Arms Control Association a few days ago in which you said the cruise missile might eventually be included in a comprehensive arms limitation agreement . . . may I assume that you're tending to exclude the cruise missile from the next SALT agreement, or is it

Carter: I recognize the possible utility of cruise missiles of certain kinds for maintaining the effectiveness of our bomber deterrent. On the other hand, strategic range cruise missiles also present important arms control issues because of the difficulty in verifying their characteristics and the number of platforms from which they could be launched. So cruise missiles pose a case of the need for arms control factors to be considered before deployment decisions by the United States. If I were satisfied that an agreement would be adequately verified, I would accept, in return for appropriate Soviet commitments regarding controls on their weapons, some limits on strategic range cruise missile deployments in a new SALT agreement.

After SALT II, what should our goals for SALT III be?

Ford: President Ford sees the intent of SALT III as a continuation of attempts to negotiate limits on strategic nuclear arms. The particular goals will depend upon the exact achievements of the SALT II negotiations and the stage of technological development when the SALT III negotiations begin. As a general concept, SALT II is intended to apply quantitative limitations on numbers of vehicles, while SALT III would provide the upper limits on quantitative capabilities and stabilize the strategic positions of the two super-powers.

Carter: The core of our dealings with the Soviet Union must be mutual reduction of arms and halting the race in strategic technology. We should negotiate to reduce the present SALT ceilings on offensive weapons before both sides start a new arms race to reach the current maximums and before new missile systems are tested or committed for production. Attaining these objectives will require hard bargaining with the Soviets, but I'm not afraid of hard bargaining with the Soviet Union, and it would strengthen the support for the agreements that can be reached and show that SALT is not a one way street.

What steps should the United States take to prevent the spread of nuclear weapons?

still negotiable in that context?"
Ford: "I believe that the cruise missile, which we are now developing in research and development across the spectrum from air, from the sea, or from the land, can be included within a SALT II agreement. They are a new weapons system that has a great potential, both conventional and nuclear-armed. At the same time, we have to make certain that the Soviet Union's Backfire, which they claim is not an intercontinental aircraft and which some of our people contend is, must also be included if we are to get the kind of agreement which is in the best interest of both countries . . ."

Ford: President Ford believes that there are several steps the United States must take, and must continue, in order to prevent the spread of nuclear weapons:

Through diplomatic channels, encourage universal adherence to the Non-Proliferation Treaty. The recent ratification by Japan, and the accession of many of the Western European countries over a year ago, demonstrate the viability of the treaty.

Through mutual security arrangements, create the protection that permits countries to forego the acquisition of nuclear weapons. By seeking to lessen regional tensions, the President hopes to reduce the motivation for the development of nuclear weapons by states in that region.

By following a policy of imposing international safeguards on all exported nuclear facilities and avoiding the transfer of sensitive materials, help to meet the legitimate needs for electrical power generation without providing a capability for weapons development. At the same time, we must not be quixotic in our supply policy since we will drive recipients to other sources or to develop their own independent capacity, and thereby lose our influence and ability to exert control over international nuclear affairs.

Because the United States is not the only supplier of nuclear technology, President Ford wants to obtain the cooperation of other suppliers in applying safeguards and restrictions on exports. We recently have had good results in concerting the export policies of the major supplier nations, but the President will continue to press for even stricter, and more broadly based, controls and restraints.

The effectiveness of the International Atomic Energy Agency (IAEA) is an important key to achieving an international nuclear regime where power needs are met under appropriate safeguards against diversion of nuclear materials to weapons. The President believes we should work with the IAEA, both through contribution of money, and the provision of technical support continuously to update and enhance its effectiveness.

Carter: We must make halting proliferation of nuclear weapons a top national priority. As President, I would take the following eleven steps to control further nuclear proliferation:

I would call upon all nations to adopt a voluntary moratorium on the national sale or purchase of enrichment or reprocessing plants—a moratorium which should apply retroactively to the recent German-Brazilian and the French-Pakistan agreements.

I would make no new commitments for the sale of nuclear technology or fuel to countries which refuse to forego nuclear explosives, to refrain from national nuclear reprocessing, or to place their nuclear facilities under IAEA safeguards.

I would seek to withhold authority for domestic commercial reprocessing until the need for, the economics, and the safety of this technology is clearly demonstrated. If we should ever decide to go forward with commercial reprocessing, it should be on a multinational basis.

I would call for an international conference on energy, to provide a forum in which all nations could focus on the non-proliferation issue. Such a conference would also have to explore non-nuclear means of meeting energy demands of other nations so that no state would be forced into a premature commitment to atomic power.

I would support a strengthening of the safeguards and inspection authority of the IAEA and place all of our own peaceful domestic nuclear facilities under those safeguards.

I would seek to renegotiate our existing agreements as a nuclear supplier, many of which were entered into before we began insisting on reprocessing safeguards and which are now inadequate.

I would take steps to insure that the United States is once again a reliable supplier of enriched uranium—the fuel for civilian reactors which is unsuitable for weapons—by supporting enlargement of our government-owned facility.

I would explore international initiatives such as multinational enrichment plants and multinational spent fuel storage areas which could provide alternatives to the establishment of enrichment or reprocessing plants on a national basis.

I would redirect our own energy research and development efforts to correct the disproportionate emphasis which we have placed on nuclear power at the expense of renewable energy technologies. Our emphasis on the breeder reactor must be converted into a long term, possibly multinational effort.

Finally, I would follow through on my belief that the United States can and should negotiate a comprehensive test ban treaty with the Soviet Union, and reduce, through the SALT talks, strategic nuclear forces and technology.

I would encourage the Soviet Union to join us in a total ban of all nuclear explosions for at least five years. This ban would include so-called "peaceful nuclear devices."

Should the United States export nuclear fuel and equipment for nuclear power plants to countries which have refused to ratify the Non-Proliferation Treaty (NPT)?

Ford: The President has not restricted U.S. nuclear cooperation only to those countries that have ratified the Non-Proliferation Treaty, because such a policy would not effectively function as a non-proliferation tool. Other suppliers, who may themselves not be parties to the treaty, could step in and provide the nuclear facilities and materials, with fewer restraints than we require. The United States not only insists that all of its exported nuclear material be under international safeguards, but also exercises some additional bilateral controls over the development of the recipient countries' nuclear program. For example, nuclear fuel cannot be reprocessed abroad without U.S. approval.

Carter: I believe it is important that we create incentives for all countries to participate in the Non-Proliferation Treaty. For that reason, we should refuse to sell nuclear power plants and fuels to nations which do not become a party to the NPT or which will not adhere to strict provisions on international safeguards of nuclear facilities or which refuse to refrain from national nuclear reprocessing.

Should the United States insist that non-parties to the NPT to which such materials are exported be required to place all their peaceful nuclear facilities under IAEA safeguards?

Ford: The President considers it an important objective to achieve full safeguards on all nuclear facilities in non-nuclear weapon states. As the first major step in this direction, the key suppliers have undertaken to require safeguards on all their exports, thereby closing off external sources of unsafeguarded facilities. He would, of course, encourage the application of safeguards to all indigenous facilities as a condition of export, but does not believe we can enforce such a policy without the cooperation of the other suppliers. Again, a unilateral U.S. policy simply would not be effective. We are, however, continuing to meet with the other suppliers and expect further progress toward this objective.

Carter: I believe such a requirement would be a wise one, and that the United States should negotiate with other supplier nations to make it a condition of all sales. The possibility of achieving such a common position has not been fully explored by the present administration.

Do you support a comprehensive nuclear test ban, verified by national technical means? Please explain your position.

Ford: President Ford does indeed support a comprehensive test ban backed by adequate safeguards and has taken steps to bring us closer to such a goal. Such a ban would be useful in stemming the tide of the arms race, first by the ban itself, and second, by fostering a spirit of coopera- tion between the United States and the Soviet Union.

Carter: I support a comprehensive test ban agreement with the Soviet Union, covering both weapons tests and so-called "peaceful" nuclear explosions. The United States and the Soviet Union should conclude such an agreement immediately, to last for five years, during which they should encourage all other countries to join. At the end of the five year period the agreement could be continued if it served the interests of the parties. Such a ban would be a significant arms limitation agreement between the United States and the Soviet Union, and, as other nations joined, could have highly favorable effects in reducing the dangers of nuclear proliferation. National verification capabilities over the last twenty years have advanced to the point where we no longer have to rely on on-site inspection to distinguish between earthquakes and even very small weapons tests, so a comprehensive test ban verified by national technical means would be acceptable.

Do you believe that the proposed Threshold Test Ban (permitting underground tests up to 150 kilotons and Soviet peaceful explosions of multiple devices totaling higher yields with U.S. observers present) will be a useful step in controlling nuclear weapons? Please state your position.

Ford: The President sees the Threshold Test Ban as a useful step toward the ultimate goal of controlling nuclear weapons, in that it brings us closer to a comprehensive nuclear test ban with its attendant benefits to the world. As the President said on June 7, 1976:

> For twenty-five years, American Presidents have been trying to negotiate the peaceful experiments in nuclear explosions. We have been trying for twenty-five years to get on-site inspection in the Soviet Union, to see whether they were living up to those agreements. I have just signed, about ten days ago, a negotiated settlement that gives the United States the right to make certain— to make positive—in the Soviet Union, that the agreement they signed is lived up to.

President Ford is concerned that we not stop there, but continue to press forward in our negotiations to achieve still more gains under the nuclear test policy of his administration.

Carter: The so-called Threshold Test Ban Treaty represents a wholly inadequate step beyond the limited test ban of thirteen years ago. The so-called "on-site" inspection provisions of the peaceful nuclear explosions agreement signed recently may be a concession in Soviet eyes, but, contrary to administration claims, they are no compensation for the Peaceful Nuclear Explosion agreement's dangerous legitimizing of peaceful nuclear explosions, which are indistinguishable from bombs.

Would you increase, reduce, or maintain the present levels of U.S. nuclear weapons in South Korea? In Western Europe? If you favor reductions, over what time frame?

Ford: President Ford has no plans for altering the current level of U.S. military commitments overseas; the present deployment represents a careful balance of forces worked out over a period of many years and is tailored to meet the security needs of the United States and our allies. In Western Europe, however, we can visualize that under the proper circumstances such as a reduction in Warsaw Pact forces in central Europe, the United States could withdraw a limited number of tactical nuclear weapons, and in fact NATO has offered to do just this. At the same time, the President is determined to resist attempts at unilateral U.S. disarmament.

Carter: We have many tactical nuclear weapons, some of great size, both within this nation and outside the continental limits of the United States. The present deployments are more than adequate to accommodate our deterrence needs. Tactical nuclear weapons should be withdrawn from unnecessarily exposed positions and their numbers related to realistic missions for such weapons. In particular, tactical nuclear weapons should be withdrawn from Korea as a part of a gradual withdrawal of U.S. ground forces which in turn would be part of an overall coordinated plan to reduce tensions on the Korean peninsula. This would involve several steps: we must see that Korea can defend itself; we will leave adequate air support and build up South Korean air capability; we will act only in full consultation with both South Korea and Japan (it is essential that nothing be done to cause turmoil in Japan); and we will seek to encourage the Communist powers to engage their North Korean friends in a search for a reduction in tensions in the area.

Do you believe the United States should make it a policy not to be the first to use nuclear weapons in certain circumstances? If so, under what circumstances?

Ford: The policy of the United States, as expressed by the Ford administration, has always been that it will not precipitate a nuclear war. The nuclear capacity of the United States will be used only when it is seen as absolutely essential to the security of the United States and its allies; for example, an actual nuclear attack upon this nation. Except in such circumstances, the task of our nuclear forces is to act as a deterrent to an attack by any aggressor.

Carter: The use of nuclear weapons under any circumstances would be an awesome step. I am not hopeful that any nuclear war could stay limited. The present administration has been entirely too casual in discussing the possibility of nuclear war, and in appearing to threaten initiation of nuclear war for political purposes, or for fighting so-called limited nuclear wars. The concentration of our defense policy, especially our nuclear policy, must be on deterrence. Unfortunately, we cannot renounce first use of nuclear weapons in those limited situations where vital and essential U.S. interests may be threatened by military aggression against us or our allies. This is part of deterrence; of insuring that a war will never begin. However, I believe we need to insure that we and our allies have conventional capability to reduce dependence on nuclear weapons.

Should the United States initiate efforts to control the sales abroad of conventional armaments? What specific steps should be taken?

Ford: The demand for armaments of all types around the world is great, and the number of suppliers is large. Therefore, any attempt to curtail arms sales will probably be unsuccessful unless all nations involved in the sales of weapons can come to some sort of agreement. Otherwise, the market will be open only to those who choose not to participate in the agreement. President Ford is unwilling to create a situation in which the more responsible nations are forced to sit by, having agreed to cease arms sales abroad, while the less scrupulous nations who opt not to join the agreement are allowed to be the sole suppliers to the ever-increasing market. Such a unilateral curtailment would do little to restrict the traffic in arms.

Furthermore, the President is determined that the United States retain the option to provide our friends and allies with the weapons necessary to protect themselves. If we expect them to assume the burden of their own defense, they must be able to obtain the resources necessary for that defense. The United States cannot be a party to any agreement that would prevent us from aiding those who depend on our support.

The Ford Administration is, however, being very judicious in the sales of U.S. arms abroad so that arms are provided only to those who can demonstrate a valid need for them. We are encouraging other friendly supplier nations to exercise equal caution along these lines. The President has directed that all possible steps be taken to prevent acquisition of arms from us by those who would put them to illegitimate uses.

Carter: I am particularly concerned by our nation's role as the world's leading arms salesman. Our sales of billions of dollars of arms, particularly to developing nations, fuel regional arms races and complicate our relationships with other supplier nations. We cannot be both the world's leading champion of peace and the world's leading supplier of weapons of war. If I become president I will work with our allies, some of whom also sell arms, and also seek to work with the Soviets to reduce the commerce in weapons. We must assess every arms sale on an individual national basis, to insure that the only sales we make are those that promote peace in the regions and carry out our committed foreign policy. At the same time, there are certain arms sales programs, notably those to Israel, which are necessary so that Israel can pursue peace from a position of strength and security. Our diplomacy in this area should be based on a four-part approach: (a) an international conference of suppliers and consumers to put the issue to the forefront of the world's arms control agenda, (b) greater U.S. self-restraint, (c) work with Western suppliers and the Soviets to dampen down arms sales promotion, and (d) support for regional efforts to limit arms buildup.

Do you believe the United States should support the proposed world disarmament conference?

Ford: The concept of a world disarmament conference has been employed as part of a Communist propaganda campaign for many years; the United States has consistently held that such a broadside approach is unlikely to yield real results. In keeping with his policy of seeking to achieve peace through negotiations, President Ford has supported plans for various meetings in which nations could gather to formulate programs for specific disarmament objectives. In fact, the United States has participated in meetings in Geneva of this nature. The President would not favor our participation in large and unstructured conferences if they appeared to be simply a tool by which certain groups of nations would elaborate unworkable proposals and subvert such meetings to their own purposes.

The President is of the opinion that the results of arms control and reduction conferences must fully protect the security of the United States. The costs, benefits, and responsibilities of disarmament plans must be fully shared on a fair basis by all nations involved. No nation should be allowed to gain an advantage at the expense of another. An equitable agreement would be one which will bring about true world disarmament.

Carter: Arms control is a worldwide concern: Non-proliferation is important to both nuclear weapons and non-nuclear weapons states. SALT is in the interest of all, not just the USSR and the United States. Arms sales divert resources from development and build regional tensions that could lead to world war; the whole world ultimately bears the burden of expending our planet's resources on arms. Therefore, all elements of the world's population must be fully represented in arms control efforts. At the same time, we must treat arms control as a serious business, not an occasion for posturing or propaganda. For that reason, I am skeptical about very large scale disarmament conferences with no clear agenda. But if we can develop an appropriate agenda, I would favor as broad a conference as possible on the control of conventional weapons in order to move this issue to the front rank of the world's concerns. I also favor an international conference on energy to provide a forum in which all nations can focus on the non-proliferation issue as well as other energy issues. *(October 1976)*

Glossary

The writings of specialists in arms control are often peppered with acronyms; therefore, the editors considered it useful to begin the glossary with a list identifying the most common of these acronyms. Definitions may be found in the main body of the glossary. The glossary concludes with a list of arms control agreements and negotiations.

Acronyms

ABM   anti-ballistic missile
ACDA   Arms Control and Disarmament Agency
ALBM   air-launched ballistic missile
ALCM   air-launched cruise missile
ALPS   alternative launch-point system
ASW   anti-submarine warfare
AWACS   airborne warning and control system
CCD   Conference of the Committee on Disarmament
CD   Committee on Disarmament
CEP   circular error probable
C^3I command, control, communication, and intelligence
CSCE   Conference on Security and Co-operation in Europe
CTBT   comprehensive test ban treaty
DOD   Department of Defense
ELF   extremely low frequency
EMT   equivalent megatonnage
FBS   forward-based system
FOBS   fractional orbital bombardment system
GCD   general and complete disarmament
GLCM   ground-launched cruise missile
ICBM   intercontinental ballistic missile
INFCE   International Nuclear Fuel Cycle Evaluation
IRBM   intermediate-range ballistic missile
MAPS   multiple aim-point system
MARV   maneuverable re-entry vehicle
MBFR   Mutual and Balanced Force Reductions Talks
MIRV   multiple independently-targetable re-entry vehicle
MPS   multiple protective structure
MRBM   medium-range ballistic missile

MX   missile experimental

NAVSTAR   navigation system using time and ranging

NPT   Non-Proliferation Treaty

NTM   national technical means

PENAIDS   penetration aids

PGM   precision-guided munition

PNE   peaceful nuclear explosion

psi   pounds per square inch

R&D   research and development

RPV   remotely-piloted vehicle

SALT   Strategic Arms Limitation Talks

SLBM   submarine-launched ballistic missile

SLCM   sea-launched cruise missile

SRAM   short-range attack missile

SRBM   short-range ballistic missile

SSBN   a   nuclear-propelled   ballistic-missile-bearing   submarine (so designated by the U.S. Navy)

TNW   theater nuclear weapon

TTBT   Threshold Test Ban Treaty

V/STOL   vertical short take-off and landing

Arms Control Terms

active defense   The protection of civil and military targets through the use of defensive weapons, such as surface-to-air missiles, anti-ballistic missile missiles and anti-aircraft artillery. *See* passive defense.

air-breathing missile   A missile with an engine requiring the intake of air for combustion of its fuel, as in a ramjet or turbojet.

air-launched ballistic missile (ALBM)   A ballistic missile launched from an aircraft in flight. An example is the U.S. short-range attack missile (SRAM).

air-launched cruise missile   *See* cruise missile.

airborne warning and control system (AWACS)   A flying command post. AWACS has the capacity to identify hostile aircraft and to control friendly air forces in either offensive or defensive missions.

alternative launch-point system (ALPS)   A proposed method of deploying land-based missiles designed to solve the theoretical problem of ICBM vulnerability. This system is based on the construction of alternate silos around existing Minuteman silos and the random transfer of missile cannisters among the silos. Only one cannister per silo complex would contain a missile; the other cannisters would be constructed to simulate missile deployment. This system has been contemplated for use with Minuteman II and III missiles and can be adapted for the MX or a possible Minuteman IV missile.

anti-ballistic missile (ABM) system A system of missiles and radars capable of defending against a ballistic-missile attack by destroying incoming offensive missiles. The defensive missiles may be armed with either nuclear or non-nuclear warheads.

anti-submarine warfare (ASW) The detection, identification, tracking, and destruction of hostile submarines. ASW can be either strategic (aimed at neutralizing an opponent's ballistic-missile submarines), or tactical (concerned with the pursuit and destruction of submarines in a local situation for missions such as convoy defense and aircraft carrier defense).

area defense Defense of a wide geographic area against missiles and aircraft.

arms control Any unilateral action or multilateral plan, arrangement, or process, resting upon explicit or implicit international agreement, which limits or regulates any aspect of the following: the production, numbers, type, configuration, and performance characteristics of weapon systems (including related command and control, logistics support, and intelligence arrangements or mechanisms); and the numerical strength, organization, equipment, deployment or employment of the armed forces retained by the parties. A list of arms control agreements in force or being negotiated may be found at the end of the glossary.

arms limitation *See* arms control.

arms transfer The sale or grant of arms from one nation to another.

ballistic missile A missile, classified by range, that moves on a free-falling trajectory under the influence of gravity.

binary nerve gas A toxic gas created by the mixture of two relatively harmless chemicals during the final trajectory stage of a missile, bomb or shell in which the gases are loaded. Because its two components are non-toxic until they are combined, binary gas can be stored and handled more easily than other toxic gases.

bomber An aircraft, usually classified by range, capable of delivering nuclear and non-nuclear ordnance. Long-range bombers are those capable of traveling 6,000 or more miles on one load of fuel; medium-range bombers can travel between 3,500 and 6,000 miles without refueling.

U.S. Bombers

B-52G/H.   These models, with ranges between 10,000 and 12,500 miles in unrefueled flight, each carry four bombs and four short-range attack missiles.

B-52D.   This model of the B-52, delivered in 1956-1958, has recently undergone modernization. The seventy-five that are currently deployed each carry four bombs.

FB-111A.   First deployed in 1969. The sixty-six medium-range FB-111As currently deployed each carry two short-range attack missiles and two bombs and have a maximum range of 6,000 miles.

Soviet Bombers (Nicknames Assigned by NATO)

Bear.   First deployed in 1956. The 100 Bears now in service each have a maximum range of 8,000 miles.

Bison.   The Soviet Union currently deploys thirty-five Bison, which have a maximum range of 7,000 miles.

Backfire.   A bomber of undetermined range and limited fuel capacity, the Backfire's primary mission is for naval attack or theater operations.

breeder reactor   A reactor that produces more nuclear fuel than it consumes while generating power.

circular error probable (CEP)   A measure of missile accuracy. It is the radius of a circle around a target in which 50 percent of the missiles aimed at that target will land.

civil defense   *See* passive defense.

cold launch   A technique for ejecting a missile from its silo by use of low-pressure gas. Because the full ignition of the rocket occurs after the missile has been ejected from the silo, the need for extensive shielding of the missile in the silo against its exhaust is reduced. This technique causes little damage to silos, thus facilitating reloading while also increasing the silo's usable diameter by up to 50 percent.

command, control, communication, and intelligence (C³I)   The "nerves" of military operations, that is, information-processing systems used to detect, assess and respond to actual and potential military and political crisis situations or conflicts. C³I includes systems which manage materiel and manpower during crises or conflicts, as well as in peacetime.

conditional restraint   The temporary foregoing or delaying of a particular military action, usually the deployment of a weapon system, subject to an opponent's practicing restraint in the same or another acceptable area, so as to limit or reduce forces, weapons or deployments without a negotiated agreement.

confidence-building measures Measures taken to demonstrate a nation's lack of belligerent or hostile *intent,* as distinguished from measures which actually reduce military *capabilities.* Confidence-building measures can be negotiated or unilateral. The division between confidence-building measures and arms control measures is not strict; the former may involve, for example, troop withdrawals, while the latter may aim more at securing trust than limiting weaponry.

counterforce Directed against an opponent's military forces and military industry. Used to describe military strategies, attacks, weapons, etc.

countervalue Directed against an opponent's civilian and economic centers. Used to describe military strategies, attacks, weapons, etc.

crisis stability A strategic situation in which neither side has an incentive to use nuclear weapons during a crisis.

cruise missile A pilotless missile, propelled by an air-breathing jet engine, that flies in the atmosphere. Cruise missiles may be armed with either conventional or nuclear warheads and launched from an aircraft, a submarine or surface ship, or land-based platform.

damage limitation The capacity to reduce damage from a nuclear attack, by passive or active defenses or by striking the opponent's forces in a counterforce attack.

demilitarized zone An area in which the deployment of military forces or weaponry, either conventional or nuclear, is prohibited.

deployment Distribution of a weapon system to units for use in combat—the final stage in the weapon-acquisition process.

depressed trajectory The trajectory of a ballistic missile fired at an angle much lower to the ground than the normal minimum energy, or high, trajectory. Missiles fired with a depressed trajectory fly low, are harder to track with radar, and their flying time is reduced. Use of this trajectory in an attack increases the vulnerability of targeted forces which depend on warning time for their security.

deterrence Dissuasion of a potential adversary from initiating an attack or conflict, often by the threat of unacceptable retaliatory damage. Nuclear deterrence is usually contrasted with the concept of nuclear defense, the strategy and forces for limiting damage, if deterrence fails. Some hold that a strategy of nuclear defense may also have a deterrent effect, if it can reduce the destructive potential of a nuclear attack.

disarmament In UN usage, all measures related to the prevention, limitation, reduction or elimination of weapons and military forces. *See* general and complete disarmament.

dual-capable system   A weapon system capable of carrying nuclear or conventional explosives.

dual-mission system   A weapon system capable of operating in a tactical, theater, or strategic mode. Sometimes called a "gray-area" or "hybrid" system.

enhanced radiation warhead   A warhead, commonly referred to as the neutron bomb, which kills by radiation rather than by blast. This warhead is designed for deployment on the European-based U.S. Lance missile.

enrichment   A process which increases the ratio of ^{235}U to ^{238}U above that found in natural uranium. Uranium used in light-water reactors, high-temperature gas-cooled reactors, and nuclear explosives must be enriched. Methods of enrichment include gaseous diffusion, gas centrifuge, the aerodynamic process, and lasers.

equivalent megatonnage (EMT)   A common measure of the destructive effect of nuclear weapons on unprotected targets, such as cities. Destruction does not increase proportionally with an increase in the yield of nuclear weapons. EMT can increase the gross destructive potential of an entire nuclear arsenal or a single nuclear weapon. The former measure is computed by multiplying the number of warheads (N) by the specific yield (Y) raised to the two-thirds power: $EMT = NY^{2/3}$. The latter measure is defined as $Y^{2/3}$ for weapons of a yield less than one megaton and as $Y^{1/2}$ for weapons over one megaton.

essential equivalence   A balance of forces in which the capabilities of both parties are approximately equal in effectiveness, though they might not be equal numerically.

fallout   The spread of radioactive particles from clouds of debris produced by nuclear blasts. "Local fallout" falls to the earth's surface within twenty-four hours of the blast.

first strike   An initial attack with nuclear weapons. A *disarming* first strike is one in which the attacker attempts to destroy all or a large portion of its adversary's strategic nuclear forces before they can be launched. A *preemptive* first strike is one in which a nation launches its attack first on the presumption that the adversary is about to attack.

first use   The introduction of nuclear weapons into a strategic or tactical conflict. *See* first strike. A no-first-use pledge by a nation obliges it not to be the first to introduce nuclear weapons in a conflict.

fission   The process of splitting atomic nuclei through bombardment by neutrons. This process yields vast quantities of energy as well as more neutrons capable of initiating further fission.

flexible response The capacity to meet aggression or deal with conflict by choosing among a variety of options. *See* graduated response.

forward-based system (FBS) A medium-range U.S. nuclear delivery system, based in third countries or on aircraft carriers, which can strike targets in the Soviet Union. Examples of such systems are F-111 and F-4 ground-based aircraft and carrier-based A-6 and A-7 aircraft.

fractional orbital bombardment system (FOBS) A proposed weapon system wherein a missile is propelled into an orbital trajectory but is decelerated and re-enters the earth's atmosphere before completing a full orbit. Potentially, the system could reduce warning time, make it possible to attack from unexpected angles, and increase range, though at a substantial cost in payload and accuracy.

fractionation The division of bomber or missile payload into separate re-entry vehicles, or the degree of such division.

fratricide The destruction or degradation of the accuracy and effectiveness of an attacking nuclear weapon by the nearby explosion of another attacking nuclear weapon. This phenomenon would decrease the effectiveness of an attack on closely spaced targets, such as missile silos.

fusion The process of combining atomic nuclei to form a single, heavier element or nucleus and to release large amounts of energy.

general and complete disarmament (GCD) The total abandonment of military forces and weapons (other than internal police forces) by all nations at the same time, usually foreseen as occurring through an agreed schedule of force reductions. In 1961, in the so-called McCloy-Zorin Principles, the United States and the USSR agreed that their negotiations would have GCD as their ultimate objective.

graduated response An effort to prevent and to slow escalation of an armed conflict by responding to adversary actions at a similar or only slightly higher level of force.

gray-area system *See* dual-capable and dual-mission systems.

ground-launched cruise missile (GLCM) *See* cruise missile.

hard or hardened target A target protected against the blast, heat, and radiation effects of nuclear weapons of specific yields. Hardening is usually accomplished by means of earth and reinforced concrete and is measured by the number of pounds per square inch of blast overpressure which a target can withstand.

heavy missile A missile with a large payload which can carry nuclear warheads capable of destroying fixed, hardened targets. In the SALT I negotiations a common definition of heavy missile was not reached; however, certain ICBMs (such as the U.S. Titan II and

Soviet SS-9) were designated heavy missiles. Under the SALT II treaty the new Soviet ICBM, the SS-18, will be counted as a heavy missile.

independent initiative   A measure undertaken by a nation with the aim of reducing or limiting armaments or increasing military stability, independent of negotiated agreements.

inertial guidance   The basic guidance system for ballistic missiles. This system is capable of detecting and correcting deviations from the intended velocity or trajectory.

intercontinental ballistic missile (ICBM)   A ballistic missile with a range of 4,000 or more nautical miles. Conventionally, the term ICBM is used only for land-based systems, to differentiate them from submarine-launched ballistic missiles, which also have an intercontinental range.

U.S. ICBMs

Titan II. Deployment began in 1962. There are at present fifty-four Titans in the U.S. nuclear force. Under the SALT I agreement, Titan was defined as a heavy missile.

Minuteman II.   Four hundred and fifty are currently deployed; deployment began in 1966.

Minuteman III.   This MIRVed ICBM is the backbone of the U.S. ICBM force; it was first deployed in 1970. The 550 Minuteman IIIs each carry three warheads of 170 kilotons each.

Soviet ICBMs

SS-9.   First deployed in 1965, the single-warhead SS-9, with a throw-weight of 12,000 pounds, was defined as a heavy missile in SALT I.

SS-11.   The Soviets have deployed 780 single-warhead SS-11s since 1966.

SS-13.   Sixty have been deployed since 1968. A successor to the SS-13, the SS-16, is reportedly ready for deployment, possibly in a land-mobile mode.

SS-17.   First deployed in 1975, this MIRVed missile has been positioned in modified SS-11 silos.

SS-18.   This heavy missile, a modernization of the SS-9, has been MIRVed since its initial deployment in 1975.

SS-19.   Two hundred of this follow-on missile to the SS-11, with greater throw-weight capacity than the SS-11, have been deployed since 1976.

intermediate-range ballistic missile (IRBM)   A ballistic missile with a range of between 1,500 and 4,000 nautical miles.

kiloton A measure of the yield of a nuclear weapon, equivalent to 1,000 tons of TNT.

launch-on-warning doctrine A strategic doctrine under which a nation's bombers and land-based missiles would be launched on receipt of warning (from satellites and other early-warning systems) that an opponent had launched its missiles. This doctrine is sometimes also called "launch on positive (or confirmed) notification of attack" to distinguish between possible and actual attack. Sometimes recommended for use when there is uncertainty over the ability of fixed-site strategic weapons (e.g., ICBMs) to survive an attack, a launch-on-warning doctrine is viewed as destabilizing in a crisis situation.

light-water reactor The most common type of nuclear power reactor. It is fueled by enriched uranium. The spent fuel of a light-water reactor contains significant amounts of plutonium which could be used to make nuclear explosives.

maneuverable re-entry vehicle (MARV) A missile-launched nuclear weapon with a warhead the course of which can be adjusted by internal or external mechanisms, enabling it to evade ABM defenses and to strike its targets with a high degree of accuracy. This ability makes MARV a potential first-strike weapon.

Mark 12A warhead A new warhead for the Minuteman III missile. The increased accuracy and yield of the Mark 12A re-entry vehicles in the warhead will increase the ability of the Minuteman III missiles to destroy hardened Soviet missile silos and other targets.

medium-range ballistic missile (MRBM) A ballistic missile with a range of between 500 and 1,500 nautical miles.

megaton A measure of the yield of a nuclear weapon, equivalent to 1,000,000 tons of TNT.

missile experimental (MX) A U.S. ICBM, now in the research and development phase, which is designed to replace the current ICBM force during the 1980s. This more accurate, powerful, and destructive missile could be deployed in either a single silo or mobile mode and would be capable of destroying Soviet missile silos.

multiple aim point system (MAPS) A proposed method of deploying U.S. ICBMs, similar to the alternative launch-point system (ALPS). The MAPS concept differs from ALPS in that it would require new missile fields for the MX missile, rather than simply new dummy silos at existing Minuteman missile fields. Both concepts are often referred to as the "shell game," since they involve protecting ICBMs through deception.

multiple independently-targetable re-entry vehicle (MIRV) A package of two or more re-entry vehicles which can be carried by a single ballistic missile and delivered on separate targets. The term MIRV is also commonly used for a missile with a MIRVed warhead or for the process of switching from single to multiple re-entry vehicles.

multiple protective structure (MPS)　Any missile-basing mode designed to provide more aim-points than actual missile launchers. The purpose of MPS is to protect U.S. land-based ICBMs against a hypothetical first strike by complicating the attacker's targeting plan. These basing modes include vertical shelters, horizontal shelters, a trench shelter, or a slope-sided pool covering missile silos. *See also* multiple aim point system and alternative launch-point system.

mutual assured destruction　A concept of reciprocal deterrence which rests on the ability of the two nuclear superpowers to inflict unacceptable damage on one another after surviving a nuclear first strike.

mutual example force restraint *or* **reduction**　A means of limiting or reducing military capabilities whereby two nations, explicitly or tacitly, agree to limit or reduce forces without a negotiated agreement. The process of mutual example force restraint or reduction is akin to conditional restraint and may begin with one nation taking the initiative. *See* conditional restraint.

national technical means (NTM)　A method of verifying compliance with negotiated arms control agreements generally consistent with the recognized provisions of international law, commonly understood as surveillance by satellite and aerial reconnaissance.

navigational system using time and ranging (NAVSTAR)　A global positioning system for providing course data to ballistic missiles and other weapon systems. NAVSTAR consists of twenty-four satellites in synchronous orbits providing near-continuous signals to passive receivers aboard ballistic missiles, allowing them to determine their positions within twenty to thirty feet and to correct their attitude or velocity.

nuclear fuel cycle　Any process for developing, utilizing, and disposing of nuclear fuels.

nuclear weapon-free zone　An area in which the production and deployment of nuclear weapons is prohibited.

on-site inspection　A method of verifying compliance with an arms control agreement whereby representatives of an international or other designated organization, or of the parties to the agreement, are given direct access to view force deployments or weapon systems.

parity　A level of forces in which opposing nations possess approximately equal capabilities.

passive defense　The protection of civil and military targets without the use of weapon systems. Measures for protecting population (evacuation, blast shelters, fallout shelters) and economic targets (dispersal, hardening, redundancy) are ordinarily termed "civil defense." Military targets can be passively defended by camouflage, hardening, dispersal, and similar techniques. *See* active defense.

peaceful nuclear explosion (PNE) The non-military use of nuclear detonations for such purposes as stimulating natural gas, recovering oil shale, diverting rivers, or excavating.

penetration aids (PENAIDS) Techniques and/or devices employed to deceive an opponent's defenses, thus increasing the probability of a weapon's penetrating the defenses and reaching its intended targets.

plutonium An element not found in nature which is created as a waste product of nuclear reactors. Plutonium can be used to make nuclear weapons.

point defense Defense of a limited geographic area. Usually refers to the defense of ICBM silos against attacking missiles.

pounds per square inch (psi) A measure of nuclear blast overpressure or dynamic pressure, used to calculate the effects of a nuclear detonation or the ability of a structure to withstand a nuclear blast.

precision-guided munition (PGM) A bomb or missile that is guided during its terminal phase. In the absence of active defenses, the probability of a PGM making a direct hit on its target is greater than 50 percent.

preemptive strike A damage-limiting attack launched in anticipation of an opponent's attack.

proliferation The spread of weapons, usually nuclear weapons. Horizontal proliferation refers to the acquisition of nuclear weapons by states not previously possessing them. Vertical proliferation refers to increases in the nuclear arsenals of those states already possessing nuclear weapons.

proof-testing The testing of warheads and other weapon components to assure the continued quality and reliability of weapon stockpiles. Also called reliability testing.

re-entry vehicle That part of a ballistic missile designed to re-enter the earth's atmosphere in the terminal portion of its trajectory.

remotely-piloted vehicle (RPV) A pilotless aircraft that is guided from a distant location by a person with equipment which provides much of the same information a pilot would have.

reprocessing plant A facility required to separate the uranium and plutonium present in spent reactor fuel. The plutonium recovered through reprocessing can be reused as reactor fuel or for nuclear explosives.

Schlesinger doctrine (*also* new strategic doctrine *or* limited nuclear war doctrine) A concept advanced in 1974 by former Defense Secretary James Schlesinger which called for a change in American targeting doctrine and weapons so as to permit a greater capability for limited strikes against high-value military targets (missile silos, etc.) on the assumption that this might limit the scope and damage of nuclear war.

Seafarer An extremely low frequency (ELF) communications system being developed. If constructed it will improve communications with U.S. submarines at greater depths to aid in assuring their survivability and will improve U.S. retargeting capability for SLBMs.

sea-launched cruise missile (SLCM) *See* cruise missile.

second strike A follow-up or retaliatory attack after an opponent's first strike. Second-strike capability describes the capacity to attack after suffering a first strike. The U.S. strategy of deterrence is premised on high confidence in the ability of the United States to deliver a nuclear second strike that would inflict unacceptable damage on the nation which struck first.

short-range attack missile (SRAM) A nuclear air-to-surface missile deployed on B-52s.

short-range ballistic missile (SRBM) A ballistic missile with a range of under 500 nautical miles.

strategic Relating to a nation's offensive or defensive military potential, including its geographical location and its resources and economic, political and military strength. The term strategic is used to denote those weapons or forces capable of directly affecting another nation's war-fighting ability, as distinguished from tactical or theater weapons or forces.

Strategic Arms Limitation Talks (SALT) Negotiations between the United States and the USSR initiated in 1969 which seek to limit the strategic nuclear forces, both offensive and defensive, of both sides.

submarine-launched ballistic missile (SLBM) Any ballistic missile launched from a submarine.

U.S. SLBMs

Polaris A3. This SLBM was initially deployed in 1964; one hundred and sixty are currently part of the U.S. force. The Polaris A3 has a range of 2,880 miles.

Poseidon C3. This SLBM carries ten MIRVed missiles, and has a range of 2,880 miles. Four hundred ninety-six have been deployed since 1971.

Trident I and II. These missiles, currently in early production and research and development stages respectively and projected for deployment in the 1980s, will improve the accuracy of the sea-based missile force if deployed.

Soviet SLBMs

SS-N-4. Currently twenty-seven of this SLBM, with a range of 350 miles, are deployed. First deployed in 1961.

SS-N-5. Deployment began in 1964; the fifty-four that are currently deployed have a maximum range of 750 miles.

SS-N-6. First deployed in 1969, this missile is now the largest part of the Soviet SLBM force with 528 missiles in the inventory of the USSR.

SS-N-8. First deployed in 1972, this single warhead SLBM increased the maximum range of the Soviet SLBM force to 4,800 miles.

SS-NX-17. The solid-fuel successor to the SS-N-6. Only sixteen have been deployed since 1977; each carries a single warhead but has been tested with MIRVs.

SS-NX-18. This successor to the SS-N-8, first deployed in 1978, carries three MIRVed missiles and has a maximum range of greater than 5,000 miles.

tactical   Relating to battlefield operations as distinguished from theater or strategic operations. Tactical weapons or forces are those designed for combat with opposing military forces rather than for reaching the rear areas of the opponent or the opponent's homeland, which require theater or strategic weapons, respectively.

tactical nuclear weapon   A short-range, low-yield nuclear weapon designed for combat use on the battlefield.

telemetry   The transmission of electronic signals by missiles to earth. Monitoring these signals aids in evaluating a weapon's performance and provides a way of verifying weapon tests undertaken by an adversary.

theater of war (*also* theater of operations)   In a war of significant geographic extent, a distinct area of operations including but not limited to tactical operations and encompassing all land, sea and air activities within that zone. Designating a given area as a theater of war is an administrative, logistical and command convenience and may vary from one nation to another or may be agreed upon among allies. A theater includes the rear areas of the combat forces but not necessarily their homelands. Theater responsibilities may be assigned in the absence of war.

theater nuclear weapon (TNW)   A nuclear weapon, usually of longer range and larger yield than a tactical nuclear weapon, which can be used in theater operations. Many strategic nuclear weapons can be used in theater operations, but not all theater nuclear weapons are designed for strategic use. The Soviet SS-16 mobile missile is generally considered a theater nuclear weapon, as are the nuclear-capable U.S. fighter/bombers deployed in the Far East and Europe and the U.S. Lance missile.

throw-weight The maximum weight of the warheads, guidance unit, and penetration aids which can be delivered by a missile over a particular range and in a stated trajectory.

Triad U.S. strategic forces which are composed of three parts: land-based intercontinental ballistic missiles; submarine-launched ballistic missiles; and long-range bombers.

vertical short take-off and landing (V/STOL) Relating to the ability (of an aircraft) vertically to clear a 50-foot obstacle within 1,500 feet after takeoff or to stop within 1,500 feet over a 50-foot obstacle in landing. An advantage of V/STOL aircraft is that they are able to operate nearer the forward edge of the battle area.

warhead That part of a missile, torpedo, rocket, or other munition which contains either the nuclear or thermonuclear system, chemical or biological agent, or inert materials intended to inflict damage.

yield The force of a nuclear explosion expressed as the equivalent of the energy produced by tons of TNT. *See* kiloton and megaton.

Arms Control Agreements in Force

The 1959 Antarctic Treaty demilitarizes the Antarctic and declares that it shall be used for peaceful purposes.

The 1963 Partial Test Ban Treaty bans nuclear weapon tests in the atmosphere, in outer space and under water.

The 1963 U.S.-Soviet Hot Line Agreement establishes a direct communications link between the governments of the United States and the USSR for use in time of emergency. A 1971 agreement further improved the communications link.

The 1967 Outer Space Treaty prohibits the placing of nuclear or other weapons of mass destruction around the earth and also outlaws the establishment of military bases, installations and fortifications, the testing of any type of weapons, and the conduct of military maneuvers in outer space.

The 1967 Treaty of Tlatelolco prohibits the testing, use, manufacture, production or acquisition by any means of nuclear weapons in Latin America. Under Protocol II the nuclear weapon states agree to respect the military denuclearization of Latin America.

The 1968 Non-Proliferation Treaty (NPT) prohibits the transfer of nuclear weapons by nuclear-weapon states and the acquisition of such weapons by non-nuclear weapon states.

The 1971 Sea-Bed Treaty prohibits the emplacement of nuclear weapons or other weapons of mass destruction on the seabed beyond a twelve-mile zone.

The 1971 U.S.-Soviet Nuclear Accidents Agreement provides for immediate notification, one of the other, in the event of an accidental, unauthorized incident involving a possible detonation of a nuclear weapon.

The 1972 Biological Weapons Convention prohibits the development, production, stockpiling, or acquisition of biological agents and any weapons designed to use such agents.

The 1972 ABM Treaty limited the deployment of anti-ballistic missile defenses by the United States and the USSR to two areas—one for the defense of the national capital, and the other for the defense of some ICBMs. A 1974 Protocol further limited both parties to a single area of deployment.

The 1972 Interim Offensive Weapons Agreement froze the aggregate number of U.S. and Soviet ballistic missile launchers for a five-year period. This agreement expired on October 3, 1977. This agreement and the ABM Treaty are known as SALT I.

The 1972 Incidents on the High Seas Agreement assures the navigational safety of ships assigned to the U.S. and Soviet armed forces. Measures providing for the safety of flight for military aircraft over the high seas are also included.

The 1972 Agreement on Basic Principles of Relations between the United States and the USSR provides the basis for relations between the United States and the USSR. Both parties agree to do the utmost to avoid military confrontations and to prevent the outbreak of nuclear war.

The 1973 Agreement on the Prevention of Nuclear War provides that the United States and the USSR will take all actions necessary to preclude the outbreak of nuclear war.

The 1974 Declaration of Ayacucho Agreement envisions the limitation of armaments in Latin America.

The 1974 Threshold Test Ban Treaty (TTBT) limits the size of U.S. and Soviet nuclear weapons tests to 150 kilotons.

The 1975 Conference on Security and Cooperation in Europe (CSCE) contains a provision on confidence-building measures which provides for notification of major military maneuvers in Europe.

The 1976 Peaceful Nuclear Explosions Treaty (PNE) complements the 1974 Threshold Test Ban Treaty by prohibiting any individual underground nuclear explosion for peaceful purposes which has a yield of more than 150 kilotons, or any group explosion with an aggregate yield exceeding 1,500 kilotons.

The 1977 Environmental Modification Convention prohibits the hostile use of techniques which could produce substantial environmental modifications.

Arms Control Negotiations

Baruch Plan called for placing all atomic resources of the world under the control of an independent international authority. Soviet displeasure with certain provisions led to an eventual deadlock in the talks. Initiated in 1946.

Conference of the Committee on Disarmament (CCD), the central forum dealing with multilateral arms control, co-chaired by the United States and the USSR, created to discuss general and complete disarmament. Initiated in 1961.

Talks on Mutual and Balanced Force Reductions (MBFR), multilateral negotiations seeking to limit NATO and Warsaw Pact forces within a limited geographic region. Initiated in 1973.

Indian Ocean Negotiations, bilateral talks between the United States and the USSR which seek to find mutually acceptable limits on weapons deployed in the Indian Ocean. Initiated in 1976.

Comprehensive Test Ban Negotiations (CTB), talks between the United States, the USSR, and Great Britain which seek to ban all nuclear testing. Initiated in 1977.

Negotiations to Limit Conventional Arms Transfers, bilateral negotiations between the United States and the USSR which seek to place constraints on arms transfers to certain areas. Initiated in 1978.

Committee on Disarmament (CD), created by the 1978 UN Special Session on Disarmament to replace the Conference of the Committee on Disarmament. This new negotiating forum will operate under a rotating chairmanship. Initiated in 1979.

International Nuclear Fuel Cycle Evaluation (INFCE), a two-year, forty-nation study of the future of the international nuclear trade and nuclear technology. Scheduled to conclude in 1979, INFCE is responsible for surveying the feasibility of proliferation-resistant nuclear fuel cycles.

Bibliography

SALT

Aaron, David. "SALT: A New Concept." *Foreign Policy* 17 (Winter 1974-75): 157-165.

Allison, Graham. "Cold Dawn and the Mind of Kissinger." *Washington Monthly* 6 (March 1974): 38-47. (Review of *Cold Dawn* by John Newhouse and *Kissinger: Portrait of a Mind* by Stephen Graubard.)

Arbatov, Georgy. "The Soviet View of Our SALT Policy." *Long Island Newsday,* April 6, 1978.

Aspin, Les. "SALT or No SALT." *Bulletin of the Atomic Scientists,* June 1978, pp. 34-38.

Bertram, Christoph, ed. "The Future of Arms Control: Part 1—Beyond SALT II." *Adelphi Paper Number 141.* London: International Institute for Strategic Studies, 1978.

Brennan, Donald G. "The Soviet Military Build-Up and Its Implications for the Negotiations on Strategic Arms Limitations." *Orbis* 21 (Spring 1977).

Burns, Richard Dean and Susan Hoffman. *The SALT Era: A Selected Bibliography,* Political Issues Series, IV, 5. Los Angeles: Center for the Study of Armament and Disarmament, University of California, 1977.

Burt, Richard. "Arms Control and Soviet Strategic Forces: The Risks of Asking SALT to Do Too Much." *Washington Review of Strategic and International Studies* 1 (January 1978): 19-33.

———. "One Trouble with Arms Control Talk: There's So Much of It." *New York Times,* February 19, 1978.

———. "SALT II and Offensive Force Levels." *Orbis* 18 (Summer 1974): 465-481.

———. "The Scope and Limits of SALT." *Foreign Affairs* 61 (July 1978): 751-770.

———. "Snag in Arms Talks: Missile Modernizing." *New York Times,* November 2, 1977.

Caldwell, Lawrence T. "Soviet Attitudes to SALT." *Adelphi Paper Number 75.* London: International Institute for Strategic Studies, 1971.

Carter, Barry. "What Next in Arms Control?" *Orbis* 17 (Spring 1973): 176-196.

Carter, Luther J. "Strategic Weapons: Verification Keeps Ahead of Arms Control." *Science,* March 14, 1975, pp. 936-939.

Cranston, Alan. "A Different Perspective on SALT I." *Congressional Record,* February 17, 1976, S 1683-1684.

Davis, Jacquelyn K. "SALT and the Balance of Superpower Strategic Forces." *NATO's Fifteen Nations* 23 (February/March 1978): 56-61.

Drew, Elizabeth. "An Argument Over Survival." *New Yorker,* April 4, 1977, pp. 99-117.

Frye, Alton. "Strategic Restraint, Mutual and Assured." *Foreign Policy* 27 (Summer 1977): 3-24.

Garthoff, Raymond L. "Negotiating with the Russians: Some Lessons from SALT." *International Security* 1 (Spring 1977): 3-24.

————. "SALT and the Soviet Military." *Problems of Communism,* January/February 1975, pp. 21-37.

Gelb, Leslie H. "Own Arms Offer Rejected by U.S." *New York Times,* January 18, 1976.

Glagolev, Igor S. "The Soviet Decision-Making Process in Arms Control." *Orbis* 21 (Winter 1978): 767-776.

Gray, Colin S. "Detente, Arms Control, and Strategy: Perspectives on SALT." *American Political Science Review* 70 (December 1976): 1242-1256.

————. "The Limits of Arms Control." *Air Force Magazine,* August 1975, pp. 70-72.

————. "A Problem Guide to SALT II." *Survival* 17 (September/ October 1975): 230-234.

————. "SALT I Aftermath: Have the Soviets Been Cheating?" *Air Force Magazine,* November 1975, pp. 28-33.

Hallett, Douglas. "Kissinger Dolosus: The Domestic Politics of SALT." *Yale Review* 65 (Winter 1976): 161-174.

Jackson, Henry. "SALT: An Analysis and a Proposal." *Congressional Record,* December 4, 1973, S 39426-39428.

Kennedy, Edward M. "Address Before the Overseas Press Club." Reprinted in the *Congressional Record,* April 12, 1976, S 5449-5452.

Kissinger, Henry A. "The Vladivostok Accord: Background Briefing by Henry Kissinger, December 3, 1974." *Survival* 17 (July/ August 1975): 191-198.

Kruzel, Joseph. "SALT II: The Search for a Follow-On Agreement." *Orbis* 17 (Summer 1973): 334-363.

Laird, Melvin R. "Arms Control: The Russians Are Cheating!" *Reader's Digest,* December 1977.

Lambeth, Benjamin. "The Soviet Challenge under SALT I." *Current History* 63 (October 1972): 150-155.

Leader, Stefan H. "SALT: A Race Against the Arms Race." *Defense Monitor.* Washington, D.C.: Center for Defense Information, July 1977.

Leitenberg, Milton. "Soviet Secrecy and Negotiations on Strategic Weapon Arms Control and Disarmament." *Bulletin of Peace Proposals* 4 (1974) : 377-380.

Lodal, Jan M. "Verifying SALT." *Foreign Policy* 24 (Fall 1976) : 40-64.

Lord, Carnes. "Verification and the Future of Arms Control." *Strategic Review* 6 (Spring 1978) : 24-33.

Luttwak, Edward N. "SALT and the Meaning of Strategy." *Washington Review of Strategic and International Studies* 1 (April 1978) : 16-28.

————. "Why Arms Control Has Failed." *Commentary,* January 1978, pp. 19-28.

Milshetyn, M. A. and L. S. Semeyko. "SALT II—A Soviet View." *Survival* 16 (March/April 1974) : 63-70.

Nacht, Michael L. "The Vladivostok Accord and American Technological Options." *Survival* 17 (May/June 1975) : 106-113.

Newhouse, John. *Cold Dawn: The Story of SALT.* New York: Holt, Rinehart and Winston, 1973.

Nitze, Paul H. "SALT: The Strategic Balance Between Hope and Skepticism." *Foreign Policy* 17 (Winter 1974-75) : 136-156.

————. "Soviet's Negotiating Style Assayed." *Aviation Week & Space Technology,* February 17, 1975, pp. 40-43.

Panofsky, W. K. H. "From SALT I to SALT II." *Survey* 19 (Spring 1973) : 160-187. (Followed by a description of Soviet arms control attitudes by Marshall D. Shulman.)

Payne, Samuel B., Jr. "The Soviet Debate on Strategic Arms Limitation: 1969-72." *Soviet Studies* 27 (January 1975) : 27-45.

Pfaltzgraff, Jr., Robert L. and Jacquelyn K. Davis. *SALT II: Promise or Precipice.* Washington, D.C.: Center for Advanced International Studies, University of Miami, 1976.

Robinson, Clarence, Jr. "Backfire Draws Focus in SALT." *Aviation Week & Space Technology,* August 25, 1975, pp. 14-15.

Scoville, Herbert, Jr. "The Balance of Arms." *New Republic,* March 30, 1974, pp. 11-13.

————. "Beyond SALT One." *Foreign Affairs* 50 (April 1972) : 488-500.

————. "An 'Iffy' Arms Control Agreement." *New Republic,* January 18, 1975, pp. 19-21.

————. "The SALT Negotiations." *Scientific American,* August 1977, pp. 24-31.

Sienkiewicz, Stanley. "SALT and Soviet Nuclear Doctrine." *International Security* 2 (Spring 1978) : 84-100.

Slocombe, Walter. *Controlling Strategic Nuclear Weapons.* New York: Foreign Policy Association, Headline Series 226, June 1975.

Smith, Gerard C. "SALT After Vladivostok." *Journal of International Affairs* 29 (Spring 1975) : 7-18.

Sonnenfeldt, Helmut. "Russia, America and Detente." *Foreign Affairs* 56 (January 1978) : 275-294.

Szulc, Tad. "Carter's SALT Mines." *New Republic,* March 18, 1978, pp. 14-15.

Ulsamer, Edgar. "SALT II's Gray-Area Weapon Systems." *Air Force Magazine,* July 1976, pp. 80-85.

U.S., Congress. House, Committee on International Relations, Subcommittee on International Security and Scientific Affairs. *The Vladivostok Accord: Implications to U.S. Security, Arms Control, and World Peace, Hearings,* 94th Cong., 1st sess.

U.S., Congress. Senate, Committee on Foreign Relations. *Strategic Arms Limitation Agreements,* 92nd Cong., 2nd sess.

Van Cleave, William R. "SALT on the Eagle's Tail." *Strategic Review* 9 (Spring 1976) : 44-55.

———. "The SALT Papers: A Torrent of Verbiage or a Spring of Capital Truths?" *Orbis* 17 (Winter 1974) : 1396-1401. (Review of John Newhouse's *Cold Dawn: The Story of SALT.*)

Willrich, Mason and John B. Rhinelander, eds. *SALT: The Moscow Agreements and Beyond.* New York: The Free Press, 1974.

Wilson, Charles H. "The Honorable Paul H. Nitze Testifies before the Subcommittee on Arms Control and Disarmament on SALT." *Congressional Record,* July 2, 1974, E 4445-4446.

Wolfe, Thomas W. *The SALT Experience: Its Impact on U.S. and Soviet Strategic Policy and Decisionmaking,* R-1686-PR. Santa Monica, California: Rand Corp., 1975.

———. "Soviet Interests in SALT" in William R. Kintner and Robert L. Pfaltzgraff, Jr., eds. *SALT: Implications for Arms Control in the 1970's.* Pittsburgh: University of Pittsburgh Press, 1973, pp. 21-54.

Other Arms Control Efforts

Atlantic Council, Working Group on Security. *Arms Control and the Gray Area Weapons Systems.* Washington, D. C.: Atlantic Council, 1978.

Barnaby, Frank. "Nuclear Test Ban's Last Chance?" *New Scientist,* April 1, 1976, pp. 11-12.

Barton, John H. and Lawrence D. Weiler. *International Arms Control: Issues and Agreements.* Stanford, California: Stanford University Press, 1976.

Bellany, Ian. "Peace Research: Means and Ends." *International Affairs,* January 1976, pp. 13-26.

Bertram, Christoph. "The Future of Arms Control: Part II: Arms Control and Technological Change: Elements of a New Approach." *Adelphi Paper Number 146.* London: International Institute for Strategic Studies, 1978.

――――. "Mutual Force Reductions in Europe: The Political Aspects." *Adelphi Paper Number 84.* London: International Institute for Strategic Studies, 1972.

Bezboruah, Monoranjan. *U.S. Strategy in the Indian Océan: The International Response.* New York: Praeger, 1977.

Blechman, Barry M. *The Control of Naval Armaments: Prospects and Possibilities.* Washington, D. C.: The Brookings Institution, 1975.

Bloomfield, Lincoln P. and Harlan Cleveland. "A Strategy for the United States." *International Security* 2 (Spring 1978): 32-55.

Brennan, Donald. "A Comprehensive Test Ban: Everybody. or Nobody." *International Security* 1 (Summer 1976): 92-117.

Brodie, Bernard. "On the Objectives of Arms Control." *International Security* 1 (Summer 1976): 17-36.

Bull, Hedley. "Arms Control and World Order." *International Security* 1 (Summer 1976): 3-16.

――――. *The Control of the Arms Race,* 2nd edition. New York: Praeger, 1966.

Burns, Richard D., compiler. *Arms Control and Disarmament: War/Peace Bibliography Series #6.* Santa Barbara, California: ABC-Clio Press, 1978.

Cahn, Anne, F. A. Long, and George Rathjens. "The Search for a New Handle on Arms Control." *Science and Public Affairs,* April 1974.

Canby, Steven L. "Mutual Force Reductions: A Military Perspective." *International Security* 2 (Winter 1978): 122-135.

Carlton, David and Carlo Schaerf, eds. *Arms Control and Technological Innovation.* London: Croom Helm, 1977.

Chayes, A., F. A. Long, and G. W. Rathjens. "Threshold Treaty: A Step Backwards." *Bulletin of the Atomic Scientists,* January 1975, p. 16.

Clemens, Walter, Jr. *The Superpowers and Arms Control: From Cold War to Interdependence.* Lexington, Massachusetts: D. C. Heath & Co., 1973.

Clough, Ralph N., A. Doak Barnett, Morton H. Halperin, and Jerome H. Kahan. *The United States, China, and Arms Control.* Washington, D. C.: The Brookings Institution, 1975.

Coffey, Joseph I. *Arms Control and European Security: A Guide to East-West Negotiations.* New York: Praeger, 1977.

Cohen, S. T. and W. R. Van Cleave. "The Nuclear Test Ban: A Dangerous Anachronism." *National Review,* July 8, 1977, pp. 770-775.

Evron, Yair. "The Role of Arms Control in the Middle East." *Adelphi Paper Number 138*. London: International Institute for Strategic Studies, 1977.

Fisher, Adrian S. "Arms Control, Disarmament and International Law." *Virginia Law Review* 51 (November 1964): 1200-1219.

Garthoff, Douglas F. "The Soviet Military and Arms Control." *Survival* 19 (November/December 1977): 242-250.

Gray, Colin S. "Of Bargaining Chips and Building Blocks: Arms Control and Defense Policy." *International Journal* 28 (Spring 1973): 266-296.

Haass, Richard. "Naval Arms Limitation in the Indian Ocean." *Survival* 20 (March/April 1978): 50-57.

Halsted, Thomas A. "Why No End to Nuclear Testing?" *Survival* 19 (March/April 1977): 60-66.

Hill, R. J. "MBFR." *International Journal* 29 (Spring 1974): 242-255.

Holzman, Franklyn D. *Financial Checks on Soviet Defense Expenditures*. Lexington, Massachusetts: Lexington Books, 1975.

Hopkins, John C. "Why Not Stop Testing." *Bulletin of the Atomic Scientists,* April 1977, pp. 30-31.

Ikle, Fred C. *How Nations Negotiate*. New York: Harper & Row, 1964.

International Institute for Strategic Studies, the Brookings Institution, and the Japan Institute for International Affairs. "SALT and MBFR: The Next Phase." *Survival* 17 (January/February 1975): 14-24.

Kincade, William H. "Thinking About Arms Control and Strategic Weapons." *World Affairs* 136 (Spring 1974): 364-376.

Kistiakowsky, G. B. and H. F. York. "Strategic Arms Race Slowdown through Test Limitations." *Science,* August 2, 1974, pp. 403-406.

Kolkowicz, Roman *et al. The Soviet Union and Arms Control: A Superpower Dilemma*. Baltimore: The Johns Hopkins University Press, 1970.

Lambert, Robert W. and Jean E. Mayer. *International Negotiations on the Biological Weapons and Toxin Convention*. U.S. Arms Control and Disarmament Agency, Publication 78, May 1975.

Long, Franklin and George W. Rathjens, eds. *Arms, Defense Policy and Arms Control*. New York: W. W. Norton & Co. Inc., 1976.

Marder, Murrey and Robert Kaiser. "Carter and Arms Control: A Test of His Presidency." *Washington Post,* April 10, 1977.

Martin, Laurence. *Arms and Strategy: The World Power Struggle Today*. New York: David McKay Co., 1973.

Multan, W. and A. Towpik. "Western Arms Control Policies in Europe Seen from the East." *Survival* 16 (May/June 1974): 127-132.

Myrdal, Alva. "The International Control of Disarmament." *Scientific American,* October 1974, pp. 21-33.

National Technical Information Service. *Arms Control, A Bibliography with Abstracts, 1964-1977.* Springfield, Virginia: National Technical Information Service, Publication PS-77/0454/7GA.

Nitze, Paul H., John F. Lehman, and Seymour Weiss. *The Carter Disarmament Proposals: Some Basic Questions and Cautions.* Miami: University of Miami, Center for Advanced International Studies, 1977.

Pugwash Council. "Peace and Security in a Changing World." *Bulletin of the Atomic Scientists,* December 1977, pp. 33-39.

Ravenal, Earl C. "The Case for Unilateral Arms Control Initiatives." *World Issues,* June/July 1977, p. 3.

————. "Does Disarmament Have A Future?" *Nation,* May 27, 1978, pp. 636-640.

Roberts, Chalmers. *The Nuclear Years.* New York: Praeger, 1970.

Robinson, J. P. Perry. "The Special Case of Chemical and Biological Weapons." *Bulletin of the Atomic Scientists,* May 1975, pp. 17-23.

Schelling, Thomas C. *Arms and Influence.* New Haven: Yale University Press, 1966.

———— and Morton H. Halperin. *Strategy and Arms Control.* New York: The Twentieth Century Fund, 1961.

Sharp, Jane M. O. "Isaiah Revisited." *Bulletin of the Atomic Scientists,* April 1978, pp. 18-21, 52-57.

————, ed. *Opportunities for Disarmament.* New York and Washington, D. C.: Carnegie Endowment for International Peace, 1978.

Singer, J. David. "An Assessment of Peace Research." *International Security* 1 (Summer 1976): 118-137.

Sohn, Louis B. "Disarmament at the Crossroads." *International Security* 2 (Spring 1978): 4-31.

Stockholm International Peace Research Institute. *Armaments and Disarmament in the Nuclear Age: A Handbook.* Cambridge, Massachusetts: The MIT Press, 1976.

————. *Arms Control: A Survey and Appraisal of Multilateral Agreements.* London: Taylor & Francis, 1978.

————. *Chemical Disarmament: New Weapons for Old.* Stockholm: Almqvist & Wiksell, 1975.

————. *Outer Space: Battlefield of the Future?* London: Taylor & Francis, 1978.

————. *World Armaments and Disarmament: SIPRI Yearbook 1978.* London: Taylor & Francis, 1978.

Thee, Marek. "Crisis in Arms Control." *Bulletin of Peace Proposals* 7 (1976): 99-102.

————. "Disarmament Through Unilateral Initiatives." *Bulletin of Peace Proposals* 4 (1974): 381-384.

U.S., Arms Control and Disarmament Agency. *Verification: The Critical Element of Arms Control.* Washington, D.C.: Government Printing Office, 1976.

U.S., Congress. House, Committee on International Relations, Subcommittee on International Organizations. *Prohibition of Weather Modification as a Weapon of War, Hearings,* 94th Cong., 1st sess.

Viorst, Milton. "Politics of Disarmament." *Nation,* June 3, 1978.

Weiss, Edith Brown. "International Responses to Weather Modification." *International Organization* 29 (Summer 1975): 805-826.

Wilkes, Owen. "Military Research and Development Programs: Problems of Control." *Bulletin of Peace Proposals* 9 (1978): 3-10.

Nuclear Proliferation

Baker, Steven. "Nuclear Proliferation: Monopoly or Cartel?" *Foreign Policy* 23 (Summer 1976): 202-220.

Betts, Richard K. "Paranoids, Pygmies, Pariahs & Nonproliferation." *Foreign Policy* 26 (Spring 1977): 157-183.

Bloomfield, Lincoln P. "Nuclear Spread and World Order." *Foreign Affairs* 53 (July 1975): 743-755.

Bull, Hedley. "Rethinking Non-Proliferation." *International Affairs* 51 (April 1975): 175-189.

Burt, Richard. "Proliferation and the Spread of New Conventional Weapons Technology." *International Security* 1 (Winter 1977): 119-139.

Carter, Jimmy. "Nuclear Energy and World Order." Address to the United Nations, May 13, 1976, reprinted in the *Congressional Record,* June 4, 1976, S 8541-8544.

Doub, William O. and Joseph M. Dukert. "Making Nuclear Energy Safe and Secure." *Foreign Affairs* 53 (July 1975): 756-772.

Dowty, Alan. "Nuclear Proliferation: The Israeli Case." *International Studies Quarterly* 22 (March 1978): 79-120.

Dunn, Lewis A. "Nuclear 'Gray Marketeering.'" *International Security* 1 (Winter 1977): 107-118.

Endicott, John E. *Japan's Nuclear Option: Political, Technical, and Strategic Factors.* New York: Praeger Special Studies, 1975.

Epstein, William. *The Last Chance: Nuclear Proliferation and Arms Control.* New York: The Free Press, 1976.

————. "Nuclear-free Zones." *Scientific American,* November 1975, pp. 25-35.

Falk, Richard. "A World Order Problem." *International Security* 3 (Winter 1977): 79-93.

Freedman, Lawrence. "Israel's Nuclear Policy." *Survival* 17 (May/ June 1975) : 114-120.

Gall, Norman. "Nuclear Proliferation: Atoms for Brazil, Dangers for All." *Foreign Policy* 23 (Summer 1976) : 155-201.

Goldschmidt, Bertrand. "A Historical Survey of Nonproliferation Policies." *International Security* 2 (Summer 1977) : 69-87.

Greenwood, Ted, Harold A. Feiveson, and Theodore B. Taylor. *Nuclear Proliferation: Motivations, Capabilities, and Strategies for Control.* New York: McGraw-Hill, 1977.

————, George Rathjens, and Jack Ruina. "Nuclear Power and Weapons Proliferation." *Adelphi Paper Number 130.* London: International Institute for Strategic Studies, 1977.

Jaipal, Rikhi. "The Indian Nuclear Situation." *International Security* 1 (Spring 1977) : 44-51.

Jensen, Lloyd. *Return from the Nuclear Brink: National Interest and the Nuclear Non-Proliferation Treaty.* Lexington, Massachusetts: D. C. Health & Co., 1973.

Joskow, Paul L. "The International Nuclear Industry Today." *Foreign Affairs* 54 (July 1976) : 788-803.

Kaiser, Karl. "The Great Nuclear Debate: German-American Disagreements." *Foreign Policy* 30 (Spring 1978) : 83-110.

Kennedy, Edward M. "The Nuclear Non-proliferation Treaty." *Congressional Record,* July 30, 1975, S 14462-14464.

Lodgaard, S. and M. Thee. "The Arms Race and Nuclear Proliferation." *Bulletin of Peace Proposals* 8 (Spring 1977) : 3-6.

Long, Clarence D. "Nuclear Proliferation: Can Congress Act In Time?" *International Security* 1 (Spring 1977) : 52-76.

Maddox, John. "Prospects for Nuclear Proliferation." *Adelphi Paper Number 113.* London: International Institute for Strategic Studies, 1975.

Marhaw, Onkar and Ann Schultz, eds. *Nuclear Proliferation and the Near-Nuclear Countries.* Cambridge: Ballinger Publishing Co., 1975.

McCracken, Samuel. "The War Against the Atom." *Commentary,* September 1977, pp. 33-47.

Meeker, Thomas A. *The Proliferation of Nuclear Weapons and the Non-Proliferation Treaty (NPT): A Selective Bibliography and Source List.* Los Angeles, California: Center for the Study of Armament and Disarmament, California State University, 1973.

Myrdal, Alva. *The Right to Conduct Nuclear Explosions: Political Aspects and Policy Proposals.* Stockholm: Stockholm International Peace Research Institute, 1975.

The Non-Proliferation Treaty: A Preview of the 1975 Review Conference. Washington, D.C.: The Arms Control Association, 1974.

"The NPT Review Conference and Nuclear Proliferation." *Orbis* 19 (Summer 1975) : 316-320.

Nuclear Energy Policy Study Group. *Nuclear Power: Issues and Choices.* Cambridge: Ballinger Publishing Co., 1977.

Nuclear Suppliers Group. "Guidelines for Nuclear Transfers." *Survival* 20 (March/April 1978) : 85-87.

Nye, Joseph S. "Nonproliferation: A Long-Term Strategy." *Foreign Affairs* 56 (April 1978) : 601-623.

Pranger, Robert J. and Dale R. Tahtinen. *Nuclear Threat in the Middle East.* Washington, D.C.: American Enterprise Institute for Public Policy Research, 1975.

Primack, Joel. "Nuclear Reactor Safety: An Introduction to the Issues." *Bulletin of the Atomic Scientists,* September 1975, pp. 5-19.

"Proliferation and the Indian Test." *Survival* 16 (September/October 1974) : 210-216. ("A View from India" by R. V. R. Chandrasekhara Rao and "A View from Japan" by Ryukichi Imai.)

Quester, George. "Can Proliferation Now Be Stopped?" *Foreign Affairs* 53 (October 1974) : 77-97.

Ribicoff, Abraham A. "A Market-Sharing Approach to the Nuclear Sales Problem." *Foreign Affairs* 54 (July 1976) : 763-787.

Rosenbaum, H. J. and G. M. Cooper. "Brazil and the Nuclear Non-Proliferation Treaty." *International Affairs* 46 (January 1970) : 74-90.

Schelling, Thomas C. "The Limits of Non-Proliferation." *New Republic,* January 22, 1977, pp. 38-40.

————. "Who Will Have the Bomb?" *International Security* 1 (Summer 1976) : 77-91.

Stevenson, Adlai E. III. "Nuclear Reactors: America Must Act." *Foreign Affairs* 53 (October 1974) : 64-76.

Stockholm International Peace Research Institute. *Nuclear Proliferation Problems.* Cambridge: The MIT Press, 1974.

————. *Safeguards Against Nuclear Proliferation.* Cambridge: The MIT Press, 1975.

Symington, Stuart. "The Washington Nuclear Mess." *International Security* 1 (Winter 1977) : 71-78.

U.S., Comptroller General. *An Evaluation of the Administration's Proposed Nuclear Non-Proliferation Strategy.* Washington, D.C.: Government Printing Office, 1977.

U.S., Congress. House, Committee on International Relations and Senate, Committee on Governmental Affairs. *Nuclear Proliferation Factbook,* 95th Cong., 1st sess.

————. Joint Committee on Atomic Energy. *Proliferation of Nuclear Weapons, Hearings,* 93rd Cong., 2nd sess.

————. "Who's Afraid of the Cruise Missile?" *Orbis* 21 (Fall 1977): 517-531.

Holst, Johan Jorgen. "What Is Really Going On?" *Foreign Policy* 19 (Summer 1975): 155-163.

Johnson, David. "U.S. Strategic Momentum." *Defense Monitor*. Washington, D.C.: Center for Defense Information, 1974.

Kahan, Jerome H. *Security in the Nuclear Age: Developing U.S. Strategic Arms Policy*. Washington, D.C.: The Brookings Institution, 1975.

Kaplan, Fred. "Enhanced Radiation Weapons." *Scientific American*, May 1978, pp. 44-51.

Kemp, Geoffrey. "Nuclear Forces for Medium Powers: Part I: Targets and Weapons Systems." *Adelphi Paper Number 106*. London: International Institute for Strategic Studies, 1974.

————. "Nuclear Forces for Medium Powers: Parts II and III: Strategic Requirements and Options." *Adelphi Paper Number 107*. London: International Institute for Strategic Studies, 1974.

Kistiakowsky, George B. "Enhanced Radiation Warheads, Alias the Neutron Bomb." *Technology Review* 80 (May 1978): 24-31.

Lambeth, Benjamin S. "The Evolving Soviet Strategic Threat." *Current History* 69 (October 1975): 121-125, 152-153.

Leitenberg, Milton. "The Race to Oblivion." *Bulletin of the Atomic Scientists*, September 1974, pp. 8-20.

————. "Modernization of U.S. Tactical Nuclear Weapons, The New Debate, 1970-1977" in Stockholm International Peace Research Institute. *Tactical Nuclear Weapons: European Perspectives*. London: Taylor & Francis, 1978.

Lodal, Jan M. "Assuring Strategic Stability: An Alternative View." *Foreign Affairs* 54 (April 1976): 462-481.

Luttwak, Edward N. "Nuclear Strategy: The New Debate." *Commentary*, April 1974, pp. 53-59.

————. *Strategic Power: Military Capabilities and Political Utility*. Beverly Hills: SAGE Publications, 1976.

————. *The U.S.-U.S.S.R. Nuclear Weapons Balance*. Beverly Hills: SAGE Publications, 1974.

McGlinchey, Joseph J. and Jakob W. Seelig. "Why ICBMs Can Survive a Nuclear Attack." *Air Force Magazine*, September 1974, pp. 82-85.

McGovern, George S. "Members of Congress for Peace Through Law, Report on the B-1 Bomber Program." *Congressional Record*, May 20, 1974, S 8655-8674.

McLucas, John L. "The Case for a Modern Strategic Bomber." *AEI Defense Review* 2 (1978): 13-24.

Miller, Barry. "Advanced Reentry Vehicle Tests Planned." *Aviation Week & Space Technology,* May 24, 1976, pp. 22-23.

Nacht, Michael L. "The Delicate Balance of Error." *Foreign Policy* 19 (Summer 1975): 163-177.

"The Neutron Bomb Arms Control Impact Statement." *Congressional Record,* August 3, 1977, H 8498-8502.

Nitze, Paul H. "Assuring Strategic Stability in an Era of Detente." *Foreign Affairs* 54 (January 1976): 207-232.

————. "The Relationship of Strategic and Theater Nuclear Forces." *International Security* 2 (Fall 1977): 122-132.

"Nuclear War by 1999?" *Harvard Magazine,* November 1975, pp. 19-25.

"The Physical and Medical Effects of the Hiroshima and Nagasaki Bombs." *Bulletin of the Atomic Scientists,* December 1977, pp. 54-56.

Polmar, Norman. *Strategic Weapons: An Introduction.* New York: Crane, Russak & Co. Inc., 1975.

Ra'anan, Uri. "Soviet Decision-Making and the Strategic Balance: Some Reflections" in Robert L. Pfaltzgraff, Jr., ed. *Contrasting Approaches to Strategic Arms Control.* Lexington, Massachusetts: D. C. Heath & Co., 1974.

Rathjens, G. W. "Flexible Response Options." *Orbis* 18 (Fall 1974): 677-688.

Record, Jeffrey. "Theatre Nuclear Weapons: Begging the Soviet Union to Pre-empt." *Survival* 19 (September/October 1977): 208-211.

Robinson, Clarence A., Jr. "Strategic Force Structure to Face Stiff Debate." *Aviation Week & Space Technology,* April 18, 1977, pp. 16-19.

Rosecrance, Richard. "Strategic Deterrence Reconsidered." *Adelphi Paper Number 116.* London: International Institute for Strategic Studies, 1975.

Rummel, R. J. "Will the Soviet Union Soon Have a First Strike Capability?" *Orbis* 20 (Fall 1976): 579-594.

Schandler, Herbert Y. *U.S. Policy on the Use of Nuclear Weapons, 1945-1975,* Congressional Research Service Publication No. 75-175 F. Washington, D.C.: Library of Congress, 1975.

Schroeder, Pat. "Shooting at Empty Silos." *Washington Monthly* 6 (May 1974): 43-47.

Shapley, Deborah. "Cruise Missiles: Air Force, Navy Weapon Poses New Arms Issue." *Science,* February 7, 1975, pp. 416-418.

Sherman, Robert. "A Manual of Missile Capability." *Air Force Magazine,* February 1977, pp. 35-39.

Smart, Ian. "The Future of the British Nuclear Deterrent." *Survival* 20 (January/February 1978): 21-24.

Stockholm International Peace Research Institute. *World Armaments:*

The Nuclear Threat. Stockholm: Stockholm International Peace Research Institute, 1977.

Tsipis, Kosta. "The Accuracy of Strategic Missiles." *Scientific American,* July 1975, pp. 14-34.

―――. "The Long-Range Cruise Missile." *Bulletin of the Atomic Scientists,* April 1975, pp. 14-26.

Tucker, Robert C., Klaus Knorr, Richard A. Falk, and Hedley Bull. *Proposal for No First Use of Nuclear Weapons: Pros and Cons,* Policy Memorandum No. 28. Princeton, New Jersey: Princeton University, Center of International Studies, 1963.

Ulsamer, Edgar. "Our ICBM Force—the Vulnerability Myth." *Air Force Magazine,* August 1974, pp. 65-70.

U.S., Arms Control and Disarmament Agency. *Worldwide Effects of Nuclear War . . . Some Perspectives.* Washington, D.C.: Government Printing Office, 1976.

U.S., Congress. Congressional Budget Office. *Counterforce Issues for the U.S. Strategic Nuclear Forces.* Washington, D.C.: Government Printing Office, 1978.

―――. Congressional Budget Office. *Planning U.S. Strategic Nuclear Forces for the 1980s.* Washington, D.C.: Government Printing Office, 1978.

―――. Congressional Budget Office. *Retaliatory Issues for the U.S. Strategic Nuclear Forces.* Washington, D.C.: Government Printing Office, 1978.

―――. Senate, Committee on Foreign Relations. *Briefing on Counterforce Attacks, Hearings,* 93rd Cong., 2nd sess.

―――. Senate, Committee on Foreign Relations, Subcommittee on Arms Control, International Organizations and Security Agreements. *Analyses of Effects of Limited Nuclear Warfare,* 94th Cong., 1st sess.

Van Cleave, William R. and Roger W. Barnett. "Strategic Adaptability." *Orbis* 18 (Fall 1974): 655-676.

Vershbow, Alexander R. "The Cruise Missile: The End of Arms Control?" *Foreign Affairs* 55 (October 1976): 133-146.

Warner, Edward L. III. "Soviet Strategic Force Posture: Some Alternative Explanations" in Frank B. Horton III, Anthony C. Rogerson, and Edward L. Warner III, eds. *Comparative Defense Policy.* Baltimore: The Johns Hopkins University Press, 1974.

Wohlstetter, Albert. "How to Confuse Ourselves." *Foreign Policy* 20 (Fall 1975): 170-198.

―――. "Rivals, But No 'Race.' " *Foreign Policy* 16 (Fall 1974): 48-81.

York, Herbert. *The Advisors: Oppenheimer, Teller & the Superbomb.* San Francisco: W. H. Freeman and Company, 1976.

Other Weapons Systems and Force Levels

Baker, David. "Killer Satellites." *Flight International,* October 15, 1977, pp. 1129-1135.

Berman, Robert P. *Soviet Air Power in Transition.* Washington, D.C.: The Brookings Institution, 1978.

Booth, K. *Navies and Foreign Policy.* New York: Crane, Russak & Co., 1977.

Burke, John T. "Smart Weapons: A Coming Revolution in Tactics." *Army* 23 (February 1973): 14-20.

Burt, Richard. "New Weapons Technologies: Debate and Directions." *Adelphi Paper Number 126.* London: International Institute for Strategic Studies, 1976.

Covault, Craig. "Military Efforts in Space on Increase." *Aviation Week & Space Technology,* May 1, 1978, pp. 53-54.

Digby, James. "Precision-Guided Weapons." *Adelphi Paper Number 118.* London: International Institute for Strategic Studies, 1975.

Finney, John W. "Dreadnought or Dinosaur." *New York Times Magazine,* January 18, 1976, pp. 6, 30-35.

Freedman, Lawrence. "The Soviet Union and 'Anti-Space Defense.'" *Survival* 19 (January/February 1977): 16-23.

Garwin, Richard L. "Effective Military Technology for the 1980s." *International Security* 1 (Fall 1976): 50-77.

Gorshkov, S. G. "The Sea Power of the State." *Survival* 19 (January/February 1977): 24-29.

Gratzl, J. "T-64: Some Thoughts on the New Soviet Battle Tank." *International Defense Review,* February 1976, pp. 24-26.

Hofmann, Oberst K. "The Battlefield of the 1980s." *International Defense Review,* June 1977, pp. 431-435.

Hart, Gary. "The U.S. Senate and the Future of the Navy." *International Security* 2 (Spring 1978): 175-184.

International Institute for Strategic Studies. *Strategic Survey 1977.* London: International Institute for Strategic Studies, 1978.

Klass, Philip J. "Special Report: Laser Weapons." *Aviation Week & Space Technology,* August 18, 1975, pp. 34-39.

Leopold, Revven. "Technologically Improved Warships: A Partial Answer to a Reduced Fleet." *International Security* 2 (Spring 1978): 185-194.

MccGwire, Michael and John McDonnell, eds. *Soviet Naval Influence: Domestic and Foreign Dimensions.* New York: Praeger Publishers, 1977.

Panyalev, Georg. "The SU-19 Fencer: Threat to Western Europe." *International Defense Review,* February 1976, pp. 67-69.

Polmar, Norman, ed. *World Combat Aircraft Directory.* Garden City, New York: Doubleday & Co., 1976.

Record, Jeffrey. *Sizing Up the Soviet Army.* Washington, D.C.: The Brookings Institution, 1975.

Sellers, Robert C., ed. *Armed Forces of the World: A Reference Handbook.* New York: Praeger Publishers, 1977.

Stockholm International Peace Research Institute. *Anti-Personnel Weapons.* London: Taylor & Francis, 1978.

Sundaram, G. S. "Electronic Warfare: A Key to Combat Survival." *International Defense Review,* February 1976, pp. 51-54.

Turner, Stansfield. "The Naval Balance: Not Just a Numbers Game." *Foreign Affairs* 55 (January 1977): 339-354.

Verble, Keith E. and Charles J. Malven. "Precision Laser Target Designation—a Breakthrough in Guided Weapons Employment." *International Defense Review,* April 1974, pp. 204-209.

Young, S. H. H. "Gallery of USAF Weapons." *Air Force Magazine,* May 1978, pp. 114-130.

Defense Budget and the Decision-Making Process

Aspin, Les. "Address to Pacem in Terris IV" in the *Congressional Record,* December 4, 1975, H 11906-11908.

Betts, Richard K. *Soldiers, Statesmen, and Cold War Crises.* Cambridge, Massachusetts: Harvard University Press, 1977.

Blechman, Barry M. *et al. The Soviet Military Build-up and U.S. Defense Spending.* Washington, D.C.: The Brookings Institution, 1977.

———— and Edward R. Fried. "Controlling the Defense Budget." *Foreign Affairs* 54 (January 1976): 233-249.

Boffey, Philip M. "Arms Control Impact Statements Again Have Little Impact." *Science,* June 10, 1977, p. 1181.

Brown, George S. *United States Military Posture for FY 1979.* Washington, D.C.: Government Printing Office, 1978.

Brown, Harold. *Department of Defense Annual Report Fiscal Year 1979.* Washington, D.C.: Government Printing Office, 1978.

Burt, Richard. "Defence Budgeting: The British and American Cases." *Adelphi Paper Number 112.* London: International Institute for Strategic Studies, 1975.

———— and Geoffrey Kemp, eds. *Congressional Hearings on American Defense Policy: 1947-1971: An Annotated Bibliography.* Lawrence, Kansas: University Press of Kansas, 1974.

Cahn, Anne Hessing. *Congress, Military Affairs and (a Bit of) Information.* Beverly Hills: SAGE Publications, A Sage Professional Paper, 1974.

Coulam, Robert F. *Illusions of Choice: The F-111 and the Problem of Weapons Acquisition Reform.* Princeton, New Jersey: Princeton University Press, 1977.

Garthoff, Douglas F. "The Soviet Military and Arms Control." *Survival* 19 (November/December 1977): 242-250.

Hollist, W. Ladd. "An Analysis of Arms Processes in the United States and the Soviet Union." *International Studies Quarterly* 21 (September 1977): 503-528.

Holloway, David. "Technology and Political Decision in Soviet Armament Policy." *Journal of Peace Research* 11 (1974): 257-279.

Laurence, Edward J. "The Changing Role of Congress in Defense Policy-Making." *Journal of Conflict Resolution* 20 (June 1976): 213-253.

Luttwak, Edward N. "Defense Reconsidered." *Commentary,* March 1977, pp. 51-58.

Members of Congress for Peace Through Law Task Force on Defense Policy. "Defending America: An Alternative U.S. Foreign Policy and Defense Policy Posture Statement" in the *Congressional Record,* May 19, 1976, S 7507-7533.

Muskie, Edmund S. and Bill Brock. *What Price Defense?* Washington, D.C.: American Enterprise Institute for Public Policy Research, 1974.

"NSC-68: A Report to the National Security Council." *Naval War College Review* 27 (May/June 1975): 51-108.

Ognibene, Peter J. *Scoop: The Life and Politics of Henry M. Jackson.* New York: Stein and Day, 1975.

Pechman, Joseph A., ed. *Setting National Priorities: The 1979 Budget.* Washington, D.C.: The Brookings Institution, 1978.

Perry, William J. *The FY 1979 Department of Defense Program for Research, Development, and Acquisition.* Washington, D.C.: Government Printing Office, 1978.

U.S., Congress. House, Committee on Foreign Affairs, Subcommittee on National Security Policy and Scientific Developments. *Arms Control and Disarmament Agency, Hearings,* 93rd Cong., 2nd sess.

————. House, Committee on International Relations and Senate, Committee on Foreign Relations. *Fiscal Year 1979 Arms Control Impact Statements,* 95th Cong., 2nd sess.

————. Joint Economic Committee, Subcommittee on Priorities and Economy in Government. *Allocation of Resources in the Soviet Union and China—1977, Parts I, II, and III, Hearings,* 95th Cong., 1st sess.

————. Senate, Committee on Armed Services. *Department of Defense Authorization for Fiscal Year 1979, Part I, Authorization Posture Statement,* 95th Cong., 2nd sess.

Conventional Arms Transfers

"The Arms Sales Numbers Game." *New Republic,* February 18, 1978, pp. 5-6.

Cahn, Anne Hessing, Joseph J. Kruzel, Peter M. Dawkins, and Jacques Huntzinger. *Controlling Future Arms Trade.* New York: McGraw-Hill, 1977.

Farley, Philip J., Stephen S. Kaplan, and William H. Lewis. *Arms Across the Sea.* Washington, D.C.: The Brookings Institution, 1978.

Gwertzman, Bernard. "U.S. & Soviet Agree to Hold Regular Talks to Curb Arms Trade." *New York Times,* May 12, 1978.

Johnsen, Katherine. "Arms Exports Increase 60% in Decade." *Aviation Week & Space Technology,* July 31, 1978, p. 19.

―――. "Congress to Expand Arms Sales Monitoring." *Aviation Week & Space Technology,* August 14, 1978, pp. 14-15.

Kemp, Geoffrey. "Arms Traffic and Third World Conflict." *International Conciliation* 577 (March 1970).

―――, Robert L. Pfalzgraff, Jr., and Uri Ra' anan. *The Other Arms Race.* Lexington, Massachusetts: Lexington Books, 1975.

Kissinger, Henry A., "Security Assistance and Foreign Policy. *Department of State Bulletin,* April 19, 1976, pp. 501-505.

Leiss, Amelia C. with Geoffrey Kemp, *et al. Arms Transfers to Less Developed Countries, Arms Control and Local Conflict, Vol. III.* Cambridge: Center for International Studies, 1970.

Louscher, David. "The Rise of Military Sales as a U.S. Foreign Assistance Instrument." *Orbis* 20 (Winter 1977): 933-964.

Oberdorfer, Don. "Exports of U.S. Arms Pose Thorny Questions of Control." *Washington Post,* May 14, 1978.

Ra' anan, Uri. *The USSR Arms the Third World.* Cambridge: The MIT Press, 1969.

Rosen, Steven J. *The Proliferation of Land-Based Technologies: Implications for Local Military Balances.* Los Angeles: Center for Arms Control and International Security, University of California, 1978.

Rothschild, Emma. "The Boom in the Death Business." *New York Review of Books,* October 2, 1975, pp. 7-12.

Sampson, Anthony. *The Arms Bazaar: From Lebanon to Lockheed.* New York: Viking Press, 1977.

Stanley, John and Maurice Pearton. *The International Trade in Arms.* New York: Praeger Publishers, 1972.

Stockholm International Peace Research Institute. *The Arms Trade with the Third World.* New York: Humanities Press, 1971.

Thee, Marek, ed. "Arms Trade and Transfer of Military Technology." *Bulletin of Peace Proposals* 13 (1977).

U.S., Arms Control and Disarmament Agency. *The International Trans-fer of Conventional Arms.* Washington, D.C.: Government Print-ing Office, 1974.

————. *World Military Expenditures and Arms Transfers 1967-1976.* Washington, D.C.: Arms Control and Disarmament Agency, 1978.

U.S., Congress. Congressional Budget Office. *The Effect of Foreign Military Sales on the U.S. Economy, Staff Working Paper.* Wash-ington, D.C.: Government Printing Office, 1976.

————. House, Committee on International Relations. *International Transfer of Technology: An Agenda of National Security Issues,* 95th Cong., 2nd sess.

————. House, Committee on International Relations. *Review of the President's Conventional Arms Transfer Policy,* 95th Cong., 2nd sess.

————. House, Committee on International Relations. *United States Arms Policies in the Persian Gulf and Red Sea Areas: Past, Present, and Future,* 95th Cong., 1st sess.

————. House, Committee on International Relations. *United States Arms Transfer and Security Assistance Programs,* 95th Cong., 2nd sess.

————. Senate, Committee on Foreign Relations. *The International Security Assistance Act of 1978,* 95th Cong., 2nd sess.

U.S., Defense Security Assistance Agency. Data Management Division. *Foreign Military Sales and Military Assistance Facts.* Washington, D.C.: Data Management Division, 1975.

U.S., General Accounting Office. *Arms Sales Ceiling Based on Incon-sistent and Erroneous Data.* Washington, D.C.: Government Print-ing Office, 1978.

————. *Military Sales—An Increasing U.S. Role in Africa.* Washing-ton, D.C.: Government Printing Office, 1978.

Military Strategy and Security Matters

Amiel, Saadia. "Deterrence by Conventional Forces." *Survival* 20 (March/April 1978): 58-62.

Arbatov, Georgi. "The Dangers of a New Cold War." *Bulletin of the Atomic Scientists,* March 1977, pp. 30-40.

Bagley, Worth H. "Sea Power and Western Security: The Next Decade." *Adelphi Paper Number 139.* London: International Institute for Strategic Studies, 1977.

Barber, Ransom E. "The Myth of Soviet Nuclear Strategy." *Army,* June 1975, pp. 10-17.

Barnett, Roger W. "Trans-SALT: Soviet Strategic Doctrine." *Orbis* 19 (Summer 1975): 533-561.

Blechman, Barry M. and Stephen S. Kaplan. "Armed Forces as Political Instruments." *Survival* 19 (July/August 1977): 169-173.

Brodie, Bernard. "The Development of Nuclear Strategy." *International Security* 2 (Spring 1978): 65-83.

Brown, Thomas A. "Number Mysticism, Rationality and the Strategic Balance." *Orbis* 21 (Fall 1977): 479-496.

Cline, Ray S. *World Power Assessment: A Calculus of Strategic Drift.* Washington, D.C.: Georgetown University .Center for Strategic Studies, 1975.

Davis, Lynn Etheridge. "Limited Nuclear Options: Deterrence and the New American Doctrine." *Adelphi Paper Number 121.* London: International Institute for Strategic Studies, 1976.

Erickson, John. "The Chimera of Mutual Deterrence." *Strategic Review* 6 (Spring 1978): 11-17.

Etzold, Thomas H. "Soviet Civil Defense and U.S. Strategy." *Air Force Magazine,* October 1977, pp. 38-41.

―――. "The Vagaries of Deterrence: Toward a More Viable Strategy." *Strategic Review* 5 (Summer 1977): 71-76.

Garrett, Stephen A. "Detente and the Military Balance." *Bulletin of the Atomic Scientists,* April 1977, pp. 10-20.

Goure, Leon. *War Survival in Soviet Strategy—USSR Civil Defense.* Washington, D.C.: Center for Advanced International Studies, University of Miami, 1976.

Gray, Colin S. "Across the Nuclear Divide—Strategic Studies, Past and Present." *International Security* 2 (Summer 1977): 24-46.

―――. *The Geopolitics of the Nuclear Era: Heartland, Rimlands, and the Technological Revolution.* New York: Crane, Russak & Co., 1977.

―――. "New Weapons and the Resort to Force." *International Journal* 30 (Spring 1975): 238-258.

―――. "The Strategic Forces Triad: End of the Road?" *Foreign Affairs* 56 (July 1978): 771-789.

Gray, Robert C. and Robert J. Bresler. "Why Weapons Make Poor Bargaining Chips." *Bulletin of the Atomic Scientists,* September 1977, pp. 8-9.

Greenwood, Ted and Michael L. Nacht. "The New Nuclear Debate: Sense or Nonsense?" *Foreign Affairs* 52 (July 1974): 761-780.

Head, Richard G. "Technology and the Military Balance." *Foreign Affairs* 56 (April 1978): 544-563.

Holst, Johan J. and Uwe Nerlich, eds. *Beyond Nuclear Deterrence: New Aims, New Arms.* New York: Crane, Russak & Co., 1977.

Ikle, Fred C. "Can Nuclear Deterrence Last Out the Century?" *Foreign Affairs* 51 (January 1973): 267-285.

International Institute for Strategic Studies. "The Diffusion of Power:

Proliferation of Force." *Adelphi Paper Number 133*. London: International Institute for Strategic Studies, 1977.

Jervis, Robert. *Deterrence Theory Revisited*. Los Angeles: Center for Arms Control and International Security, University of California, 1978.

Johansen, Robert C. "Countercombatant Strategy: A New Balance of Terror?" *Worldview* 17 (July 1974): 47-53.

Kaplan, Fred M. "The Soviet Civil Defense Myth." *Bulletin of the Atomic Scientists*, March 1978, pp. 15-20. (Part 2 of this article appears in the April 1978 issue of the *Bulletin*, pp. 41-48.)

Kemp, Geoffrey. "Scarcity and Strategy." *Foreign Affairs* 56 (January 1978): 396-414.

Kincade, William H. "Repeating History: The Civil Defense Debate Renewed." *International Security* 2 (Winter 1978): 99-120.

————. "A Strategy for All Seasons: Targeting Doctrine and Strategic Arms Control." *Bulletin of the Atomic Scientists*, May 1978, pp. 14-20.

Kistiakowsky, G. B. "Is Paranoia Necessary for Security?" *New York Times Magazine*, November 27, 1977, pp. 52-54, 76-86.

Knorr, Klaus. "Is International Coercion Waning or Rising?" *International Security* 1 (Spring 1977): 92-110.

————. "The Limits of Economic and Military Power." *Daedalus* 104 (Fall 1975): 229-243.

————. "On the International Uses of Military Force in the Contemporary World." *Orbis* 21 (Spring 1977): 5-27.

Lall, Betty Goetz. "Mutual Deterrence: The Need for a New Definition." *Bulletin of the Atomic Scientists*, December 1977, pp. 10-11.

Luttwak, Edward N. "Perceptions of Military Force and U.S. Defense Policy." *Survival* 19 (January/February 1977): 2-8.

————. *The Political Uses of Sea Power*. Baltimore: The Johns Hopkins University Press, 1974.

Martin, Laurence. *Arms and Strategy*. New York: David McKay Co., 1973.

————. "Changes in American Strategic Doctrine—An Initial Interpretation." *Survival* 16 (July/August 1974): 158-164.

Middleton, Drew. *Can America Win the Next War?* New York: Charles Scribner's Sons, 1975.

Moore, William C. "Counterforce: Facts and Fantasies." *Air Force Magazine*, April 1974, pp. 49-52.

Panofsky, Wolfgang K. H. "The Mutual Hostage Relationship between America and Russia." *Foreign Affairs* 51 (October 1973): 109-118.

Perlmutter, Amos. *The Military and Politics in Modern Times*. New Haven: Yale University Press, 1977.

Pfaltzgraff, Robert L., Jr. "The United States and a Strategy for the West." *Strategic Review* 5 (Summer 1977): 10-25.

Pillsbury, Michael. "U.S.-Chinese Military Ties?" *Foreign Policy* 20 (Fall 1975): 50-64.

Pipes, Richard. "Why the Soviet Union Thinks It Could Fight and Win a Nuclear War." *Commentary,* July 1977, pp. 21-34.

Pranger, Robert J. and Roger P. Labrie. *Nuclear Strategy and National Security—Points of View.* Washington, D.C.: American Enterprise Institute for Public Policy Research, 1977.

Ravenal, Earl C. "After Schlesinger: Something Has to Give." *Foreign Policy* 22 (Spring 1976): 71-95.

—————. "Toward Nuclear Stability: A Modest Proposal for Avoiding Armageddon." *Atlantic Monthly,* September 1977, pp. 35-41.

Salomon, Michael D. "New Concepts for Strategic Parity." *Survival* 19 (November/December 1977): 255-262.

Scott, William F. "Soviet Military Doctrine and Strategy: Realities and Misunderstandings." *Strategic Review* 3 (Summer 1975): 57-66.

—————. *Soviet Sources of Military Doctrine and Strategy.* New York: Crane, Russak & Co., 1975.

Scoville, Herbert, Jr. "Flexible MADness?" *Foreign Policy* 14 (Spring 1974): 164-177.

Sienkiewicz, Stanley. "SALT and Soviet Nuclear Doctrine." *International Security* 2 (Spring 1978): 84-100.

Sparkman, John. "Schlesinger Views Future Foreign Policy." *Congressional Record,* December 5, 1975, S 21247-21249.

Steinbruner, John D. "Beyond Rational Deterrence: The Struggle for New Conceptions." *World Politics* 28 (January 1976): 223-245.

————— and Thomas M. Garwin. "Strategic Vulnerability: The Balance between Prudence and Paranoia." *International Security* 1 (Summer 1976): 138-181.

Ullman, Richard H. "No First Use of Nuclear Weapons." *Foreign Affairs* 50 (July 1972): 669-683.

U.S., Air Force, trans. *The Offensive (A Soviet View).* Washington, D.C.: Government Printing Office, 1973.

U.S., Congress. Senate, Committee on Foreign Relations. *Briefing on Counterforce Attacks, Hearings,* 93rd Cong., 2nd sess.

U.S., Navy. Office of the Chief of Naval Operations. *Understanding Soviet Naval Deployments.* Washington, D.C.: Government Printing Office, 1975.

Yergin, Daniel. *Shattered Peace: The Origins of the Cold War and the National Security State.* Boston: Houghton Mifflin Co., 1977.

European Security Issues

Burt, Richard. "New Weapons Technologies and European Security." *Orbis* 19 (Summer 1975): 514-532.

Canby, Steven. "The Alliance and Europe: Part IV, Military Doctrine and Technology." *Adelphi Paper Number 109*. London: International Institute for Strategic Studies, 1975.

――――. "Damping Nuclear Counterforce Incentives: Correcting NATO's Inferiority in Conventional Military Strength." *Orbis* 19 (Spring 1975): 47-71.

Cliffe, Trevor. "Military Technology and European Balance." *Adelphi Paper Number 89*. London: International Institute for Strategic Studies, 1972.

Coffey, J. I. "New Approaches to Arms Reduction in Europe." *Adelphi Paper Number 105*. London: International Institute for Strategic Studies, 1974.

Cohen, Eliot. "NATO Standardization: The Perils of Common Sense." *Foreign Policy* 31 (Summer 1978): 72-90.

Dyer, Philip W. "Tactical Nuclear Weapons and Deterrence in Europe." *Political Science Quarterly* 92 (Summer 1977): 245-257.

Ellsworth, Robert. "New Imperatives for the Old Alliance." *International Security* 2 (Spring 1978): 132-148.

Enthoven, Alain C. "U.S. Forces in Europe: How Many? Doing What?" *Foreign Affairs* 53 (April 1975): 513-532.

"Europe's Deterrents: Cruising into the Next Generation." *Economist,* July 30, 1977, pp. 44-45.

Fischer, Robert Lucas. "Defending the Central Front: The Balance of Forces." *Adelphi Paper Number 127*. London: International Institute for Strategic Studies, 1976.

Geneste, Marc E. "The City Walls: A Credible Defense Doctrine for the West." *Orbis* 19 (Summer 1975): 477-496.

Goodman, Elliot R. *The Fate of the Atlantic Community*. New York: Praeger Publishers, 1975.

Gray, Colin S. "Nuclear Weapons in NATO Strategy." *NATO's Fifteen Nations* 23 (February/March 1978): 82-92.

Hattinger, Hans. "Armaments, Detente, and Bureaucracy: The Case of the Arms Race in Europe." *Journal of Conflict Resolution* 19 (December 1975): 571-595.

Heyhoe, D. C. R. "The Alliance and Europe: Part VI, The European Programme Group." *Adelphi Paper Number 129*. London: International Institute for Strategic Studies, 1977.

Hillenbrand, Martin J. "NATO and Western Europe in an Era of Transition." *International Security* 2 (Fall 1977): 3-24.

Hunt, Kenneth. "The Alliance and Europe: Part II, Defense with Fewer

Men." *Adelphi Paper Number 98*. London: International Institute for Strategic Studies, 1973.

International Institute for Strategic Studies. "New Conventional Weapons and East-West Security." *Adelphi Papers Numbers 144 and 145*. London: International Institute for Strategic Studies, 1978.

Karber, Phillip A. "The Soviet Anti-Tank Debate." *Survival* 18 (May/June 1976): 105-111.

Khlestov, O. "Mutual Force Reductions in Europe." *Survival* 16 (November/December 1974): 293-298.

Knorr, Klaus. "The Atlantic Alliance: A Reappraisal." New York: Headline Series 221, Foreign Policy Association, 1974.

Komer, R. W. "Treating NATO's Self-Inflicted Wound." *Foreign Policy* 13 (Winter 1973/74): 34-48.

Lawrence, Richard D. and Jeffrey Record. *U.S. Force Structure in NATO: An Alternative*. Washington, D.C.: The Brookings Institution, 1974.

Martin, Laurence. "Theatre Nuclear Weapons and Europe." *Survival* 16 (November/December 1974): 268-276.

Miettinen, Jorma K. "Time for Europeans to Debate the Presence of Tactical Nukes." *Bulletin of the Atomic Scientists,* May 1976, pp. 18-22.

Morse, John H. "New Weapons Technologies: Implications for NATO." *Orbis* 19 (Summer 1975): 497-513.

Nerlich, Uwe. "The Alliance and Europe: Part V, Nuclear Weapons and East-West Negotiations." *Adelphi Paper Number 120*. London: International Institute for Strategic Studies, 1975/76.

Newhouse, John. *U.S. Troops in Europe*. Washington, D.C.: The Brookings Institution, 1971.

Nunn, Sam. "NATO Strategy." *Survival* 19 (January/February 1977): 30-32.

Pipes, Richard, ed. *Soviet Strategy in Europe*. New York: Crane, Russak & Co., 1976.

Record, Jeffrey. *U.S. Nuclear Weapons in Europe: Issues and Alternatives*. Washington, D.C.: The Brookings Institution, 1974.

Sinnreich, Richard Hart. "NATO's Doctrinal Dilemma." *Orbis* 19 (Summer 1975): 461-476.

Shreffler, R. G. "The Neutron Bomb for NATO Defense: An Alternative." *Orbis* 21 (Winter 1978): 959-967.

U.S., Congress. Congressional Budget Office. *Assessing the NATO/Warsaw Pact Military Balance*. Washington, D.C.: Government Printing Office, 1977.

―――. Congressional Budget Office. *U.S. Air and Ground Conventional Forces for NATO: Air Defense Issues, Firepower Issues, and*

Mobility and Logistics Issues. (3 volumes) Washington, D.C.: Government Printing Office, 1978.

Vincent, R. J. "Military Power and Political Influence: The Soviet Union and Western Europe." *Adelphi Paper Number 119.* London: International Institute for Strategic Studies, 1975.

Wolf, Charles, Jr. and Derek Leebaert. "Trade Liberalization as a Path to Weapons Standardization in NATO." *International Security* 2 (Winter 1978): 136-159.

York, Herbert F. "The Nuclear 'Balance of Terror' in Europe." *Bulletin of the Atomic Scientists,* May 1976, pp. 16-17.

Other Regional Security Issues

Bhargava, G. S. "India's Security in the 1980's." *Adelphi Paper Number 125.* London: International Institute for Strategic Studies, 1976.

Carus, W. Seth. "The Military Balance of Power in the Middle East." *Current History* 74 (January 1978): 29-32, 35-36.

Chubin, Shahram. "Iran's Security in the 1980's." *International Security* 2 (Winter 1978): 51-80.

Clough, Ralph N. *Deterrence and Defense in Korea: The Role of U.S. Forces.* Washington, D.C.: The Brookings Institution, 1976.

Fraser, Angus M. "Military Capabilities in China." *Current History* 69 (September 1975): 70-74, 102.

Gasteyger, Curt. "The Super-Powers in the Mediterranean." *Survival* 17 (November/December 1975): 270-275.

Grant, Bruce. "The Security of South-East Asia." *Adelphi Paper Number 142.* London: International Institute for Strategic Studies, 1978.

Ha, Joseph M. "U.S. Withdrawal from Korea: A Means, Not an End." *Orbis* 21 (Fall 1977): 607-622.

International Institute for Strategic Studies. "The Middle East and the International System: I, The Impact of the 1973 War." *Adelphi Paper Number 114.* London: International Institute for Strategic Studies, 1975.

Kapur, Ashok. *India's Nuclear Option: Atomic Diplomacy and Decision Making.* New York: Praeger Publishers, 1976.

Kennedy, Edward M. "The Persian Gulf: Arms Race or Arms Control?" *Foreign Affairs* 54 (October 1975): 14-35.

Larrabee, F. Stephen. "Balkan Security." *Adelphi Paper Number 135.* London: International Institute for Strategic Studies, 1977.

Leitenberg, Milton and Nicole Ball. "The Military Expenditures of Less Developed Nations." *Bulletin of Peace Proposals* 8 (1977): 310-315.

Mangold, Peter. "The Soviet Record in the Middle East." *Survival* 20 (May/June 1978) : 98-104.

Monroe, Elizabeth and A. H. Farrar-Hookley. "The Arab-Israel War, October 1973: Background and Events." *Adelphi Paper Number 111.* London: International Institute for Strategic Studies, 1975.

Rosen, Steven J. "What the Next Arab-Israeli War Might Look Like." *International Security* 2 (Spring 1978) : 149-174.

U.S., Congress. Congressional Budget Office. *Force Planning and Budgetary Implications of U.S. Withdrawal from Korea.* Washington, D.C.: Government Printing Office, 1978.

———. House, Committee on Foreign Affairs, Subcommittee on the Near East and South Asia. *Proposed Expansion of U.S. Military Facilities in the Indian Ocean, Hearings,* 93rd Cong., 2nd sess.

Weinstein, Franklin B. "The United States, Japan and the Security of Korea." *International Security* 2 (Fall 1977) : 68-89.

Notes on Contributors

Robert L. Arnett is a Soviet-area specialist at the Library of Congress and a Ph.D. candidate at Ohio State University.

Les Aspin, congressman from Wisconsin since 1970, serves on the House Armed Services Committee, the Government Operations Committee, and the Permanent Select Committee on Intelligence. He holds a B.A. degree from Yale University, M.A. from Oxford University, and a Ph.D. in economics from the Massachusetts Institute of Technology. He is the author of numerous articles on arms control and military issues.

John C. Baker is currently examining U.S. and Soviet strategic force policies as a member of the Foreign Policy Studies staff of the Brookings Institution. He was editor of *Arms Control Today* from 1974 to 1977.

Steven J. Baker is assistant professor in the Government Department and director of International Studies at the University of Texas at Austin. In 1975–76 he was a research fellow at the Program for Science and International Affairs, John F. Kennedy School of Government, Harvard University. He has published widely on the problem of nuclear proliferation.

Monoranjan Bezboruah holds a Ph.D. in international affairs and is the author of *U.S. Strategy in the Indian Ocean: The International Response* (N.Y.: Praeger, 1977). Having completed his LL.M. degree in international law, he is presently planning to practice law.

Hans Günter Brauch is a research associate at the Institut für Politische Wissenschaft, Heidelberg University, and teaches at the Institut für Politikwissenschaft, Darmstadt University. An honorary research fellow at the Center for Science and International Affairs, John F. Kennedy School of Government, Harvard University, and a research associate at the Arms Control and Disarmament Program, Stanford University, he has written policy analyses on arms control and American foreign policy for several German- and English-language journals.

Robert Brennis is an education program specialist in the Office of Education, Department of Health, Education and Welfare. He formerly served in a research capacity at the Arms Control Association.

Richard Burt is at present covering national security affairs for the *New York Times* in Washington. He was formerly the assistant director of the International Institute for Strategic Studies in London. He has worked as a consultant for the executive branch and Congress and is the author of several journal articles dealing with arms control and military strategy.

Anne H. Cahn is chief of the Social Impact Staff, U.S. Arms Control and Disarmament Agency. Prior to joining the administration she held research positions at Harvard University and the Massachusetts Institute of Technology. She directed the American Academy of Arts and Sciences' summer study, "New Directions in Arms Control," and has been a consultant to the U.S. Senate Committee on the Budget. She co-authored *Controlling Future Arms Trade* (N.Y.: McGraw-Hill, 1977) and has published widely on arms control matters.

Frank Church is the senior senator from Idaho and chairman of the Senate Foreign Relations Committee. He has also served on the Committee on Energy and Natural Resources and has been a leading advocate of strategic arms limitations throughout his twenty-two-year career in the Senate.

Dick Clark, former senator from Iowa, served as a member of the Senate Foreign Relations Committee and was chairman of the Subcommittee on African Affairs. He has an M.A. degree in history from the University of Iowa and taught at the University and at Upper Iowa University before entering the political arena. He is a former chairman of Members of Congress for Peace Through Law.

Arthur S. Collins, Jr., is a retired U.S. Army officer. He served in the army from 1938 to 1974 and was a lieutenant general at time of retirement. His last assignment was deputy commander-in-chief, U.S. Army, Europe. He has written a book, *Common Sense Training* (San Rafael, Calif.: Presidio Press, 1978), has contributed articles to military journals, and has written editorials on various aspects of current social-political-military matters.

Thomas J. Downey represents the Second District of New York (Suffolk County) in the U.S. Congress. He is a member of the Armed Services Committee and is an official congressional adviser to SALT. A leading opponent of the B-1 bomber and advocate of the cruise missile, he has written widely on arms control and military matters, particularly as they relate to crisis stability.

Thomas A. Halsted is the public affairs adviser and director of the Office of Public Affairs, U.S. Arms Control and Disarmament Agency. He was the first executive director of the Arms Control Association and Arms Control Program director for the Carnegie Endowment from 1972 to 1977. Under his direction, *Arms Control Today* was conceived and launched in January 1974.

Christopher D. Jones is assistant professor of political science at Marquette University. He has written several articles on Soviet military affairs and on Soviet-East European relations. He is currently writing a book-length study of the mechanisms of Soviet influence in East Europe for Praeger Publishers.

Edward M. Kennedy is the senior senator from Massachusetts. Since 1973 he has served as chairman of a special joint congressional organization, the Technology Assessment Board, which aims to provide the Congress with independent expertise in evaluating complex technical programs and policies. He is a member of the Human Resources Committee, Judiciary Committee, Joint Economic Committee, and the Select Committee on Nutrition and Human Needs.

William H. Kincade has been the executive director of the Arms Control Association since September 1977. Prior to joining the association, he served as a consultant on national security policy to various congressmen and as staff director of the Joint Committee on Defense Production. He is a contributor to journals on international security affairs.

Ann Hallan Lakhdhir is a Ph.D. candidate in international relations at Columbia University. She is president of a chapter of the United Nations Association and active in the League of Women Voters. She represented the Unitarian Universalist Women's Federation at the United Nations during the Special Session on Disarmament and during prior meetings of Committee 1 and of the Preparatory Committee.

Betty G. Lall is associate director for labor and urban affairs of the Metropolitan District Office of Cornell University's New York State School of Industrial and Labor Relations. Formerly she was staff director of the U.S. Senate Subcommittee on Disarmament, a senior official of the U.S. Arms Control and Disarmament Agency, and disarmament editor of the *Bulletin of the Atomic Scientists*. She serves on the national board of the Arms Control Association.

Franklin A. Long is Henry Luce Professor of Science and Society at Cornell University's Program on Science, Technology and Society and director of Cornell's Peace Studies Program. He is currently involved in research on U.S. programs of military research and development and has co-authored an article published this year in the *Bulletin of the Atomic Scientists,* "U.S. Military R & D: A Set of Questions." He is actively involved in various aspects of research on topics of science and technology for development, appropriate technology and science policy.

Edward C. Luck has been the deputy director of policy studies for the United Nations Association (UNA) of the USA since March 1977. Prior to this position, he was project director of the UNA-USA National Policy Panel on Conventional Arms Control. He previously served as a consultant for the Social Science Department of the Rand Corporation. He has published widely in the fields of arms control, national security policy and Soviet foreign policy.

Matthew Meselson, Thomas Dudley Cabot Professor of the Natural Sciences at Harvard University, was from 1963 to 1973 consultant on biological and chemical warfare to the U.S. Arms Control and Disarmament Agency. He has written articles on the control of chemical and biological weapons, particularly from the point of view of U.S. national security interests. He recently edited the volume *Chemical Weapons and Chemical Arms Control* (Washington, D.C.: Carnegie Endowment, 1978).

Robert S. Metzger is at present an attorney with the firm of Latham & Watkins in Los Angeles, California. During the 1977–78 academic year he was a research fellow at the Center for Science and International Affairs, John F. Kennedy School of Government, Harvard University. He has written extensively on arms control impact statement legislation and is currently completing work on articles concerned with the arms control implications of "gray-area weapons."

John Gorham Palfrey, professor of law at Columbia University, was a U.S. Atomic Energy Commissioner in the 1960s. In 1976–77 he was a fellow at the Woodrow Wilson International Center for Scholars. Since 1975, he has been a consultant to the U.S. Arms Control and Disarmament Agency and has written numerous articles on U.S. nuclear energy policies.

Jeffrey D. Porro was a research consultant to the Rand Corporation while completing work on his Ph.D. at the University of California, Los Angeles, from 1973 to 1975. Before becoming editor of *Arms Control Today* in January 1978, he worked as a legislative assistant for national security affairs on the staff of Senator Howard M. Metzenbaum. He has recently taken a position with the Bureau of Politico-Military Affairs in the State Department.

George Rathjens is professor of political science at the Massachusetts Institute of Technology. Involved for more than twenty years in defense and arms control problems, he has most recently been particularly concerned about the problems of nuclear power and its relation to weapons proliferation. He has been a frequent witness before congressional committees dealing with military programs, arms control, and nuclear energy policy and has written widely on these subjects.

Jeffrey Record is legislative assistant for military affairs to Senator Sam Nunn. Before going to work for Senator Nunn in 1976, he served on the defense analysis staff of the Brookings Institution Foreign Policy

Studies Program, where he wrote several books, including *Sizing Up the Soviet Army* (1975), *U.S. Force Structure in NATO* (1974), *U.S. Nuclear Weapons in Europe* (1974), and numerous articles on military history and tactics.

John R. Redick is research director of the Stanley Foundation and editor of its occasional paper series. He is the author of articles dealing with nuclear proliferation in Latin America including "Desarme y el Tratado de no Proliferacion," *Revista de Occidente* (Madrid, January 1977), and "Regional Restraint: U.S. Nuclear Policy in Latin America," *Orbis*, Spring 1978. He has also helped organize and has been a rapporteur for national and international conferences dealing with non-proliferation and Latin America.

John B. Rhinelander is now an attorney in private practice in Washington, D.C. He has previously served in five departments of the executive branch, including Defense and State, and served as legal adviser to the U.S. delegation during SALT I. He was co-editor of *SALT—The Moscow Agreements and Beyond* (Riverside, N.J.: Macmillan Co., 1974).

Herbert Scoville, Jr., is vice president of the Arms Control Association. He is a writer and consultant to many organizations on national security affairs, particularly on the control of nuclear weapons. He was formerly assistant director of the U.S. Arms Control and Disarmament Agency, deputy director for research of the Central Intelligence Agency, and technical director of the Department of Defense Armed Forces Special Weapons Project.

Jane M. O. Sharp, formerly national director of the Council for a Livable World, is currently a research fellow at the Center for Science and International Affairs, John F. Kennedy School of Government, Harvard University, and a doctoral candidate at the Graduate Institute of International Studies, Geneva, Switzerland. She has published articles in the *Bulletin of the Atomic Scientists* and *Alternatives*.

Marshall D. Shulman is special adviser to the secretary of state on Soviet affairs. He is currently on leave from his position as Adlai E. Stevenson Professor of International Relations at Columbia University. At the time of the writing of this article, he was also director of the Russian Institute at Columbia University.

Angus Simmons is currently in Taiwan doing research. He worked for the National Council for U.S.-China Trade. He travelled in China in 1976 with a graduate student group from Johns Hopkins University.

Walter Slocombe was, at the time the articles in this book were published, a Washington, D.C., attorney. He is now principal deputy assistant secretary of defense for international security affairs and director, Department of Defense SALT Task Force.

Michael J. Sullivan III is an associate professor of political science at Drexel University where he teaches courses in science, technology, and international politics. A former naval officer and NATO Fellow, he has written on arms control, national defense, and global security matters for *International Organization, Pacific Affairs, Asian Survey, Strategic Digest* (New Delhi), and the *Journal of International Studies* (Seoul).

Ronald L. Tammen is Senator William Proxmire's legislative assistant for military and foreign affairs. His prior employment includes service as a strategic weapons analyst with the Central Intelligence Agency. He is the author of *MIRV and the Arms Race* (N.Y.: Praeger, 1973), the editor of *The Economics of Defense Spending* (N.Y.: Praeger, 1971) and a contributor to various journals. Since 1969 he has been deeply involved in the congressional debate on the B-1 bomber.

Lawrence Weiler is special assistant for public and academic liaison, U.S. Arms Control and Disarmament Agency. He was special U.S. coordinator for the United Nations Special Session on Disarmament. At the time these articles were written, he was associate director of the Stanford Arms Control Program. He was a member of the U.S. SALT I Delegation, at which time he was counselor of the U.S. Arms Control and Disarmament Agency. He is co-editor of *International Arms Control* (Stanford University Press, 1976) and *Congress and Arms Control* (Boulder, Colo.: Westview Press, 1978).

Nancy V. Yinger was the editor of *Arms Control Today* in 1977. She travelled in China in 1976 with a graduate student group from Johns Hopkins University. She is currently working in Boston.

Index

ABM. *See* Anti-ballistic missiles
ABM Treaty, 85; charged Soviet violations of, 38, 40-41; effect of, 28, 171; and limited counterforce capability, 50-51; and mutual deterrence, 102; proposed amendments to, 76; provisions of, 27-28
Accident Measures Agreement, *1971*, 36
ACDA. *See* Arms Control and Disarmament Agency
Action-reaction theory, 25
Airborne Warning and Control System (AWACS), 194
Air Force: and B-1 program, 80; and MX ICBM, 71-72
Air-launched cruise missile (ALCM), 88; and arms control, 91-92; extended and standard, 89; military effectiveness of, 91; proposed mission for, 91; SALT II limits on, 5; U.S. versus Soviet, 94
ALCM. *See* Air-launched cruise missile
Anti-ballistic missile (ABM); expenditures on, 106; and ICBM force, 76; limitations on, 27
Anti-submarine warfare: by active trailing, 69, 71; U.S.-Soviet capability for, 20, 103
Argentina: and nuclear arms control, 240; and nuclear-free zone treaty, 145, 212; nuclear program, 214
Arms control: action-reaction theory of, 25; and ALCM, 91-92; and arms impact statements, 234-37; by ban on active trailing, 69, 71; and cruise missiles, 85, 95-96; and MX ICBM, 74; and neutron warheads, 133-34; opponents of, 10; qualitative, 18. *See also* Regional arms control; Verification of arms control agreements
Arms Control Association, 11, 141, 144, 170
Arms Control and Disarmament Act, 41, 43, 46
Arms Control and Disarmament Agency (ACDA), 22, 187; and

arms impact statements, 234, 235-36; and binary nerve gas, 208; and future disarmament objectives, 233; presidential views on, 253; proposed expansion of, 232; reorganization of, 41; responsibilities, 230-31
Arms Export Control Act, 184
Arms, non-nuclear: "advanced" missile, 202; chemical, 205-09; technological changes in, 201, 203-05; versus nuclear weapons, 204-05; world-wide proliferation of, 184. *See also* Arms transfers, conventional
Arms race: presidential views on, 252-53; psychology of, 4
Arms transfers, conventional: in bilateral diplomacy, 195; to China, 196-201; competition over, 194; by country, 186; effect on nonproliferation, 160-63; efforts to regulate, 184, 188, 191; extent of, 185, 187; and likelihood of armed conflict, 191-93; by region, 221; volume of U.S., 192
"Assured destruction" capability: deterrence through, 25; and limited retaliation, 50
Atomic Energy Commission, 151
AWACS. *See* Airborne Warning and Control System

B-1 bomber program, 9; cancellation of, 79-80, 84; cost, 81-82
B-52 fleet: proposals for, 103; modifications in, 80-81
Backfire bomber, Soviet, 15: ALCM-equipped, 94; threat to U.S., 101
Binary nerve gas, 206-07
Biological weapons, 206, 207, 224
Biological Weapons Convention of *1972*, 206, 207
Bombers: comparison of, 79; ICBM strike capability against, 18; SALT II ceilings on, 5, 7; SLBM strike capability against, 18. *See also* B-1 bomber program
Brazil, 158; and nuclear-free zone treaty, 145, 212; nuclear power reactors, 152-53, 214; and nuclear weapons control, 240; West Ger-